OPPOSING
VIEWPOINTS®
SERIES

| Organ Donation

Other Books of Related Interest

Opposing Viewpoints Series

Genetic Engineering
Health Care
Medical Technology

At Issue Series

Embryonic and Adult Stem Cells
Extending the Human Life Span
Organ Transplants

Current Controversies Series

Human Trafficking
Medicare
Vaccines

"Congress shall make no law ... abridging the freedom of speech, or of the press."

First Amendment to the US Constitution

The basic foundation of our democracy is the First Amendment guarantee of freedom of expression. The Opposing Viewpoints Series is dedicated to the concept of this basic freedom and the idea that it is more important to practice it than to enshrine it.

OPPOSING
VIEWPOINTS®
SERIES

| Organ Donation

Laura Egendorf, Book Editor

GREENHAVEN PRESS
A part of Gale, Cengage Learning

GALE
CENGAGE Learning·

Detroit • New York • San Francisco • New Haven, Conn • Waterville, Maine • London

Elizabeth Des Chenes, *Director, Publishing Solutions*

© 2013 Greenhaven Press, a part of Gale, Cengage Learning

Gale and Greenhaven Press are registered trademarks used herein under license.

For more information, contact:
Greenhaven Press
27500 Drake Rd.
Farmington Hills, MI 48331-3535
Or you can visit our Internet site at gale.cengage.com.

For product information and technology assistance, contact us at:

Gale Customer Support, 1-800-877-4253.
For permission to use material from this text or product, submit all requests online at www.cengage.com/permissions.

Further permissions questions can be emailed to permissionrequest@cengage.com.

Articles in Greenhaven Press anthologies are often edited for length to meet page requirements. In addition, original titles of these works are changed to clearly present the main thesis and to explicitly indicate the author's opinion. Every effort is made to ensure that Greenhaven Press accurately reflects the original intent of the authors. Every effort has been made to trace the owners of copyrighted material.

Cover Image © Jeff Banke/Shutterstock.com.

LIBRARY OF CONGRESS CATALOGING-IN-PUBLICATION DATA

Organ donation / Laura Egendorf, book editor.
   pages cm. -- (Opposing viewpoints)
   Includes bibliographical references and index.
   ISBN 978-0-7377-6332-4 (hardcover) -- ISBN 978-0-7377-6333-1 (pbk.)
  1. Donation of organs, tissues, etc.--Popular works. I. Egendorf, Laura K., 1973-
   RD129.5.O738 2013
   362.17'83--dc23

                                  2013002332

Printed in the United States of America
1 2 3 4 5 6 7 17 16 15 14 13

Contents

Why Consider Opposing Viewpoints?

> *"The only way in which a human being can make some approach to knowing the whole of a subject is by hearing what can be said about it by persons of every variety of opinion and studying all modes in which it can be looked at by every character of mind. No wise man ever acquired his wisdom in any mode but this."*
>
> *John Stuart Mill*

In our media-intensive culture it is not difficult to find differing opinions. Thousands of newspapers and magazines and dozens of radio and television talk shows resound with differing points of view. The difficulty lies in deciding which opinion to agree with and which "experts" seem the most credible. The more inundated we become with differing opinions and claims, the more essential it is to hone critical reading and thinking skills to evaluate these ideas. Opposing Viewpoints books address this problem directly by presenting stimulating debates that can be used to enhance and teach these skills. The varied opinions contained in each book examine many different aspects of a single issue. While examining these conveniently edited opposing views, readers can develop critical thinking skills such as the ability to compare and contrast authors' credibility, facts, argumentation styles, use of persuasive techniques, and other stylistic tools. In short, the Opposing Viewpoints Series is an ideal way to attain the higher-level thinking and reading skills so essential in a culture of diverse and contradictory opinions.

In addition to providing a tool for critical thinking, Opposing Viewpoints books challenge readers to question their own strongly held opinions and assumptions. Most people form their opinions on the basis of upbringing, peer pressure, and personal, cultural, or professional bias. By reading carefully balanced opposing views, readers must directly confront new ideas as well as the opinions of those with whom they disagree. This is not to argue simplistically that everyone who reads opposing views will—or should—change his or her opinion. Instead, the series enhances readers' understanding of their own views by encouraging confrontation with opposing ideas. Careful examination of others' views can lead to the readers' understanding of the logical inconsistencies in their own opinions, perspective on why they hold an opinion, and the consideration of the possibility that their opinion requires further evaluation.

Evaluating Other Opinions

To ensure that this type of examination occurs, Opposing Viewpoints books present all types of opinions. Prominent spokespeople on different sides of each issue as well as well-known professionals from many disciplines challenge the reader. An additional goal of the series is to provide a forum for other, less known, or even unpopular viewpoints. The opinion of an ordinary person who has had to make the decision to cut off life support from a terminally ill relative, for example, may be just as valuable and provide just as much insight as a medical ethicist's professional opinion. The editors have two additional purposes in including these less known views. One, the editors encourage readers to respect others' opinions—even when not enhanced by professional credibility. It is only by reading or listening to and objectively evaluating others' ideas that one can determine whether they are worthy of consideration. Two, the inclusion of such viewpoints encourages the important critical thinking skill of objectively evaluating an author's credentials and bias. This evaluation will illuminate an author's reasons for taking a particular stance on an issue and will aid in readers' evaluation of the author's ideas.

It is our hope that these books will give readers a deeper understanding of the issues debated and an appreciation of the complexity of even seemingly simple issues when good and honest people disagree. This awareness is particularly important in a democratic society such as ours in which people enter into public debate to determine the common good. Those with whom one disagrees should not be regarded as enemies but rather as people whose views deserve careful examination and may shed light on one's own.

Thomas Jefferson once said that "difference of opinion leads to inquiry, and inquiry to truth." Jefferson, a broadly educated man, argued that "if a nation expects to be ignorant and free . . . it expects what never was and never will be." As individuals and as a nation, it is imperative that we consider the opinions of others and examine them with skill and discernment. The Opposing Viewpoints Series is intended to help readers achieve this goal.

David L. Bender and Bruno Leone,
Founders

Introduction

"Facebook's goal to help solve the problem of organ donation is laudable, but to be effective users will have to embrace the idea of sharing information that some may see as incredibly personal."

Ian Paul, PCWorld, *May 1, 2012.*

One of the challenges facing organ donation is finding ways to educate people on the need for organ donors and how they can become potential donors. The most effective solutions may involve the Internet, as hundreds of millions of people can be reached in an instant. On May 1, 2012, the social network behemoth Facebook suggested a new way to harness the power of social media when it introduced a feature that lets people sign up as organ donors. However, questions remain as to whether social media is an effective long-term answer for the shortage in donor organs and whether people who participate in these programs could risk a loss of privacy.

At Facebook's organ donation page, members can register as organ donors and share their organ donor status with other Facebook members. The page also details why the company decided to add this option, asserting:

More than 114,000 people in the United States, and millions more around the globe, are waiting for the heart, kidney or liver transplant that will save their lives. Many of those people—an average of 18 people per day—will die waiting, because there simply aren't enough organ donors to meet the need. Medical experts believe that broader awareness about organ donation could go a long way toward solving this crisis.

Given that Facebook has one billion members worldwide, this initiative could potentially impact many lives. In fact, the immediate results were impressive. In their article in the *Hastings Center Report*, "Can Social Media Increase Transplant Donation and Save Lives?," Blair L. Sadler and Alfred M. Sadler Jr. write:

> What has happened after the May 1 announcement? According to David Fleming, CEO of Donate Life America, the initial response "dwarfs any past organ donation initiative." By the end of the day of the announcement, 6,000 people had enrolled through 22 state registries. Charlene Zettel, the CEO of Donate California, reported that California had experienced a remarkable uptick. Typically, about 70 people register as organ donors online each day; in the 24 hours following the Facebook announcement, about 3,900 Californians signed up.

Beyond Facebook's efforts, there have also been smaller regional programs that are trying to use social media and the Internet to increase the numbers of people registering as organ donors. For example, the Center for Donation and Transplant (CDT), a federal organization that coordinates the recovery of donated organs and tissues in northeastern New York and western Vermont, worked with a social media company to increase awareness of Vermont's online registry; its six-month effort resulted in a 525 percent increase in donor registrants.

However, these social media efforts may not be sustainable. The Sadler brothers observed that the Facebook impact lasted only two weeks, before organ registrant numbers returned to their pre-May 2012 numbers. Meanwhile, Vermont's numbers rose, but the state still has the lowest percentage of potential organ donors, at only 3 percent. Facebook has countered these assertions, pointing out that 275,000 people registered worldwide between May and September 2012. Still, for social networking to be a long-term answer to the organ shortage, further steps may need to be made. For example, Facebook could develop ways for people to share how organ donation has impacted their lives or the lives of relatives and friends. The Sadlers offer several further suggestions, including having state donor organizations provide Facebook with real-time updates on the number of donors; they also suggest that state registries need to be more user-friendly. Facebook is also working on a version of its organ donation page for mobile phones, which would make signing up even easier.

However, there could be drawbacks to involving social networks in the organ donation process. The growth of the Internet has been paralleled by an increase in the loss of privacy, with many people being too quick to reveal personal information that could fall into the wrong hands. In an article for the Internal Medicine News Digital Network, Miriam E. Tucker addresses this concern. She cites a study of Facebook pages that were seeking a living kidney donor for a specific person, either for themselves, a family member, or friend. The study found that the people creating these pages often included detailed medical histories and photographs, perhaps not understanding the potential risk of making such personal information available to the general public—particularly because the content of those pages is not covered by US medical privacy laws.

At the same time, these concerns about privacy could be overstated. The Internet may have made lives less private, but it could also be argued that people who belong to social networking sites have come to accept the tradeoff of less privacy for more information. Matthew Weinstock, senior editor of *Hospitals and Health Networks* magazine, observes, "As [Facebook founder Mark] Zuckerberg so poetically stated a couple of years ago, privacy is 'no longer a social norm.' The challenge, it seems, for the health care industry, is how to navigate this landscape that seems to change in the blink of eye."

The approach that Facebook is taking to increase the number of organ donors may be controversial, but it has also helped increase awareness about the need for organs. *Opposing Viewpoints: Organ Donation* examines the issues surrounding organ donation in the following chapters: Is the Organ Allocation System

Fair?, How Can Organ Donation Be Increased?, What Ethical Issues Surround Organ Donation?, and What Is the Future of Organ Donation? Authors explore, among other issues, the challenges of finding organs for those who need them while also considering the rights of potential donors and recipients.

1

Is the Organ Allocation System Fair?

Chapter Preface

A major concern that many people have about the US organ transplantation system is whether organs reach the people most in need. The March 2012 heart transplant surgery of former US vice president Dick Cheney raised questions concerning both Cheney's fame and his age—and the impact those two factors may have had on his surgery.

Cheney was seventy-one and had had five heart attacks—and surgery to implant a partial artificial heart—before the transplant. Heart transplants for patients over the age of sixty-five are rare but not uncommon—332 out of 2,332 people in that age group received transplants in 2011, according to the United Network for Organ Sharing. One reason that relatively few older patients receive heart transplants is because recipients can have no other health problems, such as liver or lung damage—a state of good health that becomes less likely as patients age.

In the opinion of bioethicist Art Caplan, the vice president's operation was troubling not just because of his age—more than 3,100 people are on the waiting list for a heart, with most up to twenty years Cheney's junior—but also because his wealth and top-of-the-line health insurance gave him advantages most people don't have. According to Caplan, in a post on the NBC News blog *Vitals*, "It is possible that Cheney was the only person waiting for a heart who was a good match in terms of the donor's size, blood type and other biological and geographical factors. If not, then some tough ethical questions need to be asked. When all are asked to be organ donors, both rich and poor, shouldn't each one of us have a fair shot at getting a heart?"

However, not everyone agrees that Cheney had advantages unavailable to most potential organ recipients. Cheney was on the waiting list for twenty months, which is considerably longer than the average wait of six months to one year. On the blog *Postmodern Conservative*, Peter Lawler argues: "Did he cut in line? Is he too old? Nobody, in my opinion, should be asking such questions. He's too visible a guy to have been able to cut in line. Twenty months is a long wait—one that was pretty close to too long for Cheney. There appears to be nothing much physically wrong with Cheney beyond a long-standing bum ticker."

The debate over Dick Cheney's heart transplant is a microcosm of the issues surrounding the fairness of the US organ transplant system. In the following chapter, authors debate whether organ allocation is fair and discuss ways in which the system can be improved.

> *"[US government agencies] recognize the gaps in oversight that existed when serious problems were exposed at transplant centers."*

Government Oversight into Organ Transplants Needs Improvement

United States Government Accountability Office

In the following viewpoint, the United States Government Accountability Office (GAO) asserts that several government agencies must work together to improve government oversight into organ transplants and reduce the wait time for transplants. The GAO believes that the Centers for Medicare and Medicaid Services (CMS), the Organ Procurement and Transplantation Network (OPTN), and the Health Resources and Services Administration (HRSA) need to address problems such as understaffing, inadequate internal communication, and failure to protect living donors. According to the GAO, sharing information among the three agencies will help them reach this goal. The GAO is an independent, nonpartisan agency that works for Congress; its primary mission is to investigate how the federal government spends taxpayer dollars.

United States Government Accountability Office, "Organ Transplant Programs: Federal Agencies Have Acted to Improve Oversight, but Implementation Issues Remain," April 2008, pp. 13, 24–20.

As you read, consider the following questions:
1. According to the GAO, why did OPTN increase its staff size in 2007?
2. Why is it important for CMS and OPTN to exchange information on their oversight activities, per the GAO?
3. What is the difficult challenge facing CMS and HRSA, in GAO's opinion?

C MS's [Centers for Medicare and Medicaid Services] and, to a lesser extent, the OPTN's [Organ Procurement and Transplantation Network] oversight of transplant programs was not comprehensive at the time high-profile problems came to light in 2005 and 2006. CMS did not actively monitor extra-renal [non-kidney] transplant programs' compliance with criteria for Medicare approval. CMS monitored renal transplant programs through contracts with state agencies, but the surveys reviewed compliance with requirements that had not been substantially updated in decades and were limited in scope; also, not all programs were actively monitored. At the same time, the OPTN actively monitored transplant programs and took action to resolve identified problems, but its oversight activities fell short in some respects—the OPTN's monitoring did not include methods capable of promptly detecting problems at transplant programs that prolonged the time that patients waited for transplants, and the OPTN did not always meet its goals for conducting on-site reviews. . . .

Developing a Set of Indicators

To address shortcomings in the OPTN's ability to detect problems affecting patients waiting for transplants, such as understaffing, the OPTN and HRSA [Health Resources and Services Administration], along with another HRSA contractor, are working to develop and implement a set of activity-level indicators. The set of indicators would be used to monitor programs for problems, such as understaffing, indicated by lower-than-expected activity levels in a manner similar to how the OPTN currently monitors programs for performance problems indicated by lower-than-expected survival rates. The set of indicators includes two existing indicators already developed by the OPTN, one of which, although available, was not previously reviewed by the MPSC [Membership Professional Standards Committee], and a new organ acceptance rate indicator. The new indicator, which is intended to identify programs exhibiting lower-than-expected rates of organ acceptance, is a key component of the set of activity-level indicators and has been under development since January 2006. According to the OPTN, the organ acceptance rate indicator had been developed but not yet implemented for kidney and liver transplant programs as of February 2008.

With HRSA's encouragement, the OPTN has also taken steps to increase its capacity to conduct on-site monitoring activities and to improve internal communication. The OPTN substantially increased its staff in 2007 in order to get back on schedule in conducting on-site reviews once every 3 years. According to OPTN officials, the increase in staff will also help the OPTN address its backlog of peer review site visits and achieve its goal of conducting all peer review site visits within 3 months of the visit being recommended by the MPSC. To improve internal communication, the OPTN reported that since 2006, its leadership has emphasized the importance of shared communication, particularly across departments. As a result, according to the OPTN, staff responsible for managing the waiting list, including handling patient transfers, now meet frequently with staff responsible for monitoring policy compliance to share information about potential policy violations.

Three Key Areas Need Improvement

Although CMS, HRSA, and the OPTN have taken steps to improve oversight of transplant programs since the high-profile cases came to light, three important areas remain in progress.

- One key unresolved question is the extent to which CMS will conduct on-site reapproval surveys of transplant programs (as part of its new review procedures) after transplant programs gain initial Medicare approval under the new regulations. According to CMS's new regulations, CMS may choose not to conduct on-site reapproval surveys for transplant programs meeting data submission, clinical experience, and outcomes requirements. This means that CMS could potentially choose not to conduct any reapproval surveys for programs meeting these requirements. While CMS officials said that they see value in conducting reapproval surveys, just how CMS will apply its discretion remains unclear. As of January 2008, CMS officials said that the agency had not decided how many reapproval surveys it would conduct or how it would choose which programs to survey among those that meet the aforementioned requirements. They emphasized the agency's need to carefully consider resource constraints in making these decisions. A decision by CMS not to conduct an on-site reapproval survey at a transplant program means that compliance with some CoPs [condition of participation] would not be reviewed unless there was a complaint investigation. As a result, problems at transplant programs unrelated to the data submission, clinical experience, and outcomes requirements—for example, a transplant program failing to provide required protections for living donors or to sufficiently staff its program—could go undetected. In two of the high-profile cases, staffing problems that ultimately affected patients' access to transplants would not have been detected by the outcomes indicator that CMS has now adopted, and the numbers of transplants performed per year at these programs exceeded or were close to CMS's clinical experience requirement.

- Additional questions remain regarding the extent to which CMS will accurately track on-site surveys to avoid the misclassification errors we identified in our review and complete the surveys on a timely basis. As a result of the new transplant regulations, renal transplant programs will no longer share Medicare identification numbers with dialysis facilities, and previously misclassified renal transplant programs will at some point receive a new accurate classification in CMS's survey database once they are approved. However, the potential for transplant programs to be mistakenly classified may remain because transplant programs within the same hospital will share one transplant center Medicare identification number, according to CMS officials. CMS officials said that they were highly aware of the need for their systems to accurately track the status of each transplant program separately. They said that they plan to test for this capability in their new tracking system for transplant programs, which remains under development. What also remains to be seen is the extent to which surveys will occur on a timely basis. Prior to the new regulations, state agencies did not always meet CMS goals for surveying ESRD facilities. Now, under the new regulations, the responsibilities of state agencies that will be conducting on-site surveys of transplant programs will increase, since they will be required to survey both renal and extra-renal transplant programs. With respect to initial approval surveys, CMS's stated plan is that high-priority surveys of transplant programs will be completed by the end of fiscal year 2008, but as of January 2008, CMS officials expressed some uncertainty about meeting this goal. Initial surveys of transplant programs have been given a relatively high priority in the state agency workload, but it is not definite that this high priority level will continue because CMS has revised state agency workload priorities in the past. Further, the priority level for reapproval surveys is not yet known; a lower priority could affect how frequently surveys occur.

• The last unresolved question concerns the OPTN's and HRSA's planned organ acceptance rate indicator, which as part of a set of activity-level indicators, could potentially improve the OPTN's ability to detect transplant programs experiencing problems that prolong the time patients wait for transplants. According to the OPTN, the organ acceptance rate indicator for kidney and liver transplant programs has been developed but, as of February 2008, has not yet been implemented; HRSA officials expect the indicator to be in place within 1 year. HRSA and OPTN officials reported that they are considering developing organ acceptance rate indicators for transplant programs for other organ types. Before extending the indicator to other types of programs, however, the OPTN will first assess the effectiveness of the indicator at detecting potential problems at kidney and liver transplant programs, which perform larger volumes of transplants, and determine the feasibility of developing an indicator for programs with lower transplant volumes, such as heart and lung transplant programs.

Data Should Be Shared

CMS, HRSA, and the OPTN have recognized the importance of sharing data on transplant programs with one another and have taken initial steps to share basic data. To help CMS assess programs' compliance with its new Medicare requirements, the OPTN (through HRSA) is now sending CMS certain basic transplant program data on a quarterly basis. For example, the new Medicare regulations require transplant centers to be OPTN members, so the OPTN is providing data on the status of each transplant center's membership in the OPTN.

While this basic data sharing represents progress, CMS, HRSA, and the OPTN have additional information resulting from their oversight activities that could be shared. The exchange of this information is important because CMS and the

Medicare Requirements for Transplant Programs for Which the OPTN Is Providing Data to CMS

Medicare requirement	Data provided to CMS on each OPTN member
Transplant programs must be a member of the OPTN	OPTN membership status
Transplant programs must submit OPTN-required date to the OPTN within 90 days of OPTN deadlines	Member's compliance with OPTN data submission policies
The hospital in which a transplant program operates must have a written agreement with an organ procurement organization to receive organs	The organ procurement organization with which the transplant center has an agreement
Transplant programs must ensure that all individuals who provide services at the program, supervise services, or both, are qualified to provide or supervise such services	The names of the primary surgeon and primary physician at the transplant program

TAKEN FROM: GAO analysis of Medicare CoPs for transplant centers and information from CMS and HRSA.

OPTN conduct different monitoring activities and, as a result, may have different information about transplant programs that could be relevant to each other. For example, while both CMS and the OPTN conduct on-site reviews of transplant programs, the OPTN's on-site reviews focus largely on medical records review while CMS's on-site surveys are more broadly scoped. If the OPTN determined during an on-site review that the medical urgency assigned to patients by a transplant program was not supported by its medical records, this information could be of interest to CMS if this practice inappropriately reduced the chances of others on the waiting list to receive a transplant. As another example, the OPTN and HRSA are working to put into place their organ acceptance rate indicator, which CMS officials said they would be interested in using. Information from CMS's and the OPTN's investigations could also be potentially important to share. For example, if CMS investigated a complaint from a patient about the length of time he or she had been waiting for a transplant and determined that the delay was caused by the program failing to update the patient's health status, a violation of OPTN policy, the OPTN might want to flag the program for closer monitoring.

CMS and HRSA have recognized the importance of sharing information from their oversight activities, but the agencies have not yet reached agreement on how they would do so. CMS submitted a draft proposal to HRSA in April 2007 describing how CMS and HRSA could potentially share information about organ transplant programs. CMS and HRSA officials have since discussed the initial proposal, including possible revisions, but their progress has been slow. As of February 2008, CMS and HRSA had yet to reach agreement or establish a time frame for doing so. According to HRSA officials it had taken the agencies several months to better understand each other's oversight processes, and both agencies needed to further explore their information needs. CMS officials also indicated that further issues would need to be resolved before an agreement could be reached.

Some Issues Have Not Been Resolved

As part of any agreement to share information from their oversight activities, CMS and HRSA will need to determine precisely what information from their oversight activities they will share and at what point in their oversight processes they will share it. CMS and HRSA have discussed but not resolved these issues:

- *Nature of information to be shared.* It will be important for CMS and HRSA to determine specifically what information they will share from their oversight activities. For example, while CMS's initial proposal addressed how CMS and HRSA could share information from CMS's and the OPTN's investigations of serious complaints, such as those involving threats to patient health and safety, CMS and HRSA officials have since discussed whether to share information from all complaints. In addition, CMS and HRSA have not determined to what extent information from routine inspections, such as the OPTN's on-site reviews and CMS's on-site surveys, will be shared and at what level of detail. For example, CMS's initial proposal called for CMS to notify the OPTN about its completed on-site surveys and to indicate whether the transplant program surveyed had a plan of correction, but it did not call for CMS to provide information on the deficiencies CMS found. HRSA officials have since expressed their interest in having this more detailed information.

- *Timing of information sharing.* A more difficult challenge that CMS and HRSA face is agreeing when to share information about potential problems at transplant programs. Officials from both CMS and HRSA consider the severity of the identified problem(s) with a program to be a key factor in determining the appropriate time for information sharing. In this regard, officials from both agencies stated a willingness to promptly share information on potentially serious problems. Agreeing on just when to exchange information on less serious problems has been more problematic for the agencies in part because of differences in their approaches to oversight. On the one hand, CMS officials emphasize their agency's obligation to investigate any indications of noncompliance with Medicare requirements and prefer to be notified as soon as possible if the OPTN discovers a potential problem indicating noncompliance with Medicare CoPs. On the other hand, HRSA officials have emphasized that the viability and success of the OPTN's performance improvement process depends upon transplant programs sharing openly about their practices or past events. HRSA officials contend that the possibility of such information being shared with CMS, a regulatory agency, could cause transplant programs to be less candid about discussing real or potential problems, making it more difficult for the OPTN to help them return to compliance.

CMS, HRSA, and the OPTN recognize the gaps in oversight that existed when serious problems were exposed at transplant centers and have taken significant steps to strengthen federal oversight. The actions they have taken will help improve standards for transplant programs and should improve detection of potential problems. These actions include CMS's issuance of new regulations that expand and update requirements for transplant programs. In addition, CMS plans to conduct on-site surveys of all transplant programs seeking initial Medicare approval under the new regulations and to regularly review certain transplant program data, which should reduce the chances of problems going undetected by the agency. Similarly, if the OPTN's and HRSA's efforts to develop and implement a set of activity-level indicators to detect problems that prolong the time patients wait for transplants are successful, the indicators will likely result in earlier detection of these more subtle problems.

> *"Although bias against transplanting people with intellectual disability has been reduced, it is still a factor."*

The Organ Donation System Remains Biased Against the Disabled

Steven Reiss

The organ donation system is biased against the intellectually disabled, Steven Reiss argues in the following viewpoint. Reiss cites the case of a three-year-old girl with an intellectual disability who was denied a place on a transplant list. While he acknowledges that this prejudice is not as great as it once was, Reiss asserts that it is a sign of the wider problem of access to health care. Reiss is a professor of psychology and psychiatry at Ohio State University.

As you read, consider the following questions:

1. According to the author, how many Americans underwent a liver transplant in 2002?
2. In Reiss's view, what should organ allocation not take into account?

3. What is the solution to saving lives, in the author's opinion?

In 2004 Linda Jones and I started the nation's only formal program on organ transplantation and intellectual disabilities (mental retardation). Linda was a nurse who had retired as head of "Lifeline Ohio," the organ procurement program for central Ohio. I was a professor and head of a university center on intellectual disabilities. In 2002 I underwent liver transplantation at the Ohio State University because an autoimmune disease was destroying my birth liver.

Over the course of three years Linda spoke with many physicians and policy people about the topic. She spoke with people in North America, Europe, and Asia. I hired Marilee Martens to collect data for us for a literature review, which we published in 2006.

Here is what I think about the case of Amelia, the three-year old who has an intellectual disability and was denied listing for a transplant at Children's Hospital in Philadelphia.

The Intellectually Disabled Can Have Successful Transplants

Organ transplantation is as effective with people with intellectual disability as with the general population. It is much more effective than most people realize. I was one of about 16,000 Americans who underwent liver transplant in 2002. A year later more than 90 percent of us were alive.

I think it is likely Children's Hospital will reverse its decision and list Amelia. Huge numbers of people care passionately about this issue. I don't understand what the hospital administrators are waiting for. The longer this goes on, the more will be the damage to the reputation of their hospital.

In the past the system of listing people for transplants and allocating organs had significant bias against people with disabilities, especially those with intellectual disabilities. It was biased against people with certain personality traits and/or mental illness. Clearly, the trend has been toward less bias. People with intellectual disabilities have been successfully transplanted. I don't think the bias has been eliminated but I believe it is greatly reduced from where it was.

Although bias against transplanting people with intellectual disability has been reduced, it is still a factor and needs to be reduced further. Many doctors have expressed such bias to me personally. Many don't share this bias. Freeing the system of bias is a work in progress.

Organ allocation should not take into account disability, personality, or the insurance status of the patient.

If you have a loved one who has an intellectual disability and is denied listing for a transplant by one center, go to another center without delay. The decisions are not the same from one center to another.

A Lack of Health-Care Access Worsens the Problem

The discrimination against people with intellectual disabilities being listed for organ transplants may be part of a larger problem of access to health care, especially for adults. The more Lives Worth Saving looked at transplants, the more we noticed people dying from, say, a cancer that had been diagnosed only a day before death. We heard stories of parents losing their jobs because they had children with special needs posting too many bills with the health insurer.

The United States has a number of federally funded programs in the field of developmental disabilities. Policy makers need to re-direct some of this money and create a national priority on health care for adults with developmental disabilities. My take-away thought from the three years I participated in Lives Worth Saving was, "What is going on with health care for this population? How big must a tumor be before somebody notices it?" I don't think this was about bias. I think it was about access to care.

I believe Amelia's life is worth saving. Nothing in her medical records will change my mind on that point, because it is not a medical judgment. The solution isn't to discover a better way for deciding who gets a kidney and who doesn't. The solution is to find more kidneys.

*"We need legislation or folks are going
to be negative about organ donations."*

Organ Donors Should Consider Where Their Organs End Up

Laura Schlessinger

In the following viewpoint, Laura Schlessinger, also known as Dr. Laura, argues that the organ donation process is unfair and should be more discerning about who receives organ transplants. She believes that potential organ donors should be able to specify categories of people—such as those with a criminal history or substance abuse issues—who may not receive organs from that donor. She further asserts that legislation addressing this issue is needed so that the public will not feel negatively about organ donation. Schlessinger is a radio personality and best-selling author.

As you read, consider the following questions:

1. How many New Yorkers died while waiting for liver transplants as of July 2010, according to data cited by the author?

2. How many people does the author state that Johnny Concepcion passed on New York's transplant waiting list?

3. What recipients would the author like to specify for her organ donations?

As of July, 50 New Yorkers waiting for liver transplants died waiting for an organ, according to the Organ Procurement and Transplant Network.

Johnny Concepcion is not one of them. Concepcion is 42 and a confessed wife killer. He stabbed his wife to death and then drank rat poison in a suicide attempt. The rat poison destroyed his liver so he needed a transplant to survive.

Kerry Sullivan, a fine, upstanding citizen of NYC, has waited a year for a transplanted liver.

The available liver went to . . . Johnny Concepcion—just days after he admitted murdering his wife and destroying his own liver in suicide action.

What?

I remember the furor when a liver transplant was given to Mickey Mantle of baseball fame, when the media revealed that he destroyed his own liver with eons of alcohol abuse.

Obviously, judgment calls have to be made. And they are not supposed to consider religion, gender, financial status, celebrity and so forth—that makes totally fair sense—but really.

Let's go through this again. On July 5, the man murders a woman with 15 stab wounds (after a history of abusing her). Two days later, July 7, he tries to kill himself with rat poison, and he goes immediately to a hospital to get a transplant, passing almost 2,000 people on New York's transplant list and gets an organ and then goes to jail.

I saw a newspaper photo of him in the hospital after the transplant—smiling and giving a V for victory hand signal.

What?

This is a comment from a citizen responding to this news story from the *New York Post*:

> F-d-up World!!! It's funny how they don't put the truth in Commercials for Organ Donation . . . Donate an organ!! Save a Murderer! I have changed my mind on organ donation. I want absolute certainty that my organ goes to someone without criminal history! OR NO THANKS!

I have changed my mind on organ donation. I want absolute certainty that my organ goes to someone without a criminal history—or no thanks.

I believe it is time for people to put caveats on their organ donations: no convicted or confessed murderers, rapists, child molesters, homegrown terrorists, national traitors, long-term alcoholics who destroy their own livers and might likely destroy a new one. . . . We need legislation or folks are going to be negative about organ donations.

If he were to get the death penalty . . . Could we give the liver back to someone he passed on the list?

Just asking.

I am wondering about the dot on my drivers license which indicates me as a potential organ donor. I frankly am going to find out if I can specify that the recipients all be small children. I'll let you know.

> *"Since older candidates on the waiting list are less likely to live long enough to receive a kidney, making them less eligible for transplants will probably result in more deaths on the list."*

How Not to Assign Kidneys

Lainie Friedman Ross and Benjamin E. Hippen

A new proposal to change the way kidneys are allocated could result in more deaths for older patients on the waiting list, Lainie Friedman Ross and Benjamin E. Hippen opine in the following viewpoint. Ross and Hippen argue that the two-pronged system proposed by the United Network for Organ Sharing would result in more deceased-donor kidneys going to patients under the age of fifty, while also reducing the number of live kidney donations. The authors suggest that a more equitable approach would entail expanding living donor transplantations by encouraging kidney swaps and donor chains. Ross is a pediatrician and professor of ethics at the University of Chicago, and Hippen is a transplant nephrologist at the Carolinas Medical Center in Charlotte, North Carolina.

As you read, consider the following questions:

1. How long can deceased-donor kidneys last, as stated by the authors?

2. What is "first-person consent legislation," as explained by Ross and Hippen?

3. According to the authors, what are kidney swaps?

The United Network for Organ Sharing, the nonprofit group that manages the nation's organ transplant system, wants to change the system for allocating kidneys from deceased donors. While organs from living donors are usually directed to a particular person, kidneys from the deceased are distributed under a formula devised by the network. The proposal is supposed to provide deceased-donor kidneys of higher quality to healthier, younger patients instead of to elderly ones who presumably have fewer years to live.

It sounds simple enough. But the strategy could result in fewer kidneys going from living donors to young candidates, and could lead to more deaths of older or sicker candidates on the waiting list. Moreover, it would do nothing to address the fundamental problem: the persistent shortage of kidneys from donors, both living and deceased.

A Two-Pronged Strategy for Kidney Donations

The proposal would set up a two-pronged strategy that is intended to increase the number of life-years gained for every donor kidney. Under the proposal, the top 20 percent of kidneys from deceased donors who had been young and healthy would be assigned to the top 20 percent of young healthy candidates. In other words, the best deceased-donor kidneys would be given to patients likeliest to have long lives ahead of them.

The other 80 percent of deceased-donor kidneys would be allocated first to local candidates within a 15-year age range of the donor, and if no potential candidate were identified, then to the broader pool of candidates. (For example, candidates aged 25 to 55 would get priority for a kidney from a 40-year-old donor who had just died.)

But while the goal is understandable, the proposal is flawed. For one thing, our ability to forecast the success of any particular transplant is limited. The models used to predict whether both the kidney and the recipient survive in any individual operation are correct only 60 percent to 70 percent of the time; sometimes kidneys don't last as long as expected. So basing a vast shift in policy on a model that is just two-thirds accurate should give us pause.

Donations from Living Donors Could Decrease

In addition, giving healthy young patients first dibs on kidneys from young deceased donors might reduce donation rates from living donors to the young candidates, which is at cross-purposes with the goal of extending years of life after transplant. In 2005, the network started giving pediatric transplant candidates priority for kidneys from deceased donors younger than 35. While the pediatric patients received more organs from deceased donors, they got fewer organs from living donors. The likely explanation is that the donors, including many parents, held off, figuring that they could donate later, when the deceased-donor kidney eventually failed. (Those kidneys can last up to 20 years.)

The new proposal would effectively expand the 2005 rule to all healthier, younger candidates, potentially reducing living-donor transplantation to the very group that stands to benefit the most from it. This would only increase their need for another transplant later, since kidneys from deceased donors do not last as long as kidneys from living ones.

Giving more organs to young recipients would also come at the expense of "older" recipients, which in this context can mean 50 to 64. (Only a tiny fraction of all kidneys go to recipients older than 70.) Since older candidates on the waiting list are less likely to live long enough to receive a kidney, making them less eligible for transplants will probably result in more deaths on the list, and more pressure on available living donors to donate to older candidates.

Ways to Reduce the Kidney Shortage

What should be done instead?

First, allocate kidneys on a broader basis. Under both the current and proposed systems, kidneys are allocated locally. But while a New Yorker with end-stage renal disease will typically wait at least six years for a transplant, her counterpart in Minnesota might wait just two to three. Since a kidney from a young deceased donor would probably be allocated to a young local candidate, young candidates in areas with long waiting lists would still be at a substantial disadvantage under the new proposal. Turf disputes among regional and state networks are the main reason geographic disparities haven't been addressed.

Second, the network should continue to support first-person consent legislation under which people who have properly declared their willingness to donate their organs in case of an unexpected death cannot have their wishes overruled by their bereaved families.

But for now, the only sure way to reduce the shortage of organs is to expand transplantation from living donors, which requires more resources from the network. The public needs better education about the benefits of donation by the living and assurances that it is almost always safe. And the network should identify and remove disincentives to donation, like the expenses donors incur for travel or for taking unpaid leave from work for the operation preparation, the procedure and recuperation. We also support tracking the long-term health of living donors, which the network should do more to promote.

The network should also keep encouraging innovative efforts like "kidney swaps" or "donor chains." Kidney swaps involve two donor-recipient pairs who are incompatible within the pair, but can donate to the other pair's recipient. (Think of it as a square dance where the couples switch partners halfway through.)

Donor chains begin with a living donor willing to donate to anyone on the waiting list. Instead of simply giving that donor's kidney to the next patient in line, the kidney can go to the

Fewer Kidneys for Older Patients

The United Network for Organ Sharing (UNOS) is considering a kidney-allocation plant that would give preference to younger patients in an effort to get more life-years from each transplant. Below is how UNOS estimates the new system could affect the percentage of kidney transplants that go to patients in different age groups.

% OF KIDNEY RECIPIENTS BY AGE GROUP

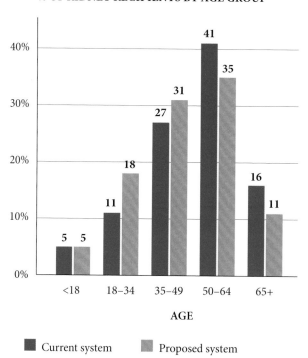

TAKEN FROM: *American Medical News*, "Reallocation Proposition," March 28, 2011.

would-be recipient in an incompatible donor-recipient pair; that donor, in turn, can then give to another recipient of an incompatible donor-recipient pair, with the chain continuing indefinitely. (Consider it the medical equivalent of "pay it forward.")

Patients count on doctors to be not only compassionate in providing care, but also dispassionate in examining data and vigilant in considering the undesirable consequences of any treatment. On these points, the new proposal for allocating kidneys from deceased donors falls short. And on the really pressing issues, it is not nearly ambitious enough.

Periodical and Internet Sources Bibliography

The following articles have been selected to supplement the diverse views presented in this chapter.

Ruth Carol	"Giving Patients a Second Chance at Life," *Minority Nurse*, Winter 2008.
Matthew Cooper and Cynthia L. Forland	"The Elderly as Recipients of Living Donor Kidneys: How Old Is Too Old?," *Current Opinion in Organ Transplantation*, April 2011.
Janice D'Arcy	"Denying an Organ to a 'Mentally Retarded' Child," *Washington Post*, January 17, 2012.
Robert Davis	"More Elderly Having Transplant Surgery," *USA Today*, February 5, 2008.
Charlotte Hays	"Is Denial of Life-Saving Care for Mentally Disabled Girl a Sign of Things to Come?," *National Catholic Register*, February 1, 2012.
Greg A. Knoll	"Is Kidney Transplantation for Everyone?," *Clinical Journal of the American Society of Nephrology*, vol. 4, 2009.
Wayne Kondro	"Plan Proposed to Make Organ Donation Less 'Ad Hoc,'" *Canadian Medical Association Journal*, August 7, 2012.
Danielle Ofri	"When Readiness to Give Can Help Save Your Life," *International Herald Tribune*, February 22, 2012.
Jennifer Wider	"Organ Donation: A Crisis Among Minorities," *JADE*, January–February 2008.
Alan Zarembo	"Dick Cheney: Are Heart Transplants Unusual for Older Patients?," *Los Angeles Times*, March 26, 2012.

CHAPTER 2

How Can Organ Donation Be Increased?

Chapter Preface

For parents, few tragedies can be worse than giving birth to an anencephalic infant. Babies born with this condition lack a forebrain and cerebrum; they posses only a brain stem, which allows for autonomic functions such as breathing and sucking. However, without the higher-level brain functions, death is inevitable and typically occurs within days, if not hours. The desire of some families to find meaning in this tragedy has led to a debate on whether anencephalic infants should become organ donors. The issue is one that is both morally and medically complicated.

The primary issue facing the use of anencephalic newborns as organ donors is that they are not technically brain dead—the standard criterion used to determine whether someone can donate organs. Typically, by the time one of these infants is considered brain dead, their organs have deteriorated too much to be of use. Redefining brain death for anencephalic newborns would be one way to increase the size of the donor pool. Fazal Khan and Brian Lea, in an article in the *Indiana Health Law Review*, suggest classifying these infants as "'brain-absent' to a degree sufficient to justify their treatment as brain dead." Khan and Lea argue that this reclassification recognizes that newborns with anencephaly are very similar to brain-dead individuals. The authors conclude: "Allowing donation of organs from anencephalic infants seems proper as it benefits the recipients of the organs and the families of both the donor and recipient, while burdening the anencephalic donor herself to little or no degree." The Florida Pediatric Society's Commission on Bioethics concurs, suggesting that pediatricians ought to advocate for parents who want to donate their infant's organs.

However, there are also arguments against anencephalic organ donations from both a medical and religious perspective. In contrast to the Florida society, the Canadian Paediatric Society (CPS) opposes anencephalic donation. According to a position paper by the CPS, allowing this type of organ donation could result in "application of similar arguments in favour of organ donation from other seriously brain-damaged living patients [and] serious risk of loss of public trust in transplantation programs." In the view of the organization Catholics United for the Faith, anencephalic donation is not just an issue of medical ethics but morality as well. The organization contends, "Removing the organs of an anencephalic infant, even if it is doubtfully human conceptus, includes the willingness to destroy it even if it is human, and thus, incurs the moral malice of murder."

There are more people in the United States that need organs than there are organs available, and finding ways to bridge that gap can be very controversial, as shown in the debate over using anencephalic infants as organ donors. In the following chapter, authors evaluate ways to increase organ donation.

> *"The truly decent route would be to allow people to withhold or give their organs freely, especially upon death, even if in exchange for money."*

The Selling of Organs Should Be Legalized

Anthony Gregory

In the following viewpoint, Anthony Gregory argues that the creation of a legal organ market would help solve the transplant organ shortage in the United States. He asserts that the health of a kidney donor is not harmed by the donation, and that self-ownership should include the right to sell one's organs. He believes that a legal and legitimate market will rectify the negative and criminal aspects of the organ trade, such as the exploitation of donors. Anthony Gregory is a research editor at the Independent Institute, a libertarian think tank based in California.

As you read, consider the following questions:

1. How many people died in 2008 while waiting for a kidney transplant, according to the viewpoint?
2. How did Iran solve its kidney shortage, as explained by the author?

3. According to the World Health Organization, as cited by Gregory, the black market accounts for what percent of kidney transplants worldwide?

Last month, New Yorker Levy Izhak Rosenbaum pled guilty in federal court to the crime of facilitating illegal kidney transplants. It has been deemed the first proven case of black market organ trafficking in the United States. His lawyers argue that his lawbreaking was benevolent: "The transplants were successful and the donors and recipients are now leading full and healthy lives."

Indeed, why are organ sales illegal? Donors of blood, semen, and eggs, and volunteers for medical trials, are often compensated. Why not apply the same principle to organs?

The very idea of legalization might sound gruesome to most people, but it shouldn't, especially since research shows it would save lives. In the United States, where the 1984 National Organ Transplantation Act prohibits compensation for organ donating, there are only about 20,000 kidneys every year for the approximately 80,000 patients on the waiting list. In 2008, nearly 5,000 died waiting.

A global perspective shows how big the problem is. "Millions of people suffer from kidney disease, but in 2007 there were just 64,606 kidney-transplant operations in the entire world," according to George Mason University professor and Independent Institute research director Alexander Tabarrok, writing in the *Wall Street Journal*.

A Legal Market Can End Organ Shortages

Almost every other country has prohibitions like America's. In Iran, however, selling one's kidney for profit is legal. There are no patients anguishing on the waiting list. The Iranians have solved their kidney shortage by legalizing sales.

Many will protest that an organ market will lead to exploitation and unfair advantages for the rich and powerful. But these

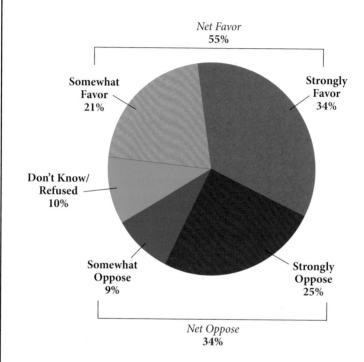

Fifty-Five Percent of the Public Supports an Organ Market

Would you favor or oppose allowing healthy people under medical supervision to sell their organs to patients who need them for transplants?

Net Favor
55%

Somewhat Favor
21%

Strongly Favor
34%

Don't Know/ Refused
10%

Somewhat Oppose
9%

Strongly Oppose
25%

Net Oppose
34%

TAKEN FROM: Reason Foundation, Reason-Rupe Public Opinion Research Project, March 2012 Questionnaire. http://reason.com/poll.

are the characteristics of the current illicit organ trade. Moreover, as with drug prohibition today and alcohol prohibition in the 1920s, pushing a market underground is the way to make it rife with violence and criminality.

In Japan, for the right price, you can buy livers and kidneys harvested from executed Chinese prisoners. Three years ago in India, police broke up an organ ring that had taken as many as 500 kidneys from poor laborers. The World Health

Organization estimates that the black market accounts for 20 percent of kidney transplants worldwide. Everywhere from Latin America to the former Soviet Republics, from the Philippines to South Africa, a huge network has emerged typified by threats, coercion, intimidation, extortion, and shoddy surgeries.

Although not every black market transaction is exploitative—demonstrating that organ sales, in and of themselves, are not the problem—the most unsavory parts of the trade can be attributed to the fact that it is illegal. Witnessing the horror stories, many are calling on governments to crack down even more severely. Unfortunately, prohibition drives up black-market profits, turns the market over to organized crime, and isolates those harmed in the trade from the normal routes of recourse.

Several years ago, transplant surgeon Nadley Hakim at St. Mary's Hospital in London pointed out that "this trade is going on anyway, why not have a controlled trade where if someone wants to donate a kidney for a particular price, that would be acceptable? If it is done safely, the donor will not suffer."

Bringing the market into the open is the best way to ensure the trade's appropriate activity. Since the stakes would be very high, market forces and social pressure would ensure that people are not intimidated or defrauded. In the United States, attitudes are not so casual as to allow gross degeneracy. Enabling a process by which consenting people engage in open transactions would mitigate the exploitation of innocent citizens and underhanded dealing by those seeking to skirt the law.

Organ Sales Are Consistent with the Ideals of Civil Liberty and Free Markets

The most fundamental case for legalizing organ sales—an appeal to civil liberty—has proven highly controversial. Liberals like to say, "my body, my choice," and conservatives claim to favor free markets, but true self-ownership would include the right to sell one's body parts, and genuine free enterprise would imply a market in human organs. In any event, studies show that this has become a matter of life and death.

Perhaps the key to progress is more widespread exposure to the facts. In 2008, six experts took on this issue [in] an Oxford-style debate hosted by National Public Radio. By the end, those in the audience who favored allowing the market climbed from 44 to 60 percent.

Yet, the organ trade continues to operate in the shadows and questionable activities occur in the medical establishment under the color of law. Even today, doctors sometimes legally harvest organ tissue from dead patients without consent. Meanwhile, thousands are perishing and even more are suffering while we wait for the system to change.

The truly decent route would be to allow people to withhold or give their organs freely, especially upon death, even if in exchange for money. Thousands of lives would be saved. Once again, humanitarianism is best served by the respect for civil liberty, and yet we are deprived both, with horribly unfortunate consequences, just to maintain the pretense of state-enforced propriety.

| *"Many doctors worry that paying for organs is too dangerous a path."*

Tax Cuts for Organs?

Priya Shetty

In the following viewpoint, Priya Shetty argues that offering people financial incentives, such as tax cuts or free health insurance, in exchange for donating their kidney or portion of their lung, pancreas, or liver, could cause potential ethical problems. According to Shetty, poor people could risk being exploited by an incentive system, while a black market could also emerge. Shetty suggests that another option might be to introduce a system of presumed consent but also notes that might introduce its own set of problems. Shetty is a science journalist whose work has appeared in The Lancet *and the* Guardian.

As you read, consider the following questions:

1. In what year did the United States ban the sale of organs, as stated by Shetty?
2. Why does Benjamin Hippen think poor people would not be ideal organ donors, as explained by the author?
3. As stated by the author, what proportion of donated kidneys is from the black market?

Sally Satel is one of the lucky ones. After being diagnosed with kidney failure in 2004, and facing years of dialysis, she was offered a kidney by someone she barely knew. She had already had a few heartbreaking near-misses with friends offering their kidney, only to later retract the offer. She finally had a transplant in 2006, when a journalist acquaintance made good on her offer to donate.

Satel, a psychiatrist at the Oasis Clinic, Washington, DC, and lecturer at the Yale University School of Medicine, New Haven, CT, USA, realises that she could easily have become one of the thousands dying on waiting lists because of the severe organ shortage.

Although buying and selling organs is still illegal in most countries, including the USA, a controversial proposal to reduce organ shortages by offering donors a financial incentive has been gaining ground with advocates like Satel. With the demand for organs far rapidly outstripping supply, it is a compelling argument, but many doctors worry that paying for organs is too dangerous a path.

In 1984, the US National Organ Transplant Act banned the sale of organs. Although living donors can donate a portion of their liver, lung, or pancreas, the need for kidneys is by far the highest. This year, over 100,000 people in the USA are waiting for an organ, of whom about 80,000 need a kidney. According to the United Network on Organ Sharing, based in the USA, which manages organ procurement and transplants on behalf of the government, between January and September there have only been another 7,000 donors.

As the crisis in the supply of organs worsens, some transplant surgeons are calling for a radical effort to increase donations by offering substantial financial rewards in exchange for organs. There is some precedent for the commercialisation of human body parts. For instance, women help other women conceive by selling their eggs or acting as paid surrogates. This June , the state of New York made it legal for women to be paid for donating eggs for research.

The incentives proposed for organ donors are substantial tax cuts, free lifetime health insurance, or free college tuition. Cash could be included too, although Satel says it could appeal to people who are desperate for quick money such as those with large gambling debts. Donors do incur some costs (panel) and even those who oppose incentives, such as the US National Kidney Foundation, agree that compensating donors for loss of earnings or paying for donation-related health-care insurance costs is fair.

But the idea of financially motivating donors to give organs is anathema to many doctors. "Donors are human beings, they are not pigs on a farm", says Gabriel Danovitch, director of the kidney transplant programme at the University of California, Los Angeles, CA, USA. Arthur Caplan, director of the University of Pennsylvania's Center for Bioethics, PA, USA, agrees. "Paying people to maim themselves for money is a violation of the do no harm ethic of medicine", he says.

International organisations are also yet to be convinced. WHO and the World Medical Association have ruled against payments to donors. Last year, the Istanbul Declaration, which was signed by 77 countries in an effort to eliminate organ trafficking and transplant tourism (when people from high-income countries travel to low-income countries to procure organs), also ruled against the commercialisation of living donations. And a European Union resolution last year said that any payment should be confined "solely to compensation strictly limited to making good the expense and inconvenience associated with the donation".

One concern is the potential for exploiting the poor. Even non-cash benefits could be valuable enough (e.g., free health care in the USA) to hold a powerful appeal for the least well off. But Benjamin Hippen, a nephrologist at Metrolina Nephrology Associates based in Charlotte, NC, USA, says that extremely poor people would not be ideal donors in any case because "low socioeconomic status around the world is an independent risk factor for kidney disease. In the long term, the recipient may not be better off with a kidney from someone at high risk, and the donor themselves might develop kidney failure".

The overriding concern among critics of the proposal, however, is the danger a US organ market could unleash. A special issue of *Current Opinions on Organ Transplantation* highlighted concerns about the organ trade in developing countries. In one paper, Ejaz Ahmed, at the Sindh Institute of Urology, and colleagues say that in Pakistan, the poor are heavily exploited—in 2007, over 70% of the 2,500 kidney transplants came from the extremely poor. In the same issue, Benita Padilla, at the National Kidney and Transplant Institute in the Philippines, argued for legislation against transplant commercialism for similar reasons.

The shortage of organs means that trafficking has skyrocketed—WHO estimates that a fifth of the 70,000 kidneys transplanted around the world every year are from the black market. Hippen argues that paying donors in the USA could eliminate organ trafficking. "What provides the economic support [for trafficking] is wealthy people from North America and western Europe".

Iran is the only country that has any semblance of a regulated paid donor system, but Ahmed's team say the country has seen deceased donations plummet as a result. And, although Iran has theoretically outlawed transplant tourism, "that isn't quite the case in reality", says Francis Delmonico, professor of surgery at Harvard Medical School, Boston, MA, USA.

Advocates of financial incentives argue that a US market would be saved by regulation. Caplan disagrees, saying that "given the failure to regulate the mortgage industry, savings and loans, banking, and stock markets in nearly every nation why would anyone think a kidney market could be regulated?" Delmonico also thinks black markets are inevitable. "Once you say it's okay to have a market, you won't be able to fix a price and ensure that price is the only game in town". Crucially, if the law were changed to allow financial incentives, there would be no going back if it

Tax Incentives for Organ Donors Would Prevent Low-Income Donors from Profiting

While there are contexts in which paternalism may be justified ... [tax incentives are] not one of them because it involves adults who are fully competent to enter into contracts. Indeed, financial decisions as to cadaveric donations are significantly less risky and harmful than countless other decisions the law permits competent adults to make each day—for example, to drink alcohol, scuba dive, or work in a coal mine or on construction projects. Put another way, if we are going to commercialize human bodies by providing financial incentives for harvesting organs, those incentives should be available to all who qualify based on relevant factors (like health) and not based on an individual's tax bracket. Our bodies are uniquely ours, and preventing low income persons from profiting because we do not believe they can make as free and as informed of a choice as middle or high income persons is paternalistic and demeaning.

Lisa Milot, "The Case Against Tax Incentives for Organ Transfers," Willamette Law Review, *vol. 45, Fall 2008.*

did not work, says Danovitch. "It would be like putting an egg back together after you've cracked it".

The American Medical Association has been pushing for pilot studies to gauge whether financial incentives would work in practice, although none have yet been started. Until major organisations get behind the concept, it seems unlikely that incentives will be introduced. However, Mark Cherry, professor of philosophy at Saint Edward's University in Austin, TX, USA, says that although no big organisation has yet come out in favour, transplant surgeons have admitted to him in private that they support incentives. He believes they do not go public with their views for fear of professional vilification.

One way to boost the organ supply could be a system of presumed consent, where everyone is considered a potential donor unless they opt out. The idea has political backing in the USA. In September, Cass Sunstein, Barack Obama's nominee to head the Office of Information and Regulatory Affairs, came out strongly in favour of it. But the system has had mixed results in Europe. Spain, which introduced presumed consent in 1990 has seen donations double, but Sweden saw hardly any increase in donation rates.

The notion that organs "belong to the state" after death is difficult to enforce in the face of grieving family members who do not want to give consent, says Hippen. Pressing the issue is likely to undermine trust in the medical profession, he says.

The UK decided last year not to introduce presumed consent for this very reason. It plans to focus instead on recruiting extra donor transplant coordinators and 24-h organ retrieval teams—factors that some believe explain Spain's high donor rates.

Presumed consent "is a way of the government taxing even your body parts, which strikes me as horrific and coercive", says Cherry. He would prefer "organ futures", where a person agrees that their organs can be sold after death. This approach could be especially useful for heart and lung transplants, says Robert Sade, head of the Medical University of South Carolina, Charleston, SC, USA. "Cash contributions to the estates of deceased donors, substantial tax benefits, or payment of funeral expenses might clear those waiting lists", he says.

Meanwhile, the severe organ shortage seems to have already created a black market in the USA. Earlier this year, the Federal Bureau of Investigation (FBI) arrested a group of fraudulent politicians and rabbis, one of whom allegedly bought a kidney from an impoverished Israeli for US$10,000, and tried to sell it for $160,000.

This revelation did not surprise Satel. The waiting list for a kidney can be as long as 10 years, which is longer than people who need one are likely to live. "Everyone was so shocked [by the FBI's discovery], but do people really think we are going to sit by and die?" she asks.

The desperation Satel speaks of is felt by many on waiting lists. On Sept 13, the Irish screenwriter Frank Deasy wrote of the trauma of waiting for an organ in the UK newspaper *The Observer*. "Whole families are living on the list", he wrote, "struggling to carry on normal life, their hopes and dreams, their children's futures, in the balance". Deasy died 4 days later, when the long-awaited transplant materialised, but failed to save him.

> *"Presumed consent, financial compensation for living and deceased donors and point systems would all increase the supply of transplant organs."*

The Meat Market

Alex Tabarrok

In the following viewpoint, Alex Tabarrok contends that one way to reduce the organ shortage in the United States is by following the lead of countries such as Singapore and adopting a policy of presumed consent. He explains that under presumed consent everyone is a potential organ donor unless they opt out. According to Tabarrok, countries with presumed consent laws have seen modest increases in organ donations. Tabarrok further argues that financial compensation and point systems that give potential organ donors higher placement on organ waiting lists would also help solve the shortage. Tabarrok is a professor of economics at George Mason University.

As you read, consider the following questions:

1. What is cardiac death, as defined by the author?

2. In Tabarrok's opinion, what do the Iranian donation system and the black market demonstrate?
3. What is "no give, no take," as explained by the author?

Harvesting human organs for sale! The idea suggests the lurid world of horror movies and 19th-century grave robbers. Yet right now, Singapore is preparing to pay donors as much as 50,000 Singapore dollars (almost US$36,000) for their organs. Iran has eliminated waiting lists for kidneys entirely by paying its citizens to donate. Israel is implementing a "no give, no take" system that puts people who opt out of the donor system at the bottom of the transplant waiting list should they ever need an organ.

Millions of people suffer from kidney disease, but in 2007 there were just 64,606 kidney-transplant operations in the entire world. In the U.S. alone, 83,000 people wait on the official kidney-transplant list. But just 16,500 people received a kidney transplant in 2008, while almost 5,000 died waiting for one.

To combat yet another shortfall, some American doctors are routinely removing pieces of tissue from deceased patients for transplant without their, or their families', prior consent. And the practice is perfectly legal. In a number of U.S. states, medical examiners conducting autopsies may and do harvest corneas with little or no family notification. (By the time of autopsy, it is too late to harvest organs such as kidneys.) Few people know about routine removal statutes and perhaps because of this, these laws have effectively increased cornea transplants.

Routine removal is perhaps the most extreme response to the devastating shortage of organs world-wide. That shortage is leading some countries to try unusual new methods to increase donation. Innovation has occurred in the U.S. as well, but progress has been slow and not without cost or controversy.

Organs can be taken from deceased donors only after they have been declared dead, but where is the line between life and death? Philosophers have been debating the dividing line between baldness and nonbaldness for over 2,000 years, so there is little hope that the dividing line between life and death will ever be agreed upon. Indeed, the great paradox of deceased donation is that we must draw the line between life and death precisely where we cannot be sure of the answer, because the line must lie where the donor is dead but the donor's organs are not.

In 1968 the *Journal of the American Medical Association* published its criteria for brain death. But reduced crime and better automobile safety have led to fewer potential brain-dead donors than in the past. Now, greater attention is being given to donation after cardiac death: no heart beat for two to five minutes (protocols differ) after the heart stops beating spontaneously. Both standards are controversial—the surgeon who performed the first heart transplant from a brain-dead donor in 1968 was threatened with prosecution, as have been some surgeons using donation after cardiac death. Despite the controversy, donation after cardiac death more than tripled between 2002 and 2006, when it accounted for about 8% of all deceased donors nationwide. In some regions, that figure is up to 20%.

The shortage of organs has increased the use of so-called expanded-criteria organs, or organs that used to be considered unsuitable for transplant. Kidneys donated from people over the age of 60 or from people who had various medical problems are more likely to fail than organs from younger, healthier donors, but they are now being used under the pressure. At the University of Maryland's School of Medicine five patients recently received transplants of kidneys that had either cancerous or benign tumors removed from them. Why would anyone risk cancer? Head surgeon Dr. Michael Phelan explained, "the ongoing shortage of organs from deceased donors, and the high risk of dying while waiting for a transplant, prompted five donors and recipients to push ahead with surgery." Expanded-criteria organs are a useful response to the shortage, but their use also means that the shortage is even worse than it appears

"Recycling—Glass Cans Organs," cartoon by Grizelda. www.cartoonstock.com.

because as the waiting list lengthens, the quality of transplants is falling.

Routine removal has been used for corneas but is unlikely to ever become standard for kidneys, livers or lungs. Nevertheless more countries are moving toward presumed consent. Under that standard, everyone is considered to be a potential organ donor unless they have affirmatively opted out, say, by signing a non-organ-donor card. Presumed consent is common in Europe and appears to raise donation rates modestly, especially when combined, as it is in Spain, with readily available transplant coordinators, trained organ-procurement specialists, round-the-clock laboratory facilities and other investments in transplant infrastructure.

The British Medical Association has called for a presumed consent system in the U.K., and Wales plans to move to such a system this year. India is also beginning a presumed consent program that will start this year with corneas and later expand to other organs. Presumed consent has less support in the U.S. but experiments at the state level would make for a useful test.

Rabbis selling organs in New Jersey? Organ sales from poor Indian, Thai and Philippine donors? Transplant tourism? It's all part of the growing black market in transplants. Already, the black market may account for 5% to 10% of transplants world-wide. If organ sales are voluntary, it's hard to fault either the buyer or the seller. But as long as the market remains underground the donors may not receive adequate postoperative care, and that puts a black mark on all proposals to legalize financial compensation.

Only one country, Iran, has eliminated the shortage of transplant organs—and only Iran has a working and legal payment system for organ donation. In this system, organs are not bought and sold at the bazaar. Patients who cannot be assigned a kidney from a deceased donor and who cannot find a related living donor may apply to the nonprofit, volunteer-run Dialysis and Transplant Patients Association (Datpa). Datpa identifies potential donors from a pool of applicants. Those donors are medically evaluated by transplant physicians, who have no connection to Datpa, in just the same way as are uncompensated donors. The government pays donors $1,200 and provides one year of limited health-insurance coverage. In addition, working through Datpa, kidney recipients pay donors between $2,300 and $4,500. Charitable organizations provide remuneration to donors for recipients who cannot afford to pay, thus demonstrating that Iran has something to teach the world about charity as well as about markets.

The Iranian system and the black market demonstrate one important fact: The organ shortage can be solved by paying living donors. The Iranian system began in 1988 and eliminated the shortage of kidneys by 1999. Writing in the *Journal of Economic Perspectives* in 2007, Nobel Laureate economist Gary Becker and Julio Elias estimated that a payment of $15,000 for living donors would alleviate the shortage of kidneys in the U.S. Payment could be made by the federal government to avoid any hint of inequality in kidney allocation. Moreover, this proposal would save the government money since even with a significant payment, transplant is cheaper than the dialysis that is now paid for by Medicare's End Stage Renal Disease program.

In March 2009 Singapore legalized a government plan for paying organ donors. Although it's not clear yet when this will be implemented, the amounts being discussed for payment, around $50,000, suggest the possibility of a significant donor incentive. So far, the U.S. has lagged other countries in addressing the shortage, but last year, Sen. Arlen Specter circulated a draft bill that would allow U.S. government entities to test compensation programs for organ donation. These programs would only offer noncash compensation such as funeral expenses for deceased donors and health and life insurance or tax credits for living donors.

World-wide we will soon harvest more kidneys from living donors than from deceased donors. In one sense, this is a great success—the body can function perfectly well with one kidney so with proper care, kidney donation is a low-risk procedure. In another sense, it's an ugly failure. Why must we harvest kidneys from the living, when kidneys that could save lives are routinely being buried and burned? A payment of funeral expenses for the gift of life or a discount on driver's license fees for those who sign their organ donor card could increase the supply of organs from deceased donors, saving lives and also alleviating some of the necessity for living donors.

Two countries, Singapore and Israel, have pioneered non-monetary incentives systems for potential organ donors. In Singapore anyone may opt out of its presumed consent system. However, those who opt out are assigned a lower priority on the transplant waiting list should they one day need an organ, a system I have called "no give, no take."

Many people find the idea of paying for organs repugnant but they do accept the ethical foundation of no give, no take— that those who are willing to give should be the first to receive.

In addition to satisfying ethical constraints, no give, no take increases the incentive to sign one's organ donor card thereby reducing the shortage. In the U.S., Lifesharers.org, a nonprofit network of potential organ donors (for which I am an adviser), is working to implement a similar system.

In Israel a more flexible version of no give, no take will be phased into place beginning this year. In the Israeli system, people who sign their organ donor cards are given points pushing them up the transplant list should they one day need a transplant. Points will also be given to transplant candidates whose first-degree relatives have signed their organ donor cards or whose first-degree relatives were organ donors. In the case of kidneys, for example, two points (on a 0- to 18-point scale) will be given if the candidate had three or more years previous to being listed signed their organ card. One point will be given if a first-degree relative has signed and 3.5 points if a first-degree relative has previously donated an organ.

The world-wide shortage of organs is going to get worse before it gets better, but we do have options. Presumed consent, financial compensation for living and deceased donors and point systems would all increase the supply of transplant organs. Too many people have died already but pressure is mounting for innovation that will save lives.

> *"'Presumed consent' proposals such as Colorado's . . . actually reduce the overall number of available organs."*

Presumed Consent Is the Wrong Way to Increase Organ Donation

Daniel Sayani

A proposed law in Colorado that would presume all Coloradans with a driver's license or ID card have consented to become organ donors is a threat to individual liberty, Daniel Sayani argues in the following viewpoint. According to Sayani, the legislation ignores individuals' rights to bodily autonomy and could result in doctors viewing patients as potential sources of organs, rather than lives worthy of being saved. He also argues that presumed consent will not solve the organ shortage, and most Coloradans are willing to donate organs without being coerced. Sayani is a contributor to The New American *magazine.*

As you read, consider the following questions:

1. According to Sayani, from where do Colorado legislators believe bodily freedom stems?

2. What was the conclusion of a study conducted in the Netherlands, as cited by Sayani?
3. What proportion of Coloradans has voluntarily expressed interest in organ donation, as stated by the author?

Some Colorado state legislators are proposing to make theirs the first state in which people become organ donors by default. The proposal, introduced in the state Senate last week [January 2011], would change the process for renewing driver's licenses and ID cards so applicants are assumed to be organ and tissue donors unless they initial a statement saying they want to opt out, according to the *Huffington Post*.

Entitled "A Bill Concerning Presumed Consent for Organ and Tissue Donation," SB 11-042 was introduced in the General Assembly by Democrat State Representative Dan Pabon, and initially was supported by Democrat State Senator Lucia Guzman. Guzman, however, last night declared that she has changed her mind. The *Washington Post* reports:

> Democratic Sen. Lucia Guzman told Denver's KUSA-TV that she is dropping her proposal that the state change to a "presumed consent" system.
>
> That system automatically classifies all applicants for driver's licenses and state ID cards as organ and tissue donors unless they opt out. Such donations are used in several European countries but have raised ethical concerns in the US.

The Colorado proposal was introduced last week and sparked fears and opposition from many. According to the text of the legislation:

> The bill changes the organ donation program so that a person is presumed to have consented to organ and tissue donation at the time the person applies for or renews a driver's license or identification card unless the person initials a statement that

states that the person does not want to be considered as a possible organ and tissue donor.

The text of the bill amends driver's license and photo ID renewal forms to read:

> You are automatically deemed to have consented to being an organ and tissue donor and this designation will appear on your driver's license or identification card.

Giving Up Bodily Autonomy

The legislation makes no explicit exemptions or provisions stating that if individuals die prior to being able to sign or initial the state-run DMV form, their organs will be protected from state-sanctioned organ harvesting, even if it violates their ethical or religious beliefs, or their dying wishes to not donate organs.

The state mistakenly assumes that unless individuals initial the specific document provided by the Department of Motor Vehicles, they are expressing their desire to donate organs and living tissue, resting on the fallacious notion that "silence equals (or implies) consent." Colorado wants its citizens to effectively surrender their bodily autonomy to the state if they fail to sign a state-sanctioned document.

The proposal is a revelatory example of positivism. The individual's right to bodily autonomy is not a factor at play in the minds of the bill's sponsors; instead, they do not view the individual's right to control his own body as existing from Natural Law or from God, believing rather that state-issued documentation from the Department of Motor Vehicles is the only binding, admissible, and significant element at play in the corporal freedoms of the governed.

In other words, to these legislators, one's bodily freedom stems not from God, but from the Colorado DMV—and not even one's own organs are safe from the clutches of the state.

The Colorado proposal is yet another example of an Orwellian [reminiscent of George Orwell's works depicting an authoritarian state] assault on individual liberty, including religious liberty and patients' rights. It also indicates a step in the direction of the overall aim of so-called "Healthcare Reform": the inevitable slump toward rationing care and sacrificing the individual's access to life-saving treatments and services in the interest of the "greater good of others."

People are essentially being threatened with becoming organ donors against their wishes. Bioethicists and health policy experts have warned that if doctors view all patients as prospective donors, they will no longer consider them as patients worthy of having their lives prolonged, but instead will see them as walking organ banks—mere commodities that fulfill the utilitarian function of providing organs to others.

Once again, government is acting contrary to the fundamental Lockean (referring to the philosopher John Locke) notion that the individual is the effective owner of his body, and has the right to determine what he will do with it (while acknowledging that God, as Creator, is ultimately in control of the body, and prohibits individuals from doing anything contrary to self-preservation, according to John Locke's *Second Treatise on Government*).

Presumed Consent Is Ineffective

"Presumed consent" proposals such as Colorado's, widely considered by experts to be unethical, actually *reduce* the overall number of available organs, as individuals are less likely to volunteer as donors when they are aware of such coercive Orwellian policies as state-sanctioned organ harvesting.

According to an article in the *British Medical Journal* by Linda Wright, Director of Bioethics for the Toronto-based University Health Network, and Assistant Professor of Surgery at the University of Toronto Medical School, presumed consent is also ineffective at ameliorating the plight of those on waiting lists for organ transplants. She notes:

Research indicates that Presumed Consent will not answer the organ shortage. It has not eliminated waiting lists despite evidence that it increased organ donation in some countries.

Wright's argument also posits that efforts to utilize "presumed consent" as a quick fix to the nation's organ shortage are merely superficial and neglect to address the root causes of the shortage. As summarized by the *New York Times*:

> She also says encouraging people to talk to their families about their wishes on donation, engaging communities to help build the necessary trust to favor organ donation, and increasing our knowledge of what influences donation rates are also important. Finally, meeting the demand for organs may require not only increasing organ supply but also optimizing disease prevention and recipient selection, she adds. "Given the multi-factorial nature of the problem, presumed consent alone will not solve the organ shortage," she concludes.

A [2005] study conducted in the Netherlands, published in the journal *Transplant International* examined whether different consent systems explain the difference in organ donation rates among countries when taking into account the difference in relevant mortality rates. Researchers, who analyzed data on donation and relevant mortality rates for 10 different countries as well as information on the existing consent systems, concluded,

> International comparative legal research has shown that the differences between decision systems are marginal. When the national organ donation rates are corrected for mortality rates, these findings are confirmed: the donor efficiency rate shows that opting-out systems do not automatically guarantee higher donation rates than opting-in systems.

Organ Transplants Are a Gift

Informed consent respects and acknowledges the essential formality of the transplanted organ as a *gift* that one person gives to another. A necessary dimension of a gift as gift is that it must be given. It must be endowed; one cannot receive a gift from the other if the other has not consented to the giving. In effect, without the giver's consent, the so-called gift has been taken rather than been received. . . . Without informed consent, a transplanted organ ceases to be a gift; it is something taken. Some may even say that it is something stolen.

Nicanor Austriaco, "Presumed Consent for Organ Procurement," National Catholic Bioethics Quarterly, *Summer 2009.*

Consent Must Be Voluntary

Agreeing with the professional opinion of Wright is virologist Gee Yen Shin, who authored an editorial entitled "Presumed Consent is too Paternalistic," in which he wrote that while presumed consent is an "attractive utilitarian approach to solving a perennial dilemma," it is nonetheless unethical. He continued:

What of the autonomy of individuals and patients? Is it acceptable or just to presume that the sick and the dying are content to surrender their organs after death? I believe that government, "the State," exists to serve the people, not the other way around. Harvesting organs from citizens who have died on the basis of presumed consent is the most macabre manifestation of the latter that one could imagine.

Given the shortage of organs in the UK, the preoccupation with the preservation of patient autonomy may seem dogmatic and possibly eccentric, but this inconvenient concept underpins the ethics behind modern medical practice. The State brushes autonomy and free will aside at its peril. If the Government goes ahead with presumed consent for organ donation, it will irrevocably alter the relationship between the State and its citizens.

Philosopher Hugh McLachlan is also of the opinion that presumed consent is:

> . . . a very troublesome notion. Consent must be voluntarily and knowingly expressed in order to serve the function of morally authorizing actions of other people towards and concerning the consenting person that otherwise would be morally wrong. To say that it can reasonably be presumed that we consent to donate our organs if we do not specifically say that we do not consent is absurd. It is a deceitful piece of sophistry.

Similar Legislation Has Been Rejected

The proposed legislation is also suspect because Colorado already has one of the highest organ donation rates of any state in the country. According to the Colorado Donor Alliance, over two-thirds of Coloradans have already expressed their voluntary desire to donate organs on driver's licenses and identification cards, and as a result, the organization, Colorado's premier advocacy group for organ donation, opposes the legislation. According to Sue Dunn, President and CEO of the Donor Alliance, the legislation may even reduce the number of organ donors:

> I don't think it should pass right now. And that is an awkward [thing] for me to say running an organ and tissue recovery agency. What we don't know and what has not been shown in any state in the country, is will rates go up or down. Would the way that it gets presented at the driver's license office actually increase the number of people who say no?

Such legislative efforts have also been proposed by Democrats in New York and Delaware, and have soundly been rejected in both states. In New York, the Catholic League for Civil and Religious Rights and the Orthodox Jewish groups Agudath Israel of America and the Rabbinical Alliance of America effectively lobbied for the bill's defeat—a victory for the Lockean principle of corporal liberty.

New York Assemblyman Dov Hikind expressed fear that such bills result in "protracted legal battles over organ harvesting," and Professor McLachlan seconds this claim, arguing that "presumed consent" paves a path for organ harvesting as an "opt-out" system.

In light of State Senator Guzman's withdrawal from supporting the Colorado bill, its fate remains uncertain. [Editor's Note: In February 2011, Colorado's Senate Committee on Health and Human Services voted to postpone the bill indefinitely.] Colorado's Republican State Senator Shawn Mitchell says,

> If enough people aren't volunteering, that doesn't mean the government can suddenly lay claim to their body and to their organs after they die. People, I would hope, would be willing to make this choice, but if they're not, the government doesn't own their bodies. They do and after they're dead, their families do.

Those who believe in the religious and ethical liberties of human beings, as well as in public health decisions that are empirically and ethically validated, will continue to stand firm against "presumed consent" efforts.

Periodical and Internet Sources Bibliography

The following articles have been selected to supplement the diverse views presented in this chapter.

Ted Alcorn	"China's Organ Transplant System in Transition," *The Lancet*, June 4, 2011.
Nicanor Pier Giorgio Austriaco	"Presumed Consent for Organ Procurement," *National Catholic Bioethics Quarterly*, Summer 2009.
Alexander Berger	"Why Selling Organs Should Be Legal," *New York Times*, December 5, 2011.
Sarah Boehm	"Presumed Consent: A Bad Thing," *British Medical Journal*, February 16, 2008.
The Economist	"Opting Out of Opting Out," November 20, 2008.
The Economist	"The Gap Between Supply and Demand," October 9, 2008.
Benjamin Hippen and Arthur Matas	"The Point of Control: Can a Regulated Organ Market Be Moral?," *Hastings Center Report*, November–December 2009.
Ana Lita	"The Dark Side of Organ Transplantation," *The Humanist*, March–April 2008.
David Schwark	"Organ Conscription: How the Dead Can Save the Living," *Journal of Law and Health*, Summer 2011.
Wesley J. Smith	"Presumptuous Consent," *First Things*, May 18, 2010.

OPPOSING
VIEWPOINTS®
SERIES

CHAPTER 3

What Ethical Issues Surround Organ Donation?

Chapter Preface

Like many medical issues, organ donation has a set of ethical complications. One of the biggest ethical controversies in organ donation involves China. Each year, approximately 1.5 million people in China are in need of transplants. However, only ten thousand of those people undergo the procedure, in part because the cadaver organ donation rate is one of the world's lowest, at a mere 0.03 per 1 million people. In the past, the Chinese government has sought to close this gap by harvesting organs from executed prisoners, a policy that has garnered widespread criticism. However, the government vowed in March 2012 to stop that practice by 2017 and focus its efforts on building a voluntary organ donation system. Despite that major change, organ donation in China is likely to remain ethically complex.

One challenge facing China is Confucian views on organ donation. Confucianism, which can be considered both a philosophy and a religion, opposes organ donation based on the view that the body should remain intact from birth through burial. Li Li, writing for the weekly newsmagazine *Beijing Review*, explains: "Chinese customs call for people to be buried or cremated with the body intact. One die-hard superstition has it that if an organ is taken from a body after death, the person in question will be reborn with a handicap in that organ in his or her next life." However, in 2000, South Korea, another nation in which Confucianism predominates, formally recognized brain death for the purposes of organ donation, so it is possible that the Chinese view may eventually change.

Another ethical issue facing China is the black-market organ trade. Li cites the story of a teenage boy who sold one of his kidneys for approximately $3,500. While the boy sold his kidney voluntarily to have money to buy a new computer, other stories have involved coercion. In an article for the medical journal *The Lancet*, Ted Alcorn observes: "The scarcity of organs in China has also fostered a black market for illegal transplants, glimpsed by the public only through occasional reports such as the March, 2011, investigation by the Chinese newspaper *Southern Weekend*, which chronicled the story of a migrant worker named Hu Jie who was forced by traffickers to sell his kidney." The Chinese government has increased its efforts to fight illegal organ trafficking, including charging people with homicide if they compel another person to donate an organ. It is also considering financial incentives as a way to spur legal organ donation, which could reduce the appeal of a black market.

China is not alone in struggling to find the balance between increasing the availability of organs and ensuring its citizens donate organs in an ethical fashion. The authors in the following chapter debate the ethical challenges surrounding organ donation.

| *"A diagnosis of death by neurological criteria is theory, not scientific fact."*

Organ Donation: The Inconvenient Truth

John B. Shea

In the following viewpoint, John B. Shea contends that the brain death and cardiac death criteria for organ donation are immoral. According to Shea, the Catholic Church permits organ donation from a deceased donor as long as the person is "certainly dead." However, he argues that there is scientific and medical evidence that people who are brain dead still have parts of their brain that are active, and some patients who have suffered cardiac death could still be revived. Shea is a physician who has written about bioethics for Catholic Insight.

As you read, consider the following questions:

1. As quoted by Shea, what does Alan Shewmon say is the result of brain death?
2. Which brain functions are ignored when a patient is declared brain dead, according to the author?
3. According to Shea, why are organ donors sometimes anesthetized?

Ever since organ donation after a declaration of "cardiac death" was first practised in the Ottawa Hospital in June 2006, Canadians have been subjected to an incessant drumbeat of rhetorical manipulation in the media in favour of organ donation. The following commentary is offered in order to inform the public about the truth in regard to both the moral principles and scientific facts pertaining to both the donation and harvesting of human organs for transplantation purposes. Many physicians have serious and well-considered concerns about the morality of human organ transplantation and about the fact that the general public has not been properly informed about what really happens when organs are retrieved.

Editor: *In July 2007, Britain's Chief Medical Officer repeated an earlier proposal to make a patient's consent for donating organs a* presumed *consent, in order to overcome a backlog of requests for organs. All patients, therefore, are counted as organ donors un-less they specifically opt out. In Ontario, three legislators recently introduced private member's bills with similar provisions. Under this regime, organ donations become mandatory—an extremely dangerous development. The following essay explains why.*

Pope John Paul II, addressing the 18th International Congress of the Transplantation Society on August 29, 2000, stated that, "*Vital organs which occur singly* in the body can be removed only after death; that is, from the body of someone who is certainly dead . . . the death of a person is a single event consisting in the total disintegration of that unity and integrated whole that is the personal self. . . . The death of a person is an event which *no scientific technique or empirical method can identify directly.* . . . The "criteria" for ascertaining death used by medicine today should not be understood as the technical scientific determination of that *exact moment* of a person's death, but as a scientifically secure means of *identifying the biological signs that a person has died.*" He further stated that "the criterion adopted in more recent times for ascertaining the fact of death—namely the *complete* and *irreversible* cessation of all brain activity—if rigorously applied, does not seem to conflict with the essential elements of a sound anthropology."[1] This was only a superficially apparent endorsement.

Alan Shewmon, vice-chair of neurology at the University of California, has stated that any attempt to define the unity of the "organism as a whole" versus multiplicity, a collection of organs and tissues, is, in theory, translatable from the philosophical to the physical domain. But he suspects that any attempt to operationally define "organism as a whole" with the goal of enabling unequivocal, non-arbitrary, dichotomous, categorization of all cases, is an exercise in futility. Shewmon also states "healthy living organisms are obviously integrated unities, that decomposing corpses are obviously not unities, and that there is a fuzzy area in between that is intrinsically undecidable."[2]

Church Re-Opens Debate

The arguments of some that complete cessation of brain activity was not equivalent to death was apparently enough to persuade Pope John Paul II to re-open the debate five years later. Just months before his death in April, 2005, he asked the Pontifical Academy for the Sciences to restudy the signs of death and get scientific verification that those signs were still valid.

Also, Pope Benedict XVI has asked that this debate be revived. On September 14, 2006, Bishop Sanchez, chancellor of the Academy, stated that the Academy had reaffirmed that brain death was equivalent to the death of a person. The debate is not over, however: Dr. Alan Shewmon, a participant in the Vatican study in 2006, has stated that brain death alone "results in a terminally ill patient, deeply comatose, but not a dead person." Bishop Sanchez said that he will have "to wait and see from the Vatican."

In his message on the World Day of the Sick, February 4, 2003, Pope John Paul II said, "It is never licit to kill one human being in order to save another." *The Catechism of the Catholic Church* states (paragraph 2296): "It is morally inadmissible directly to bring about the disabling mutilation or death of a human being, even in order to delay the death of other persons.[3]

Methods of Organ Retrieval

Today, organs are retrieved under four different sets of circumstances.

- From a living donor; for example, a single kidney or part of a liver. This presents no moral problem, provided there is properly informed consent and there is no major risk to the life or health of the donor
- From a person who is declared dead using the older criteria of loss of respiration and cardiac function along with *rigor mortis*. Tissues such as bone marrow, corneas, heart valves and skin may be removed. This procedure is morally acceptable
- After the patient has been declared "brain dead"
- After the patient has been declared to have suffered "cardiac death." The moral status of both "brain death" and "cardiac death" is questionable

Theory and Practice

Organs are obtained from an unconscious patient after he or she has been called "brain dead" using clinical and technologically acquired information, regarded as diagnostic. The public in general is not aware of the following serious criticisms of this kind of organ harvesting. The theory of brain death is highly controversial and can be used for utilitarian purposes.[4] The Pontifical Academy of Sciences declared brain death to be "the true criterion for death" in 1985 and again in 1989. However, in February of 2005, Pope John Paul II called for more precise means of establishing that the donor is dead before vital organs are removed. Organ transplants, he continued, are acceptable only when they are conducted in a manner "so as to guarantee respect for life and for the human person."[5]

The concept that whole brain death (irreversible loss of function of the cerebrum, cerebellum and brain stem) means the loss of integrated organic unity in a human being has been subjected to a powerful critique by neurologist Alan Shewmon.[6] Some physicians question whether we can be sure the entire brain is really dead in patients declared dead in the U.S. by "whole brain," or in the U.K. by "brain stem," criteria.[7] Neurological criteria are not sufficient for declaration of death when an intact cardio-respiratory system is functioning. These criteria test for the absence of some specific brain reflexes. Functions of the brain that are not considered are temperature control, blood pressure, cardiac rate and salt and water balance. When a patient is declared brain dead, these functions are not only still present, but also frequently active.

There is no consensus on diagnostic criteria for brain death. They are the subject of intense international debate. Various sets of neurological criteria for the diagnosis of brain death are used. A person could be diagnosed as brain dead if one set is used and not be diagnosed as brain dead if another is used.[8,9,10,11]

A diagnosis of death by neurological criteria is theory, not scientific fact. Also, irreversibility of neurological function is a prognosis, not a medically observable fact. There is also evidence of poor compliance with accepted guidelines of brain death.[12]

Utilitarian Rationale

Brain death can be used for purely utilitarian purposes. In 2005, Dr. Robert Spaemann, a former philosopher at the University of Munich, told the Pontifical Academy of Sciences that the brain death approach to defining death reflects a new set of priorities. It was no longer the interest of the dying to avoid being declared "dead" prematurely, but the community's interest in declaring a dying person dead as soon as possible.

Two reasons are given: 1) guaranteeing legal immunity for discontinuing life-prolonging measures that would constitute a financial and personal burden for family members and society alike, and 2) collecting vital organs for the purpose of saving the lives of other human beings by transplantation.[13]

The goal is to move to a society where people see organ donation as a social responsibility and where donating organs would be accepted as a normal part of dying. In cases where a person chose to withhold recording a specific choice about donating his or her organs, the surviving family members would agree to donation.[14] In the U.S., federal regulations require institutions to contact local organ procurement organizations concerning death, or impending death, to insure that the family will be approached at the appropriate time by a professional skilled in presenting the proposal of organ donation.

Vatican Debate

Bishop Fabian Bruskewitz of Lincoln, Nebraska told the Pontifical Academy at its 2005 meeting that "no respectable, learned and accepted moral Catholic theologian has said that the words of Jesus regarding laying down one's life for one's friends (John 15:13) is a command or even a licence for suicidal consent for the benefit of another's continuation of earthly life." The bishop then observed that current technology enables doctors to monitor brain activity "in the outer one or two centimetres of the brain." He asked, "Do we have, then, moral certitude in any way that can be called apodictic, regarding even the existence, much less the cessation, of brain activity?"[15]

In 2006, the Pontifical Academy published a statement titled, "Why the concept of brain death is valid as a definition of death." Breaking protocol, several participants in a 2005 Vatican-sponsored conference on the ethics of declaring someone brain dead have published the papers they delivered at the debate. The publication of those papers, which the Vatican had decided not to publish, is evidence of strong feelings about brain death by a minority of members of the Pontifical Academy for Life. Roberto De Mattei, vice-president of the National Research

There Is No Consensus on Brain Death

One can be declared "brain dead" by one set of criteria, but alive by another or perhaps all others; in other words, one could be declared dead in one state and alive in another. This quandary has persisted to the present. In the January 2008 edition of *Neurology*, it was reported that there is no consensus about which of the hundreds of disparate sets of criteria should be used to declare a person "brain dead." The pro-life author warned that Western society is reaching a point, if it is not already there, where the moment of death will be determined not by objective bodily changes but rather the philosophy of personhood by those in power.

American Catholic, *"What Happened to the Hippocratic Oath?," May 5, 2010.*

Council of Italy, told *Catholic News Service* on April 20, 2007 that, "The concern of many is that the Vatican has not taken the appropriate position when doubts exist about the end of human life. . . . The moment of separation of the soul from the body is shrouded in mystery, just as the moment when a soul enters a person is."[15]

Harvard's Oxymoron

The 1968 Harvard Ad Hoc Committee for Irreversible Coma published criteria that held that any organ that no longer functions, or has the possibility of functioning again, is, for all practical purposes, *if not in reality*, dead. They then described the criteria for the diagnosis of irreversible coma and its concomitantly permanent non-functioning brain. They equated the state of coma with brain death and then declared the patient brain-dead. They implied that brain death should be regarded as death, because it inevitably leads to death and that the person in irreversible coma is, for all practical purposes, *if not in reality*, dead. Untold semantic confusion has followed this oxymoronic notion.[16]

The Deadly Apnea Test

Every set of criteria for "brain death" includes an apnea test, considered the most important step in the diagnosis of brain death. The ventilator is discontinued. "Apnea" is the absence of breathing. The only purpose of this test is to determine if the patient is unable to breathe on his or her own, in order to declare "brain death." It aggravates the patient's condition and is commonly done without the knowledge or consent of family members. The ventilator is turned off for up to 10 minutes, carbon dioxide increases in the blood and the blood pressure may drop, indicating that cardiac arrest has occurred. The test significantly impairs the possibility of recovery and can lead to the death of the patient through a heart attack or irreversible brain damage. Dr. Yoshio Watenabe, a cardiologist from Natoya, Japan, stated that if patients were not subjected to the apnea test, they could have a 60 per cent chance of recovery to normal life if treated with timely therapeutic hypothermia (cooling). Note the similarity to cardiac death, later described.[17]

Some form of anesthesia is needed to prevent the donor from moving during removal of the organs. The donor's blood pressure may rise during surgical removal. Similar changes take place during ordinary surgical procedures only if the depth of anesthesia is inadequate. Body movement and a rise in blood pressure are due to the skin incision and surgical procedure if the donor is not anesthetized. Is it not reasonable to consider that the donor may feel pain? In some cases, drugs to paralyze muscle contraction are given to prevent the donor from moving during removal of the organs. Yet, sometimes no anesthesia is administered to the donor. Movement by the donor is distressing to doctors and nurses. Perhaps this is another reason why anesthesia and drugs to paralyze the muscles are usually given.

Organ Harvesting After "Cardiac Death"

Brain death has been used as a means for the moral validation of the retrieval of human organs for transplant since the late 1960s, and "brain dead" patients have been the main source of organs over the years ever since. However, demand for organs has increasingly exceeded supply. In 1993, a new way for categorizing patients as "dead" was conceived. According to a protocol developed at the University of Pittsburgh, a patient could be declared dead, even though not "brain dead," if he or she was declared to have suffered "irreversible loss of circulatory and respiratory function." The Institute of Medicine found that in so-called "controlled non-heartbeating donation," a typical patient would be five to 55 years old, would have suffered a severe head injury, would not be brain dead, would not be a drug user or HIV-positive and would be free from cancer or sepsis. This patient would frequently be unconscious as a result of a car crash.

Typically, the patient would be in an emergency department, in coma, and on a ventilator. If the physician decided that treatment was futile, he asked the relatives' permission to withdraw ventilation and then for their permission to remove organs, if the patient's heart had stopped beating. Ventilation was then withdrawn. If the heart stopped beating within an hour, the surgeon waited two to five minutes before taking out the organs. If the heart had not stopped beating within an hour, the patient would be returned to a hospital bed to die without any further treatment. Note that the patient's physician has a conflict of interest. The longer he waits, the less suitable the organs are for transplant due to damage from lack of oxygenation. The sooner the doctor declares treatment futile, the less chance the patient has of spontaneous recovery.[18]

These procedures are performed despite animal studies and clinical experience that shows even complete recovery of consciousness is possible several minutes after the heart stops, if resuscitative efforts succeed. This kind of resuscitation has been reported after more than 10 minutes of cardiac electric asystole in humans.[19] The fact that the heart stops beating due to ventricular fibrillation, as occurs in a heart attack, does not indicate irreversible cessation of cardiac activity.[20] The application of criteria for organ donation after cardiac death becomes questionable since artificial circulatory and ventilatory support is sometimes resumed after death in order to maintain the viability of abdominal and thoracic organs in potential donors.[21] Extracorporeal circulatory support can lead to return of neurological function in people who were neurologically intact before cardiac death.[22,23]

Finally, it is now widely known that a patient whose heart has stopped beating for 15 minutes after a heart attack can recover if he is treated by cooling the body to 33°C, cardio-pulmonary bypass, cardioplegia (stopping the heart beat chemically) and a slow increase in oxygenation for 24 hours. Up to 80 per cent of these patients can be discharged from hospital, 55 per cent having a good neurological outcome. Clearly, the assumption made by physicians that a patient is dead five minutes after the heart has stopped beating is incorrect.[24]

An ominous and disturbing development is a recent widespread move to involve *palliative caregivers* in the organ donation process. Those care givers are said to provide "skills and principles applicable to donation after cardiac death." In effect, they are to be the agents of a soft-sell program to make the family "feel comfortable and supported during this extremely difficult time." This movement is in keeping with the Institute of Medicine Report Brief, 2006, on "Organ Donation: Opportunities for Action." The IOM goal is "to move toward a society where people see organ donation as a social responsibility" and where "donating organs would be accepted as a normal part of dying and, in cases where a patient died without recording a specific choice about donation of his or her organs, the surviving family members would be comfortable giving permission."[25]

Comment: *Organ donation can be a moral good if the means used to obtain the organs is itself morally good. The circumstances under which this holds true have been described. The critical question is whether a person is truly dead when declared "brain dead" or to have suffered "cardiac death." The answer, in light of the scientific evidence, is that it has not been established cardiac or brain death criteria indicate the real death of a patient with certainty. Mauro Cozzoli, writing about the status of the embryo, has stated, "The uncertainty with regard to whether we are dealing with a human individual is not an abstract doubt, regarding a theory, principle, or doctrinal position* (dubium uris). *As such, it is a doubt about a fact concerning the life of a human being, his existence here and now* (dubium facti)." *As such, "it creates the same obligations as certainty."[26]*

The object of the will is determined by both the agent's motive (finis operantis) *and by the physical character, the integral nature of the external act* (finis operis). *The physical and clinical realities of an action, whether actual or potential, must not be ignored or denied.[27] Those caregivers in Catholic hospitals who administer levonorgestrel, an abortifacient, to a woman who has been raped, ignore or deny the fact that it is impossible to exclude the possibility that she has ovulated and may be pregnant. Those who harvest organs after brain death or cardiac death similarly ignore or deny the possibility that the "donor" may be alive. Professor Joseph Seifert, from the International Academy of Philosophy in Lichtenstein, states that medical ethicists should invoke the traditional moral teaching of the Catholic Church that "even if a small, reasonable doubt exists that our acts kill a living human person, we must abstain from them."[28]*

The declaration of brain death or cardiac death is not sufficient to arrive at moral certitude. The recovery of organs based on that declaration is, therefore, immoral.

References

1. Address of the Holy Father, John Paul II, to the 18th International Congress of the Transplantation Society. August 29, 2000.
2. Dr. Alan Shewmon and Elizabeth Seitz Shewmon. "The Semiotics of Death and Its Medical Implications," *Brain Death and Disorders of Consciousness.* Edited by Machado and Shewmon. Kluwer Academic/Plenum publishers, New York, 2004, pp. 105–6.
3. Carol Glatz. "Vatican resuscitates issue of whether brain death means total death." Vatican Letter, Catholic New Service. Sept. 15, 2006, backgrounder xxxi.
4. Capron, A.M. "Brain Death—Well Settled, Yet Still Unresolved." *New England Journal of Medicine.* April 19, 2001, vol. 344 (16).
5. Pope John Paul II. Letter to the Pontifical Academy of Sciences. Feb. 3, 2005.
6. D. Alan Shewmon. "Recovery from Brain Death. A Neurologist's Apologia." *Linacre Quarterly,* Feb. 1997, 30–96.
7. Donald W. Evans, retired physician, Queen's College, Cambridge. *Journal of Medical Ethics.* April 11, 2007.
8. Wijdicks, E.F. *Neurology.* 2002, Jan. 8; 58(1): 20–25.
9. Haupt, W.F., Rudolf J. "European brain death codes: a comparison of national guidelines." *J. Neurol.* 1999, June; 246(6): 432–7.
10. Evans, D.W. and Potts, M. Brain death. *BMJ,* 2002; 325:598.
11. David W. Evans. Open letter to Prof. E. F. M. Wijdics. Dec. 11, 2001, www.bmj.com.
12. Wang M.Y. et al. Neurosurgery. 2002, Sept; 51(3): 751–5.
13. Institute of Medicine, National Academy of Sciences, Report Brief, Organ Donation: Opportunities for Action, Committee on Increasing Role of Organ Donation. May, 2006.
14. D. Truog et al. Recommendations for End-of-Life Care in the Intensive Care Unit. The Ethics Committee of the Society of Critical Care. *Crit. Care Med.* 2001, vol. 29, no. 12, pp. 2332–2334.
15. Paul A. Byrne *et al.* "Brain Death is Not Death!" Source: Essay—Meeting of the Political Academy of Sciences, in early February, Paul Byrne to the *Compassionate Health Care Network.* March 29, 2005, via email.
16. See reference 6.
17. Ari R. Joffe, critical care physician, Stollery Children's Hospital, University of Alberta, e-letter to J.R. Cuo *et al.* Time dependent validity in the diagnosis of brain death using transcranial Doppler. *J. Neurol Neurosurg Psychiatry.* 2006; 77: 646–649.
18. Institute of Medicine. "Non-Heart-Beating Organ Transplantation—Medical and Ethical Issues of Procurement." 1997, National Academy Press, Washington, D.C.
19. Adhiyaman V., Sundaram R. The Lazarus phenomenon. *J. R. Coll. Physicians Edinb.* 2002, 32: 9–13.
20. American Heart Association. Management of Cardiac Arrest. *Circulation.* 2005; 112:IV 58-IV66.
21. Institute of Medicine Committee on Non-Heart-Beating Transplantation. *The scientific and ethical basis for practice and protocols, executive summary.* Washington, (D.C.): National Academy Press, 2000.
22. Magliocca, J. F. et al. Extracorporeal support for organ donation after cardiac death effectively expands the donor pool. *J Trauma.* 2005; 58:1095–1201.
23. Younger, J.G. et al. Extracorporeal resuscitation of cardiac arrest. *Acad Emerg Med.* 1999: 6: 700–7.
24. Weisfeldt, M.L., Becker L. "Resuscitation After Cardiac Arrest" A 3-phase Time-Sensitive Model. *JAMA.* Dec. 18, 2002, vol. 288, no. 23, pp. 3035–8.

25. Catherine McVearry Kelso, MD. et al. Palliative Care Consultation in the Process of Organ Donation after Cardiac Death. *Journal of Palliative Medicine*, vol. 10, no. 11, 2007.

26. Prof. Mauro Cozzoli, The Human Embryo: Ethical and Normative Aspects. The Identity and Status of the Human Embryo. Proceedings of the Third Assembly of the Pontifical Academy for Life, Vatican City. Feb. 14–16, 1997, p. 271, *Libreria Editrice Vaticana*, 00120. Citta Dei of Vaticano.

27. Steven Long, Regarding the Nature of the Object of the Moral Act According to St. Thomas Aquinas. The Thomistic Institute, 2001, maritain.nd.edu/jiuc/ti01/long.htm.

28. See reference 15.

Addendum

The case for considering "brain death" as equivalent to true death has undergone further trenchant scientific and philosophical critique.[1,2,3]

The notion of irreversible loss of circulatory and respiratory function as a criterion for determining death has also been seriously challenged. This notion means either that the heart cannot be restarted spontaneously (a weaker definition) or that the heart cannot be started despite standard cardio-pulmonary resuscitation (a stronger definition.) The stronger definition of irreversibility as meaning "can never be done" implies that *at no time* can organ procurement be permissible, because future possibilities of resuscitation can never be ruled out. The weaker definition, in practice, considers the patient dead based on the patient's moral choice to forego resuscitative interventions. The problem is that, first, the issue is not whether to resuscitate a person, but is the person truly dead? And secondly, that resuscitative interventions *are performed* during the procurement process to keep organs viable for transplantation after cessation of vital functions; for example, the use of cardio bypass machines, etc. This can result in a return of heart and brain function and even a return to consciousness.[4]

The application of criteria for irreversible cessation of neurologic, circulatory and respiratory functions requires a waiting time well in excess of 10 minutes to give more precision to the determination of death or organ procurement.[5,6,7,8,9,10]

References

1. Potts M., Byrne P.A., Nilges R.G. *Beyond brain death: the case against brain based criteria for human death.* Dordecht: Kluwer Academic Publishers, 2000.

2. Shewmon, D.A. "Brain body disconnection: implications for the theoretical basis of 'brain death'" in De Mattia R., *Finis Vitae—is brain death still life?* 211-50. Roma: Consiglio Nazionale della Richerche, 2006.

3. Truog, R.D., "Brain death—too flawed to endure, too ingrained to abandon." *J Law Med. Eth.* 2007: 35(2): 273–81.

4. Verheijde J.L., Rady, M.Y., McGregor, J. "Recovery of transplantable organs after cardiac or circulatory death: transforming the paradigm of the ethics of organ donation." *Philosophy, Ethics and Humanities in Medicine.* 2007, 2:8, http://www.peh.med.com /content/2/1/8.

5. Kootstra, G. The asystolic or non-heart beating donor. *Transplantation.* 1997, 63(7): 917–21.

6. Weber, M. et al. Kidney Transplantation from Donors Without a Heartbeat. N Eng J Med. 2002, 347 (4): 248–255.

7. Daar, A. S: Non-heartbeating donation: 10 evidence-based ethical recommendations. *Transplant Proceed.* 2004, 26: 1885–1887.

8. Wijdics, E.F., Diringer, M.N. Electro-cardiographic activity after terminal cardiac arrest in neurocatastrophies. *Neurology.* 2004, 62(4): 673–674.

9. Bos, M.A. Ethical and legal issues in non-heartbeating organ donation. *Transplantation.* 2005, 79(9): 1143–1147.

10. Bell, M., MD. Non-heartbeating organ donation: clinical process and fundamental issues. *Br J Anaesth.* 2005, 94(4): 474–478.

| *"Brain death criteria are used legally in all 50 states to pronounce patients dead."*

Recovery of Organs Based on Brain Death Is Ethical

James M. DuBois

Brain death is an ethical way to determine that a patient is eligible to become an organ donor, James M. DuBois argues in the following viewpoint. He maintains that while the general public does not understand facts about brain death, Catholic pro-life groups' objections are based on incorrect assumptions about what it means to be human. DuBois concludes that rejecting organ donation based on this criticism would negatively impact those most in need. DuBois is the department chair of health-care ethics at Saint Louis University.

As you read, consider the following questions:

1. As quoted by DuBois, what does the Catechism of the Catholic Church say about organ donation?
2. What is the difference between brain-dead patients and patients in permanent vegetative states, as explained by the author?

3. In DuBois's view, how do some opponents to brain-death criteria misunderstand human biology?

Few medical procedures have proven to be as effective in saving lives as organ transplantation. Patients on the verge of death from organ failure often live a decade or longer after receiving a transplant. The Catholic Church, and the late Pope John Paul II in particular, have been enthusiastic proponents of this extraordinary medical procedure. According to the *Catechism of the Catholic Church*, "organ donation after death is a noble and meritorious act and is to be encouraged as an expression of generous solidarity." Yet despite the church's longstanding support for organ donation, some Catholic pro-life groups challenge practices essential to it.

Challenging the Brain-Death Criteria

The latest challenge pertains to so-called brain-death criteria, which are used to declare death in over 90 percent of all cases of organ donation in the United States. In a front-page article in *L'Osservatore Romano*, Lucetta Scaraffia, a professor of history at La Sapienza University in Rome and a frequent contributor to the Vatican newspaper, argued that the Catholic Church must revisit the question of brain death because it rests on an understanding of human life that is contrary to Catholic teaching. While Federico Lombardi, S.J., director of the Vatican press office, quickly stated that Scaraffia spoke for herself and not for the magisterium, her article shows there is disagreement within the church on the question of organ donation.

Earlier this year [2009], Paul Byrne, M.D., a former president of the Catholic Medical Association and a long-time opponent of brain-death criteria, published a letter on the Web site Renew America arguing that God's law and the natural law preclude "the transplantation of unpaired vital organs, an act which causes the death of the 'donor' and violates the fifth commandment of the divine Decalogue, 'Thou shalt not kill' [Deuteronomy]." The letter was signed by over 400 individuals, including at least three Catholic bishops and many pro-life program directors.

In 1985 and 1989 the Pontifical Academy of Science studied the question of brain death and concluded that neurological criteria are the most appropriate criteria for determining the death of a human being. In the academy's view, one really should not speak of "brain death"—as if only the brain had died—but rather of the death of the human being, which may be determined neurologically.

In 2000 Pope John Paul II expressed support for organ donation and the use of neurological criteria. He wrote: "The criterion adopted in more recent times for ascertaining the fact of death, namely the complete and irreversible cessation of all brain activity, if rigorously applied, does not seem to conflict with the essential elements of a sound anthropology." He concluded that "a health worker professionally responsible for ascertaining death can use these criteria. . . ." Moreover, he strongly reasserted his support for organ donation, calling it a "genuine act of love" and noting that he had earlier called it a "way of nurturing a genuine culture of life."

To be fair, the Pontifical Academy of Science has no moral teaching authority, and a papal allocution is not the same as a papal encyclical or conciliar teaching. Still, it is ironic that many of the same people who continue to question brain-death criteria after John Paul II's allocution argue that the same pope's allocution on artificial nutrition and hydration for patients in a permanent vegetative state has decisively settled that matter.

Addressing the Objections to Brain-Death Criteria

For many people, concerns about brain death arise from a simple misunderstanding of the facts. I have spent years studying how the general public and health professionals understand death and organ donation. People in focus groups and surveys often confuse brain death with P.V.S. [persistent vegetative state]. Yet

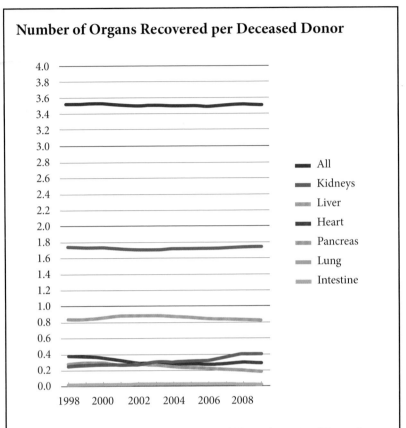

Number of Organs Recovered per Deceased Donor

Legend:
- All
- Kidneys
- Liver
- Heart
- Pancreas
- Lung
- Intestine

TAKEN FROM: Organ Procurement and Transplantation Network and Scientific Registry of Transplant Recipients, "OPTN/SRTR 2010 Annual Report: Deceased Organ Donation," 2010.

P.V.S. patients breathe spontaneously and have sleep-wake cycles. Brain-dead bodies depend upon artificial ventilation; without it there would be no respiration and no heartbeat. Moreover, many think it is possible to recover from brain death, just as patients sometimes recover from deep coma. Yet there is no documented case of a patient recovering from brain death, despite some popular reports of misdiagnosed brain death. An organ that has been deprived of oxygen sufficiently long will die, and it is medically impossible to change dead brain cells to living brain cells. Finally, about half of Americans do not know that brain death criteria are used legally in all 50 states to pronounce patients dead. They are also used in nearly all Catholic hospitals in the United States.

While these factual misunderstandings are common among the general public, they are not the source of the concerns expressed by Catholic pro-life groups. Their objections to brain-death criteria tend to be more philosophical. In a recent article in *The National Catholic Bioethics Quarterly*, I have tried to address some of these concerns. Here I will summarize three key points.

Human development. Lucetta Scaraffia and others have voiced concern that if we decide a human being is dead because he or she lacks a functioning brain, then we will deny that embryos are human until they form a brain. However, we are developmental creatures: in our earliest days of development in the uterus, we do not depend upon a brain to live. Yet as we grow, we come to depend upon a functioning brain; and when it dies, we die. To argue that support for brain death criteria calls into question the status of early human life is to misunderstand basic human biology.

The unity of the human being. According to some Catholic pro-life advocates, the brain death criteria accepted by the larger medical community rest on a "dualistic" view of the human being that assumes the human soul is radically distinct from the human body. They argue that if the soul is the life principle of the body and if an artificially maintained brain-dead body shows some signs of life, like a beating heart, then the soul must be present. Like many members of the Catholic medical community, I do not dispute the Catholic understanding of life and death; we take seriously the fact that the soul and its proper functions are intimately bound with the body. Yet a mature human body that is functionally decapitated is no longer a living human being.

Ken Iserson, M.D., a professor of emergency medicine at the University of Arizona, cites the Talmud when describing brain death: "The death throes of a decapitated man are not signs of life any more than is the twitching of a lizard's amputated tail." If one rejects the notion that a decapitated body is a dead body, then one is left with a conclusion repugnant to common sense and good metaphysics: a severed head and a decapitated body would both have to be considered living human beings if separately maintained alive (a view held by at least one opponent of brain death criteria). In fact, to be wholly consistent, one would need to hold that each is independently the same living human being that existed prior to the decapitation—a view that flatly contradicts the unity required to be human.

Strange case reports. Following brain death, most bodies spontaneously lose circulation within days, even when they are artificially ventilated and provided with aggressive critical care. But there have been exceptional case reports of prolonged "survival" of the ventilated body. These are not misdiagnoses. In some cases, the entire brain liquefies and extremities begin to turn black. Despite continued circulation, there is no room for speculation that such bodies are any more conscious than a corpse that has been buried, and the likelihood of recovery is the same. Professor Scaraffia has noted that there have also been cases of pregnant women who were pronounced brain dead; yet with artificial ventilation and aggressive support their bodies sustained pregnancies until viability. But the fact that many parts of the body may survive and function for a time is wholly compatible with death of the human being. This is precisely what makes organ transplantation possible. The human heart may beat outside of the human body in a bucket of ice, and may even be transplanted and made to function again inside another human being. That the placenta and womb may survive and function in a body maintained artificially is similarly amazing, but it does not indicate that the womb belongs to a living human being. Importantly, none of these cases present "new data" that became available only after John Paul II's allocution, and thus they do not merit a re-examination of church teaching. They are well known, even if strange and rare, phenomena.

Treating Donors with Respect

In the end, I think these philosophical disputes about brain death are actually motivated by a much deeper, more fundamental opposition to organ donation. This is illustrated by the resistance pro-life groups have offered to other kinds of organ donation, including donation after cardiac death. This opposition ultimately is driven by two deeper concerns that often go unarticulated.

First, organ donation risks treating human beings or their deceased bodies as "objects." In John Paul II's 2000 allocution on organ donation and brain death, he stated that "any procedure which tends to commercialize human organs or to consider them as items of exchange or trade must be considered morally unacceptable, because to use the body as an 'object' is to violate the dignity of the human person." He also noted that organ donation requires the informed consent of the patient or the patient's family. Yet the continual shortage of organs leads some policymakers to consider payments for organs and even organ procurement without expressed consent. Overly hasty pronouncements of brain death—which are rare but have received considerable attention in recent years—also reinforce suspicions that a concern for organ donation is trumping care for patients.

The ethical question at hand is how we should deal with the risk of treating persons as objects or commodities. It is worth recalling that Hans Jonas, one of the more famous opponents of brain-death criteria, also expressed deep reservations about medical research in general, which has yielded numerous treatments, vaccines and cures. Jonas feared that such research tends by its very nature to treat human subjects as "objects" or things. But the Catholic Church does not view medical research as intrinsically wrong for that reason; rather, it suggests how research may be conducted respectfully. It is the same with organ donation.

A second obstacle to organ donation within some Catholic circles rests on a misunderstanding of the so-called precautionary principle. This principle has been used in Catholic social teaching and basically urges caution in the face of uncertainty regarding grave risks of harm (for example, the possible harm from genetic modification). Paul Byrne, M.D., and colleagues seem to seek an absolute certainty that death has occurred, one marked by the destruction of all major organ systems. This is why Dr. Byrne opposes not only brain death, but also deceased-organ donation; by the time he would consider a body dead, no organs would be healthy enough to transplant. Yet this desire for absolute certainty conflicts with what Pope John Paul II wrote on the subject. He stated that "a health worker professionally responsible for ascertaining death can use these [neurological] criteria in each individual case as the basis for arriving at that degree of assurance in ethical judgment which moral teaching describes as 'moral certainty.'" He added that this "moral certainty is considered the necessary and sufficient basis for an ethically correct course of action."

Determining death in the context of organ donation is challenging and will likely remain controversial for the simple reason that death must be determined quickly lest all transplantable organs die with the human being. Nevertheless, the decision to reject organ donation in the name of precaution is not without cost. Patients in need of an organ transplant will die years earlier than necessary, and families who often find organ donation consoling will be bereft of the opportunity to find some meaning in their loss. We may not do evil that good may come of it, but neither should we bury our talents out of fear.

> "Through organ donation, prisoners
> can preserve a sense of self worth and
> dignity."

Organ Donation by a Prisoner: Legal and Ethical Considerations

Stuart J. Bagatell, Donald P. Owens, and Marc J. Kahn

In the following viewpoint, Stuart J. Bagatell, Donald P. Owens, and Marc J. Kahn recount an experience serving on an ethics committee where they allowed a prisoner to donate a kidney. According to the authors, the donor in this particular case was compensated fairly, without it being a prohibited sale. In addition, they argue that the donor was not coerced into making the decision and was undergoing a low-risk operation. The authors conclude that prisoners have the autonomy to make the decision to donate organs. Bagatell is on the staff at JFK Medical Center in Atlantis, Florida; Owens is an associate professor of medicine and psychiatry at Tulane University's school of medicine; and Kahn is a professor of medicine and a senior associate dean at the Tulane School of Medicine.

As you read, consider the following questions:
1. What is "compensation," as defined by the authors?
2. In the case described by the authors, why did coercion not play a role?
3. What is the mortality rate for kidney donation, according to the authors?

It is axiomatic that the act of surgery is legal assault unless the consent of the patient or his legal representative is obtained. Consent has been defined as informed consent obtained without duress. How voluntary a contribution does a brother make when he is informed that unless he offers his kidney, his twin brother will die? Can there be greater coercion that the sanction of family and friends in such a situation where the probability of successful transplantation is indeed very good? Yet what value judgment would society place in the rich industrialist who buys a kidney for his dying son for $100,000 from a poor employee in one of his factories? What about prisoners who volunteer?[1]

Rabbi Tendler

Being a member of an ethics committee is something which most physicians probably have not experienced. Academic physicians are frequently called upon to serve on committees in addition to taking care of patients and teaching. However, as most physicians are not theologians or moralists, ethics committees strive to include individuals with varied backgrounds including members of the clergy, nurses, psychologists, psychiatrists, oncologists, neonatologists, lawyers, business administrators, and students. With a collective intelligence, common sense, and experience, the goal of an ethics committee is to come to the "right" conclusion, similar to deliberations of a jury. This is often difficult when the motives of the patients involved are in question.

The Case

The Tulane abdominal transplant team had identified a potential kidney donor. This potential donor, however, had been arrested in Louisiana on charges of theft over $500. In addition, the potential donor had a warrant outstanding in Tennessee for probation violation after a conviction of theft over $1000. During the time between leaving Tennessee and his arrest in Louisiana, the potential donor befriended the potential recipient. The recipient allowed the potential donor to live in a house on his property, providing the potential donor with gainful employment and the chance for a brighter future. Over the course of a few months, the potential donor learned about the recipient's medical ailment, and for reasons unknown to the ethics committee, offered to donate a kidney to the recipient. To complicate matters further, the recipient made a promise to the potential donor that he would become the "godfather" of the donor's child following the transplant. Although the terms of this agreement were not specified, we assumed this meant that the recipient agreed to help care for and raise the potential donor's child which would likely involve some monetary assistance.

The charges in Louisiana were eventually dropped. The district attorney in Louisiana and the district attorney in Tennessee discussed the matter, and the potential donor was released from prison on his own recognizance with the understanding that once the potential donor was fit enough (assuming the kidney transplant went forward) to face the charges against him in Tennessee, the potential donor would be expected to appear in court. The question posed by the transplant team to the ethics committee was: "Would it be ethical to allow this particular living kidney donation to take place?"

Legal Implications

The first issue to address in the case presented is the legality of the proposed organ donation. In this regard, there are two main questions to consider: 1) Does the "deal" between the donor and recipient (exchange of "godfather" designation for kidney) constitute a sale of a human organ, rendering it illegal under current US law? Although the potential donor was no longer a prisoner, it was still interesting and relevant to answer. 2) Can a prisoner legally donate an organ?

As for the first question, the distinction between gift, sale, and compensation needs to be made. The definition of a *gift* is something voluntarily transferred by one person to another without compensation. In this case, the potential donor is not gifting his kidney as there is a quid pro quo, namely the promise of continued care for the potential donor's son in exchange for the organ. Therefore, a discussion concerning the ethics and legality of gift giving is not necessary in this case.

Unlike a gift, a sale refers to the transfer of ownership and title to property from one person to another for a price. Referring to the sale of organs for transplantation, Al Gore said, "It is against our system of values to buy and sell parts of human beings. It is wrong." In 1984, the same year Gore made his statement, the National Organ Transplant Act prohibited the sale of several organs and body parts for purposes of transplantation (42#U.S.C. 274 (1984)).[2,3] Therefore, according to US law, the idea of body parts being relegated to the status of "property" that can be sold for money is wrong. In other cultures, however, there are differences in ethical principles. For example, in Iran, there has been a program of compensated kidney donation from living unrelated donors since 1997. In that nation and culture, it is believed that depriving an organ donor of legitimate compensation is not ethically defensible.[4] Similarly, with respect to organ transplantation, Pope Pius XII declared in 1956 that "It would be going too far to declare immoral every acceptance or demand of payment. It is not necessarily a fault to accept it."[5] In this case, there is no evidence of a sale taking place.

Compensation is defined as something that constitutes an equivalent exchange of one thing for another. Compensation does not necessarily imply a direct exchange of money for goods and services. Recognizing the need for transplantable organs, in 2002 the United States considered compensation by way of a tax incentive for organ donation when two bills proposed within the House of Representatives called for an amendment to the IRS Code. The Gift of Life Tax Credit (GOLTC) Act and the Help Organ Procurement Expand (HOPE) Act both presented a refundable credit to individuals or to the estates of those who agree either to be living donors or to donate their organs upon death. The GOLTC act would have refunded $10,000 to the estates of individuals and the HOPE Act would have offered a refund of $2500 to qualified persons.[6] Although both bills died in committee, it seems that our government at least considered compensation for organ donation. This idea of a tax credit for organ donors appears to be more palatable than the direct selling of organs.

Returning to our case, a fair arrangement for compensation was agreed upon; the potential donor giving the potential recipient a new start to his life, and the recipient giving the donor's child a chance for a new start to his life. Section 274e(a) of the National Organ Transplant Act of 1984 states:

> It shall be unlawful for any person to knowingly acquire, receive, or otherwise transfer any human organ for valuable consideration for use in human transplantation if the transfer affects interstate commerce.

It is fair to say that caring for the donor's child would not affect interstate commerce. Thus, the recipient's agreement to care for the donor's child in exchange for receipt of the donor's kidney

Preliminary Results of a Survey of Death Row Inmates About Organ Donation

Surveys were mailed to all 37 inmates serving time on death row in Oregon as of September 2011. . . . 23/37 responded to the survey (62% response rate), 22/37 (or 59.5%) completed the survey in its entirety.

In your opinion, should inmates on death row be allowed to register as organ donors?

    20/23 responded "yes" (86.9%)

Which of the following statements characterize your attitude toward organ donation by inmates on death row? (select all that apply)

Inmates on death row should not be allowed to register as organ donors

    2/23 (8.7%) selected this response

Inmates on death row should not be encouraged to become organ donors

    18/23 (78.2%) selected this response

Organ donation is one way death row inmates can help other people

    19/23 (82.6%) selected this response

Inmates on death row should be allowed to become organ donors

    17/23 (73.9%) selected this response

Inmates on death row should be allowed and encouraged to become organ donors

    8/23 (34.8%) selected this response

Western Oregon University, "Organ Donation Survey Preliminary Findings," www.gavelife.org, 2012.

does not fall within the Act's definition of a prohibited sale of an organ.

The next issue to consider is the legality of a prisoner donating an organ. Both district attorneys involved with this case were in agreement about the release of the potential donor on his own recognizance. Therefore, the potential donor would no longer be a prisoner at the time of transplant. Regardless, Louisiana Revised Statute 15:831 regarding medical care of inmates expressly permits inmates to donate organs for transplant:

> No monies appropriated to the department from the state general fund or from dedicated funds shall be used for medical costs associated with organ transplants for inmates or for the purposes of providing cosmetic medical treatment of inmates, unless the condition necessitating such treatment or organ transplant arises or results from an accident or situation which was the fault of the department or resulted from an action or lack of action on the part of the department. However, nothing in this Section shall prohibit an inmate from donating his vital organs for transplant purposes.

Ethical Considerations

A recent consensus on live organ donation states, that "a person who gives consent to be a live organ donor should be competent, willing to donate, free from coercion, medically and psychosocially suitable, fully informed of the risks and benefits as a donor, and fully informed of the risks, benefits and alternative treatment available to the recipient."[7] Therefore, in order to properly respond to the request from the transplant team, we needed to account for each of these facets of the case.

Before any transplant at Tulane University Hospital, a psychologist performs a thorough evaluation of the donor and comments on whether or not he is suitable for transplant. The psychosocial evaluation of the potential donor includes, among other things, assessment for vulnerability to coercion and the nature of the relationship between the donor and the recipient. In this case, we received a report that affirmed the donor was in fact competent to make the decision to donate his kidney.

Another question that remained to be answered was whether or not the donor was free from coercion. Prisoners are in a very vulnerable position. The conditions of imprisonment are themselves coercive and not conducive to free decision making, but this should be seen as a vulnerability that should not disqualify a person from becoming an organ donor.[8] There is a fine line between coercion and the reciprocal nature of friendship. In this case, there was a question concerning the relationship between the potential donor and potential recipient making it unclear whether or not the donor was free from coercion. An argument could be made that the donor was being coerced by the recipient through the promise of the recipient serving as godfather to the donor's son. Friendships, however, are based on mutual respect, and reciprocal exchange of care and concern. In this case, the friendship was forged over a period of months when the recipient gave lodging and gainful employment to the potential donor. The result was the building of a trust between the two which resulted not only in the willingness to donate a kidney, but to the potential donor trusting the recipient to care for his son when he could not. As a result of this friendship, coercion did not appear to play a role.

Regarding the issue of safety of the procedure, the physicians on the transplant team attested to the medical suitability of both donor and recipient. Additionally, laparoscopic nephrectomy now accounts for 50% of the donor nephrectomy procedures done in the United States. With this procedure, hospital stays are brief and perioperative mortality reported for living kidney donors including both open and laparoscopic methods is 0.03%. Therefore, it is a safe procedure for the donor to undertake.

One major ethical principle relevant to this case is beneficence—prevent harm, remove harm, and do good. In this case, all three of these aspects are present. The potential donor prevents harm to the recipient by removing the specter of untimely death and hence removes harm by circumventing the diseased kidney. Therefore, by definition, he is doing good by the act of donation. Although in and out of police custody, the potential donor was able to exert his autonomy, become aware of the risks involved, and agree to give his kidney. The potential donor entered this project fully informed of its risks and potential hazards for both himself and his friend.

Importantly, even though prisoners are relieved of certain civil rights, they are not "owned" body and soul by the state. Prisoners still possess the autonomy to make certain decisions. Through organ donation, prisoners can preserve a sense of self worth and dignity which could become part of their rehabilitation as an offender against society.

Another subtle psychological issue that is raised in this case is the possibility of secondary gain. For the prisoner, the facts suggest no indication of secondary gain in terms of being released or privileged in jail or prison. The prisoner was released from the Louisiana parish jail and the charges were dismissed prior to any decision regarding his suitability as an organ donor. The Tennessee courts expected him to return to their jurisdiction for arraignment following resolution of the organ donation question. Therefore, there was no indication of secondary gain through the judicial system. The only level of secondary gain that seemed to exist was the pleasure of giving a gift, in this case his kidney, so that a friend might live. The ability and willingness to give the gift of life to someone is fundamental to ethical and religious traditions throughout the world. If this level of secondary gain is prohibited in this and similar cases, the social consequences become enormous, affecting the whole of voluntarism that has proved to be such a benefit in the wake of natural disasters, among other things, experienced worldwide throughout history.

So what was the "right" answer in this case? In this particular case, we determined that there were no ethical or legal issues prohibiting the donation to take place. Autonomy, beneficence, legality, morality, and gifting in friendship were all consistent with the notion that the donation could go forward. Individuals, regardless of their standing within society, have the ultimate privilege and responsibility of making decisions that affect the well being and life of others. This case highlights the basic transcultural principle; to do unto others as you would have others do unto you.

References

1. Tendler MD. Medical ethics and Torah morality. In: Carmell A, Domb C, editors. *Challenge: Torah Views on Science and Its Problems*. New York, NY: Feldheim Publishers;1978:492–499.
2. Cohen CB. Public policy and the sale of human organs. *Kennedy Inst Ethics J* 2002;12:47–64.
3. Delmonico FL, Arnold R, Scheper-Hughes N, et al. Ethical incentives, not payment, for organ donation. *New Engl J Med* 2002;346:2002–2005.
4. Bagheri A. Compensated kidney donation: an ethical review of the Iranian model. *Kennedy Inst Ethics J* 2006;16:269–282.
5. Healy GW. Moral and legal aspects of transplantation: prisoners or death convicts as donors. *Transplatation Proc* 1998;30:3653–3654.
6. Curtis AS. Congress considers incentives for organ procurement. *Kennedy Inst Ethics J* 2003;13:51–52.
7. Abecassis M. Consensus statement on the live organ donor. *JAMA* 2000;284:2919–2926.
8. Castro LD. Human organs from prisoners: kidneys for life. *J Med Ethics* 2003;29:171–175.
9. Davis CL, Delmonico FL. Living-donor kidney transplantation: a review of the current practices for the live donor. *J Am Soc Nephrology* 2005;16:2098–2110.

| "Coerced donation puts the United States in company with the People's Republic of China."

Forcing Prisoners to Donate Organs as a Condition for Release Is Unethical

St. Louis Post-Dispatch

In the following viewpoint, the editorial board of the St. Louis Post-Dispatch *asserts that prisoners should not be compelled to donate organs as a condition for early release. The board cites the case of sisters Gladys and Jamie Scott, who were granted early release from a Mississippi prison if Gladys donated a kidney to her sister. The board contends that placing such a condition on prisoners is unethical, because it could lead to widespread abuse and be particularly coercive to poor and minority prisoners. The* St. Louis Post-Dispatch *is a major newspaper in St. Louis, Missouri. It is one of the largest newspapers in the Midwest.*

As you read, consider the following questions:

1. As stated by the editorial board, how much did the Scott sisters net in the armed robbery for which they received life sentences?

2. Why are minorities often reluctant to undergo organ transplants, according to the author?

3. As explained by the editorial board, why is an ethics committee from the United Network for Organ Sharing concerned about prisoners donating organs?

G ladys Scott is being forced to donate a kidney as a condition of her early release from prison.

Just before the close of 2010, Mississippi Gov. Haley Barbour granted an early prison release to a pair of sisters serving two life sentences each for an armed robbery that netted $11.

An Early, but Unethical Release

It wasn't just the long-overdue release of Gladys Scott and Jamie Scott that has drawn national attention. Rather, it was the unusual nature of their conviction and the barbaric, unethical condition for their release.

The Scott sisters, neither of whom had prior criminal convictions, were sentenced to two life terms each for a robbery in which no one was seriously injured. They were not alleged to have used force or a weapon; they were charged with luring two men to a place where they were robbed.

As an official condition of their release, 36-year-old Gladys Scott will be required to "donate" a kidney to 38-year-old Jamie Scott, whose kidneys have failed.

Jamie Scott now receives daily dialysis at a cost to the state of about $200,000 a year. Mr. Barbour, a former lobbyist who is considering a run for president in 2012, cited the cost of that treatment in a statement announcing their early release.

The NAACP campaigned to win the sisters' release from what it argued—with strong justification—are unreasonably harsh prison sentences.

Requiring Prisoners to Donate Organs Violates Human Rights

While donating a kidney is extremely safe when donors are healthy and a rigorous evaluation has taken place, it does have a small risk of death. Requiring a prisoner to agree to take this risk in return for parole violates international transplant standards and human rights. The idea that prisoners are able to consent to risky medical treatment in return for benefits is one that ethicists have long questioned.

Frances Kissling, "How Haley Babour's Freedom-For-Kidney-Deal for Scott Sisters Makes U.S. Like China," www.alternet.com, January 7, 2011.

There Is Potential for Widespread Abuse

A spokesman for the Scotts told the *Washington Post* that requiring the organ donation as a condition of release was Gladys Scott's idea.

Mr. Barbour said that the offer to "donate" a kidney, which was contained in an application for early release sent to the governor's office, bolstered their appeal.

No matter who broached the idea first, making it a condition of early release is barbaric and unethical. It sets the stage for even more widespread abuse.

It's not uncommon for convicts facing long prison terms to offer to "donate" organs in return for a lighter sentence.

Such proposals have been widely circulated in recent years as the shortage of transplantable organs, especially kidneys, has grown worse.

More than 110,000 people were awaiting transplants as of Monday afternoon [January 2011]; about 88,000 of them were waiting for a kidney.

African-Americans are disproportionately represented on waiting lists for kidneys, just as they are in prison and on death row.

Minorities, especially African-Americans, wait longer for available organs and often experience worse outcomes.

Part of the reason is that more are uninsured. But many also are reluctant to undergo treatments like organ transplants. That's part of the lingering legacy of the Tuskegee study, in which African-American men who thought they were receiving care became unwitting subjects of a medical experiment.

Letting Prisoners Donate Organs Would Be Coercive

An ethics committee from the United Network for Organ Sharing, which manages the nation's transplant system, raised concerns about allowing prisoners, especially those facing death, reduced sentences in return for "donating" an organ.

The inconsistent ways the death penalty and life sentences are applied "suggest that these proposals would be coercive to particular classes of individuals—minorities and the poor," the committee wrote.

Coerced donation puts the United States in company with the People's Republic of China, the only other nation that makes the organs of prisoners available for transplantation. That's not company we want to keep.

For the sake of the Scott sisters and his own state's humanity, Mr. Barbour should rescind his barbaric edict and issue another one not conditioned on organ donation.

| "Creating a savior sibling is a direct
violation of the dignity of that person."

The Use of Children as Sibling Donors Is Unethical

Jennifer Lahl

"Savior siblings" are children created via in vitro fertilization to become a match for a brother or sister in need of a donor. In the following viewpoint, Jennifer Lahl argues that this process is immoral. According to Lahl, the process of creating a matching embryo is a form of eugenics that leads to the discarding of less-desirable embryos. She also argues that savior siblings, unlike most organ donors, are not making the decision freely. Lahl is the president of the Center for Bioethics and Culture, an organization that facilitates conversations on issues relating to medicine, science and technology, and other bioethical matters.

As you read, consider the following questions:

1. According to Lahl, why was Adam Nash born?
2. How many embryos did the Nash family create, as stated by the author?
3. What ethical line does Lahl assert has been crossed in the creation of savior siblings?

hat does it say about a society which permits, no, which condones the use of medicine and technology for the sole purpose of creating human life just to destroy it? It says we are the culture that has morally and tragically lost its way.

My Sister's Keeper, Jodi Picoult's 2004 novel, just came out on the big screen. Joining other profoundly bioethical films such as *Gattaca* (1997; addresses genetic engineering of super humans), *Million Dollar Baby* (2004; tackles assisted dying), and *The Island* (2005; deals with the creation of human clones to be spare parts for the wealthy sick), *My Sister's Keeper* takes on a real-life issue commonly known as "savior sibling."

How Savior Siblings Are Created

A "savior sibling" refers to the creation of a genetically matched human being, in order to be the savior of a sick child in need of a donor. This requires creating human embryos *in vitro*, which literally means "in glass" (i.e. a test tube), using the egg from the mother and fertilizing the egg with the father's sperm. Then, using pre-implantation technology, the embryos are tested, and the one deemed genetically compatible is implanted into the mother's womb in order for the embryo to grow and develop. Once that baby is delivered, the cord blood is often collected because it provides a perfect match for the sick sibling. Later on, bone marrow, blood, or even organs, can also be taken and used for transplantation for the sick sibling.

Savior siblings are already a reality, and the use of such practices in the United States is not prohibited. Adam Nash was the first savior sibling in the U.S. Adam was born in 2000 to rescue his sister Mollie, who was diagnosed with Fanconi's anemia. Mollie would have otherwise succumbed to death if not for a matched donor. The Nashes created 30 embryos and went through four rounds of in vitro fertilization (IVF) to finally produce Adam, who was the match Mollie needed. Of course, the ethics of the disposition of the 29 other embryos is quite problematic. Adam was chosen, 29 other human lives were not, simply because their DNA was not able to rescue Mollie from a deadly diagnosis.

In Picoult's story, the film opens with a voice-over narration of Anna Fitzgerald, the savior sibling. Anna describes herself as a "designer baby." Note to self—Beware of euphemisms. Euphemisms are rampant in the world of IVF. Selective reduction refers to a situation in which many embryos are transferred into a mother's womb, and then if too many of them implant, the physician, (with the parents' consent), removes the "extra" embryos. Although the removed embryos die because a lethal dose of potassium chloride is injected into the fetal heart, we politely talk about *selective* reductions. Family balancing, social sex-selection and gender selection are terms used to discuss the use of these technologies to intentionally select your children based on their sex and your preference for a boy or a girl. Of course, these euphemistic phrases are used to play down the fact that people are ordering—that is, shopping for—their children purely based on parents' desires. If you want a boy, you screen the embryos, select the male embryo, and discard the female ones in order to "balance" your family. Heaven forbid we should have unbalanced families! The practice of social sex-selection is banned in Canada, so Canadians who wish to order the sex of their children come to the U.S. Social sex-selection is just another euphemism with deadly ramifications. Healthy babies discarded because they are the wrong sex? Surely these are symptoms of a culture in decline!

The Emergence of High-Tech Eugenics

Anna Fitzgerald, the self-described designer baby in Picoult's story—designer not as in Prada, or Coach, or Gucci, but more or less like a cafeteria-style menu selection—was designed for the purpose of being the donor for her sister, Kate. Kate, diagnosed as a young child with leukemia, needs a bone marrow transplant, but NOD[1] is not conventional. . . . Most babies born are unwanted; [Anna] at least was a wanted child. But she is wanted as a product; as a medical treatment; as a donor. Actually, the most recent statistics, taken from a study done in 2001, show that overall 49 percent of babies born in the U.S. are from unintended pregnancies. After that report came out, steps were taken to reduce that number to 30 percent by 2010. We shall see how successful the educational efforts have been when the next report comes out. But of course, as all studies of this nature go, the actual statistics break out quite differently when looked at from educational, economic and age categories.

Also, Anna is not quite accurate in her description of how she was made. She suggests that the doctors took the best part of her mom's DNA and the best part of her dad's DNA and voila—the perfect match was made. If we as a society are going to be able to have an earnest conversation on the ethics of creating savior siblings, we must be intellectually honest with the facts and accuracy of the procedure. Embryos—as in *multiple* embryos, were created, and then tested, and only the one that would provide the genetic match was brought to term. The other embryos were discarded. As was the case with the Nash family, 30 embryos were created and only Adam was selected. This is high-tech eugenics: being selected only because of your "good" genes or being destined for demise because you had the wrong or "bad" genetic make-up.

From this point on, the film does a good job of addressing some real issues head on, showing the complexity of the ethical realities, while fortunately not leaving the audience with a romanticized "happily ever after" ending.

The film poignantly shows the absolute devastation parents face when told that their child has a dreadful disease that will most likely kill her. There is no sugar coating of the stress that is placed on a marriage or other children in the family, and the strained family dynamics when a child is seriously or chronically ill. That means gut-wrenching decisions, and the constant suggestion that all hope is lost and all you have to grasp for are straws.

The film deals directly with Anna's life and experience, as she has lived it knowing that she is a product who only exists because someone else desperately needed her—or parts of her at least.

"Congratulations! It's a saviour sibling," cartoon by Grizelda. www.cartoonstock.com.

Creating People as a Means to an End

And here is the heart of the ethical matter at hand. Technology, apart from any ethical or moral compass, has progressed to the point where, for the first time in history, we are able to intentionally create human life and allow it to fully develop solely because we need that life to save another. And perhaps even more worrisome is the reality that other lives were created, and then destroyed because it did not perfectly meet the need of another.

119

Realistically, there could be several embryos which provided the genetic match, but since only one is needed; even embryos which make the cut are discarded. In our desire to relieve suffering, to seek healing and cures, and to avoid death, we have crossed a bright ethical line by seeking to use one human life for the good of another.

Whether we look for moral guidance from our religious texts or to secular historical documents, it is important that we as a society remain rooted in the belief in the inherent dignity of all persons. The U.N. Declaration on Human Rights warns that wherever there is "disregard and contempt for human rights," "barbarous acts" are sure to follow. Surely, the rights of the savior sibling have been denied when from their first breath they are being used as a means to an end. The World Medical Declaration of Helsinki claims that, "the duty of the physician is to promote and safeguard the health of patients." Isn't there an immediate conflict of interest between the doctor and the patient, not to mention the savior sibling, who has nothing to gain, but perhaps is exposed to medical risk while not even being a patient? Organ donation is perhaps one of the greatest altruistic deeds a person can do. But in organ donation, the gift is freely given. It is never taken, coerced or bought. Creating a savior sibling is a direct violation of the dignity of that person. It treats human life as something to be made, manufactured and used as a commodity.

Early in the film, Anna hires an attorney and announces, "I want to sue my parents for the rights to my own body." From the moment of birth, the savior sibling has been denied the full rights to her own body, and to willingly and freely be her sister's keeper.

Note

1. Nucleotide-binding oligomerization domain (NOD) deficiency is linked to various autoimmune diseases such as leukemia.

> *"Parents have kids for all sorts of reasons. . . . Are these [reasons] inherently more ethically sound than the idea of a 'saviour sibling'?"*

Concerns About Savior Siblings Should Be Based on Facts

Erin Nelson and Timothy Caulfield

In the following viewpoint, Erin Nelson and Timothy Caulfield argue that discussions about the ethics of "savior siblings" should be based on facts. According to the authors, the debate over the issue ignores the laws that govern organ donation in the United States, Canada, and Great Britain. The authors further point out that donation of umbilical cord blood causes no harm to a newborn donor, and society cannot judge whether having a child that is a perfect donor match for an older sibling is a less valid reason for having a child. Nelson is a research fellow at the University of Alberta's Health Law Institute, and Caulfield is the Canada research chair in health law and policy and a research director at the institute.

As you read, consider the following questions:

1. As stated by the authors, under what circumstance does the Human Fertilization and Embryology Authority permit the selection of embryos?
2. Why do Nelson and Caulfield have mixed feelings about popular portrayals of medical ethics?
3. What is the Canadian law that gives the federal government jurisdiction over reproductive technology, according to the authors?

The debate over embryo selection is going to heat up again with tomorrow's [June 2009] opening of *My Sister's Keeper*. The film depicts the story of a young girl who is the product of pre-implantation genetic diagnosis. She was selected as an embryo by her parents because she is a perfect genetic match for her older sister, who suffers from leukemia. She is, in other words, a "saviour sibling."

Selecting Embryos to Create Donors

The debate around saviour siblings (and designer babies) flared with particular heat in England several years ago. Two families asked the Human Fertilisation and Embryology Authority (HFEA) for permission to select embryos that were perfect tissue matches for older siblings who suffered from blood disorders. Only one family was granted permission; the second sought treatment in the United States, and the older sibling now appears cured of Diamond-Blackfan anemia. The first family, after a court battle between the HFEA and an organization called Comment on Reproductive Ethics, eventually tried to use various reproductive technologies to create a cord blood donor sibling, but without success.

Since these cases, the HFEA has revised its views and now clearly permits the selection of embryos that may lead to the birth of a child who can provide compatible tissue "for the treatment of an existing child who is affected by a serious or life-threatening condition."

The parents in the British cases were seeking a tissue-matched cord blood donor. Umbilical cord blood is a rich source of stem cells that can produce all types of blood cells and thus can treat and potentially cure many types of blood disorders, including blood cancers such as leukemia. Cord blood is usually discarded at birth. There is no risk of harm to a newborn cord blood donor.

In the book on which *My Sister's Keeper* is based, the parents sought a cord blood donor for their daughter. But as time goes on, Anna, the "saviour sibling," undergoes more and more invasive procedures to help her sister. Ultimately, she is told by her parents that she will need to donate a kidney to save her sister's life.

There Is a Distorted Portrayal of Legal Issues

As academics, we have mixed feelings about popular and media portrayals of complex issues in health law and ethics. On the one hand, public conversation about ethical and legal issues is essential and can further sound public policy. And popular media can provide an ideal vehicle to engage the public. On the other hand, it is too easy for issues to be distorted in such a way as to derail that useful conversation.

My Sister's Keeper is a perfect example of the latter. The very idea that parents are free to decide that one of their children could be forced to donate an organ to a sibling is foreign to Canadian law. There is no way that a cord blood donor could become an organ donor simply based on parental desires. In Canada, living organ donation is governed by provincial and territorial laws that require consent from the donor, and that (for the most part) preclude living donation by minors. Even in the United States, where minors can be living organ donors, we would be shocked to see a court decide—over the objections of the potential donor—that a child should undergo unnecessary surgery solely for the benefit of someone else.

Savior Siblings Are Valued

The donor or savior sibling seems, at first blush, to be the only party in whom the burdens might outweigh the benefits. Granted they are "selected" because of their potential to help their sibling, but are also more likely than the average newborn to be free of discoverable genetic disease. There is no evidence that they are less valued than other children in the family and one could imagine them being more valued. There are no reports that savior children are wanted or valued only because of their role as rescuers.

Peter C. Williams, "Saviors as Saints or Sinners?," Pediatric Transplantation, *2008.*

But these issues, no doubt, will be the focus of the ethical debate that will surface in the wake of the movie's release.

The sensationalized portrayal of the legal issues also makes a consideration of the central ethical question—the moral acceptability of "designer" babies—more difficult to consider in a rational manner. Parents have kids for all sorts of reasons. Some are looking for a hockey star. Others need children to work in the fields or for long-term security. Still others have children by accident. Are these, or the myriad other reasons, inherently more ethically sound than the idea of a "saviour sibling"?

The Debate Should Be Based on Facts

In Canada, the Assisted Human Reproduction Act gives the federal government jurisdiction to oversee reproductive technologies, leaving it free to decide whether saviour siblings should be allowed in this country. As parents, we are both grateful that this debate remains in the realm of the hypothetical. But we also feel deep empathy for those parents who find themselves in a situation that leads them to consider these options.

We hope the movie stirs interest in these issues, but public debate should be informed by the facts—both scientific and legal.

Periodical and Internet Sources Bibliography

The following articles have been selected to supplement the diverse views presented in this chapter.

Lindsay Abrams	"Could You Love Someone Without a Face? Making Facial Transplants Common Practice," *The Atlantic*, September 10, 2012.
John L. Allen	"The Nightmare Scenario of Organ Donation," *National Catholic Reporter*, November 16, 2007.
Hannah Beech	"Are Executed Prisoners' Organs Still Being Harvested in China?," *Time*, June 7, 2011.
The Economist	"O Death, When Is Thy Sting? Defining Death," October 4, 2008.
Maggie Fazeli Fard	"Face Transplant for Virginia Man Is Lauded as Most Extensive in History," *Washington Post*, March 27, 2012.
Raffi Khatchadourian	"Transfiguration," *New Yorker*, February 13, 2012.
Sarah Levitt	"Saviour Siblings: Genetic Screening and Policy," *The Meducator*, vol. 1, 2008.
Bohdan Pomahac, et al.	"Three Patients with Full Facial Transplantation," *New England Journal of Medicine*, February 23, 2012.
Darshak Sanghavi	"When Does Death Start?," *New York Times Magazine*, December 16, 2009.
Dick Teresi, interviewed by Brian Bethune	"On the Debate over When Life Really Ends, and the Possibility Cadavers Can Feel Pain," *Maclean's*, March 19, 2012.
Stephanie Warren	"The Face of Progress," *Science World*, November 14, 2011.

OPPOSING
VIEWPOINTS®
SERIES

CHAPTER 4

What Is the Future of Organ Donation?

Chapter Preface

Patients who are ineligible for a heart transplant or are on a delayed waiting list may receive a total artificial heart (TAH) as an alternative. TAHs are devices that replace the two lower chambers, or ventricles, of the heart. The first use of an artificial heart for a patient waiting for a transplant was in 1969. However, that patient only lived a combined ninety-six hours with the artificial heart and the transplanted heart. In 1982, what can be considered the first genuine success occurred when Barney Clark survived for 112 days on a Jarvik-7 artificial heart.

As of late 2012, two types of artificial hearts are currently in use in the United States with US Food and Drug Administration approval. The AbioCor is restricted to patients who are ineligible for transplants. The other artificial heart is the CardioWest TAH-t, which is approved both as an alternative to a donor heart and as a bridge to transplantation. A study in the *New England Journal of Medicine* found that the one-year survival rate of patients who received the CardioWest artificial heart was 70 percent, compared to a 31 percent survival rate for patients who did not get that implant. In addition, for patients who later received a donor heart, the one- and five-year survival rates were 86 percent and 64 percent, respectively, compared to 84 percent and 69 percent for patients who had a heart transplant without first getting a TAH.

The prospects for TAHs continue to improve. A French company, Carmat, is developing an artificial heart that could be available in Europe by 2013. According to Bruce Crumley, writing for *Time* magazine, this artificial heart more accurately mimics a real heart by using two pumps instead of one. If successful, this new device could save thousands of lives each year. As Crumley explains, "an estimated 20,000 people worldwide . . . are each year in urgent need of a heart transplant for survival. Currently, only about a quarter of those patients receive transplanted hearts from donors. The need for a viable artificial alternative is clear."

Whether it's due to the implantation of artificial organs or to technology that has yet to be developed, organ transplants in the coming decades may be vastly different from our current understanding. The authors in the following chapter consider the future of organ donation.

"*Pig organs have multiple potential advantages over organs derived from brain-dead human donors.*"

Xenotransplantation Has Potential

William Edward Beschorner

Xenotransplantation (using organs and tissues from another species) could be a viable solution to the organ shortage, but several barriers must first be addressed, William Edward Beschorner asserts in the following viewpoint. He argues that pig organs in particular offer a variety of advantages, including resistance to human pathogens and the ability to be raised in a controlled environment. However, Beschorner acknowledges, xenotransplantation will not occur on a large scale until the barriers of unrealistic regulation, inadequate funding, and inadequate source herds are addressed. Beschorner was an associate professor of medicine at the Johns Hopkins University School of Medicine.

As you read, consider the following questions:

1. According to Beschorner, in what ways are pig organs similar to human organs?

2. What medical event occurred in 1963, as stated by the author?

3. How could xenotransplantation be combined with stem cell technology, as detailed by Beschorner?

Organ transplantation has been called a victim of its own success. Transplanted human organs can replace failed organs and eliminate the need for insulin administration in patients with insulin-dependent diabetes; however, because of a severe shortage of human donors, less than 1 in 20 individuals who require transplantation are able to undergo the procedure.

Many Patients Are Left Waiting

Patients who require heart transplantation and are designated on the waiting list as 1A priority (urgent) have a life expectancy of less than a week. If they undergo transplantation, they typically experience more than 10 additional years of active life. Less than 2,000 heart transplants are performed annually in the United States. The Organ Procurement and Transplantation Network/ United Network of Organ Sharing (OPTN/UNOS) waiting list has nearly 3,000 heart transplant candidates. However, this barely explains the true need because these are the candidates of highest priority. The International Heart and Lung Transplant society has estimated that more than 50,000 Americans annually could benefit from heart transplantation if donors were available.

For primary organs and tissues, 27,958 organ and tissue transplants were performed in the United States in 2008, excluding corneal transplants. More than 101,000 Americans are currently on the OPTN/UNOS waiting list. As with the hearts, the waiting list greatly underestimates the true need. For hearts, kidneys, livers, and pancreatic islets, approximately 500,000 transplants or more could be performed annually in the United States and more than 1.3 million transplants could be performed annually in the developed world if organs were available.

Pig Organs Have Potential

Although stem cell technology and tissue engineering are potential solutions to the organ shortage, xenotransplantation (transplanting organs and tissues from a different species) has generated considerable interest as a potential solution. Pigs are considered the optimal source of xenotransplant organs. Many pig organs are similar to the human counterparts in size, anatomy, and physiology. Large numbers of pigs can be quickly produced under standardized clean conditions. Pigs can be readily modified. Genes can be added or removed. Human cells can be grown in the pig.

Contrary to common belief, pig organs have multiple potential advantages over organs derived from brain-dead human donors. With human organs, little can be done before the donor is declared brain dead. After brain death, organs are procured in an emergency manner and are immediately transported to the medical center performing the transplant. The transplant is also performed with little warning. The transplant organ may come from a suboptimal donor with advanced age and chronic medical conditions or from a carrier with undetected infectious agents or malignant cells. A donor pig is raised under controlled conditions, specifically for use as an organ donor. Potential pathogens can be eliminated from the herd. The donor pig can be extensively analyzed. Organs are procured from young, robust donors. In xenotransplants, the procurement and transplant is performed on a scheduled elective basis.

Xenografts may provide medical advantages as well. These grafts are resistant to many human pathogens specific to human tissues, such as HIV, hepatitis, and human cytomegalovirus. Tumors such as melanoma have also been transferred to the recipient through human allografts. Pigs can be produced that are free of potential pathogens. Xenografts may be resistant to autoimmune reactions, such as the autoimmune destruction of beta cells with type 1 diabetes.

Despite these advantages, relatively few xenotransplants have been successfully performed in experimental models and none have been performed in the clinical arena. This is due to 3 main causes. First, xenotransplantation is subject to severe rejection, involving many different antigen disparities between humans and pigs that elicit multiple mechanisms of immune rejection. Current opinion dictates that severe immune suppression is required to prevent rejection, and this subjects the recipient to a high risk of infection and toxicity. Second, the perceived need for increased immune suppression leads to concern about infectious agents from the pig, including exogenous viruses (e.g., circoviruses, hepatitis E) and endogenous viruses (e.g., porcine endogenous retrovirus [PERV], which may lead to novel infectious diseases in humans (i.e., xenozoonoses). Third, for some tissues such as the liver, the physiological function of the pig organ is insufficiently close to the human to provide long-term support.

Fortunately, significant progress has been made on all fronts. Several xenotransplant technologies are now in clinical trials. . . .

Xenotransplantation Is Not a New Concept

The use of animals as organ and tissue donors is not a new idea. At a time when medical technology and understanding of immunology and physiology were primitive, animals were the preferred source.

Jean-Babtiste Denys performed the first blood transfusion into a patient in 1667 using blood taken from a sheep. In 1906, [M.] Jaboulay performed the first vascular xenotransplants, transplanting kidneys from a pig and a dog into patients with renal insufficiency. In 1963, [C.R.] Hitchcock transplanted a kidney from a baboon into 65-year-old woman; it functioned for 4 days. [K.] Reemtsma and [T.E.] Starzl achieved a measure of clinical success transplanting kidneys from nonhuman primates into human recipients.

However, over the next 25 years, focus turned to transplanting organs and tissues from human donors. In the early 1990s, porcine islets prepared from fetal pigs were transplanted into diabetic patients with modest immune suppression. Porcine C-peptide was monitored in the urine until the grafts eventually rejected. In 1992 and 1993, 2 orthotopic xenotransplants were performed placing baboon livers into patients with liver failure related to hepatitis B virus infection. Multidrug therapy was administered to prevent cellular and antibody-mediated rejection. The patients survived 70 and 26 days, respectively. The grafts provided at least partial function. Although the grafts did not undergo rejection, one of the patients developed a terminal aspergillosis related to the immune suppression.

Baboon marrow was transplanted into a patient with AIDS with the knowledge that the baboon CD4$^+$ lymphocytes were resistant to HIV. Although the patient rejected the baboon cells, his clinical condition improved, and he continued to do well at the time of publication [January 14, 2010].

Dopaminergic neurons from a fetal pig were transplanted into the brain of a patient with Parkinson's disease. The transplant significantly improved the clinical course of the patient. Seven months later, the fetal pig neurons were identified. The implantation of pig neural tissue into an immune privileged environment of the brain reduced the risk of rejection. Unfortunately, a subsequent controlled trial failed to demonstrate a statistically significant difference with the control group.

Patients in acute liver failure have been supported for a few hours to days with extracorporeal liver perfusion (ECLP) while a human liver donor is sought. Blood from the patient is perfused through the pig liver and returned. These procedures indicate that the pig liver is functional on a short-term basis. Patients typically show clinical improvement with reduction of blood ammonia and lactic acid levels, conjugation and excretion of bilirubin, and stabilization of prothrombin time.

Devices that incorporate cells or tissue from animals or incorporate human cells or tissues that have been cocultured with animal cells are considered xenografts. One promising device provides short-term support for patients with acute liver failure.

Initial clinical trials were promising, providing time to bridge to a human liver transplant. Others showed spontaneous recovery during the support period.

Following a series of public hearings by the National Institutes of Health (NIH), the Centers for Disease Control and Prevention (CDC), and the FDA [Food and Drug Administration], the FDA published guidelines for xenotransplantation to address concerns raised about infectious diseases from donor animals. The latest guidelines were published in 2003. For a clinical trial to be allowed, the investigator must demonstrate evidence of efficacy of the xenotransplants in nonhuman primates. The investigator must also demonstrate compliance with the safety guidelines, including a certified source herd, prolonged archiving of tissues and records, and current good manufacturing practice (cGMP) facilities and procedures.

Most likely, the first successful clinical trials will be with cellular transplants, such as pancreatic islets, neural cells, or hepatocytes. Because vascular xenografts are sensitive to rejection of the endothelial cells, the threshold is set higher. Heart xenografts and kidney xenografts will likely be the first tested. Lung xenografts are presently the most challenging xenografts because of the extensive capillary network and sensitivity of endothelial cells to hyperacute rejection.

Regenerative medicine urgently needs an alternative technology to supplement the transplantation of human allografts for the cure of organ and tissue failure. The leading technologies to provide tissues and organs include xenotransplantation, stem cell technology, and tissue engineering. Xenotransplantation is the first such technology to be pursued and the most advanced. . . .

There Are Barriers to Large-Scale Applications

The large-scale clinical application of xenotransplantation is threatened by 3 fiscal and logistical barriers: unrealistic federal

The Risk of Xenotransplantation Cannot Be Completely Eliminated

Risk will be an unavoidable artifact of xenotransplantation research. We cannot be rid of it and neither can we minimize it in order to optimize a xenotransplantation product's level of safety. If we place the burden of safety optimization on xenotransplantation, we will never reap any of its potential benefits. From a traditionally rational perspective, laboratory research would continue ad infinitum because increasing safety will always be the more rational choice procedure. However, what immediately strikes me as irrational in this behavior is the lack of any clearly defined stopping point for one's inquiry, the incessant insistence on the better option. This method of decision-making offers no point at which laboratory research can cease and clinical trials may commence, and is thus of no pragmatic use to us.

Ololade Olakanmi, "Xenotransplantation:
A Rational Choice?," Penn Bioethics Journal,
vol. 2, no. 2, Spring 2006.

regulation, inadequate funding by industry and government, and inadequate qualified source herds of clean swine.

The federal guidelines that regulate xenotransplantation were formed following workshops that were concerned about the potential public health hazards of zoonotic infections, particularly concern about the potential threat of PERV. At the time of those discussions, prolonged acceptance of pig xenografts in preclinical studies could be achieved only with high doses of antirejection drugs. Speculation held that if xenotransplantation was performed on a large scale, recombination of the PERV subtypes could lead to a new virus that was contagious, pathological, and a threat to the public health. The resulting guidelines called for patient followup for as long as 50 years and severe restrictions on xenograft recipients, such as travel. Although the guidelines were appropriate for the information at that time, they unfortunately discouraged large pharmaceutical and medical device companies from investing in xenotransplantation.

In addition to the stringent requirements for monitoring recipients, companies were concerned about the liability of pursuing a technology perceived to be a potential hazard to the public health. However, since PERV was initially described, numerous studies have shown no evidence of PERV becoming contagious or being pathological. Many strains fail to pass PERV to human cells in coculture. The molecular virology of PERV passage is now understood. Swine strains have been produced that are free of the PERV-C that is needed for passage. Indeed, in the near future, swine strains will likely be produced with no genomic PERV.

The risk of a public health hazard from PERV needs to be re-examined in light of current information and developments. The risk of a public health hazard from PERV in pigs is not measurably greater than a public health hazard from technologies based on human cells and tissues. Indeed, the risk for transmitting exogenous pathogens such as hepatitis, HIV, and malignant cells to patients is much less for porcine xenografts than with human based transplants. One could speculate that some unknown virus or mutational event could still produce a public health hazard. Totally ruling out the unknown is impossible. Fear of the unknown, however, is irrational and effectively blocks all technological development. Should blood transfusions and human tissue transplants also be severely restricted because of this unknown factor? The infinitesimal risk of the unknown must be balanced against the tremendous potential for regenerative medicine.

The second barrier is lack of funding. Although xenotransplantation is the closest to clinical reality of the 3 major regenerative technologies, it is also the least-supported technology.

Large corporations have ceased their support of xenotransplantation. The NIH supports xenotransplantation at a level far below that for stem cell and tissue engineering. For example, the recent economic stimulation package (American Recovery and Reinvestment Act of 2009) provided $200 million for 200 challenge grants. Although multiple challenge topics address issues with stem cell and tissue-engineering technology, no challenges are posted for improving xenotransplantation. As stem cell and tissue engineering are at a speculative stage of development with major technical hurdles to overcome, abandoning xenotransplantation, which is at an advanced stage of development, is absurd.

The third major barrier to xenotransplantation is lack of sufficient qualified source herds. At this time, only a handful of swine herds are qualified to be used for clinical trials. All of these are small herds with less than 100 pigs. Several small clinical trials are currently being pursued. The likelihood that at least one of these trials will be successful and lead to a new device approval is great. However, when such approval is achieved, not nearly enough qualified pigs will be available to satisfy the unmet need. Maintaining and developing qualified herds with the appropriate barrier facilities and husbandry is very expensive. The current herds need to be greatly expanded for widespread clinical application. This will take several years and much more support.

Regrettably, the 3 regenerative medicine technologies are usually considered in competition with each other. The underlying assumption is that one will "win" and become the standard technology for alternate tissues whereas the others will "lose" and be abandoned. Considering the enormity of the unmet need in regenerative medicine, this assumption is unfortunate. Most likely, each technology will prove to be optimal for different select diseases.

The Potential for Hybrid Technologies

A more promising approach would be to combine these technologies. Xenotransplantation could provide a cost-effective and sterile bioreactor for maturing stem cells into tissues that can be transplanted. Xenotransplantation could also provide the scaffolding for tissue engineering.

Several developments in recent years support such hybrid technologies.

Our program has been growing human hematopoietic lymphocytes and stem cells from the transplant recipient, with the goal of producing human antigen-specific T-regulatory cells that prevent rejection of pig xenografts after transfer from the chimeric pig back into the recipient. Prolonged survival and function of pig islet cell clusters has been realized in nonhuman primates without posttransplant immune suppression.

As an example, the pig liver differs from human livers in several critical aspects. Although pig livers have provided short-term life support, they are unlikely to be effective for long-term support. Human hepatocytes grow within the fetal pig liver and demonstrate normal sinusoidal architecture. Expansion is limited though by competition by the native pig hepatocytes. Transgenic pigs have been produced that express suicide genes (thymidine kinase or cytosine deaminase) in the pig hepatocytes. By providing the chimeric pig with a prodrug such as ganciclovir for thymidine kinase, selectively and conditionally destroying the pig hepatocytes is possible, giving the human hepatocytes an edge to expand.

Human hepatocytes may not be essential to develop hybrid livers. For example, when fetal lambs were injected with human CD34-positive bone marrow cells, the livers of the newborn lambs were shown to contain human hepatocytes.

With stem cell technology, the pluripotent stem cells would not be directly transplanted into the recipient because of the risk of developing teratomas. The challenge has been to differentiate the stem cells outside of the patient. Although the production of human islets or insulin producing glucose sensitive beta cells remains a challenge, the transplantation of pancreatic primordia can provide good glucose control to diabetic recipients. Fetal pigs could be used as a cost effective bioreactor to expand human stem cells or primordia and differentiate them into mature beta cells or islets. . . .

With sufficient support, xenotransplantation will address the large unmet need for many of the diseases requiring replacement of failed tissues and organs. In some devices, xenotransplantation may be a stand-alone technology. In other technologies, it may be combined with stem cell or tissue engineering technology. The future of xenotransplantation and regenerative medicine could potentially be very exciting.

"Consent of an individual to a xenotransplant has significant bearing on the protection of society."

Ethical Debate: Ethics of Xeno-Transplantation

Murali Krishna and Peter Lepping

In the following viewpoint, Murali Krishna and Peter Lepping opine that xenotransplantation—using an organ from an animal, typically a pig—is not the right answer to the organ shortage. Krishna and Lepping assert that even though xenotransplantation may save lives, the risk of infections and the need for long-term immunosuppressant therapy could greatly reduce the patient's quality of life. In addition to the impacts xenotransplantation might have on the individual, the authors also argue that the effects on society as well as the rights of animals must be considered. Krishna is a consultant psychiatrist at CSI Holdsworth Memorial Hospital in Mysore, India, and Lepping is a visiting professor in psychiatry at Glyndĉr University in Wrexham, North Wales.

As you read, consider the following questions:

1. What are allotransplantations, as defined by Krishna and Lepping?

Murali Krishna and Peter Lepping, "Ethical Debate: Ethics of Xeno-Transplantation," *British Journal of Medical Practitioners*, vol. 4, no. 3, September 2011, pp. 425–426. Copyright © 2010 by JMN Medical Education Ltd. All rights reserved. Reproduced by permission.

2. In the view of the authors, what steps would be necessary to produce pathogen-free donor organs?
3. How might Muslims and Jews respond to xenotransplantations, according to the authors?

Interest in cross-species transplantation has recently been rekindled.[1] This is due to many developments including the shortage of donor organs, advances in transplant medicine, investment in biotechnology research, and the non-availability of more ethically suitable alternatives to human organs.[1,2] Increasing success rates in allotransplantations (organs from different member of the same species) has increased the demand on donor organs. Other types of transplantation include autotransplants (a person's own organs or tissues are used for transplantation) and isotransplants (organs from one person are transplanted into another genetically identical person, like an identical twin). These options are limited in terms of body parts used and numbers.

Good facts inform good ethics. It is therefore obligatory to look into the current research knowledge about xenotransplants (organs from one species to another, for example animal to human) in more detail. The advocates of xenotransplantation argue that it could provide organs "relatively quickly" and hence save more lives. If animal organs were easily available for transplantation most eligible recipients would receive the transplantation much earlier on in their illness. It is argued that this may decrease distress and suffering. Whilst xenotransplantation may theoretically increase the survival time, it is unclear, however, whether the negative impact on recipients' quality of life due to long-term immunosuppressant therapy and the risk of zoonotic infections would in fact worsen the overall long-term outcome.[3] Recent research suggests that xenotransplantation may be associated with the transmission of pig microorganisms including viruses, bacteria, fungi, and parasites. Because of the recipient's likely immunosuppressed state, infection and pathologic consequences may be more pronounced. Transmission of most microorganisms with the exception of the porcine endogenous retroviruses may be prevented by screening the donor pig and qualified pathogen-free breeding. However, porcine endogenous retroviruses represent a special risk as they are present in the genome of all pigs and infect human cells in vitro. Until now, no porcine endogenous retrovirus transmission was observed in experimental and clinical xenotransplantations as well as in numerous infection experiments.[4] Nevertheless, strategies need to be developed to prevent their transmission to humans. It is equally possible that many eligible recipients may be denied having a trial of xenotransplantation by doctors who believe that there is in unfavourable risk-benefit ratio. The limited long-term data on outcomes of xenotransplants thus renders ethical analysis difficult.

There is some evidence to suggest that the recipients of animal organ donation may develop a different sell image with possible consequences for their identity.[5,6] This happens with human organs at times, but may be a more significant problem with animal organs, as the recipient knows that they have been given a non-human organ. Loss of identity jeopardises the core principle of autonomy, which underpins all medical treatment.

The risk of zoonosis to the recipient and to the wider society cannot be accurately estimated.[7] Hence there is a requirement for vigilant post-operative monitoring[8] with a possibility of engaging article 5 and 8 of the European Convention of Human Rights (for England and Wales; Human Rights Act 1998).† Article 12 may also be engaged as the recipients may be restricted from having physical relationships, carrying out their routine day to day activities and socialisation. This is because the prevention of possible risk to the wider public from zoonosis may require the recipient to be put under restrictions with regard to their engagement with others. This may include restrictions to go out, which can result into de facto temporary detentions at home. Hence consenting to xeno-transplantation would be "binding

"Animal Transplants," cartoon by Ed Fischer. www.cartoonstock.com.

and contractual" over a long period of time. The subject may not have the right to withdraw. This is entering into a de facto contract with potential restrictions or even deprivation of human rights. This would restrict the ability to give informed consent even for a well informed patient, as it is difficult to be fully appreciative of future restrictions of one's liberty.

Autonomous decision making and thus informed consent may also be put at risk by other factors surrounding xenotransplantation. The decision to embark on xenotransplantation may be primarily driven by an instinctual wish to survive due to a lack of other viable alternatives. Patients in these circumstances may have little or no consideration to medium and long-term effects on themselves and society. However, it is the consideration of such long-term consequences that make a truly autonomous decision, and differentiate it from a decision that is purely based on immediate instinct. Whilst the wish to survive is legitimate it is difficult to make decisions free of the pressure to survive when there is a lack of alternatives.

It also brings up an even more important question: Can any person *ever* consent to a future restriction or deprivation of their liberty or other human rights? Even if there were an option to define acceptable future restrictions it would be likely that patients could still challenge the legality of any such agreements. They could quite reasonably argue that they have agreed to the restrictions under duress because of a lack of viable alternatives to their xeno-transplants.

Xenotransplantation touches questions of utilitarianism (greatest good for the greatest numbers) and public protection.[2] Utilitarianism takes into account the reasonable interests of society in good outcomes, fairness in the distribution of resources, and the prevention of harm to others. The Nuffield council on bio-ethics embraces a utilitarian approach. However, there are limits to the utilitarian argument for xenotransplants. Even if they were widely available, the treatment would be immensely expensive. Production of a pathogen-free donor organ would involve rearing animals in strictly controlled environments, subjecting them to rigorous standards of examination and surveillance. The additional costs of developing a sustainable work force to provide transplantation and post-transplant surveillance of the patient and the community would be high. The insurance providers may not cover expenses of a xenotransplant. Public health care providers may decline to provide this treatment as it may not be recommended by expert groups as cost effective. Xenotransplantation may commence in the developing world where the regulations are lax and the poor can be more easily exploited.[8] Patients who would potentially benefit from xenotransplantation may not be able to afford it due to its cost with serious implications for fairness.

Xenotransplantation also raises other critical questions in relation to the wider community. We have seen that consent of an individual to a xenotransplant has significant bearing on the protection of society.[7] Should the members of a community therefore be consulted if there were any xeno-transplantation experiments in their region? The risk is primarily due to the risk of zoonotic infections, the need for surveillance, and possible quarantine of contacts.[7,9] In addition, if health authorities were to fund expensive experimental interventions like xenotransplantation, other routine treatments of greater potential benefits to society may be jeopardised. Society may also have views about particular animals being used as donor animals.[10] For example religions like Islam and Judaism may feel that pigs are 'ritually unclean'. They may therefore not approve of certain animals to be used for donation, and more worryingly may fail to socially accept recipients with such 'unclean' transplants.[11]

From a deontological perspective (this judges the morality of an action based on the action's adherence to a rule or principle) some authors assert that animals have rights similar to those considered appropriate for humans.[12,13] The protection of animals has legal status in many countries. Consequentialists may view the suffering and death of an animal as acceptable for the betterment of a human patient, as they would judge the morality of an action primarily by its end result. They would argue that potential benefits and improvement in human welfare arising from xenotransplantation may justify the loss of animal life. However, this will never satisfy the animal rights lobby; especially as whilst minimising the risk of acquired infections, the animals have to forgo greater suffering in the form of isolation, monitoring and investigations. Furthermore, genetic modification can have both immediate and long-term negative effects on animals.

In summary, xenotransplantation has significant ethical consequences. On an individual level, there are the questions of pressure to consent that may negate autonomy and the validity of that consent as well as the difficulties that arise when patients are asked to consent to future restrictions of their human rights. On a societal level there are questions of cost and benefit analysis as well as risks from zoonotic infections. In addition, questions of animal rights need to be addressed before any programs are likely to go ahead.

† **Appendix of Articles of the Human Rights Act.**
- Article 8 of the Human Rights Act 1998 (The right to respect for private and family life, home and correspondence)
- Article 5 (The right to liberty)
- Article 12 (The right to marry and found a family)

References

1. Advisory Group on the Ethics of Xenotransplantation: Animal Tissues into Humans. London, Stationery Office, 1997
2. Nuffield Council on Bioethics-Animal-to-Human Transplants: The ethics of xenotransplantation. London, Nuffield Council on Bioethics, 1996
3. Chapman, L.E.E., Folks, T.M., Salomon, D.R., Paterson, A.P., Eggerman, T.E., Noguchi, P.D.: Xenotransplantation and xenogeneic infections. N. Engl. J. Med. 333: 1498, 1995
4. Denner J.: Infectious risk in xenotransplantation—what post-transplant screening for the human receipient? Xenotransplantation. 2011 May; 18(3):151–7
5. Franklin, P.: Psychological aspects of kidney transplantation and organ donation. In Kidney Transplantation, Principles and Practice (4th ed.), P.J. Morris, editor, Philadelphia, Saunders, pp. 532–541, 1994
6. Nature Biotechnology Editorial P403, 1996
7. Public Health Service: Draft guidelines on infectious disease issues in xenotransplantation: Fed. Register 61:49919, 1996
8. Oman Daily Observer: Organ transplant doctor held. January 11, 1997
9. Witt, C.J., Meslin, F-X., Heyman, D.: Emerging and Other Communicable Disease Surveillance and Control (EMC). Draft WHO Recommendations on Xenotransplantation and Infectious Disease Prevention. Geneva, World Health Organization, 1997
10. Institute of Medicine: Xenotransplantation: Science, Ethics and Public Policy. Washington, DC, National Academy Press, 1996
11. Daar, A.S.: Xenotransplantation and Religion: The major monotheistic religions, Xenotransplatation 2(4): 61, 1994
12. Singer, P.: Animal Liberation. New York, Random House, 1975
13. Regan, T.: The case for animal rights. University of California Press, Los Angeles, 1983

> *"Those waiting for transplants are unlikely to worry too much about what replacement body parts look like, so long as they work."*

Artificial Organs Could Save Lives

The Economist

In the following viewpoint, The Economist *explains how in the future, people in need of an organ might be able to get an artificial one made by a three-dimensional bio-printer. The printer uses stem cells from adult bone marrow and fat, along with a hydrogel, to create the desired structure. According to the magazine, this technology will first be used to make skin, muscles, and blood vessels but could eventually create more complicated body parts. The* Economist *is a weekly newspaper that focuses on international politics and business news.*

As you read, consider the following questions:

1. What will the bio-printer be able to produce by 2015, according to the magazine?
2. As stated by *The Economist*, how many cells are in the droplets created by the Organovo machine?

3. What features might be missing from a man-made kidney, as stated by the magazine?

The great hope of transplant surgeons is that they will, one day, be able to order replacement body parts on demand. At the moment, a patient may wait months, sometimes years, for an organ from a suitable donor. During that time his condition may worsen. He may even die. The ability to make organs as they are needed would not only relieve suffering but also save lives. And that possibility may be closer with the arrival of the first commercial 3D bio-printer for manufacturing human tissue and organs.

The new machine, which costs around $200,000, has been developed by Organovo, a company in San Diego that specialises in regenerative medicine, and Invetech, an engineering and automation firm in Melbourne, Australia. One of Organovo's founders, Gabor Forgacs of the University of Missouri, developed the prototype on which the new 3D bio-printer is based. The first production models will soon be delivered to research groups which, like Dr. Forgacs's, are studying ways to produce tissue and organs for repair and replacement. At present much of this work is done by hand or by adapting existing instruments and devices.

To start with, only simple tissues, such as skin, muscle and short stretches of blood vessels, will be made, says Keith Murphy, Organovo's chief executive, and these will be for research purposes. Mr. Murphy says, however, that the company expects that within five years, once clinical trials are complete, the printers will produce blood vessels for use as grafts in bypass surgery. With more research it should be possible to produce bigger, more complex body parts. Because the machines have the ability to make branched tubes, the technology could, for example, be used to create the networks of blood vessels needed to sustain larger printed organs, like kidneys, livers and hearts.

How the Printer Works

Organovo's 3D bio-printer works in a similar way to some rapid-prototyping machines used in industry to make parts and mechanically functioning models. These work like inkjet printers, but with a third dimension. Such printers deposit droplets of polymer which fuse together to form a structure. With each pass of the printing heads, the base on which the object is being made moves down a notch. In this way, little by little, the object takes shape. Voids in the structure and complex shapes are supported by printing a "scaffold" of water-soluble material. Once the object is complete, the scaffold is washed away.

Researchers have found that something similar can be done with biological materials. When small clusters of cells are placed next to each other they flow together, fuse and organise themselves. Various techniques are being explored to condition the cells to mature into functioning body parts—for example, "exercising" incipient muscles using small machines.

Though printing organs is new, growing them from scratch on scaffolds has already been done successfully. In 2006 Anthony Atala and his colleagues at the Wake Forest Institute for Regenerative Medicine in North Carolina made new bladders for seven patients. These are still working.

Dr. Atala's process starts by taking a tiny sample of tissue from the patient's own bladder (so that the organ that is grown from it will not be rejected by his immune system). From this he extracts precursor cells that can go on to form the muscle on the outside of the bladder and the specialised cells within it. When more of these cells have been cultured in the laboratory, they are painted onto a biodegradable bladder-shaped scaffold which is warmed to body temperature. The cells then mature and multiply. Six to eight weeks later, the bladder is ready to be put into the patient.

The Benefits of Bio-Printing

The advantage of using a bio-printer is that it eliminates the need for a scaffold, so Dr. Atala, too, is experimenting with inkjet technology. The Organovo machine uses stem cells extracted from adult bone marrow and fat as the precursors. These cells can be coaxed into differentiating into many other types of cells by the application of appropriate growth factors. The cells are formed into droplets 100–500 microns in diameter and containing 10,000–30,000 cells each. The droplets retain their shape well and pass easily through the inkjet printing process.

A second printing head is used to deposit scaffolding—a sugar-based hydrogel. This does not interfere with the cells or stick to them. Once the printing is complete, the structure is left for a day or two, to allow the droplets to fuse together. For tubular structures, such as blood vessels, the hydrogel is printed in the centre and around the outside of the ring of each cross-section before the cells are added. When the part has matured, the hydrogel is peeled away from the outside and pulled from the centre like a piece of string.

The bio-printers are also capable of using other types of cells and support materials. They could be employed, Mr. Murphy suggests, to place liver cells on a pre-built, liver-shaped scaffold or to form layers of lining and connective tissue that would grow into a tooth. The printer fits inside a standard laboratory biosafety cabinet, for sterile operation. Invetech has developed a laser-based calibration system to ensure that both print heads deposit their materials accurately, and a computer-graphics system allows cross-sections of body parts to be designed.

Some researchers think machines like this may one day be capable of printing tissues and organs directly into the body. Indeed, Dr. Atala is working on one that would scan the contours of the part of a body where a skin graft was needed and then print skin onto it. As for bigger body parts, Dr. Forgacs thinks they may take many different forms, at least initially. A man-made biological substitute for a kidney, for instance, need not look like a real one or contain all its features in order to clean waste products from the bloodstream. Those waiting for transplants are unlikely to worry too much about what replacement body parts look like, so long as they work and make them better.

| "[The] biggest challenges right now, for any solid organ, is . . . the blood vessel supply."

Some Artificial Organs Are Years Away from Viability

Anthony Atala, interviewed by Marissa Cevallos

In the following viewpoint, Anthony Atala asserts that artificial organs are years from being a viable alternative to donor organs. According to Atala, simpler structures such as skin, windpipes, and bladders have successfully been created in labs and transplanted into patients. However, he explains, solid organs such as kidneys are not yet viable because it is more difficult to replicate their blood vessel supply. Atala is the W.H. Boyce professor and director of the Wake Forest Institute for Regenerative Medicine and chair of the Department of Urology at the Wake Forest University School of Medicine in North Carolina. Marissa Cervallos is a writer for the Los Angeles Times.

As you read, consider the following questions:

1. What is the first way to create organ tissues, as explained by Atala?
2. According to Atala, what organs are in the second level of complexity?

3. How many tissue and organ types are being developed at the Institute for Regenerative Medicine, as stated by Atala?

The windpipe transplanted into a terminal cancer patient in Sweden is garnering much buzz—and small wonder. The surgery marks the first time a trachea grown from a patient's stem cells and seeded onto a synthetic, rather than a donor, structure has been transplanted in a human. And it saved a 36-year-old man's life.

The trachea isn't the first organ born in a lab—and experts say there are many more to come. We talked to Dr. Anthony Atala, a pioneer in the field who in 1999 transplanted the first of several synthetic bladders into young people with bladder disease.

Atala now directs the Institute for Regenerative Medicine at Wake Forest University; in March [2011], he and colleagues announced they'd transplanted laboratory-grown urethras in five boys.

Advances in Transplants

In this edited transcript of a phone interview, he elaborates on the significance of the latest transplant and explains why some other organs will be more difficult to craft in the lab.

[Marissa Cevallos]: What is new in the trachea transplant that hadn't been done before?

[Anthony Atala]: It's another advance. He [Professor Paolo Macchiarini of the Karolinska Institute] had done a segment of a trachea before. He has made it a larger segment.

The scaffold he used before, the biological material he used before, was a donor organ where they took the cells away and they put the patient's own cells. This time they did the same process, but they created a scaffold, a spongy scaffold.

Basically, there are a couple of ways of creating these tissues. One of the ways is to take a very small biopsy from a patient's own tissue, grow the cells outside the body, and then place those cells back on that mold that replicates the patient's organ.

Now the mold can be either something you create, something you weave like a piece of material, or it could be a donor tissue that you take the cells off and add cells to it.

What other organs have been made in the lab?

There are several organs. We did the bladder. We are 12 years out for using molds in bladders. We are seven years out in urethras, an experience just published. We showed that we transplanted urethras, using their own cells, but using molds.

Organs Have Different Complexities
Which organs are next, and which will take more time?

At this point, there are four levels of complexity.

The first level are the flat structures, like skin. They are the easiest to make because they are flat.

The next level of complexity are tubular structures, like the blood vessel, the windpipe. They are usually acting as a conduit, allowing blood or air to go through.

Next are hollow non-tubular organs like the bladder or stomach because they have to act on demand. They have much more complex functionality.

The most complex are the solid organs like the heart. They require many different cell types.

At this point, we've been able to do all the first three: Flat, tubular and hollow non-tubular. Skin, urethra, windpipes and bladders. Solid organs are most complex.

The fourth level—that's going to take time—that's still years away.

There are definitely more in the pipeline. At our institute we're working at over 30 different tissue and organ types. There's definitely a long list of organs that are scheduled to go into patients.

It's just a matter of getting more tissue types and more patients treated over time.

There Is a Major Need for Kidneys
Which organs will have the biggest clinical impact?

Well, of course for any patient who needs this tissue, it's a major clinical impact. If you need a specific tissue, it's a big thing.

The kidneys by far, if you look at the need—90% of the patients on a transplant list are waiting on a kidney. That's a fourth category. We are absolutely, working very hard on that.

What are the biggest challenges in making these organs?

Biggest challenges right now, for any solid organ, is basically the vascularity, the blood vessel supply. There are a lot more cells per centimeter in solid than flat tissue, and therefore, a lot of what needs to be done—how do you keep so many cells fed.

In the solid organ, if you can picture the branches of a tree, and then the branches have branches, and those branches have leaves, it's a very complex branching system. If you can picture the leaf being the tissue and the tree being the blood vessel supply tree, it's a complex organization so you have blood flowing through the tiny cell.

How did you react when you heard about the latest transplant?

We were very pleased to hear about this work because it just represents advances in the field and further validates the fact that these technologies may have a role in treating larger numbers of patients in the future.

> *"Bioengineered stem cells . . . could be
> the game changer with regard to organ
> and tissue transplantation."*

Stem Cells Could Solve the Organ Donation Problem

*Andre Terzic, Brooks S. Edwards, Katherine C.
McKee, and Timothy J. Nelson*

*In the following viewpoint, Andre Terzic, Brooks S. Edwards,
Katherine C. McKee, and Timothy J. Nelson contend that stem
cells could be used to create new organs. According to the authors,
these cells come from a variety of sources, including embryos, umbilical cords, and bone marrow, and can also be bioengineered.
They further argue that by using the patient's own stem cells, the
risk of rejection is eliminated. Thus far, this technology has already
been used to replace tracheas. Terzic is the director of the Center
for Regenerative Medicine at the Mayo Clinic in Rochester, Minnesota; Edwards is the director of the Mayo Clinic Transplant Center; McKee is the operations manager of the transplant center; and
Nelson is the E. Rolland Dickson scholar in transplant medicine at
the clinic.*

As you read, consider the following questions:

1. What are pluripotent cells, as defined by the authors?
2. According to Terzic et al., what are some of the adult stem cell therapies that have been developed?
3. What is the "ultimate goal of regenerative medicine," in the view of the authors?

Transplant medicine has laid the foundation for the emerging field of regenerative medicine, as the central aim of transplantation is replacing defective tissue with functional tissue in order to heal patients with end-stage disease. Over the years, tissue and solid-organ transplantation have been used to treat patients with otherwise incurable diseases such as leukemia, cirrhosis, end-stage kidney disease, and cardiopulmonary failure. Although transplantation has proved to be extraordinarily successful for some patients, the limited availability of appropriate organs and tissues and the problem of rejection have created a need for new strategies to meet the demands. Regenerative medicine offers potential solutions to these critical challenges.

Once, stem cell research and solid organ transplantation were separate endeavors. Materials science and developmental biology have bridged those fields, creating the new field of regenerative medicine. The initial application of regenerative medicine occurred five decades ago when hematologists began using bone marrow-derived stem cells as a replacement for defective progenitor cells. Advances in cell, tissue, and organ engineering have since led to new possibilities. Today, a variety of regenerative applications are being used and tested. In many cases, standards of care and best practices have yet to be established for cell-based regenerative therapies; however, clinical trials conducted by reputable institutions are actively enrolling patients in order to accelerate the translation of these promising applications. Regrettably, unproven therapies also are being marketed directly to patients, who may need to travel to other countries to get them.

As a result of the increased awareness on the part of patients, clinicians increasingly find themselves having to provide opinions about these therapies, some of which may be harmful or inappropriate for certain conditions. Thus, primary care providers and other specialists need to be informed about the state of regenerative medicine and emerging therapies that hold promise as well as those that are merely hype.

Exploring Stem Cell Research

Stem cells are the building blocks of regenerative medicine. As research on stem cells progresses, new information is becoming available daily regarding breakthrough technologies that will have an impact on our ability to translate stem cell science into clinical products and services. Regenerative medicine largely draws from four stem cell populations that function as tissue progenitors: embryonic stem cells, perinatal stem cells, adult stem cells, and bioengineered stem cells. Each cell type has unique properties.

As their name implies, embryonic stem cells are stem cells derived from embryos that are the product of in vitro fertilization. These cells are pluripotent, meaning they can differentiate into all adult tissue types. Because of their differentiation capacity, embryonic stem cells are suitable for deriving tissues that are difficult to obtain such as retinal pigment epithelial cells lost in macular degeneration and other tissues damaged by disease. However, the ethical and social considerations surrounding the use of embryonic stem cells continue to foster debate and challenge our legal system.

Perinatal stem cells are derived from umbilical cord blood. Although it is frequently discarded after birth, umbilical cord blood can be stored in private facilities or in public biobanks for later use in treating diseases such as leukemia. Perinatal stem cells are considered multipotent—that is, they can differentiate into many but not all tissue types.

Adult stem cells are present in many tissues including bone marrow, adipose tissue, and circulating blood. Unlike embryonic stem cells, adult stem cells are considered multipotent or oligopotent because their differentiation potential is restricted. This class of stem cells is most commonly used for treating lymphoma, leukemia, or autoimmune diseases that require cytotoxic treatments followed by rescue of the hematopoietic lineages and immune system. Currently, mesenchymal cells, which are derived from adult sources such as bone marrow or adipose tissue, are favored in clinical applications because they are widely accessible and because they have multipotent differentiation capacity, favorable growth characteristics, and an encouraging safety/efficacy record in clinical transplantation.

Bioengineered stem cells are a recent development. Scientists have been able to create induced pluripotent stem (iPS) cells using ordinary tissues such as the fibroblasts obtained from a dermal biopsy. With reprogramming or by applying genes typically expressed in embryonic tissues, adult fibroblasts can undergo a dramatic transformation and be reset to look and feel like embryonic stem cells. In other words, bioengineered iPS cells acquire the traits of pluripotent stem cells and the ability to differentiate into all types of tissue. These cells could be the game changer with regard to organ and tissue transplantation, as their use could offer a virtually unlimited renewable pool of tissues derived from the patient's own cells, eliminating the problems of donor shortages and rejection. They also offer a way around the ethical and political concerns associated with embryonic stem cell technology. Since the advent of iPS cell technology, bioengineered stem cells have become a source for progenitor derivation, tissue-specific differentiation, and repair in preclinical studies.

Clinical trials using adult stem cells to treat diverse conditions have established that this approach is safe and practical; early results of treatments for ischemic heart disease show promise. Therapies using umbilical cord blood stem cells, embryonic

Stem Cells Have Helped Heart Patients

Real progress has been seen in therapies derived from adult stem cell research. For one thing, [David] Prentice explained, "repairing the existing, damaged organ in the body replaces the need to do a whole-organ transplant." Several thousand heart patients have been treated with adult stem cells and subsequently taken off transplant waiting lists.

A study released last December [2009] in the *Journal of the American College of Cardiology* described how stem cells from bone marrow were used to help repair heart damage. And at the annual World Congress on Anti-Aging Medicine & Regenerative Biomedical Technologies last December, Zannos Grekos, MD, director of Cardiac and Vascular Disease for Regenocyte Therapeutic, showed the successful engraftment of stem cells into damaged organs and subsequent regeneration of tissue.

Daniel Allott, "A Vexing Problem,"
Catholic World Report, *July 15, 2010.*

stem cells, and tissue-specific progenitors derived from adult stem cell populations are being developed for early-phase clinical studies.

New Uses for Stem Cells

A number of developments are enabling investigators to envision new therapies and applications. The advent of bioengineered pluripotent stem cells is particularly significant. The ability to re-create pluripotent stem cells from ordinary somatic tissues such as blood or dermal fibroblasts makes it possible to create therapies that might one day eliminate the need for allogeneic transplantation. Tissues that have been created using iPS technology include dopaminergic neurons (to replace those damaged by Parkinson disease), beta cells from the pancreas (diabetes), cardiomyocytes (ischemic heart disease), retinal pigment epithelial cells (macular degeneration or Stargardt disease), red blood cells (hemophilia and sickle cell disease), and hepatocytes (chronic liver diseases). At Mayo Clinic, we have pioneered the use of bioengineered iPS cells for treating cardiovascular diseases in preclinical studies. We are now applying this technology to ischemic and nonischemic cardiomyopathy and congenital heart diseases. Furthermore, the ability to program human iPS cells into glucose-responsive insulin-secreting progeny has been recently refined.

Advances in materials science are opening new avenues of research in regenerative medicine. Matrices produced from natural or synthetic sources now provide platforms for growing tissue grafts and even engineering organs. In fact, preclinical studies have demonstrated that it is possible to decellularize organs and leave behind only the extra-cellular matrix backbone. This natural three-dimensional scaffold provides a framework for progenitor cells to engraft and recreate the structure and function of organs such as the myocardium. The ultimate goal of this work is to one day build replacement organs.

Such breakthroughs are setting the stage for new clinical applications. One of the most innovative ones was a whole-organ replacement of the upper airway. Using a decellularized scaffold from a cadaver trachea, a team of clinicians, scientists, and engineers repopulated the matrix with mesenchymal stem cells derived from the patient's bone marrow. After months of reconstruction in the laboratory, the trachea was surgically transplanted in the patient without requiring immunosuppression.

In addition to such therapeutic applications, regenerative medicine may also lead to better methods of testing pharmaceuticals. As part of safety testing, all new pharmaceuticals must be evaluated for their toxicity. With the ability to produce human tissues using bioengineering processes, we may be able to test drugs in the laboratory before they are administered to the patient. For example, scientists are now testing cardiotoxicity of certain drugs using bioengineered cardiomyocytes.

Regenerative medicine also may help identify patients within the transplant population who will have more aggressive disease or who may be at risk for complications following organ transplantation. In other words, we may be able to use bioengineered constructs in the lab made from tissue from the patient's own body to predict such things as the long-term effect of exposure to immunosuppression medications. This ability to identify deficiencies in the tissue-renewal process also may be useful for creating individualized therapies for a variety of other diseases as well.

Regenerative Medicine Promises Better Treatment

Therapeutic uses are the ultimate goal of regenerative medicine. First-generation technologies are currently being studied with the aim of defining safety profiles of biologic agents while determining their efficacy in order to guide next-generation applications. This work will no doubt expand the number and type of patients who can be safely managed with tissue or organ transplantation. Autologous and allogeneic stem cells obtained from adipose tissue, bone marrow or peripheral blood, or bioengineered stem cells are already being used in applications designed to improve tissue healing in patients with ischemic heart disease, liver disease, neurological disorders, endocrinopathy, progressive lung conditions, and dermal wounds. Mayo Clinic physicians and scientists are developing procedures and infrastructure to support and accelerate clinical trials related to human stem cell therapies.

Regenerative medicine is redefining the future for patients with end-stage organ disease. It promises better, safer treatment at earlier stages and the possibility of cure rather than palliation of symptoms. Because its applications cross all medical disciplines, realizing the full potential of regenerative medicine will require collaboration among experts from multiple fields.

Clinical services may need to be restructured as new products and services become available, and as those products and services do more than treat specific organs or diseases. In addition, hospitals and clinics may need to dedicate resources to the field in order to efficiently navigate the regulatory processes for investigational new drug applications, FDA (Food and Drug Administration) reporting, and monitoring the safety of their clinical activities.

In addition, they may need personnel dedicated to dealing with the growing number of patients inquiring about new treatments and services. All physicians will need to know about advances in regenerative medicine and stay well-informed of developments in bench research and clinical trials as well as the limitations of therapies. How the medical community responds may be the key to whether regenerative medicine fully realizes its potential for returning patients to health.

Periodical and Internet Sources Bibliography

The following articles have been selected to supplement the diverse views presented in this chapter.

Alex Ballingall	"Heart in a Box," *Maclean's*, November 21, 2011.
Dan Bilefsky	"Black Market for Body Parts Spreads Among the Poor in Europe," *New York Times*, June 29, 2012.
D.A. Budiani-Saberi and F.L. Delmonico	"Organ Trafficking and Transplant Tourism: Commentary on the Global Realities," *American Journal of Transplantation*, vol. 8, 2008.
Jim Burdick	"Face Transplants: Part of a Brave New World," *Transplant News*, April–May 2011.
Mark Cohen	"My Illegal Heart," *Men's Health*, April 2010.
Henry Fountain	"A First: Organs Tailor-Made with Body's Own Cells," *New York Times*, September 15, 2012.
Josie Glausiusz	"The Big Idea: Organ Regeneration," *National Geographic*, March 2011.
Jeneen Interlandi	"Not Just Urban Legend," *Newsweek*, January 19, 2009.
Aamir M. Jafarey, Farhat Moazam, and Riffat Moazam Zaman	"Conversations with Kidney Vendors in Pakistan: An Ethnographic Study," *Hastings Center Report*, May–June 2009.
Medical Ethics Advisor	"Organ Trafficking—Truth or Urban Myth?," October 1, 2011.
Hari Pulakkat	"Cells Of Hope," *Business World*, June 27, 2011.

For Further Discussion

Chapter 1

1. The United States Government Accountability Office (GAO) asserts that more cooperation is needed among the government agencies that oversee organ donation. Of the problems detailed by the GAO, which do you think is the most pressing? Please provide a detailed answer.

2. The viewpoints by Steven Reiss and by Lainie Friedman Ross and Benjamin E. Hippen concern biases that they believe exist in the allocation of organs. After reading the viewpoints, whose argument did you find most compelling and why?

Chapter 2

1. Anthony Gregory and Priya Shetty debate the merits of organ markets. Whose argument do you find more convincing, and why? If there were a legal organ market in the United States, would you consider using it as a seller or buyer? Please explain your answer.

2. Do you agree with Daniel Sayani's argument that presumed consent is a violation of individual liberty? Why or why not?

Chapter 3

1. After reading all the viewpoints in this chapter, what do you consider to be the most serious ethical issue surrounding organ donation? Please explain your answer, drawing from the viewpoints and any other relevant readings.

2. The viewpoints by Jennifer Lahl and by Erin Nelson and Timothy Caulfield use a popular book-turned-movie as the impetus for their arguments on "savior siblings." Have you ever read a book or watched a movie that influenced how you feel about a controversial issue? Please explain your answer.

Chapter 4

1. After reading the pair of viewpoints on xenotransplantation, do you think it could be a viable alternative to using human organs? Regardless of your view, what do you believe would be the biggest impediment (medical, ethical, or social) to using animal organs in human patients? Please explain your answer, drawing from the viewpoints and any other related reading.

2. The final three viewpoints in this book present arguments on how advancements in science and technology may or may not change the future of organ donation. Of these viewpoints, which one do you think offers the most convincing arguments? Why did those arguments stand out for you?

Organizations to Contact

The editors have compiled the following list of organizations concerned with the issues debated in this book. The descriptions are derived from materials provided by the organizations. All have publications or information available for interested readers. The list was compiled on the date of publication of the present volume; names, addresses, phone and fax numbers, and e-mail and Internet addresses may change. Be aware that many organizations take several weeks or longer to respond to inquiries, so allow as much time as possible.

Alliance for Paired Donation
3661 Briarfield Blvd., Suite 105
Maumee, OH 43537
(419) 866-5505 • fax: (419) 383-3344
e-mail: admin@paireddonationg.org
website: www.paireddonation.org

The Alliance for Paired Donation helps people in need of kidneys through the use of kidney paired donations, where one incompatible donor/recipient pair is matched to another incompatible pair. In other words, the donor of the first pair gives to the recipient of the second, and vice versa. The alliance is also a pioneer in the use of non-simultaneous extended altruistic donor chains (NEAD chains). News and articles are available on the website.

American Organ Transplant Association (AOTA)
Administrative Service Center
PO Box 418
Stilwell, KS 66085
(713) 344-2402
e-mail: aotaonline@gmail.com
website: www.aotaonline.org

The American Organ Transplant Association provides transplant patients and their families with the resources they need to cope with this costly and difficult surgery. Among the services they provide are free transportation to and from transplant centers, fundraising information, a medical assistance program, and a list of patient support groups. The website also features links to transplant centers and other sites that provide information on developments in organ transplantation.

American Society of Transplantation (AST)

15000 Commerce Pkwy., Suite C
Mt. Laurel, NJ 08054
(856) 439-9986 • fax: (856) 439-9982
website: www.a-s-t.org

The American Society of Transplantation is an organization of more than three thousand transplant professionals dedicated to issues such as education, advocacy, and research. AST offers a forum in which these professionals can exchange knowledge and expertise. Position papers are available on the website.

Association of Organ Procurement Organizations (AOPO)

8500 Leesburg Pike, Suite 300
Vienna, VA 22182
(703) 556-4242 • fax: (703) 556-4852
e-mail: aopo@aopo.org
website: www.aopo.org

The Association of Organ Procurement Organizations is a nonprofit organization that represents fifty-eight federally designated organ procurement organizations (OPOs). Serving more than 300 million Americans, AOPO provides education and information to OPOs and collaborates with other health care organizations. The association also works with members of Congress and several government agencies on issues relating to organ and tissue donation. Numerous links relating to organ donation are available on its website.

Children's Organ Transplant Association (COTA)

2501 West COTA Drive
Bloomington, IN 47403
(800) 366-2682 • fax: (812) 336-8885
e-mail: cota@cota.org
website: www.cota.org

COTA is a nonprofit organization that provides fundraising assistance and family support to children and young adults who need or have had a transplant. Since its establishment in 1986, COTA has raised more than $65 million and helped nearly 1,900 people. Press releases, videos, and an annual report are available on its website.

Donate Life America

701 E. Byrd Street, Sixteenth Floor
Richmond, VA 23219
(804) 377-3580
e-mail: donatelifeamerica@donatelife.net
website: donatelife.net

Donate Life America is a not-for-profit alliance of national organizations and state teams that aims to increase organ, eye, and tissue donation. The alliance helps develop donor education programs and facilitate donor registries. Its website includes facts and statistics about organ donation, along with stories about organ recipients.

Kidney Foundation of Canada

300-5165 Sherbrooke Street
West Montreal, QC H4A 1T6
(514) 369-4806 • fax: (514) 369-2472
e-mail: info@kidney.ca
website: www.kidney.ca

The Kidney Foundation of Canada works with representatives from the Canadian government and health-care industry to improve the rates of organ donations. It also encourages Canadians to become organ donors and discuss their wishes with their families. Annual reports, fact sheets, and brochures can be found on the foundation's website, including the fact sheet "Eating Guidelines for Diabetes and Chronic Kidney Disease" and the brochure "Deceased Organ Donation: Let's Talk About It." Statistics on organ transplantation and waiting times are also available on the website.

Living Bank
PO Box 6725
Houston, TX 77265
(713) 528-2971
website: www.livingbank.org

The Living Bank was established in 1968 in Houston and is the United States' first organ donor registry. Its goal is to educate people about the need for organ donors and to advocate for donors and their families. The Living Bank currently has an organ donor database of 2 million people in all fifty states.

National Network of Organ Donors
PO Box 223613
West Palm Beach, FL 33422
(866) 577-9798
e-mail: info@tnnod.org
website: www.thenationalnetworkoforgandonors.org

The National Network of Organ Donors aims to eliminate the issue of liability from the decision to donate organs. It seeks to do this by lobbying the US Congress to pass laws that will give doctors and hospitals immunity from being sued by family members who are challenging a patient's intent to donate organs. The network also aims to collaborate with hospitals and other transplant listing organizations and establish a national database of organ donors. Statistics about organ donation are available on the website.

United Network for Organ Sharing (UNOS)
700 North Fourth Street
Richmond, Virginia 23219
(804) 782-4800 • fax: (804) 782-4817
website: www.unos.org

UNOS, a private, nonprofit organization, has a contract with the federal government to manage the nation's organ transplant system. Its responsibilities include matching donors to recipients on the national transplant waiting lists and maintaining the database for every transplant that occurs in the United States. In addition, UNOS oversees the Organ Procurement and Transplantation Network (OPTN). UNOS also publishes the bimonthly magazine *Update*, and the website has fact sheets and data about organ donation.

US Department of Health and Human Services, Division of Transplantation (DoT)
200 Independence Ave. SW
Washington, DC 20201
website: www.organdonor.com

The Division of Transplantation is part of the US Department of Health and Human Services. DoT oversees the organ and blood stem cell transplant systems in the United States as well as initiatives to increase organ donation. In addition, the division conducts a public awareness program with the goal of increasing donations. The division's website has links to organizations and electronic resources on organ donation.

Bibliography of Books

Firat Bilgel   *The Law and Economics of Organ Procurement.* Cambridge, UK: Intersentia, 2011.

Katrina Bramstedt and Rena Down   *The Organ Donor Experience: Good Samaritans and the Meaning of Altruism.* Lanham, MD: Rowman & Littlefield, 2011.

Scott Carney   *The Red Market: On the Trail of the World's Organ Brokers, Bone Thieves, Blood Farmers, and Child Traffickers.* New York: William Morrow, 2011.

Steve Farber and Harlan Abrahams   *On the List: Fixing America's Failing Organ Transplant System.* Emmaus, PA: Rodale, 2009.

Anne-Maree Farrell, David Price, and Muireann Quigley, eds.   *Organ Shortage: Ethics, Law, and Pragmatism.* New York: Cambridge University Press, 2011.

Sara Fovargue   *Xenotransplantation and Risk: Regulating a Developing Biotechnology.* Cambridge, UK: Cambridge University Press, 2011.

Reg Green   *The Nicholas Effect: A Boy's Gift to the World.* Bloomington, IN: AuthorHouse, 2009.

Petr T. Grinkovskiy, ed.	*Organ Donation: Supply, Policies and Practices.* Hauppauge, NY: Nova Science Publishers, 2009.
Sherine Hamdy	*Our Bodies Belong to God: Organ Transplants, Islam, and the Struggle for Human Dignity in Egypt.* Berkeley: University of California Press, 2012.
David Hamilton	*A History of Organ Transplantation: Ancient Legends to Modern Practice.* Pittsburgh: University of Pittsburgh Press, 2012.
Steven J. Jensen, ed.	*The Ethics of Organ Transplantation.* Washington, DC: Catholic University of America Press, 2011.
Andrew A. Klein, Clive J. Lewis, and Joren C. Madsen, eds.	*Organ Transplantation: A Clinical Guide.* Cambridge, UK: Cambridge University Press, 2011.
Hal Marcovitz	*Organ and Body Donation.* Edina, MN: ABDO, 2011.
Franklin G. Miller and Robert D. Truog	*Death, Dying, and Organ Transplantation: Reconstructing Medical Ethics at the End of Life.* New York: Oxford University Press, 2011.
Janet Richards	*The Ethics of Transplants: Why Careless Thought Costs Lives.* New York: Oxford University Press, 2012.

Sally Satel, ed.

When Altruism Isn't Enough: The Case for Compensating Kidney Donors. Washington, DC: AEI, 2009.

Maria Siemionow

Face to Face: My Quest to Perform the World's First Full Face Transplant. New York: Kaplan, 2009.

David Talbot and Anthony M. D'Alessandro, eds.

Organ Donation and Transplantation After Cardiac Death. Oxford, UK: Oxford University Press, 2009.

Dick Teresi

The Undead: Organ Harvesting, the Ice-Water Test, Beating Heart Cadavers—How Medicine Is Blurring the Line Between Life and Death. New York: Pantheon, 2012.

Paula T. Trzepacz and Andrea F. DiMartini, eds.

The Transplant Patient: Biological, Psychiatric and Ethical Issues in Organ Transplantation. Cambridge, UK: Cambridge University Press, 2011.

David L. Weimer

Medical Governance: Values, Expertise, and Interests in Organ Transplantation. Washington, DC: Georgetown University Press, 2010.

Beth Whitehouse

The Match: "Savior Siblings" and One Family's Battle to Heal Their Daughter. Boston: Beacon, 2010.

T.M. Wilkinson

Ethics and the Acquisition of Organs (Issues in Biomedical Ethics). New York: Oxford University Press, 2012.

Index

TEST
DRIVING
MARRIAGE

TEST DRIVING MARRIAGE

**HOW TO TELL IF YOUR LIVE-IN RELATIONSHIP
IS HEADED TO THE ALTAR**

Beliza Ann Furman

BARRICADE BOOKS, INC.
NEW YORK

Published by Barricade Books Inc.
150 Fifth Avenue
New York, NY 10011

Copyright © 1998 by

Printed in the United States of America.

Library of Congress Cataloging-in-Publication Data
Furman, Beliza Ann.
Test-driving marriage / Beliza Ann Furman.
p. cm.
ISBN 1-56980-122-3
1. Unmarried couples. I. Title.
HQ975.F87 1998
306.73'5—dc21 98-16566
CIP

First printing

TO MY DAD
Col. Albert J. Gilardi
I love you and miss you.
1914-1997

AND TO MY SISTER-IN-LAW
Ann Fulton Gilardi
Who was killed by a wreckless driver in China on May 3, 1998.
She was only 52 years old.

MY HUSBAND, SAM
Always my best friend and biggest fan. I love you.

SEAN AND ASHLEY
Our two precious children, and my greatest achievement!

LAURIE AND JILL
My special stepdaughters who gave me the reason to develop the
knack of taking a good look at everyone's side of the story.

MY BIGGEST FANS
Joanna Betesh, Joan Feldman, Tindra Lanfrank,
Ceile Miele, Liz Mazzucca, and Vivian Ruggiero
Thank you for always being there for me on both sunny
and blue days.

SPECIAL THANKS TO…
Carole and Lyle Stuart
My publishers for their continued confidence
and Pam Gallagher
Fashion Editor for the *Asbury Park Press*
Thank you for your support of *all* of my endeavors
during our 21-year long friendship.
And for encouraging me to write this book.

AND ESPECIALLY,
Tony and Lourdes

A NOTE TO MY READERS All the stories reflect true experiences of the people to whom I have spoken. In several cases, to protect their privacy, names have been changed. The cities in which these people live, physical characteristics and occupations have also been altered. Fictitious names have been marked with an asterisk the first time they appear. Any similarity in names of people living or dead is merely a coincidence.

TABLE OF CONTENTS

THE CULTURAL ASPECTS
OF LIVING TOGETHER

APPENDIX: NONNUPTIAL CONTRACTS
MAKE STRANGE BEDFELLOWS

INTRODUCTION

THE LOVE STORY
THAT SET THIS BOOK
IN MOTION

Joseph*, an award-winning, thirty-nine-year-old sculptor from Western Canada, caught me off-guard during a recent book signing and discussion for *Younger Women—Older Men*. He asked me a question that put me on the spot. "What do you think about couples living together?" I was certain he didn't want to hear my answer.

In Joseph's case, this question was loaded with conflicting agendas: a sour divorce, single parenting, lost love, and fear of being trapped. I also knew he had enticed Serena*, his twenty-nine-year-old live-in, to give up a secure job in advertising and leave her close-knit family in Miami to move to Canada, become a surrogate mother to his two kids, find a new job, and balance his checkbook. Now I felt trapped. The room full of guests, many of whom were familiar with Joseph's love sagas—past and present—became eerily silent. Everyone wanted to hear my answer. Serena, who wanted nothing more than to be married to Joseph, was sitting at the edge of her seat.

---

*Names have been changed to protect privacy.

I responded, "If lovers move in together *without* a definitive commitment about their future, I don't think their relationship will go anywhere. If you're living together because it's convenient, *both* of you better know that from the very beginning. Living together is just that—a convenience. Marriage is a commitment."

Joseph heard the dreaded '*M*' word. The irony is, he knew the answer to this question as well as I. So why did he ask it, especially in public when my answer could very well compromise what he believed to be a comfortable relationship?

Several things came to mind. Joseph, who had been married once before, was thoroughly confused about what he wanted in life—a wife or a procession of lovers. Stability or fleeting moments of balance. Midlife freedom or obligations. In short, the best of both worlds.

Or possibly, he deeply loved Serena, saw a future with her, but needed confirmation from me that if he didn't "get off the pot" real soon he'd lose her.

On the airplane home, I couldn't get my mind off Joseph and Serena. I decided living-together couples are an enigma to me. How could anyone put so much into a relationship without a firm commitment to marry? I needed to know more, especially since more and more of the subscribers seeking solace from my international, self-help network for wives of older men (W.O.O.M.) were not wives, but *live-ins*.

I went to the library and looked up "Living Together." A few books popped up on the computer screen, but they dwelled mostly on the financial aspects of living together, not the emotional implications. Within days my preliminary research unveiled the reason why: the subject of unofficial marriage has so many variables, only a tome could address all of the issues and problems that crop up. Still, I knew the subject needed to be explored in more depth to heighten awareness and to provoke unmarried couples to take an objective look at trial marriages—the good and the bad—and hear the views of those who have lived through them. The issues were a lot more complicated than the phrase "he's afraid to commit" indicated.

I went back to the couple who originally sparked my curiosity: Joseph and Serena.

"We had a global love affair," remembers Serena, who met and fell in love with Joseph while visiting friends in his hometown. "It all happened so fast. But, it wasn't a real relationship because for many months we always met within a vacationlike atmosphere. Occasionally Joey would spend a week in Miami, or I would spend a week in Canada."

It's been eight years since Joseph, a seductive, second generation Italian Canadian, broke up with a former live-in he wanted to marry. He admits he's had a lot of time to reflect upon what he is seeking in a woman if he ever decides to marry again. "I am looking for a woman whose love is unconditional, whose priorities are to direct her energy toward raising our children, and the achievement of my goals."

"I wasn't sure Serena was the ideal woman for me," he continued, "but I wanted to find out. And to do that, we had to live together. There's so much about Serena I love," smiled Joseph. He said sex is great, and she is exotically beautiful. "I didn't want to risk losing someone who could be the *one*."

After vacillating for over a year about remarriage, Joseph, who received full custody of his children after his divorce and has spent the better part of the last nine years raising them as a single father, feels his perspective on remarriage may be different from that of men who are weekend fathers.

"It was such a huge responsibility to care for those kids alone. I haven't ruled out having more children; I just want to make certain that their mother knows the responsibility for raising them will fall on her shoulders. She has to understand that."

On the other hand, Serena knows exactly what she wants. "I had marriage in mind. But before I committed myself to Joey, I made it perfectly clear I wanted children, and with that came marriage."

Contemplating her future, she murmured, "I'm not really sure what Joey has in mind. We don't touch on that."

There's a lonely, isolating aspect to living with your lover and not knowing what the future will bring. Often, one of the partners walks on eggshells while the other is making up his or her mind. Each is watching the other's every move. Efforts are made to change personality traits or physical flaws—or iron out difficulties—to achieve an unnatural level of perfection before tying the knot. "It's important to be best friends, first," thinks Joseph. "There are certain aspects of Serena's personality that will have to change before I could consider marriage."

Elaborating, he said, "Ideally my spouse will have to accept my decisions—not that I want a 'yes' woman. I just feel, strongly, someone has to be the decision-maker. And I think that should be the male. Do you think I sound chauvinistic?"

"Well," I hedged, "I suppose not—as long as you make it perfectly clear that's exactly how you feel and your mate agrees. However, it's going to be difficult to get a woman these days to agree."

A young woman's idea of being the perfect mate may include holding down a good-paying job while delegating household chores to a housekeeper or baby-sitter. "Oh! I'm very proud of Serena's job," boasts Joseph. "I wouldn't dream of asking her to quit."

Joseph's ability to embrace both old-fashioned and modern mind-sets is baffling. Surely, if I am bewildered by what he says he wants, Serena must be even more confused.

Joseph laughed at himself, "Maybe I need to go to the backwoods of Sicily to find a woman who can live up to my expectations."

Seemingly contemporary in his style, dress, lingo, taste in music, and penchant for chic, upbeat fads such as body piercing and a smoothly shaved head, Joseph continued to take me by surprise. "Would you like to clarify that?"

"It's unfortunate, this brainwashing of women who have become so 'modern.' This nation is experiencing an unprecedented disregard for what has been the foundation of the human family since the beginning of time."

"*O-kay,*" I stammered, but rebounded. Perhaps by setting expectations so high, Joseph was subconsciously trying to scare off any prospective wife.

Serena says she has been through a lot. "I'm an adult now. If anything goes wrong, it's not going to hurt me." Yet, at twenty-nine—with no assurances of becoming a mother—one has to wonder how much time she can devote to trying to please Joseph.

And at the same time, Joseph says, "I've given such serious thought to all of this, I sometimes wonder if I shouldn't spend the rest of my life unattached." Perhaps he's got a point.

Only time will tell what the future holds for Joseph and Serena. However, the uncertainty of the outcome of their love affair caught *my* attention.

A BRIEFLY CHRONICLED
ROLL IN THE HAY

As it stands, marriage is under attack. Although we are inundated with all types of advice, few visionaries have surfaced to offer a practical, workable solution. Is a marital test-drive or a permanent living-together situation a viable answer? Can the future of the traditional, nuclear family survive the implications of unsanctioned marriage? Every time we think we know, someone comes along to challenge our logic. Questions like this make us think society is going to hell in a basket.

When searching for guidance, we draw from ancestral ideologies and recent findings, tested theories and speculation. Ironically, though, when rethinking love relationships, I have discovered what goes around comes around.

A common belief is that cohabitation became popular as a result of the sexual revolution of the 1960s. But in fact, wrote Ginny Carroll for *Newsweek*, "Common law marriage was almost universally legal, accepted as practical necessity if not desirable morality in pioneer America."[1] Historians confirm that surprising fact. Common-law marriage arose on the expanding migrating frontier, where visits by circuit-riding preachers and judges were infrequent. Most states accepted informal marriage (living together without civil or religious validation) as an acceptable way to protect pioneer women from straying partners. Furthermore, children born to the couple were considered legitimate and could claim their inheritance. Similarly, various Native American communities in the nineteenth century were tolerant of trial marriages, granting their women substantial sexual and personal freedoms.[2]

This widespread acceptance of common-law marriage extended to our African American ancestors. Although as slaves they had to abandon certain tribal customs, informal marriage and community responsibility protected offspring and familial continuity.[3]

Where couples have lived together continuously for a number of years—usually, but not always, seven—common-law marriages have been recognized by some colonies and states since the seventeenth century. However, by the late nineteenth century, concerned reformist groups began petitioning state government to ban informal marriages, which they blamed for corrupting the family unit.

During the mid-1920s, Denver judge Ben Lindsey proposed that states formally recognize trial marriage as a "companionate marriage" to solve the problem of wayward and sexually promiscuous youths dallying in premarital sex.

Described by *Collier's* as "interesting and disputatious" fodder for that winter's conversation, the January, 1928 national weekly discussed the conditions: "That a couple contemplating marriage arrange a temporary contract to discover if they are really congenial. In addition to being temporary, the companionate marriage must also be childless according to the rules."

As pragmatic as it sounded, the informal marriage idea was unequivocally shot down. *Collier's* editors noted: "Nobody in complete possession of his faculties expects any lawmaking body to commit political suicide by endorsing companionate marriages, or any other bizarre proposal that seems to strike at the foundations of the family."

The increasing tendency toward and acceptability of divorce during the 1920s was cited as the reason a preposterous proposal like this came about. "First of all," insisted *Collier's*, "the modern woman is conscious of her rights. She is unwilling to accept the conditions in which her mother and her grandmother acquiesced. Then, being an earner and therefore financially independent, she does not have to tolerate a husband who has become uncongenial."

Paradoxically, women, demanding greater equality at home and in their new-found careers, were blamed for the increase in divorce. And *Collier's* concluded: "It is a mistake to postpone marriage during a trial period since everybody knows that the presence of children is the strongest tie between men and women and the surest guarantee of permanent marriage." And of course, the companionate marriage proposal was taboo.

Over seventy years later, society's concerns about divorce and informal marriages—and the persistent dichotomy of male/female relations—remain relatively unchanged.

Modern society is fighting hard for legal and societal change, however, traditional perspectives persevere from when the husband earned the income and owned all family wealth. The wife was responsible for maintaining the home and rearing children.[4]

The question looms: can a living-together couple ever attain the legal and societal status held by a married couple?

Maybe—but probably not any time soon, because over the past two hundred years, and up to the era of the Moral Majority and other fundamentalist religious groups, trial marriages have been judged to be a threat. In an effort to control family direction and deny feminism, denizens representing the religiously observant and devout have intervened, and have continually lobbied for laws that curb divorce,[5] abortion, birth control, and premarital sex.

It is interesting to note how the puritanical influence on society shifts as different cultures rise up and rebel.

Through history, we see challengers to conservative sexual ethics. Some of the more renowned include John Humphrey Noyes, who in 1848 formed the Oneida Colony, which encouraged members to engage in premarital and extramarital sexual encounters.

Before World War I, explains Mary E. Odem, researcher for the *Encyclopedia of American Social History*, radicals and bohemians influenced by Sigmund Freud and British sex theorists Edward Carpenter and Havelock Ellis flocked to Greenwich Village where they "experimented with open sexual unions based on emotional compatibility and attraction, rather than on legal marriage."

By the 1960s, the hippie culture and "the Pill" brought about significant changes in premarital predilections, and living in sin escalated. In her controversial article in the July, 1966 issue of *Redbook*, anthropologist Margaret Mead stunned society by proposing couples engage in a clearly unorthodox wedding pattern: "Marriage in Two Steps."

To some, this was a practical solution that addressed escalating teen pregnancies, shotgun weddings, and children marrying children. Premarital sex was rampant among our nation's youth. Yet, as recently as thirty years ago, their parents and laws lagged behind. In some states it was illegal for physicians to prescribe birth control devices to unmarried teens, and badly botched illegal abortions were killing or sterilizing our unmarried daughters.[6]

In Ms. Mead's two-step proposal, an *individual marriage* or temporary "student" marriage would be followed by a *parental marriage*—a lifetime commitment. By the time couples entered into it, they would be sexually aware and stable enough to become parents. The *individual marriage* would be a licensed union in which two people would be committed to each other for as long as they wished to be together but not as future parents.

Those not mature enough to accept parental responsibility could embark upon a legally tolerated sexual partnership. If the relationship did not evolve beyond that, the partners could walk away without the stigma of divorce and seek a different partner. Margaret Mead's *individual marriage* contract stated if a couple parted company, there would be no alimony or support. She urged "that we accept that attitudes toward sex and attitudes toward commitment are separate."

Ms. Mead's concept formed the basis of our present-day "palimony" and prenuptial agreements, which have changed the course of premarital history. In 1972, Los Angeles attorney Marvin Mitchelson's landmark case *Marvin v. Marvin* made front-page news; while titillating the nation's appetite for gossip, the case persisted for almost a decade.

Michelle Triola lived with actor Lee Marvin for seven years. Shortly before the relationship dissolved in 1970, Ms. Triola changed her name to Marvin. She filed suit against Mr. Marvin in 1972 claiming she was entitled to half of the $3,800,000 he had earned since they began living together and

$100,000 compensation for the singing career she interrupted while she set out to become his live-in companion.

The case was dismissed by a trial court and subsequently by the California Court of Appeals. However in 1976, the California Supreme Court rejected the earlier decisions, and sent the case back to the lower court for reconsideration. Unfortunately, Mr. Mitchelson explained to me, Ms. Marvin made little headway, and after a ten-year court battle the case was short-lived. She was awarded a mere $104,000 as an "equitable remedy," but it was ultimately expunged. Remember, there was no palimony contract and common-law marriage was banished in California in 1895. Knowing all of this, Ms. Marvin made the decision to stay in a marriage of convenience.

"Marriage in Two Steps," similar to Judge Ben Lindsey's "companionate marriage" was a progressive idea ahead of its time and it paved the way for Marvin Mitchelson to structure the modern prenuptial agreement. If prepared properly, it almost always holds up in court.

Still, the public's acceptance of cohabitation varies. Illinois is the only state including the District of Columbia that does not recognize any type of contractual relationship agreement. If you live with someone there and break up, don't expect to be awarded a nickel from the courts. "Clearly, Illinois is a very strong public policy state in favor of marriage," advised Marta Coblitz, chair of the Chicago Bar Association's Matrimonial Committee. "In a lot of ways, living together doesn't make sense," she continued. "If you really love someone enough to cohabit, why wouldn't you want to see both of you protected by marriage laws? The whole idea of denying spousal obligations is against our idea of how we are supposed to live."

"The folks in Ladue, Missouri, one of the richest communities in America, take their sin seriously, especially when it comes in the form of unmarried couples living together," states J.A. Lobbia, writer for the magazine *Mother Jones*.[7] Taking their opposition a step further, it is *illegal* to live with an unofficial spouse in Ladue. Enforcing it may be difficult, but this law certainly serves as a deterrent.[8] To some that may sound radical. However, anti-cohabitation sentiments like these stem from centuries of tradition.

By the 1970s and 1980s premarital sex and living together increased dramatically. Public apathy overshadowed any alarm over an unmarried couple living together. However, depending upon whom you ask, the 1990s have taken a conservative turn. Certain statisticians and behavioral analysts believe informal marriage is declining. *Bride's* magazine indicates lavish weddings—including younger brides and grooms—are back in vogue. One reason might be that AIDS is frightening couples into monogamous relationships, which bolster matrimony.

Political pundits are blaming everything from a hangnail to the demise of our country on the lack of morality. Single parents (the majority female) have been frowned upon—marriage is in. Yet, ironically, we shut our eyes and re-elected a president who seems to be continually facing sexual harassment charges as well as wearing the label of womanizer, justified or not. Meanwhile, Republicans are thought of by women as a party that continually meddles in women's personal matters. Yes, we certainly are a society mired in double standards.

Consider: *Roe v. Wade*, which legalized abortion in 1973, has been threatened with reversal. Fundamentalism and over-righteousness are cunningly invading our private lives. I believe inequitable palimony settlements, where there is no contract (and sometimes where there is), are litigated—consciously or subconsciously—to punish those who thumb their noses at marriage.

Is there more here that meets the eye? When temperance movements and prohibitions arise in society, does anti-cohabitation sentiment with an emphasis on repressing premarital sex follow?

"It's becoming clear that living together, a lingering artifact of the 60s, is being viewed in the cool light of the 90s much like lava lamps and Earth shoes," writes *Los Angeles Times* correspondent, Lynn Smith.[9]

If history repeats itself, and if premarital sex and trial marriages in the 1990s are truly waning, we will probably see a recycled version of other historic and controversial sexual uprisings—premarital and otherwise—reoccur around 2020 as a backlash to what some people may view as present-day narrow-mindedness.

"And you will see, for a time," remarked Dr. Joyce Chiumento, sociologist and former lecturer at Temple University and the University of Pennsylvania, "this type—or any type—of revolution will cause transitory upheaval because the folkways, the mores, the norms are all thrown into challenge. When people aren't accustomed to deviant and new ways of thinking, a period of negative and positive stimulation evolves." Because radical change is anxiety provoking, there is a level of insecurity. However, she warns, "People should also be very, very cautious not to upset the balance too extremely."

Yet, in spite of close-minded cultural and societal apprehension, Dr. Chiumento perceives, "Spurts of public turmoil and periodic change are good."[10]

Past sexual revolutions paved the way for where we stand today. Still, arguments for and against marital test drives never cease. Armed with historical facts proving that living together doesn't serve society's aims, we continue to reinvent the wheel. Meanwhile, questions remain. Is living together before marriage an answer to the escalating divorce rate? Do cohabiting couples really get to know each other well enough to stave off divorce after they marry? Can the optimistic goals of living together actually revive marriage?

Based upon the interviews I have conducted, I think not, because I found the questions surrounding living together far too controversial, even among partners who are test-driving marriage.

PHYSICAL AND EMOTIONAL IMPLICATIONS SURROUNDING LIVING TOGETHER TODAY

Viewed by some as out of touch with the twentieth century, Great Britain's Queen Elizabeth II has been forced to look at current trends publicly and privately. Banishing centuries-old, archaic doctrines that have plagued the monarchy since the abdication of the Duke of Windsor, she made the surprising decision to grant permission to her youngest son, Prince Edward, to move his girlfriend, Sophie Rhys-Jones, into his rooms at Buckingham Palace, in 1997.[1] Some in Britain were undoubtedly shocked, but polls show a greater number of people felt it was a reasonable, and perhaps pertinent decision given that her other three children were divorced.

We have to wonder, though, is this pillar of the Church of England endorsing trial marriages? Or, is Her Majesty exasperated when faced with current relationship quandaries, as many of us are?

THE FACTS
THAT MAY HAVE INFLUENCED
THE QUEEN'S DECISION

According to the latest U.S. Census, the numbers of unmarried, opposite-sex living-together couples (LTCs) are still rising, though not as rapidly as in prior decades. Current Census Bureau statistics show more than three and a half million heterosexual couples cohabit. Another source, *The American Woman*, indicates that in 1993, "more than five million households were composed of two adults living together as partners." Other surveys have proved the number is far greater. Because we cannot accurately measure how many unmarried couples live together (same sex, opposite sex, or both), no one really knows for sure. But does it really matter?

To historians, sociologists, philosophers, anthropologists, and behavioral clinical and research psychotherapists, the numbers matter only when tracking demographic shifts in premarital and marital behavior, and substantiating observations and opinions.

The numbers are also significant when describing societal shifts in popular behavior. Such shifts influence legislative referendums as legal and corporate benefit decision-makers begin to recognize these relationships and incorporate them into housing discrimination laws, health and automobile insurance benefits, inheritance issues, employee benefits, etc. The Center of Disease Control (CDC) says 33.5 percent of all women have lived with somebody.[2] [3] [4] Obviously, the more people engage in such domestic relationships, the more routine and acceptable their behavior appears.

In 1950, U.S. Bureau of the Census demographers charted 50,000 unmarried living-together couples. Morgan D.

King, Esq., author of the *Cohabitation Handbook*, states between 1960 to 1970, the number of these couples jumped by more than 700 percent, to a little more than a half a million couples.[5] Between 1970 and 1981 the number of living together couples almost tripled.[6] "And nearly doubled again in the 1980s," says David G. Myers, author of *In Pursuit of Happiness*. By the early 1980s, 44 percent of all marriages were preceded by living-together arrangements.[7]

Because of the markedly increasing number of unmarried couples living together, the Bureau of the Census added data estimating the number of cohabiting households composed of two unmarried adults of the opposite sex. The relationship category, "unmarried partner," was added for the first time to the 1990 Census Questionnaire.

In its 1994 report, *Marital Status and Living Arrangements*, "there were seven unmarried couples for every 100 married couples compared with one out of every 100 in 1970" in the United States.

Overseas, particularly in France, Britain, and Sweden, living together has skyrocketed. According to a May 2, 1992 issue of *The Economist*, three French Socialist deputies put forth proposals for a "'new contract of civil union.' This would give an unmarried couple of whatever sexual tendency the same rights as a married couple in regard to death duties, pensions, and child custody."

All of my sources concurred: Marriage—even though the 1990s has shown a slight upturn compared with the 1970s and 1980s—is down; living together is up.[8] As a result, there is a great deal of bias and deviation—including many gray areas when trying to determine the numbers of opposite and same sex living-together couples. These discrepancies cause a great deal of misinterpretation and heated discord.

Although she may have offended some of her royal subjects, Queen Elizabeth was possibly influenced by these ever-increasing numbers.

EMOTIONALLY RESPONDING TO FACTS

Taking the position LTCs are on the rise, I find marital test-drives are spurred by a generation with an over-fifty percent divorce rate. Many parents tell me they encourage their twenty-something offspring not to rush into marriage. "Why don't you two just live together for a while?"

In certain cases, living together has replaced the starter marriage.[9] However, LTCs are not influenced so much by the vow *forever after*, as much as they are by *for now*. This outlook leads to emotional complications for one or both partners when you're lovers first, soul mates later—that is, if the relationship lasts beyond the casual bond at the outset and evolves into a deeply valued and passionate union.

In 1988, I founded the international self-help network, W.O.O.M. (Wives of Older Men). Over the past ten years, five thousand spouses, brides- or grooms-to-be, and living-together partners with an age difference of ten or more years have sought my opinion about their age-disparate relationship concerns.

Because of my expertise on this subject, I have been featured in *Psychology Today*, The American Counseling Association's periodical, *Counseling Today*, The *New York Times*, Reader's Digests *New Choices*, *Glamour*, *Mademoiselle*, and *New Woman*. Barricade Books published my book, *Younger Women/Older Men* in 1995.

After hearing one horror story after another from unmarried partners, I have concluded that living-together arrangements are half-assed gutless relationships that cohabiting partners or those contemplating cohabiting need to take a longer look at.

When LTCs consult with me, I find either one partner, or both, operate in half-gear: half in love, sort of in love, think I'm in love. In spite of that, I'm open-minded enough to know what I think isn't always the last word. However, I operate from this bias: that I thought enough of myself not to have compromised my own relationship. In 1970, when I was twenty-two-years-old, I told my then lover Sam, who wanted me to move in with him, "Thank you very much, but until you marry me, I'll keep my place."

Honestly, there have been bumps in the road, but Sam and I have worked hard at our happy marriage for over a quarter century. Considering current marriage statistics, that's a milestone. Long ago, I took a stance. LTCs tend to flounder as they often dodge their personal values and ethics for the sake of a relationship.

There are many hidden agendas when couples share the rent, split the cost of a television, and vie for bathroom space without a firm commitment. Not knowing where they're headed, they can so easily become history by tomorrow and often do. Living together is a relationship of the moment that goes against all religious and spiritual covenants. Even when it makes sense, living together undermines the very foundations of our upbringing.

When I have appeared on talk radio and television shows including *Oprah, Geraldo, Regis and Kathie Lee, Donahue*, CNN, *Rolanda, Eye Witness News, Charles Perez, Good Morning New York*, CBS, and *Maury*, I have—with few exceptions—jumped at the chance to express how volatile I think it is to test-drive marriage. Why? Because routinely, one partner is persuaded by the other to live together first. If the weaker partner doesn't have the guts to say, "No. I want to get married," or, "No. I don't believe in that," power shifts to the "winner." Down the road, even years later, someone pays a price. Even if feeling powerless is a misconception, the weaker partner's control diminishes. A perceived imbalance in the relationship emerges; the "stronger" partner is blamed.

How many of these couples marry? Far fewer than you think. Marcia Lasswell, president of the American Association of Marriage and Family Therapists, told the *Los Angeles Times* that "couples who view living together as a first step toward commitment are usually deluding themselves. Many do not go on to marry later." So why do it?

One advantage for younger men and women may be learning, early on, what you *don't* want in a partner. Another is having the security of a relationship—someone to come home to. There is also the financial aspect: by splitting the rent and household costs, you can bank the other half, spend it on college tuition, or start a business. It is also convenient.

As live-ins age, successful women pursuing careers may feel they can move around more freely without domestic pressures and a husband's demands. Older couples won't lose their benefits. Inheritance hassles are kept to a minimum. Additionally, his or her kids may be a lot quicker to accept a live-in rather than a stepparent—a potential threat.

Dreamers are convinced living together is one step away from marriage. Realists use it to buy time.

One real disadvantage is you've taken yourself off the market. Potential marriage partners pass you by. You may be manipulated and prodded to change, to live up to your partner's expectations by the promise of a wedding band. Furthermore, women learn soon enough that most men aren't quick to cooperate with household chores—especially if it's only for a roommate.

However, it is most perplexing to watch women (and a few men) subjugate themselves, waste time, and squirm over live-in lovers who may never have marriage in mind. Deep down, many LTCs feel guilty. The living-together arrangement nags at their conscience. They realize it's here to stay, agree it is a popular lifestyle and their choice, but don't feel good about it while they are doing it.

When confronted to be truly honest, unofficial spouses tell me they are scared they'll get dumped if they push marriage. However, too many put up with the living-together arrangement as a second-best alternative. One woman told me her live-in lover of nine years has no plans to marry her, even though she recently became pregnant. But she tolerates his blunt candidness and her uncertain future as an acceptable trade-off. "You can't imagine what it's like to come home to an empty apartment," she remembers. "Being alone is horrible...worse than lonely. An ugly alternative I'm not willing to deal with." But again, she is only second best. Over time, that uncertainty destroys a person's self image.

Although you won't be stoned, society is far more comfortable dealing with married couples. Furthermore, certain religious organizations and fundamentalist groups who frown upon unmarried people "living in sin" may shun you. The Catholic Church is adamantly opposed to couples having pre-marital sex, let alone living together. "Marriage is a covenant," responded Father Joseph Montalbano to U.S. Catholic's Sounding Board questionnaire: "There's No Such Thing as a Trial Marriage."[10]

Moreover, hitched people constantly feel the urge to butt in, "Just when are you two gonna get married?" In retaliation, you might be dying to groan, "Misery loves company." Odds are you won't, and will just concoct a sheepish excuse. Even if you are engaged and living together before your wedding, there's no guarantee you will get married. Some couples choose to live together indefinitely.

Case in point: the common-law marriage of movie stars Goldie Hawn and Kurt Russell may be headed for the record books. Beating the odds for all types of marital unions—conventional and otherwise—this dynamic twosome has lived together for fourteen years. Too good to be true? Just ask anyone in Hollywood if Goldie and Kurt have a stable relationship (usually an L.A. County oxymoron), and you'll hear nothing but positive remarks about their love affair.

Along with her two children from her second marriage to musician Bill Hudson, Goldie and Kurt's combined family includes their love child, Wyatt. The Hawn/Russell household represents the quintessential couple living the American dream. Their union is held together by the conviction that marriage may rock the boat.

"I know how rare it is to stay together and remain this much in love," Goldie confessed to *W*. "[Kurt] meets a lot of women. And I meet a lot of men. But so far, nobody's come up for either of us. I've just lived on this planet long enough to know you never say never. If you try to hold on to a fixed position, you don't grow, you don't change, you don't move—you die."

Goldie knows. She's tried marriage twice. After two divorces and a stellar career, she says she doesn't feel pressured to get married again. In fact, Goldie feels compelled *not* to. And Kurt, who has never been married, is going along with it. Yet, most traditionalists are just itching to ask, "Why not? Why put so much effort into a relationship that has an uncertain future?"

Hollywood has such an influence on our daily lives, I find it a shame that movie stars' living arrangements become the standard for everyone else. I was amused by a recent wisecrack in *W*: "Cindy Crawford and her longtime off-and-on boyfriend Rande Gerber are *making it official*, Hollywood style. They just bought a house together, and are moving in right away."

Unfortunately, unlike the fantasies played out at the movies, celebrity love affairs are often star-crossed. There aren't but a handful of enduring relationships. Consider this recent *People* magazine headline: "As [an engaged, living-together] couple, Brad Pitt and Gwyneth Paltrow appeared to have it all; romance, elegance, and stardom. So where did their love go?" Ever think it wasn't love?

Without the vows of marriage, living together makes it less likely couples will want to work out problems. The vows of marriage force a couple to muster courage and personal forgiveness to back down from a stubborn position, and recognize you may be the one who is wrong. The infatuation of LTCs makes it so much easier to burn the bridge when faced with conflict.

Often, I am invited to speak to groups about my views regarding coping with current relationship problems such as combined families, two-career families, stepmotherhood, being a second spouse, and gaining control in your relationship. During these discussions, I emphasize how important I think it is that each partner retain his or her identity and develop autonomy within the relationship. After all, if you don't know who *you* are and what makes *you* happy, how can you insist someone else is making you miserable?

Invariably, couples stay after these discussions to "ask" me what I think about their situations. What they really want is a quick fix. "Can you make him marry me?" No.

What I might try to do is point out ways you can help yourself. A couple must assume responsibility for what happens in their relationship and for what they are doing to help or hurt each other and themselves. Without the sanctions of marriage, I find couples are less inclined to put in the effort.

Critics may say, "And you think dating someone can't push you over the edge?" Like living together, long-term dating often reveals divisive inadequacies and incompatibilities in relationships. Clearly, dating should be a regularly scheduled, fact-finding mission. A younger, unmarried couple will find the option of dating more convenient than a middle-aged, unmarried couple whose obligations such as work, business travel, and often, existing families slow the process. Middle-aged couples think living together might expedite their getting to know each other better faster. Still, it is a risk.

My fifty-year-old friend dated a man over a period of eighteen months. Supposedly, they did everything right. At the beginning, they took the relationship very slowly, including holding off having sex for a couple of months. She found many aspects of their love affair rewarding and even considered marriage, but she was opposed to moving in with him until they were married. After a year, she decided to take the summer off from work to visit her family in Texas. She laid out her itinerary so that she could rent out her condo that summer to pay her travel expenses.

Because my friend didn't have a place to stay, she lived with her male friend for three weeks, traveled for a month, and stayed with him again for three weeks. "Everything was wonderful," she said, until she moved back to her place. He never called her again. She has no idea what happened. Of course, she is crushed. "I can't believe after all those months together he didn't say good-bye—didn't tell me why." She admits he had a mean streak, but can't understand why she ignored it.

"Reflecting back," she says, "I now see cracks in the relationship. I see tell-tale signs I should have paid attention to when we dated."

She cites her former lover's ex-wife who dumped him but played a major role in his life. They were on the phone constantly discussing "the children." Furthermore, my friend was not included at frequent family parties where the ex-wife attended. She was seldom invited to spend more than a couple hours, on weekends, with his children. Then she told me that their dating was limited to once a week. Although they did speak on the phone every day, they weren't together. Add it all up and it's clear you know he wanted to keep his distance from her.

Hurt, denied, and feeling used, my friend was exposed to the volatility of life with him, even during their shortest periods of living together. She was the pawn in his game. He could deal with dating, but when they emerged as an LTC, complete with her toothbrush in his condo, that threatened his family, his ex-wife, any chance of his getting back together with his ex-wife, or his having it both ways. My friend mistook their living together as a step closer to walking down the aisle. She knows now, she had her head in the sand. Her lover never had marriage in mind.

For the past ten years, couples from all over the world have come to me with problems. After each partner vents, I always ask the other one, "Are you merely hearing what your partner has to say, or do you care enough to listen, make some changes and incorporate those concerns into your life?"

Caring is the buzzword of a relationship's success; indifference its Waterloo. If you *care* enough about your significant other you should be eager to take the risk and get married. Or *care* enough to recognize the relationship is not doing either one of you any good, and move on.

If I've done my job, *Test-Driving Marriage* will make you think about how you assess your actions and reactions. You may also learn some important things about yourself: for instance, how you establish a dialogue with those you love and why you maneuver through life the way you do.

Test-Driving Marriage examines the upside, downside, and inside of every aspect of unmarried, cohabiting love affairs for all ages. If you are auditioning for the role of either husband or wife, some of what you read may make you cry. It may demoralize you, make you laugh, or curse me. In some cases, you may think I'm off my rocker! But understand I've held too many hands of those who didn't get the part.

Of course, the final decision is yours. In this book, I show you ways to cope, accept certain outcomes, and appreciate that living together is not simply packing your bags and playing house. Even if the parameters are defined and understood from the very outset, *one partner almost always wants to get married. One partner almost always gets hurt.*

You may be in a rush to give your lover a housekey, but keep in mind, you might want to take a longer look at what you *think* will be the outcome. Couples have a moral responsibility to regard each other's self-esteem. One way to start is to know everything possible about living together.

A VARIETY OF
LIVING-TOGETHER
RELATIONSHIPS

COPING WITH THE NUANCES
OF UNOFFICIAL MARRIAGE

Throughout the following pages, you will learn about the lives of hundreds of people I've talked with. Some were casual discussions at the supermarket; others, people I know well; still others, consultations with experts in their fields. Unlike other topics I have written about, living together elicited a wide range of strong opinions, with everyone eager to share. As in romance novels, many stories had similarities, yet each had a different twist. I have included the most common living-together scenarios as well as some of the more unusual.

I discovered one common misconception among women who are cohabiting: they expect the values of marriage to bind their living-together relationships. Living together is not marriage. There are no rules. Men who choose to live with a woman do it because they want to skirt the sanctions put upon them by marriage. In short, men expect, at some time, to break up. Therefore, anything can go wrong, and sooner or later if you don't get married, it will. And if you do marry, there is no guarantee you will stay married. Statistics prove when unofficial spouses marry, they have a higher divorce rate than couples who didn't.[1]

Being a fly on the wall in the men's locker room would give women real insight into men's psyches. Not learning about men and what makes them tick is a common female shortcoming, which is why so many women are hoodwinked by the living-together relationship from day one. It's not that the men have deceived them; these women made an inaccurate assumption. "If he loves me enough to live with me, he must love me enough to marry me." Wrong. However, if you go into a living-together situation thinking, "He loves me enough to ask me to move in, but not enough to marry me," you'll save yourself a lot of heartache and you might think about *not* moving in.

Living-together issues are similar to those found in marriage: money, starting families, combining families, infidelity, etc. It became obvious to me that because these couples are not married there was less desire to address and solve problems. "I'm living with this person because I don't want the hassle of working this stuff out," was a common assumption.

In my search for men to talk about their living-together situations, I found many jumped at the chance to give their views. Their candor was eye-opening, albeit scary. "It's nice to have someone around to do the wash; cook my meals." They placed less emphasis on the gushy aspects of the love affair itself. A number of men were more comfortable discussing a past relationship than their current one.

It was startling to learn how different men perceive their love relationships. If there were current complaints, men were able to sum up the problem in a few words. They generally did not quibble about the little stuff.

Women, on the other hand, were able to articulate a current problem, and used that revelation to gripe on and on, verbally beating an issue to death, sometimes *not* realizing what the *real* problem was. Unless provoked or nagged, men generally ignore a relationship problem or internalize it, hoping it will go away. Some men deal with it by walking away from the conflict, opting to kick it around privately. Others try to offer advice.

Deborah Tannen, author of *You just don't Understand: Women and Men in Conversation*, suggests many men see themselves as problem solvers. "A complaint," she writes, "is a challenge to their ability to think of a solution. So women who seek understanding from their partner feel frustrated when they receive advice. Men likewise feel frustrated when their attempts to be caring are met with tears and anger."[2]

I found a wide range of women—from self-supporting to those who can't get it together financially—willing to put their destiny in the hands of some guy. Most women I spoke with wanted to be taken care of. Yet, in this day and age, men are less willing to do that.

When it comes to *being afraid to commit*, I have discovered this is an empty term—the diagnosis for the problems in every unofficial marriage. Commitment can be achieved without a marriage promise. However, it is *not* the solemn commitment partners pledge when they marry. Couples are fooling themselves if they think unofficial marriage is the same thing as marriage. Deep down, they know it.

My interviews with men lasted somewhere between ten to thirty minutes, longer only because I pushed to hear more. Once they trusted me, many of the men started to ramble, then caught themselves, and exclaimed, "I can't believe I am telling you my life story! I *never* do this!" True, but I got most of them to open up. We had fun with it and they were flattered. Ultimately I learned something about them and they learned something about themselves.

On the other hand, the women's interviews lasted an hour at the *very* least. And often, I had to exercise the greatest patience to piece together the truth.

I found that when a guy knows the affair is over, it's over. He moves on, but often only when he has found someone else. Wrongly or rightly, men responded, "Who cares why things aren't working? At this point it's not. Why stick around to see how badly we can destroy each other before we part company?" Men prefer to split but, if possible, remain friends. A woman may know it's over, but will prolong the pain. "Let's find out why this ill-fated relationship isn't working." Women then waste energy hating, seeking revenge, and often slam the door on a bad relationship before they have lined up another guy.

Nevertheless, men have little tact when it comes to breaking up. Some spinelessly do it over the phone, or worse yet, send a fax or an e-mail message. Others will passively ignore their live-ins, hoping they'll get the picture.

The women I talked with had one thing in mind: marriage. Some accepted whatever crumbs of a relationship were handed to them. Paradoxically, a high percentage think a marital test-drive is the secret to a successful marriage. Many guys agreed. But, significantly, I learned the *better* a man got to know his live-in mate, the *less* he wanted to marry her.

These days, private psychotherapy fees run between $90 to $150 per session. Most HMOs allow a person from one to three visits, and then you're on your own. Private health insurance companies barely cover this service, either. Therefore, many of us who can't afford extensive psychotherapy turn to less expensive support and self-help groups, or weekend encounter workshops when we have problems we can't work out ourselves.

What I have done for you in the following chapters is to create an imaginary support group of people who have traveled through the peaks and valleys while test-driving marriage. Take a look at what these people have to say about the usual and the unusual aspects of playing house. At the same time, experience the societal, cultural, and personal reasons why they do what they do.

WEIGHING THE DECISION
TO MOVE IN

At the risk of sounding maternal or preachy, we would avoid a lot of pain when we fall in love if we used our heads, not our hearts or sexual desires, to guide us through courtship. However, we all know that *love is blind*.

Calling from her crowded office, my friend Dawn*—who looks a couple of decades younger than her mid-forties—whispered into the mouthpiece, "Beliza (pronounced Bell-ee-za), I know you're writing this book about living together. I need your help!"

Bordering on a panic attack, she spewed, "I met this guy. He's really special. And now, he wants to move in with me. What should I do? I have to know now!"

Stalling, gathering my wits to answer a loaded question, I asked, "Well, uhm, tell me—what's he like?"

She gushed, "He's so cute....Oh God, it's been *twenty years* since I felt like this!"

"Yes but, what about him?" I cautioned. "Who is he? How long have you known him? I know you have a good job—does he?"

"Oh yeah, he has a good job." Dawn brushed me off, but she shouldn't have. Even though my own research belies this fact, *American Demographics* magazine claims: "Most people who live together without being married do so for economic reasons, as a precursor to marriage, or as a permanent alternative to being single. Passion has very little to do with it." Dawn's saga appeared to validate the magazine's findings—at least from Jerry's* point of view.

"The real story is," said Dawn, "before we met six weeks ago, Jerry sold his condo in Los Angeles and rented something. But he's always wanted to live on the beach. He's been looking for a place to buy near me in Malibu, but so far, hasn't found anything he likes." Recently, the couple Jerry has been renting from told him he has to be out in three or four days. "So I have to make this decision—like today," Dawn fretted. "Should I have him move in with me?"

Although she did not know it, Dawn had it all worked out: "If Beliza makes the decision for me, I can always blame her if things don't work out." But I wouldn't play into her hand.

"It'll be easier to say no—for now—Dawn, than get rid of him later." (After all, isn't this a pretty hurried decision for a woman who's been a self-supporting, single parent for over twenty years?) "Besides Dawn, if a guy really loves you, he'll appreciate an honest: 'I'm crazy about you, but I need a bit more time to think about this.' He may respect you more if you play a little hard to get. What about a hotel?"

"Well, we thought of that," she said. "But in some ways, I kind of want him here." True, Dawn isn't getting any younger. But fifty-one year-old Jerry has absolutely nothing to lose. She does: her privacy, individuality, carefree lifestyle, her teenage son and daughter's respect, their close-knit relationship, and perhaps, her home. Furthermore, Dawn's corporate public relations job requires a great deal of entertaining. Would Jerry put up with her demanding schedule? She needed to consider all of this and discuss it with Jerry.

But Dawn had her mind made up; Jerry was packing his bags and moving in. When she called to tell me, I suggested she hire a private detective to check Jerry's background, and retain a lawyer, preferably sooner than later. And for goodness sake, I told her, "Get it in writing: Jerry is not a spouse. You are not married. And never insinuate he is a spouse—even when you check into a hotel." To me, securing her post-divorce assets and equity before Jerry arrives on her doorstep was crucially important. After all, Dawn was letting a virtual stranger into her home.

My response to such euphoric good news may sound cold-hearted. However, my frankness, a result of listening to hundreds of case histories, is well founded.

W.O.O.M. TALES OF WOE

An informal poll of my W.O.O.M. members suggests over 80% of the married couples lived together first, for various lengths of time. Many of the relationships fizzled out. Sadly, the horror stories far outweigh the happy endings. Because it's so easy to walk away from a trial marriage, lovers who move in together pay less attention to the actual *character* of the individuals with whom they're involved.

Large numbers of people plunge into their love affairs. Positive they are unlike anyone else in the world, they seldom heed warning signals until they have been burned. They become victims of their own reluctance to take a hard look at what they've gotten into. Later all those "advice to the lovelorn" columns take on new meaning.

Compatible sexually, many couples are ignorant of how incompatible they are in other aspects of their relationship until, often, there is nothing to save. What surprises me, though, is how few bother to find these things out initially.[1]

TAKING CHARGE OF YOUR DESTINY

There are all kinds of living-together scenarios, beginning with on-campus relationships. These are followed by the free-spirited twenty-somethings, who may or may not have had starter marriages, the middle-aged who have never married before, middle-aged who have been married before where one or both partners have dependent children, senior couple relationships, and gay relationships.

Couples give many reasons for living together, all stemming from their desire to maintain their autonomy and independence while also wanting something more than a dating relationship. Unfortunately, when you cut the dating period short and move in too fast, you limit your chances of seeing your relationship from an objective point of view.

Dating gives you an opportunity to take a hard look at the prickly nuances in the relationship, differences that may preclude living together, and certainly marriage, unless they are worked out. Dating gives you the time to adjust to differences in opinion, culture, and style. After a while, if you love each other enough, the "little things" don't bother you as much. And if they do, you break up.

Don't ever think, "Things will be better if we live togeth-er. I'll have a better hold on him or her." Not so. Furthermore, if you move in too fast, the relationship becomes one long series of adjustments. Consider the beefs of one beleaguered woman I interviewed:

Nancy* dated Tim* for three months. She travels for her job, and so they saw each other only on weekends. The couple decided, "If this is good, living together should be wonderful!" A month later, Nancy complains, "Tim is a slob. He doesn't help around the house. He's morbidly overweight, I can't stand the way he dresses, and his table manners are from hell!" Tim hadn't changed. But by living with him day in and day out, Nancy saw Tim as he really was. And whatever positive traits she thought Tim had went by the wayside.

If Nancy had dated Tim for any length of time, she would have had time to decide whether she could live with Tim's shortcomings. Because everything hit her all at once, it was too much for her to take. Furthermore, once you move in together, the romantic side of the love affair takes a nosedive. Personal and cultural differences become more obvious and, perhaps, intolerable.

Because Nancy broke her lease, she lost her first and last month's rent. She wasted fees renting storage space for her furniture. She paid a price for her haste.

Whether you are one of the parties involved in a love affair, a parent, family member, or a concerned friend, it is important to recognize the right questions to ask before mov-ing in with someone. Moving in together should *not* be an impulsive, sexually charged decision. Raging hormones often have no conscience. Someone could get seriously hurt. Maybe you!

QUESTIONS TO ASK BEFORE YOU MOVE IN

Partners should know why they have chosen a live-in arrangement and what each expects. Level with your lover. Ask each other the following, and *listen* to the answers:

➤ Are we trying this out to get to know one another better because we think marriage is a possibility?
➤ Are we moving in together to circumvent religious laws that denounce remarriage, and will otherwise assume a committed relationship?
➤ Are we moving in together primarily to save on expenses?

Max Colpetzer, M.A., cofounder of Fort Wayne Indiana's Citadel Psychiatric Clinic suggests you ask yourself:

➤ "Can I change factors in myself my partner finds unsuitable?"
➤ "Am I afraid to commit or distrusting of love?"
➤ "Do my parents approve of this person? If not, do I think living together, rather than marriage, may appease them?"
➤ "Am I using this living-together arrangement to stall getting my divorce or pay off my ex?"

Most therapists would agree it is in your best interest to let your partner know your agendas differ. Don't ever believe your significant other knows how you feel. Express yourself freely and openly. You have little to lose. Both parties should be completely aware of why they are *not* getting married while test-driving the possibility. Don't sell yourself short, or play down the emotional ramifications of what could happen to you if it doesn't work. Too many women look for love in all the wrong places.

This fact almost forces you to have a personal protection policy from the very beginning—a financial nest egg and/or a place to park yourself when the relationship sours. Operating on these terms, though, is the most significant difference between living together and marriage. Generally, there is little emotional or financial security. You'll always be wondering what the future holds. Will we commit or split?

PLATONIC ROOMMATES TURNED LOVERS

I s there a positive side to living together? Fundamentally, I have to say no. But it can be a positive experience in certain circumstances. Earlier, I mentioned today's living-together relationship has replaced the starter marriage. If a young couple can stay within the parameters that living together sets up, each partner might learn something about love, levels of love, and what they are looking for in a partner when they do decide to get married. They must keep in mind they will probably not get married to each other.

The downside is that when a person is young, perhaps just graduated from college, this unencumbered time is the perfect opportunity to concentrate on career opportunities, standing on one's own two feet, assimilating into the workforce and society, accepting responsibility and following through on promises. It's a time for deciphering what makes you happy, what *your* ideals are—not your parents' or professors'—and

dating and meeting many different people. Juggling an impos-
ing, serious relationship at the same time takes the focus off
the development and maturity of the individual.

The upside is that living with someone can teach partners
tolerance, forgiveness, and basic relationship skills that can be
carried forth into everyday life.

At 28, Robert Taylor* has both feet firmly planted. A
rebellious teenager, he shaped up by the time he graduated
from high school. Robert put himself through college and
presently owns his own computer business. I first met him a
couple of years ago when he unscrambled a hard-drive problem for me. Very good at what he does, Robert is driven to
succeed and won't let anyone or anything interfere with this
aspiration.

Presently, Robert is living with Justine*, twenty-four, a
magazine editor who has her sights on becoming a publisher.
Her ambition rivals Robert's. Nothing is going to stop her,
either. One wonders when, in their busy lives, they have time
together.

"My college years were the best years of my life," Robert
gushes. "I loved every moment." Upon graduation, Robert
was short on funds. He wound up living with his mom and dad
and found their ways unbearable. Knowing he had to get out
of their home, Robert got a job and within a year saved
enough money to get his own place. "I was doing pretty well,"
said Robert, "but I realized I had to get a roommate," not an
easy task because his twenty-two-year-old friends could not
afford to split the rent. Robert put ads in the paper and tried
everything to find a roommate with little success. "Finally, a
woman I worked with mentioned her roommate was moving
out, and would I like her to move in?" Robert had had a platonic female college roommate and was quick to accept the

offer. "Furthermore," explained Robert, "we were pretty good friends by then. And because Justine had a boyfriend, and I was dating different women, I thought it might work."

Soon after she moved in, Justine broke up with her boyfriend, and Robert's relationship with Justine evolved into something more than "just friends." "My male friends thought I had gone crazy. Admonishing me, they said, 'Robert, what the hell have you done? Now what are you going to do? You've got to get out of that house!'"

"It was a mess," Robert remembers. "I was twenty-five years old. I couldn't bring anybody home. I couldn't get away when we had a fight. Couldn't stay out late. Couldn't flirt. I wasn't free. God, overnight, I had a live-in girlfriend!" Robert was really uncomfortable with the idea of it. Nevertheless, over the next five or six months, he and Justine were together constantly. "Our relationship just clicked," says Robert. "However, one part of me was saying, 'I've screwed up. I have to get out of this house.' Yet, another part of me was saying. 'I kind of like this.'" At that point, Robert was really uncertain. He knew he liked Justine sexually, but really didn't know if he cared about her emotionally.

"The trouble was," explained Robert, "because we were together so much, people started to think we were engaged. They treated us as if we were one step away from the altar." When in fact, according to Robert, "we had a new, fresh relationship. I had no intention of getting married, and after only four months, did not consider us an item. As a matter of fact, I still saw other women and Justine knew it."

As time went on, Robert admits he and Justine became a lot closer. However, it became obvious to him she was getting much more emotionally involved than he. Six months into the relationship, Robert realized he didn't want to be burdened with this emotional baggage and decided, after he took a short vacation without Justine, to move out of the house. "Away from her it became apparent I didn't like her as much as I thought. I didn't call her, I didn't miss her, I felt relieved to be rid of her. When I returned, I walked into the apartment and told Justine I was moving out. She was upset I hadn't even called, she knew our relationship was going in different directions. I told her I would still like to see her, but I was feeling claustrophobic and needed space. At first, Justine took it real personally. She thought I was just trying to blow her off." At the same time, Robert felt very badly about hurting Justine. "She took it wrong, cried, and was very unhappy. On the other hand, the relationship happened too fast, and for all the wrong reasons."

Within a few days, Justine moved out. They both began to see other people, but continued to date. Months later, Robert realized her moving out was the best thing that could have happened. He began comparing other dates to Justine. None of them came close to her. And then he realized how much he missed her and loved her. "That never would have happened if we had continued to live together," Robert confessed. "I didn't appreciate Justine's generosity, her good heart, nor her ability to accept people unconditionally until I started dating all types of other women."

Robert is tight with his money and himself, but admits Justine is just the opposite. "Justine paid for all the stuff in our apartment," Robert bragged: the leather couches, stereos, anything they needed to live comfortably. "I could have lived with a bed and a kitchen table." Robert admits "I am a classic snob. Justine, always seeing the good in people, will hang around with Harley Davidson-types to psychics." Her father walked out when she and her five sisters were young children; he was never seen or heard from again. From childhood, Justine was on her own with no one to fall back on. "Yet, as poor as she was, she'd give her last dime to someone who needed it." Aside from her day job and attending college, Justine earns extra money bartending and recently became a poster girl for Molsen Beer. But most disconcerting to Robert's family and friends; she also dances at topless bars and clubs. "Even though she never does it nude, I have always had a problem with that," admits Robert. "But she makes $300 a night doing what she has to do to survive. And as tough as it is for me to deal with, I know she's a good person."

"Unfortunately," Robert explained, "dancers are stereo-typed as sluts or drug addicts." It was tough for Justine to gain acceptance. "My parents didn't want her around, my friends loathed her," says Robert. "They told me, 'Bob, keep this girl as a fling on the side. But don't get involved. She's bad news.'"

"Imagine this, everyone was telling me to dump Justine when finally I had just come to realize she was the most special thing that had happened to me. The peer pressure to throw her to the curb was mind-boggling. Even so, I went against everyone's judgment when I decided we should move in together again. But this time, we both agreed we needed our space, to go out with our friends, and have a life separate and apart from our love affair." Over time, Robert's friends and family saw how happy Justine made Robert and that she was the good person he boasted about.

Justine has graduated from college and has been offered a fabulous job in Los Angeles, five airplane hours away. Torn between her leaving him and his wanting to see her obtain her goals, Robert admits it will be difficult for him to see her go. And who knows what will happen after that? Yet, they both learned so much about the hurt and pain loving someone dearly can incur. "Justine is twenty-four years old; she's very young. I can't stand in her way. And if I did, she might resent me if I hold her back."

I asked, "Have you discussed your following her to L.A.—marriage?"

Robert replied, "People are too much in a hurry to get married. It's the thing to do after you graduate from college. As committed as we are to each other, Justine and I have to get our acts together first. It wouldn't be a good marriage otherwise. I see a future for this relationship. But neither one of us is in any hurry to commit to marriage. We joke around and discuss it halfheartedly, but we're not interested now. As far as following her to Los Angeles, I can't. My friends in New York mean too much to me. Many go back to childhood." Robert, who comes from a close-knit Jewish family, says he couldn't possibly move far from his sisters and parents.

In conclusion, I asked, "What do you see as the most important lesson you learned from this three year relationship?"

"If Justine and I hadn't broken up for awhile," Robert responded, "we might never have realized the importance of balance in life. You've got to have a balance of friends and a balance in relationships. And you've got to have a balance of work and a balance of play. If one of those is more important than the other, somewhere along the line it will affect you and negatively impact how you react to those around you."

The lessons Robert learned from this relationship were many, from not judging a book by its cover to what he really wants in a wife. A future marriage may have ended in divorce if he had not learned early on about balance in life.

Timing means everything when it comes to deciding if you should enter into a living-together relationship. If you want to get married now and start a family, living together usually won't get you those things. As much as it hurts to walk away from a love affair that seems wonderful at the moment, it will only be a matter of time before you'll break up if your ideals and goals don't mesh. Think about using that expended negative energy in seeking a positive, permanent relationship.

IF WE'RE NOT MARRIED, WHY AM I WASHING HIS JOCKEY SHORTS?

YOU LIVE HERE, TOO!

Brad*, very proud of himself, called Allison* to say, "I vacuumed for you today!"

"For me?" she quips. It's funny and she laughs, but Allison firmly reminds him, "Whose house is this? Don't you live here, too?" Often she has told him, "You'll do housework, but you still think you're doing me a favor."

"So many women I know put up with working all day," Allison says, "and then come home and do housework all night. Wedding ring or no ring, I wouldn't put up with that." It's true that many men act like guests in their own homes. They push an inordinate amount of housework off on the unofficial wife who finds little satisfaction in knocking herself out for a guy who may or may not be there six months from now.

Allison is standing up to Brad; she's dead serious and determined when she says, "We're going to work at this until we get it right."

Allison met Brad six years ago at a tennis club in Chicago. At the time, she was being transferred by her company to a different state, and Brad was on his way back to live in North Carolina. She admits it wasn't love at first sight, "But one thing led to another, and neither of us ever left Chicago."

"We met in the middle of the week," thirty-one-year-old Allison remembers, "and by the weekend, Brad invited me to go out with him and one of his buddies." His buddy never made it, so Allison and Brad went alone. "I didn't give his calling me to go out again a second thought," she said. "I just knew he would." From that day forward, they saw each other every day.

From the outset, Allison says her attraction to Brad wasn't all about mad, passionate love. As a matter of fact, preferring to focus on relationship priorities and developing their friendship, they didn't sleep together until ten months after their first date. Right away, she felt she had met her soul mate. "Brad is one of those guys who attaches himself to your heart, and is with you forever."

The couple had been dating for about a year when Allison moved into a new condo. Brad, who was living in the apartment of a friend working in Atlanta, helped her get settled. Concerned Allison might be scared alone the first night, he stayed with her that night, and every night since then.

In so many cases, couples move in together to save money and split the rent. "We never discussed moving in together," Allison emphasized. "That wasn't the case here. It was completely spontaneous. Brad moved in because he wanted to. He didn't have to. It wasn't a money issue. And he always knew it was my place."

For the next four years, Allison and Brad did not talk much about marriage. "Actually," Allison says, "for two years we didn't discuss it at all." There were several reasons why. For example, Brad wasn't crazy about having children. His mother died when he was two; his father died when he was ten, and he was raised by his stepmother who was very good to him. But, Allison says, Brad never experienced the nurturing that often only natural or from-birth adoptive parents can provide. She explained that any chance he had to develop secure family ties was stolen from him at a tender age.

As a result, Brad was reluctant to share Allison with anyone else. Nor did he want her to share her time or emotions with other people. "It was difficult for him to grasp that in your heart, there's enough love for a lot of different people," Allison said.

Allison didn't think she could commit to not having children for the rest of her life, and that was a big issue. However, she revealed, "I'm not an advocate of living together, either." Morally and religiously, she didn't think living together was the message she wanted to send to her young nieces and nephews. Besides, she said, "I was pretty upset my father left my mother for his dentist, and I retaliated by almost marrying a guy just out of college who was the exact opposite of my father. But I found out I *liked* many of my father's qualities and I think there is great benefit to commitment and marriage."

For the next couple of years, Brad & Allison gave each other space to work out their individual feelings. They enjoyed being together, but avoided conflict. Gradually, Allison did notice a change in Brad. Since the birth of his nephew, Allison says, "Brad has begun to see that you can love a child, but that love doesn't have to interfere with your love for someone else." And with that, Brad came to terms with Allison's feelings. "I know that Brad still doesn't want a child," she said, "but he's come around enough to assure me that if I really insisted, he would agree."

Other conflicts about marriage and family Brad has stem from a matriarchal woman he latched onto as a young boy. Allison told me this woman is adamantly against marriage and conveyed that attitude to Brad. Brad, who is very attached to her, is fighting to find out what he wants for himself while still trying to please her. With these kinds of conflicts, it's no wonder Allison and Brad have dragged their heels on their way to the altar.

Why does she stay with him? "The unique part about our living-together relationship is, after that first year, Brad and I thought of this commitment as everlasting." So their getting married or not getting married was never an issue.

Still, I detected some hesitation when Allison said, "We'll *probably* get married within a year." Allison is the type who doesn't jump into things without a great deal of thought and planning. But how perfectly can you straighten things out? Will the expectations of marriage be unreal? Will marriage exacerbate problems that were tolerable when you lived together, but become intolerable when you realize that you are stuck with them forever?

Knowing in my heart Allison and Brad's intentions are honest, I asked, "So what do you think about living together before marriage, now that you've done it for five years?"

She assured me, "I justify it by knowing our relationship isn't a test drive. That on every other level, Brad and I might as well be married."

"With your being fully aware of the plusses and minuses, and that there is no such thing as a perfect mate, what's holding it up?"

"I want to wait until we do something big, like buy a house. Or marriage won't seem any different than living together."

"Would getting pregnant be a big event?" I asked.

"Oh that would be a very big event!"

"It appears you've been able to get into Brad's head. You know why and how he will respond to you the way he does on so many different levels. Do you think living together accelerated the process?"

"Our relationship is so balanced," she said. "Because we took our time to get to know each other."

"Would you do it again?"

"I don't know." She hesitated. "I still don't think it's right. But I also don't think a couple should get married shortly after they meet. There isn't any right amount of time to know when it's time to get married. But if you focus on what the two of you represent to each other, you'll know in your heart when you're into it forever. And if that doesn't happen, you should move on."

"With five years under your belt, what would you tell someone who was thinking about launching into a living-together relationship?"

"Some of my friends, particularly the women, go into relationships for all the wrong reasons. They're willing to compromise all the other issues as long as they've found a good provider. And even those with professional degrees will accept being treated poorly if they know a guy will take care of them.

"By the time Brad and I met, we were both financially secure," Allison said. "We were also both happy about ourselves. So we could add something to each other's lives. I think women who are independent and financially secure themselves make better relationship choices."

Bravo! I couldn't have said that better. When a woman financially needs a live-in man, she may stick with him even against her better judgment. After a while, she dislikes herself, and dislikes and distrusts him because she feels she doesn't carry her financial weight. She feels inferior. Angry that she can't take charge of her life, she blames her unofficial spouse for her own inadequacies and resentment brews. Eventually, this type of woman turns into a nag, demanding that all her happiness, security, and kudos come from her live-in. When she becomes a burden, he dumps her. I have seen this vicious cycle over and over again among the women I have worked with who belonged to my W.O.O.M. support network.

What should a woman trapped in this behavior pattern do? She should stay with her parents or rent inexpensive housing. She should manage her money and build up a financial nest egg, and not expect a man to support her. She will develop self-reliance, and become a mature, responsible, and confident partner, ready to cope with the demands of a relationship, and capable of leaving it if the relationship isn't working.

In Allison's case, she has control of her life as an individual. Getting married is the icing on the cake as long as she doesn't expect Brad's earlier insecurities to evaporate. After their marriage, she'll have to be *even more* understanding and forgiving than she was as a live-in. For Brad, any sign of trouble in his marriage may provoke bad memories, feelings of guilt, and fear of abandonment resulting from losing two parents at a young age. The onus of developing trustworthiness in this relationship is on Allison. Any words said in a fit of anger, implying "I'm leaving!" could have devastating consequences.

JUST WHAT IS HE WAITING FOR?

Hurricane Marilyn's hundred-plus mile-per-hour winds whirled through the house. Billy* had built it himself, with Lauren* by his side installing sheet rock and mixing cement. Instead of running for cover, Lauren braced one huge glass door against the winds while Billy braced the other. She risked her life waiting for the winds to pass. Isn't that the kind of girl you wouldn't want to lose? Despite that, thirty-five-year-old Billy is still test-driving marriage. To Lauren, the wait has been interminable.

It is no wonder she sounded so exasperated when we spoke. "Like," she blurted out, "what is he waiting for!

"At first," Lauren worried, "I had to prove to him I was not a gold digger" when early on, he wanted her to sign a prenuptial agreement. "Now that he has seen what kind of person I am, and the contributions I have made, I think he finally trusts me." Billy changed his mind about the prenup, but it appears the wedding certificate is not within Lauren's reach.

They went in together on furniture and many other household items. In lieu of rent, she pays all the small bills. Laughing about the title of this chapter, she boasted Billy does *her* laundry! "He built the laundry room as a birthday present—but I bought the washer and dryer." Her contribution has not only been financial, though. She says, "I have put in physical labor. I worked my ass off on that house!"—which remains in his name, although she thinks that will change if they ever get married.

Last February, when Billy was unemployed, Lauren supported them. And now that he has started his own business, she is supporting them still, "so Billy won't have to dip into his savings." Despite her allegiance, Billy has reservations about her.

But I wondered, once you've given all of that away, what's the impetus for marriage?

The couple met while they both worked at a Caribbean hotel on the island of St. John. Billy was the security manager. Lauren came to the island from San Antonio, Texas. She took a job in the hotel's restaurant. When both discovered each had gone through recent break-ups, "We'd get together and talk about it," she said. "And we became really good friends, first. After that, we fell in love."

When Billy saw how little money she had left after paying her rent at the end of the month, he invited Lauren to live with him in a small studio attached to his house. "I have a soft-spot for women who need help," Billy said. "It broke my heart to see Lauren struggling to make ends meet." At first Lauren didn't want to move in with him. "She didn't want to get involved," he said. "But I talked her into it."

Billy is from St. John. His roots go way, way, *way* back. "At first, after we got really serious, I wasn't sure Lauren would want to stay here," he says. "But now, she loves it." Still, he had to be sure she could stand the isolation of living on a small island for the rest of her life. A couple of years ago, he took a temporary job stateside as a test. As it turns out, Lauren was itching to get back to St. John even more than Billy. With that worry put to rest, I asked, "So now, what's the holdup?"

"It's been so long," Lauren says, "I just want to get it over with. We started living together six years ago. But it took us until April 1996 to get engaged. I was sure we would be married by now!" Instead, the couple has taken the focus off their relationship by making and breaking wedding plans. They have gone back and forth about whether they want a big wedding or not. Lauren even bought a really fancy wedding dress in the days when she wanted a big, old-fashioned wedding. After the first wedding date came and went, she canceled the gown and got her deposit back. Now, she has reservations about spending so much money on a big wedding, "I think I just want to go off and get married," she says. "Grab my sister. Grab Billy's brother. Get on a plane headed to a private destination and get married."

I suggested a pergola in my backyard was just itching for a bride, but Lauren has been so emotionally shuttled around, she didn't catch my enthusiasm.

"We both know that we want to spend the rest of our lives together," Lauren is sure. "But I think Billy is scared of the actual commitment. And I was scared, too. Marriage is the real thing. You're always worried: 'Is this the right person?' But now, we have waited so long, I just want to get married and get on with our lives."

Their indecisiveness sounds dreadful. I was dying to ask Billy, "Do you love her or not?" But, later when we spoke, he beat me to it when he said, "People always tell you you'll know when it's right. I know with Lauren it's right, because I feel it."

Baffled by the procrastination, I said to Lauren, "If two people fall in love, generally they get married. They don't live together for five and a half years thinking about it."

"I know," Lauren sighed. "It's weird. I'm confused myself." And now that she's waited so long she worries, "So many people have warned us marriage changes everything. Things aren't the same. What if that happens to us? Will I regret we got married?"

"Do you think if you hadn't lived together you wouldn't have these feelings?"

"I don't know the answer to that," Lauren admitted. "Right now, I think I am glad we live together because we know the ins and outs, and all the quirks. I have friends who married, and didn't live together. It takes them so much longer to get to know each other and adjust. But it bothers me that I can't know if living together will negatively impact our marriage."

"I agree that sounds good on the surface, but after so many years, what more is there to know?"

"I think," she reasoned, "you get used to living together. It's comfortable…it feels good. You take it for granted that you're always going to be together, so marriage is on the back burner. It'll happen when it happens."

More to the point, Billy isn't questioning his stalling. He has personally seen unhappy living-together-first marriages fall apart. "I've seen disasters in 90 percent of these marriages. My brother was married sixteen years ago to the perfect wife. They had two perfect kids, and then he found out his wife had been unfaithful for years.

"So I tell Lauren," Billy said, "'Look, everything's peachy now, but I have seen what I thought were the best marriages fall apart. When I see that happen, I get scared.'" Billy says he can't compare what he and Lauren have now with marriage. "And maybe everything would turn out just fine, but I see the awful problems that occur after people live together happily, then get married. People change. I don't want either of us to be in that boat."

When I asked him if he thought living together before marriage was a prerequisite, he said, "When you date, it's artificial. You can put on a show. She gets all dressed up, has her hair done a certain way, wears pretty clothes and perfume. It's not the same as when you live together and have bills to pay, have to sort out who's picking up the groceries, who's making dinner, or who's going to do the dishes. That's reality. That's life, and that's where love comes in."

I wanted to ask him, "And Lauren hasn't proven she's up to the job already?" but I held back. The truth about test-driving marriage is that one partner has the lonely burden of waiting around for the other partner to decide whether he or she *loves* that person *enough* to want to get married.

I must have hit a raw nerve when I asked Lauren, "Is more emphasis being put on whether or not you should marry rather than on the actual relationship?"

She hesitated for a very long time, then she said, "Right now it's just tough. I'm twenty-eight. I want to get married. I want to get on with my life—have a family." Her family has put a lot of pressure on her and Billy, which makes it even harder for her to cope with his indecisiveness. "And even now," she revealed, "with our second wedding date in sight, Billy talks about holding it off *another* year.

"Maybe Billy is more frightened than I think," she added. "But I would like to know what he is so frightened of. Is there something deep in there I don't understand? I have asked him, 'Are you scared I'm not the one? Are you looking at me differently? Am I not going to be a challenge anymore?'" Relieved to a point, she said, "He always answers my questions with answers I want to hear. Maybe he isn't telling me everything." All of a sudden she stopped and questioned what she had just said, as if she was beginning to doubt herself.

Lauren explained when she first met Billy he would never discuss anything. "He was a brick wall. He never would argue, until one day I told him arguing is healthy, then we started to communicate more naturally." They have worked out a big issue for most couples.

"If you had a best friend and she was in a situation similar to this, what would you say to her if she came to you looking for support?"

Lauren reiterated, "I'd ask her what's taking her so long?"

"Does it frighten you that statistics show that couples who live together and then marry have a higher divorce rate than those who didn't?"

"Yes, that frightens me. I've read it, too. But I don't know what the difference is. And not knowing that difference makes me apprehensive. I worry, have I destroyed my chances of having a long lasting marriage by living with Billy first?" Will she later blame their living together every time they don't see eye to eye, or at worst, split?

"When Billy and I first met," she said, "we talked about marriage. We both agreed we were not in any rush to get married. But we knew we were the right person for each other." So why give her an engagement ring and raise false, or in this case, ever-delayed hopes?

Lots of guys like Billy fall into that trap. They're in love, but not *that* much in love. They think an engagement ring will buy them time. Not so. It speeds up the process. And breaking off an engagement is far more humiliating than breaking up a relationship.

Billy's hesitation has wrecked Lauren's confidence. When we spoke, she was so frustrated I got the feeling she didn't know what she wanted anymore. Is that any way to start a marriage?

Billy says, "Just wanting to get it over with is not a reason to get married. Nor is worrying about what the family thinks." It's like the movie *Four Weddings and a Funeral,* where everyone was getting married because it seemed like a good idea. "Then everyone gets divorced or plays around," he said, "and that seems like a good idea, too.

I don't feel financially stable enough to have children now," Billy admitted. "And what if I want to go back to the

States every so often? Going back and forth is no life for kids. I have also begun to live by my own rules. Ninety percent of the time Lauren and I agree, but I worry about the other ten percent."

Any objective viewer knows Billy is not ready to get married, but Lauren is. And even though he proposed to her without an actual date in mind, he has offered Lauren the best commitment he's capable of at this time. Knowing this, should she push marriage? Or instead, watch his reaction as she packs her bags and moves out? Either way, she should be prepared to know that if Billy balks, she *can* live without him.

The real issue here is whether Lauren can continue to wait for Billy to decide if things will be "perfect enough" to get married. As difficult as it seems, that's a choice only Lauren can make. And once they're married, and can't live up to the level of perfection that they expect, will it all fall apart? Chances are, it will.

HOW HOUSEWORK CAN BE AN LTC'S UNDOING

At Dr. Rebecca Stafford's annual Christmas party, she told me that fifteen years before becoming president of Monmouth University, she co-wrote a paper, "The Division of Labor Among Cohabiting and Married Couples," printed in the *Journal of Marriage and the Family*. The study is as pertinent today as it was twenty years ago.

"It would seem that a personally committed, but structurally unfettered, heterosexual relationship should provide fertile soil for developing an egalitarian companionship between men and women free of traditional authority and sex-role patterning," wrote Dr. Stafford and her co-authors who described an egalitarian relationship as having three elements:

➤ Equal distribution of power
➤ Equal consideration by each partner of the other's personal needs and goals
➤ Equal division of labor in the household

When one or more of these components are not heeded or respected, and the relationship follows the traditional patterns of division of labor in marriage, according to Dr. Stafford, resentment soon erodes the reasons why a couple chooses to live together and the couple breaks up.

Dr. Stafford's study shows that "among both married and cohabiting couples, the women are taking most of the responsibility for, and performing most of, the household tasks. It also appears that the partners of the cohabiting women have very few responsibilities, mainly household repairs." Meanwhile, the brouhaha surrounding sexual equality and feminist idealism is shot in the foot by women who don't assert themselves and demand an equal division of labor. According to the study, if you are washing the dishes and he isn't drying them, chances are he will be less likely to want to get married. Often, "We broke up over doing the laundry!" is no joke.

If the cohabiting "wife" doesn't lay it on the line and refuse to take on the entire burden of housework from the very first day the couple decides to move in together, she jeopardizes her power in the relationship and her chances of ever becoming that guy's wife.

So...how much has changed in the past twenty years?

ONE MAN'S WHO'S BEEN THERE ONE TIME TOO MANY

One of the most charming men a woman could meet is fifty-three-year-old Joe Amiel. He's tall, but not svelte. Dark, where tresses exist. Handsome, but no George Clooney. So what is it about him that would put him at the top of anyone's most eligible bachelor list, year after year? To begin with, he's powerful, successful, and confident. Joe, who reminds me of Oscar de la Renta, is impeccably groomed, suave, articulate, elegant, yet commanding. Although chivalrous, brilliant, fun-loving, and generous, his most outstanding feature is his genuine love of women. He will sweep you off your feet. All women—single, happily married, and anywhere in between—can't help but vie for his attention.

Joe owns The Old Mill Inn, a hugely successful, well-known restaurant in Spring Lake, New Jersey. Aside from being a restaurateur, he is a partner in Manhattan Pictures, a movie production company, with Danny Aiello. Between the restaurant and the movie company, stunning women, models, and actresses fill his life. Joe seems to have his pick of them. Yet, he has never married—but not because he didn't try to find a wife. Over the years, Joe has been involved with several meaningful living-together relationships. But when he turned 50, he began to change his philosophy of life and love.

"I used to think living together, trying a relationship out, was the way to go," Joe confided. "But now, I don't think I would ever do it again, because I never found anyone I wanted to marry after I lived with them. Maybe I got to know them too well, too fast. Or they, me. On the other hand, women I dated—didn't live with—were women I now consider more likely marriage candidates."

In explaining his reasons, Joe told of his first live-in love affair in the 1960s with a Ford model from Austria.

"Inez* was my teacher," Joe reminisced. "Being a few years older than I was, she taught me a lot about sex…what women want; what I wanted myself." Worldly at twenty-three, but not as worldly as she was at twenty-six, Joe feels in retrospect "Inez was much too much for me at the time. She was gorgeous, sexy beyond description, rubbed elbows with European celebrities, and successful enough to have a huge, fabulous apartment on Sutton Place South."

"It was like, *hello*, what are you doing with me?" Joe chuckled. "I was losing my hair, insecure about my looks, not rich like her other boyfriends, and to top it off, just starting out in the restaurant business." Whatever Joe thought he was lacking didn't stand in Inez's way. Within two weeks the love affair was hot and heavy. "Can you believe she moved in with *me*." Joe laughed. "Into this tiny three-room apartment on East Fifty-third!"

A year later, the relationship, based for the most part on good sex, was over. "Inez wanted to get married, and I didn't," describes Joe. "But the biggest drawback was our differing work schedules."

"My hours were, *still are*, long," explained Joe… "11:00 A.M. to sometimes 2:00 in the morning." And even though Inez traveled a lot, she had a day job and resented the evenings Joe couldn't spend with her. He said, "I needed to find someone in the business who had similar hours, or at least understood my end of the business."

When Joe turned down her marriage proposal, Inez moved to Paris to work for Dior. But she persisted and would call Joe weekly from every major European capital she toured. "It was really humorous," Joe remembered. "Inez would repeatedly call the restaurant and say, 'Baby lion, you want I should come back?'" She kept these calls up for months.

When Inez returned to New York nine months later, Joe ran into her at Maxwell's Plum, now defunct, where they had a drink for old-time's sake. When the evening ended, and Joe offered to drop her off at her apartment, they got into a huge fight over why he didn't want to see her upstairs. He noticed in the rearview mirror the cab driver was incredulous that Joe had turned her down. The cabby was so upset, he leaned up against his hack parked in front of Joe's apartment, and listened intently as Joe spent over an hour explaining to him their history, and why he didn't want to have sex with her.

"I felt I had to do it to prove to this guy I wasn't gay," Joe belly-laughed. "Needless to say, that was the last time I saw Inez."

Not daunted by one relationship failure, Joe entered five more marital test-drives, some as short as six months; others as long as three years, with enough time in between to remember the good. "Let's see. After Inez came the Pan Am airline stewardess. That lasted six months. Neither one of us was concerned with marriage. It was a relationship of convenience for both us; but in the back of my head I thought, *you never know*.

"Now, the one after that was the serious one." Haltingly, with a great deal of emotion in his voice, Joe told me he really loved Janine*. "If times were different, I could have married her...wanted to marry her. But my mother had just passed away. I was only twenty-nine, and she was the last of my immediate family. I was grieving her loss, and at the same time concerned about my emotional and financial future. Because I was going through some really disconcerting, and sometimes frightening times, I felt Janine should have been more sympathetic. I felt that because she was not from a close-knit family, she couldn't understand the deep loss I was dealing with. And even though everything else between us clicked, she couldn't understand why she couldn't fill the emotional gulf. I resented that she was jealous of me for clinging to the loss of my family. I didn't want to, but I put up a wall between us." Over the next several months, Joe sensed the love affair was unraveling, "but it wasn't until nine months later, at my mother's unveiling, that Janine acted like such a bitch and I decided I could never marry her."

It's obvious, though, that Janine left an impression on Joe. They still talk over the phone frequently and are special friends to this day. Twenty-four years later, I found it interesting that neither Joe nor Janine had ever married.

After Janine, Joe dated other women but did not live with anyone until he was thirty-eight and met Tina.* "I had known Tina since she was seventeen," Joe informed me. "But I didn't date her until she was twenty-four."

"So what was so great about Tina?"

"She was the most sensuous woman I ever met." Joe laughed. "She was a total spoiled brat, candidly frank."

"What was the catch?"

"Tina was used to getting her own way—she was spoiled by her wealthy father—yet we had one of the most romantic relationships anyone could have. The idea that she was this sexy young thing and I was the older man appealed to me." As delicious as Joe felt with Tina, though, he decided, "I could never marry her, and we terminated the short-lived affair ten months later."

Is Joe seeking an impossible-to-find composite of all of the women he has loved and admired? By now, it was becoming apparent these love affairs were Joe's conquests—testosterone-driven trophies he's lined up, savored, and used as stepping stones to his next affair. "And even after they leave, they never leave because we remain good friends," Joe said. These women's long-term friendship makes it clear Joe genuinely loved, and still likes, all these women.

After Tina, there was a two-year love affair with another younger woman whom Joe thought he was crazy about, but which ended in much the same way.

"To wrap it up," Joe said, "I think you live with people, and sometimes you are attracted to them, but because you are caught up in the sexual aspect, you never really get to know them. I think if I had dated Janine and taken it slower, I might have been able to show her my past life was not a threat to our future. I would have had the time to develop our relationship, rather than jump in and lose perspective.

"The same thing with Tina. If I had taken more time to get to know her, the relationship might have had a better chance. I might have married one of these women."

Today, Joe's attitudes toward test-driving marriage have changed. "I used to say I would never marry someone unless I lived with them first. But now, I realize I was totally wrong. Living together can hurt relationships. And from now on, if I find someone I think is special enough, I want to be patient, give the relationship time to develop with a year of old-fashioned courting, rather than basing it on six weeks of electrifying sex. You are taking a chance when you live with somebody. Why not take a real chance and take your time. Why not make a real commitment, instead of a half-assed attempt?"

MOVING IN WITH SOMEONE ELSE'S KIDS

L iving with someone else's kids can cool even a rock-solid love affair. It is tantamount to throwing cold water on the relationship. Unrelated partners often find kids compromise time alone, intimacy, and spontaneous sex, and sometimes innocently, but more often intentionally, connive at turf wars between the most devoted partners.

Caring parents know their children's needs come first, and because they do, the unrelated party can feel shut out, abused, used, and unwelcome. Often, parents overextend themselves to the kids to overcome feelings of guilt for leaving a spouse. The truth is living with another person right under your kids' noses does not build their confidence in relationships.

Differing and *conflicting* ideas about discipline are the biggest problem when you move in with someone you love and his or her kids. When ex-spouses are added to the mix, plus an assortment of grandparents and relatives who may not accept an unofficial parent, you've got emotional chaos.

Enough can't be said about how difficult combining families is. Resentment is a given when children—from toddlers to teenagers—are involved.

In 1971, I married my husband *and* his two children, five and eight years old. To say that was an adjustment which has required assiduous work for the past twenty-seven years may be an understatement. My thirty-five-year-old stepdaughter, Laurie Furman, an MSW in St. Louis, now focuses on children of divorced parents.

I have found, over the years I have been a self-help consultant, that those of us who move in with someone else's kids devour learning from others' experiences. This chapter includes a range of situations people have shared with me, but in reality this subject could be a book on its own. Start here in order to gain wisdom you'll need to draw your family and your unofficial partner and perhaps his or her family closer together. But understand unmarried partners who are parents have a harder time with it. There is absolutely no reason for LTCs' children to like each other, or to get along with or listen to a live-in unless they want to. Stepparents warrant respect. He or she is a *spouse*. Live-in surrogates are another matter entirely.

CONFLICTING IDEAS ON DISCIPLINE

I recently received a letter from a W.O.O.M. member who scribbled, "please change my name back to... Mitchell* and I are getting divorced."

"Divorced!" I screeched to my office wall. "They just got married!" I could have predicted it, but would have lost the wager on how soon it would happen. The couple started dating in March 1987, lived together a total of three years on two sep-arate occasions, finally married in 1995, then shut the door on a nine-year love affair a year-and-a-half later. According to Terri, Mitchell's slack discipline with his children was the major cause of every one of their breakups. "Mitchell wanted me to get involved with their schooling, help them with their homework, cook and clean, yet when I took control, he couldn't deal with that," Terri explained. She says the chilly reception she got from the parents of his ex-wife also contributed to their break-up.

"When Mitchell's son was arrested for drinking while dri-ving with minors in the car, I felt we should ground him," Terri continued. But, she says, Mitchell, who has full custody, thought the community service penalty the teenager was given was enough. "I felt he should reinforce the discipline," Terri said, as she choked away tears of frustration while discussing what led to her divorce.

Whether Mitchell was right or wrong when it came to his kids is not the issue. The issue is Terri's role as a parent, which was never defined, made it impossible for her to feel she had stature in the household. "I felt disillusioned about my expect-ed role," she said. "I was raised very strictly. Either you did something right or you did something wrong. And if you did something wrong there were consequences." To this day, Terri isn't sure why Mitchell married her. If she was there to cook and clean, help pay the bills, help draft book reports—estab-lish a support system—then why was she not allowed to disci-pline the children when they got into trouble? "Even though we knew this was a big problem when we lived together," Terri sighed, "we married without working it out. That was the mis-take we both made."

If Terri had asked, I would have told her that was marital suicide and to see a therapist before she married Mitchell.

However, my opinion would have had little bearing on her decision. Terri wanted to be married to Mitchell no matter what.

This is a tough problem for mental health professionals. Terri was dealing with a guilt-ridden father who not only felt his kids had been through enough, but also that his behavior had caused a lot of their rebelliousness. He couldn't see that discipline and love go hand in hand.

No matter how many or few live-in lovers a parent invites home over the years, his or her children are reluctant to develop a close bond with the unattached partner. Knowing the family tie is uncertain, kids often shy away from getting close. In essence, their parent's lover has no status, not even that of a stepparent; he/she is a nonentity and likely to get blamed for every family tiff.

To many, the sole purpose of a trial marriage is to see if you and your partner's ideologies mesh. Terri's backfired because she did not heed the trial marriage's warnings. Fortunately, she has returned to therapy to work on her own strengths and weaknesses. Maybe this time she'll take a more responsible approach and not play Russian Roulette with her self-esteem and future.

YOU'RE NOT MY DADDY!

NYPD Blue star Dennis Franz and his wife Joanie, say they were in love since their first dance, but it took eleven years to change their status from unofficially married to married. Recently, he told *In Style*, "The first time I met my daughters their parents' divorce was still fresh, and they were not immediately ready to trust another person. They were protective of their relationship with their mother and not sure they wanted anyone to come into their lives. Yet they were still young enough to need someone to make a fuss over them and show them attention—which I was very happy to do."

Over the years, Tricia and Krista developed a fondness for Dennis, but the ground rules were set early. "We made it perfectly clear early on that if I was to be a part of the equation, I was going to need to be thought of as a disciplinarian. When I said things, the kids were going to have to take them as seriously as if mom were saying them, and show me some respect." He always worried that someday the kids might turn on him and say, "You don't have a right to tell me anything because you're not my father." But it never happened. And now, Dennis says, "What kept it from being a more difficult experience was that I loved coming home and having the girls greet me at the front door."[1]

In many circumstances, it's hard to get respect—no matter how hard you knock yourself out trying. However, if the unrelated partner and the parent can agree on an approach to discipline, support each other, and stick to the rules, you'll find everyone more comfortable living together in unwedded bliss.

IT WAS ME WHO HAD TO CHANGE; NOT THEM

Pete Borg*, a forty-year-old father of two kids, ages eight and thirteen, moved in with Maggie*, a thirty-eight-year-old mother of two kids, ages nine and eleven years old, two-and-a-half years ago. "The quasi-honeymoon lasted about four months when the shit hit the fan," he remembers, and was followed by his moving out, moving back, then moving out again, and only one month later, after he rented a townhouse and purchased $10,000 worth of brand new furniture, moving back in again. "It's been crazy," the cardiologist said. "I haven't been able to concentrate on my practice. I'm exhausted and stressed out from the hassle."

"So," I probed, "knowing from past experience this was a volatile relationship, why did you go back?"

"The bottom line is I have two children; she has two children. It was like Maggie and I get along fine, but the peg just wasn't fitting the hole. I always put my kids as a priority over Maggie." When Sunday morning rolled around, Pete was off with his kids, doing great things, leaving Maggie and her two kids at home.

"During the week," he said, "I always would take my kids out for dinner, but I wouldn't include Maggie and her two kids." He completely refused to accept Maggie's children, wishing they didn't exist. "In fact, I was so bad, when Maggie bought groceries for all of us, I would examine the bags to see what she bought for her kids, and refuse to pay for them. Even though she took the time to buy the groceries for me and my kids, I fumed when I saw them eating a hot dog *I* paid for."

Pete was consumed with resentment and he complained so much about Maggie's kids to his kids, the two sets of kids barely talked to each other. "It got so bad, I had to get out."

After he moved out the last time, Maggie and Pete both dated different people for a few weeks. But they weren't happy. "I didn't have any desire to go out," he said. A couple of weeks after that, Pete's thirteen-year-old daughter called and told him she didn't want to go with him that Friday night. She had a party. "And it hit me," he revealed. "She's not going to be around five years from now." Eleven years of faithful visitations, Disney World vacations, soccer games, and ballet recitals went down the drain. "I was very, very hurt," Pete admitted. "I wasn't prepared for the time when my kids wouldn't want to be with me...wouldn't need me."

After contemplating in his lonely condo, he decided, "I've got to get my priorities in order." He realized his relationship with Maggie should have come first. "I like waking up at three o'clock in the morning and finding a warm body next to me," he added. He realized his love for his children would not change, "but you just have to put things in their proper perspective."

A couple of weeks later, Pete called Maggie. They were both just miserable without each other. That's when he determined the problems all along were a result of his lousy attitude, emphasizing, "I acted like such an asshole!"

Finally recognizing how important balance is to any relationship, Pete says he had to make a radical change; it was okay to spend some time alone with his kids, but it's healthier to spend some time all together as a family. Admitting he berated Maggie's kids so badly for many months, Pete realizes, "It's obvious they shouldn't like me, and I'm not sure they ever will."

Now, when he goes home, Pete plays ball with Maggie's kids, or takes them to the pool. He's trying to establish a relationship with them by spending time alone with them, too. "It's tough," Pete admitted. "I put up so many walls to keep my kids away from her kids, it's going to take some time." Yet, surprisingly, little by little Maggie's kids are warming up. And now, when Pete calls his kids, he tells them, "*This* is what we are doing tonight. And Maggie's coming with us, and her kids are coming with us." And they roll with it.

"I was very up and down—very volatile," Pete confessed. "I poisoned our ever becoming a family—ever getting married. Until I faced that it was *I* was putting up the barriers, *I* who was destroying any chance Maggie and I had of staying together, we weren't going anywhere."

The few short weeks he was separated from Maggie, Pete said he got a good look at what was out there. "Then it became very clear how much I love her," he said. "And," he boasted, "I did all of this without any therapy!"

With self-discovery comes maturity. That's when everyone gets on with his or her life.

KERI'S ORDEAL

Keri* and her "friend," Doug* met in Baton Rouge, Louisiana in 1993. He was on a business trip from his home in Washington, she explained, "so it was kind of a chance meeting. But I was going through a hard time. My fiancé had been killed in a car crash six months before, and I hadn't really gotten over it. When Doug invited me for a drink, I told him to go away, leave me alone. Yet, he persisted and asked me again." Aggravated by now, Keri did not disclose she was underage, but she did tell him, "I don't want to have a drink with you," and gave him every indication she wanted him to get lost. About an hour later he came back to her table. "Begrudgingly, I started to talk to him," Keri remembers. "I don't know what came over me, but we talked for a few hours, then ended up having breakfast together at an all night diner. Afterward we walked on the beach, and talked even more."

From the beginning, Keri thought Doug was in his mid-thirties; he assumed she didn't drink for personal reasons, and mistook her for twenty-five. "It was a little awkward when two weeks later I found out he was forty, and let him know I was twenty," she said. Raised in the Bible Belt, Keri had a hard time dealing with the age difference. "My mother flipped out," she confided. "She didn't like that at all."

In spite of her mother's objections, Keri and Doug became close telephone friends. Soon after, he asked if she would visit him when he was on a business trip on the East Coast. She said, "What do you think I am going to do, *drive* from Baton Rouge to Boston or New York to meet you! I don't think so."

Considering her refusal, Doug suggested he use his frequent flyer miles to fly Keri to various East Coast job sites. Because she was a floor manager at a local department store, she was able to arrange her work schedule to accommodate Doug's wishes. But it was inconvenient, "He was all over the map doing computer installations. It wasn't always fun. I spent a great deal of time watching." Sometimes Keri would help him, and that was when, she admitted, "it gave me an opportunity to observe his work ethic, and over time I found I admired his aptitude and dependability. I respected his drive, too."

They entered into a pretty serious bicoastal relationship, and while it was evolving she said, "We kind of grew attached to each other. But I knew Doug did not want a committed relationship, and he made it clear we would continue to date other people." Because Doug had been through his share of relationships and a divorce, he was adamant, he didn't want to get involved. Yet, despite hearing his warning, Keri couldn't help it—she was falling for him. "It was hard not to because he broke his own rules," Keri giggled. "Every night, from wherever he was, he would call me and we would talk sometimes for over an hour."

"Sure puts a damper on dating others when a guy checks up on you nightly," I jokingly suggested. Although Doug may have wanted an uncommitted relationship, he was possessive and acted committed to Keri.

I WANT YOU TO LIVE WITH ME
BUT DON'T EXPECT A RING

By January 1995, Doug found most of his work was on the East Coast and moved to Charleston. Beforehand, he had invited Keri to join him there not only to live with him, but to establish a home base for his business. Taking into account she would be leaving a good job, he offered to pay her a commensurate salary even though he would be supporting her. He said, "I don't want people to think I'm your sugar daddy."

Although caught off guard by Doug's invitation, Keri couldn't wait to live with him, and felt, on the whole, the deal was fair. "It was an incredibly fulfilling six months," she says. Soon, the age difference became just a number, and Keri finally told her family and friends, "This is it. This is where I'm happy. The place I need to be."

MOM AND DAD DID NOT TAKE IT WELL

Her mother expressed deep disapproval, even though Keri explained the arrangement was completely sincere. She worked hard coordinating Doug's work schedule, often putting in twelve-hour days. Furthermore, Keri said, "I insisted my salary be deposited into my bank account."

In the end, Keri's mom and her stepfather accepted the arrangement more quickly than her father and her stepmother.

WHERE DO I FIT INTO THIS UNCERTAIN PICTURE?

Six months later, Doug was unhappy. "He missed his kids terribly," Keri said. "He decided, 'I can't do this anymore. I can't be away from my kids.'"

"But wait a minute," Keri said. "I'm not sure I signed up for Washington." Nonetheless, by then she was really in love with him and wanted to marry him. But the subject was never discussed. "I was *afraid* to bring it up," she admits. "Afraid he would say, 'No;' but a proposal would have been the icing on the cake."

Keri moved with Doug to Seattle, where he bought a house. She told him, "I don't want the financial burden of helping you with the mortgage if we are not going to get married. That's not fair." However, the couple made both oral and written agreements that stipulate the longer Keri lived in the house and contributes to its upkeep, the more she would be financially compensated if they split. "I came into this with almost nothing," she said. "And I have told my parents that all legacies should go to my brother until my future with Doug is settled," even though her family has visited and grown to love Doug and his kids. On the other hand, Keri feels that if something should happen to her, her parents should financially compensate Doug. "He should have the opportunity to grieve without worrying about paying bills," Keri said. "A token of my love for him."

As time progressed, though, Keri felt less and less certain about not having a notarized agreement. Doug promised she could have a car and the items she has purchased for the house. "But some of these promises are still unfulfilled," she worries. "It is awkward for me to say I want my share. I have a stake in this relationship, too."

Keri says Doug appreciates what she has given up. She says he has agreed she is entitled to a monetary settlement if the relationship sours. But so far it's just talk.

"Furthermore," she continued, "moving to Seattle was the hardest thing I have ever done. I left my friends and my family for a love affair that promised much, but delivered little. It has been a year and a half since I moved to the West Coast, three years since I met Doug. If I had come here with a husband, I would call this home. I would have gotten my library card, registered to vote—done all the things a wife would do.

Under the circumstances, my heart isn't always here." She developed mood swings.

Doug wanted to know, "Why are you being so bitchy?"

NO LONGER JUST THE TWO OF US

Keri went into therapy. After a few sessions she realized her problems were related to Doug's kids. "It's not that they are bad," she explained. "They are bright, funny, really good kids, but Doug never discussed their living with us before we moved, even though I think deep down that was his plan." When he did get around to mentioning it, Keri remembers she was still in the romantic phase, where anything goes. Partly because she thought it was a great idea, and partly because she didn't know what would happen to her if she told Doug, "*No.*" Keri agreed.

Keri didn't have a clue how drastically kids would change their lifestyle. "I was so starry-eyed. I remember feeding the squirrels in Boston at the Commons, how we would jump in a plane and go off to Bermuda or Miami for the weekend. We went out for dinner, to the theater. We got up early and watched the sunrise. Then all of a sudden I'm the housewife with curlers in my hair!"

FLOUNDERING WHILE TRYING
TO RECAPTURE TWO
MISSED CHILDHOODS

Doug's teenagers were five and six years old when he divorced their mother. They stayed with him during summer vacation, and Doug took summers off from work. Keri, on the other hand, chose to get a job, but soon found the routine of putting in a full day at the office, running home to make dinner, then doing the laundry, got old real fast. It was a shock. She said, "I wasn't prepared." Allowing herself to get dumped on, Keri sighed, "The mom thing wore me down. I wanted boundaries." She felt she was entitled to privacy for herself and time alone with Doug. "And because I felt I had to compete for Doug's attention, I began resenting his kids."

Very soon, the atmosphere became incredibly tense, especially when the kids decided they wanted to stay with their father full-time. Keri and Doug's daughter locked horns. And like most households that combine families, the tension wreaked havoc with everyone and severely tested Keri and Doug's relationship. To get even, Keri laid down the law, and now realizes she went too far. Doug complained that she was being too strict; yet he was far too permissive. Considering he hadn't been around to care for his kids since they were very young, Keri felt badly for their mother who, by this time, had been relegated to third-party status. "It didn't seem fair," Keri lamented. Overnight she was shunned by her children and their dad when *he* decided it was time to make up for lost piggyback rides and bedtime stories.

CARRYING THE BURDENS OF THE THREE
OF THEM PLUS MOM

"My heart went out to her," Keri said. After the decision the kids' mother went into a depression. "She was deeply hurt," Keri said, "and I felt responsible," and the kids didn't really know what to do. Over a period of a few months, Keri made an effort to talk to her but she was too angry and remained cool for a very long time. Keri finally asked her to resume custody, but she didn't want the kids back. Days later, overburdened by endless pandemonium, Keri went into intensive therapy and wound up on antidepressants. By now, she was seriously considering leaving Doug.

FINALLY PUTTING HER FOOT DOWN

"It was a year and a half of hell," Keri said, "when Doug and I sat down and talked out our problems. I told him surrogate motherhood sucks, that he had to stop undermining me, and had better back me up 110 percent. We established rules in the house, boundaries to be respected. A lot of what happened was not the kids' fault," Keri realizes now. "Because of my own insecurities, I let things go too far. I should have expressed my feelings a lot sooner and not wavered because Doug and I aren't married."

I told her, "A nanny would have had more status in this household." Like many live-ins, Keri did not have the confidence in her relationship, her status, or herself to establish standing.

"We're getting back on our feet," Keri said. "But Doug and I have not faced where I stand." Together, they have started therapy. And Doug plans to attend sessions himself. He has lamely hinted at marriage, knowing that if she leaves, he'll have to deal with housework and the kids by himself. But Keri has no clue what the future holds. She admits the ordeal has been hard on Doug, too. She understands he's torn between her and his kids. "Yet through it all, Doug has been incredibly supportive. I know he really loves me. But when it comes to marriage, Doug has told me, 'I can't do that right now.'"

LADIES, THINK ABOUT IT...

It is a gutsy question to ask yourself, and even more gutsy to ask him, but I would want to know "If you are not going to marry me, then why am *I* mopping the floors and babysitting while you're playing golf?" Once you know the reason, the kid problems will work themselves out. If no promise of marriage is forthcoming and you choose to stay, you probably won't give a damn about the kids and their dirty laundry and remarks anyway.

If you choose to walk out, you definitely won't care about "the kids." However, if you get a proposal and a wedding date, all the problems with the kids become half yours. Do you really want that? Knowing the answer to that question before you move in is crucial when you test-drive marriage.

YOU'RE NICE;
BUT BABY IS BETTER

HE DOESN'T WANT TO HAVE MY BABY

"It's been terrible," Diana sighed. "I've been crying every day since I stopped living with Dolph, and came back home to stay with my family near Los Angeles. But I recognize our relationship can't be about Dolph getting his way on all the important issues. Even if I was certain our deep love for each other would get us beyond most of them, I can't live with his refusal to have children. And if I did, my resentment would eventually eat away at what we had, and I'd end up leaving him anyway."

Just talk of a having a baby can be the wedge that drives a couple in separate directions, particularly when one partner wants kids and the other doesn't. As I have seen far too many times among W.O.O.M. members, there is no compromise on this subject. Eventually, if someone doesn't give in, you'll lose each other physically, emotionally, or both—even when the couple thinks everything else going on within the relationship is wonderful.

"Right now, Dolph is at home in Las Vegas trying to work this out," sighs Diana, an only child who knows she would not even have nieces and nephews to fill the void. "But every time Dolph pictures a baby toddling around, he can't fathom being a start-over dad and that's a huge roadblock. We could never get married without working out this issue. And if we were dumb enough to try it, it could mean a fourth divorce for Dolph, and I know he doesn't want that." Which means she and Dolph can't even get engaged.

"Neither Dolph nor I feel at ease living in sin," Diana lamented, and concluded their living together not only complicated and exacerbated other major issues surrounding the relationship, it eventually stirred up minor ones, too. Diana was raised Catholic, but as an adult didn't practice her faith. With Dolph, she developed a renewed spirituality, abandoning the Catholic Church to attend Dolph's Calvary Church, a nondenominational congregation. Despite their deep devotion, Diana admits she and Dolph could not get as involved in church activities as they would have liked. "Living together without at least a promise of marriage went against everything Dolph and I believe in."

The couple regularly attended church together, but after the services, "we felt hypocritical," she confided, "because we knew we were doing something terribly wrong. That upset me. I found it hard to live with myself."

IF THEY WERE SO AGAINST IT, WHY DID DIANA AND DOLPH CHOOSE TO LIVE TOGETHER?

"I was on vacation, and Dolph stopped me at a fountain at Harrah's in Laughlin, Nevada," Diana remembers. "Instantly, we were really attracted to each other." Unfortunately, geography was not in the couple's favor. Diana lived in California; Dolph, Las Vegas. "We talked on the phone every day, and Dolph would fly me to Vegas," Diana said, "but it's not the same as seeing each other every day." Nine months later, Diana resigned her job at Nordstrom's, left her friends and family in California, and moved in with Dolph, who owns a car rental agency in Las Vegas. She says, "Each day we were together, I fell more and more in love.

"At first," says Diana, "I didn't really know if I wanted children. But as our love grew, I realized how very badly I wanted to have a baby with Dolph…our baby. And the more I wanted to have a baby I knew Dolph didn't. Since I knew he was engaged to a woman before we met and had been willing to raise her three young children, I thought that he didn't love me enough to want to raise mine.

Diana observed, "I'm much younger than his daughter, and a year younger than his son. And because Dolph is not really that close to his kids, I wasn't able to develop any type of relationship with them."

My studies of W.O.O.M. couples reveal that when older men do not have a close relationship with their children, they are extremely reluctant to start a second family. For whatever reasons, they simply did not enjoy the parenting experience. As these men age (forty and over), they become less inclined—not more—to compromise on this issue. This is also a major dilemma for over-thirty career women who wait to have children, fall in love with same-age men who have had children from a previous marriage(s), and find out these men refuse to have more children.

When women move in with men before working this issue out, they are headed for real heartache. In the ten years I have dealt with couples, I have found no other issue that causes such anguish. I can guarantee when a talk-show host discusses this subject with me, the phones ring incessantly with callers looking for a solution. There isn't one.

Not being allowed to have a baby can eat many women alive. I know. My husband Sam and I went round and round on this subject. If one of us had not given in, our marriage wouldn't have made it. In our situation, he gave in and we had two children. Living with a man does not change his mind. In fact, many men have told me they break up over this issue. Women yearning to have babies should be aware of this fact.

AND THEN EVERYTHING ELSE
STARTS TO FALL APART

For six months, while living together, Diana fretted about the baby issue. Was Dolph worth giving up because of her wish to have a baby? Meanwhile, other issues surfaced. Diana admits moving to Las Vegas and trying to fit into Dolph's circle of friends and family was extremely difficult. "I'm a jealous person," Diana confessed. "It was difficult for me to cope with people coming up to Dolph saying, 'Oh hi, I knew your ex-wife. She used to do my nails,' and treat me as if I didn't exist."

Diana became resentful when Dolph decided to buy a piece of property next door to his parents' home. "I worked with Dolph at the car rental agency and we were together twenty-four hours a day, seven days a week. I had no friends or family in Vegas, yet Dolph was surrounded by family who influenced his thinking. It got on my nerves that we were always with Dolph's friends, that he made all the decisions, and was free to come and go as he pleased." Soon, even her friends from home remarked at how she had changed from being a very assertive go-getter to a doormat, letting Dolph sway her, even over matters such as the length of her hair. "I never felt more controlled," Diana says.

On the other hand, she and Dolph had a great time together. They could pick up and go whenever they wanted, and took fabulous vacations. "Dolph was really generous," Diana admits. "Besides, I felt really secure with him. I knew I would never have to worry. I would always be taken care of. That's hard to give up. He was so handsome, perfect in many ways. It will be hard not to compare every other man I meet to him."

When I look at a photograph of Diana, whose gorgeous looks remind me of a Dallas Cowboys cheerleader, and Dolph, a Tom Selleck look-alike, I see the perfect couple, but I realize how misleading snapshots of smiling couples can be. If photos could capture the darker side of our lives, would we then level with ourselves and confront the pitfalls of our relationships? Would we stand a better chance of facing how we truly treat each other, expecting more from our significant others than they can deliver, to holding ourselves back emotionally? We might scare ourselves into looking at life from our significant other's point of view.

If a man doesn't want kids, and we do, we should not become involved with him in the first place. We'll only end up feeling tormented and cheated out of one of life's greatest experiences—motherhood!

I LOVE OUR BABY, BUT I'M NOT SURE I WANT TO MARRY "HER"

Over the last several decades, living together has openly thumbed its nose at traditional values, although, compared with Woodstock's "in-your-face" mania, today's nonconformists *appear* toned-down. Perhaps we can attribute that to the popularity of psychotherapy and its spin-offs that allow us to vent more discreetly. Still, have the over-psychoanalyzed 1990s changed us for the better? We might have the answer to that question thirty years from now when we can judge the results of this trend. But for now, compared to the compulsive 1960s, it seems current solutions to love predicaments have been, in their own way, reasoned out.

Some believe that living together, in order to get to know our partner better before marriage, is the answer to the high divorce rate. For those who get bored easily, they reason that only by living together can they change partners like their underwear, and avoid the stigma of divorce. Disgruntled partners argue that children are better off in a separated household because living with constant fighting creates emotional instability. On the other hand, plenty of people think that staying together, but playing around, is a better choice when children are involved. But then what do we end up with? A well-reasoned but still dysfunctional segment of society unable to cope with the choices they made.

Since there is no easy solution to the problem of finding the perfect mate and lasting passion, more than fifty percent of our married population and countless unofficial spouses try to deal with love's enigmatic circumstances. Just take a look at Richard*'s complicated marital test drive and how he has envisioned his future with Nancy*.

Richard describes Nancy as perfect in many ways. She's good-looking with all the right curves in all the right places. She's intelligent, self-sufficient,... a hard-worker. She can handle herself in any social situation. Anyone else would call Nancy an incredible catch. "She has class," says Richard, her unofficial spouse. "But if there were a way out of this relationship, I'd race to the nearest exit." Apparently, she is not perfect enough.

Richard, a firefighter, met Nancy three years ago at a wet-down. "She came with some friends," he said. "I was unattached, looking to get into a relationship, and didn't waste a moment taking a closer look. After the party, Nancy and I went for a couple of drinks and we've been together since that night."

Up until nine months ago, Nancy maintained her own place. But shortly after she became pregnant with their baby, she moved in with Richard, even though well before the pregnancy, he realized the chemistry wasn't there; their sex life was almost nonexistent.

"So why in the world did you get her pregnant?" I burst out.

"It was just one of those times. Nancy looked great, and I was horny. I always use protection, but this time I didn't. I'd just about given up on having sex with her." However, as fate would have it, Nancy became pregnant.

"Knowing how unhappy you were as a couple, did either of you consider terminating the pregnancy?" I asked.

"No," emphasized Richard, who is thirty-five. "I was ready to have a child. And I would never have insulted Nancy like that." Richard feels sad he may never know real love.

I probed, "Do you feel you have to stay with her?"

"Right now, I feel I have to," he sighed. "God, it's so hard for me to talk about this."

"Then don't," I told him. But he seemed to want to.

"All her other qualities make up for it," Richard explained. "And in many ways, it's my fault. I rationalize the lack of sex as a trade-off. I love my baby, and I love to watch them together. It really is beautiful." However, in the past five months, since the baby was born, Richard and Nancy have made love only twice.

Knowing this is not normal for a young couple, I asked, "How long can this ecstasy over the baby last?"

"I don't know," he whispered, sounding defeated.

"What does Nancy think about all of this?"

"Well, she knows I'm unhappy. So we get pissed at each other easily. It's rough."

"And you think you can tolerate that for very long?"

"I'm not sure, but right now I'm sticking with it."

"Seems to me you're confused—bewildered."

"You're right, I am. But the more I stay at home and don't go out gallivanting, the easier it is for me to accept my life as it is. If I'm not out running around checking out the girls, I'm not reminded about should haves. So maybe something will develop." He laughed and reasoned, "Maybe I'll fall in love with her."

"If you don't, would you be willing to settle like that?"

"No. Settling will never change my attitude toward her. But you know, I've never met a girl I was totally happy with. If the sex was good, something else bothered me."

"Could it be you're looking for a level of perfection that doesn't exist?"

"Probably, but I'm not even looking, now. I couldn't because I'm more concerned with this baby. I love seeing him every day."

Realizing their baby is their only bond, though a miraculous one, Richard softened toward Nancy and his morale improved. For the first time, he smiled warmly and revealed, "Both Nancy and I are in bliss. We're so happy with the baby, and that's good enough for both of us at this point."

"Talk to me about what you see happening in the days ahead. Has the subject of marriage ever surfaced?"

"Not really. We haven't discussed it at all."

"Could you live together indefinitely?"

"Yeah, I could. But I don't think Nancy would. Being an unwed mother embarrasses her. She's putting up with me, now, but I don't know how long that will last. Right now, she's not going to argue with me over the marriage issue because she knows that's not going to do her any good."

"Do you really think she's willing to wait it out?"

"Well, you know, even if I decided to marry her, she wouldn't have me right now. I mean I'd have to be really nice for a few months before I would even bring it up. I'd have to show her I love her. And I'm not sure that's possible."

"Has she ever asked you why you can't fall in love with her?"

"No," said Richard.

"Could she be in such denial?"

"She doesn't ask a lot of questions."

"Do you think she's afraid of being a single parent and having to handle all of this responsibility on her own?"

"That won't happen. Our baby's not going anywhere. Besides, I will always pay the bills."

"And you think you have control over that?"

"Yeah."

"Could Nancy support herself if she wanted more out of a relationship than you can give her?"

"Not really."

"How much did she make before she quit her job when the baby was born?"

"About fifty," he murmured.

"Fifty thousand!"

"Yeah, but that's not a lot of money."

"Seems to me a woman could support herself and a child on that."

"Not really."

"Since Nancy quit her job to stay home and take care of your son, do you financially compensate her?"

"I take good care of the baby, but I don't give Nancy as much as I should—maybe a couple hundred a month."

I thought that was on the low side, but he informed me, "She has her own money." Nancy had saved over $100,000 before they met.

Curious, I asked Richard, "What if Nancy decides she wants more out of a relationship than you can give. What if she left you and took the baby?"

His answer surprised me. "I'd give anything if she would fall in love with another guy—get out of my life—but that's not going to happen. She's so busy taking care of the baby, there's no time, no opportunity for her to meet someone else."

"But if she did find someone else, you wouldn't be able to see the baby day to day."

"Then I'll have to deal with that," he said.

Thinking how sad and atypical this alliance is, I thought for sure there was a positive side. "Would you call this more of a friendship than a love relationship?"

"Not really," he decided. "A friend is someone I can do all kinds of things with. Go skiing. Travel to the Himalayas. Mountain climb. It bothers me Nancy doesn't do any of those things. Just think how romantic it would be exploring all of that with somebody you love."

"But that's fleeting. What about all of Nancy's attributes that aren't fleeting?"

"They are not going to satisfy my sexual urges."

"Then would you say you tolerate her?"

"No, it's more than that."

"Then you're ambiguous?"

"I don't feel anything."

"What would be the most ideal situation for you?"

"You *do not* want to know that."

"Really? Then why did I ask?"

"The most ideal situation right now would be for both of us to have an open relationship. Let me do whatever I want. And she'd do her thing."

"That's how much this child means to you?"

"Well, I'm not sure the baby has anything to do with the fact that I want to go out and have sex when I want to. If I were allowed to do that, then everything would be fine. And I'd let her do that, too." As if she needed his permission!

Curious, I asked, "How would you feel about that arrangement?"

"Well, I don't know. Here's the way it is: If you have a woman you don't have great sex with, then you really don't care. It's easy to tell her, 'go ahead.'"

"Do you have feelings of animosity about all of this?"

"You mean, am I pissed?"

"Exactly."

"No. Why should I be mad at her? I put myself in this position, knowing our sex life stunk from the day I met her. And that's my own fault. She can't help who she is, or what she's capable of. As much as I hate repeating my father's mistakes, I can be really cold. That doesn't help either." Mulling over what he had just said, Richard added, "I'm a pain in the neck. I've been spoiled with things...sex. Being chased by all kinds of women. That's a hard act to follow."

"So if you stay together, what about five years from now when your baby goes to school. How are you going to deal with his getting teased because his parents aren't married?"

"Humph. That's a tough one. I never thought about that. But I have a feeling I'll be married to Nancy by then."

"Seriously?"

"Yeah," he assured me. "We'll come together, somehow. Lots of people settle."

Richard's commitment seems risky, don't you think? In his own way, Richard, whose boyish looks and infectious smile are winning, fluctuated wildly on the maturity scale. I had to remind myself he was thirty-five. On the other hand, his level of responsibility toward his child—and Nancy, on his terms—is commendable. "Lots of married men defer to their wives as the 'mother of their children,' then screw around on the side, and sometimes it works," Richard reminded me.

I concluded, to the best of *his* ability, Richard seems to be really working at his relationship. But will his love for his baby override his discontent with Nancy in the long term? We can't answer that, and neither can Richard.

In conclusion, I asked Richard, "If you could be objective, what would you say to a guy who might be involved in a similar situation?"

"I'd tell him to make his move and get out. Don't drag it out like I did."

"Even if he loved his baby?"

"No. I was talking about the two years before Nancy got pregnant. I should have ended it, not hung around. But once a baby comes along, I can't give any advice. A guy has to decide that on his own. Decide how much his baby means to him. In my case, my baby means so much to me I'm willing to do whatever it takes to keep him in my life."

Because he seems convinced he is a martyr, Richard has lost sight of the long term discipline it is going to take to fulfill this good deed. Look at what he is up against:

► He recognizes Nancy was the wrong choice as a lifelong partner.

➤ He wants the freedom to have sex with whomever he wants.

➤ When he gets it, he finds something wrong with them.

➤ His craving for romance overshadows the ups and downs a long-term relationship demands.

➤ Because of his poor relationship with his father, he may not know what it takes to establish a healthy, loving, forgiving, and tolerant relationship.

If Richard wants this relationship to last, he'll need years of self-analysis and psychotherapy. On the other hand, he has a deep sense of loyalty, which might get him over rough times.

Rather than betray Nancy and delude himself, wouldn't a reasonable solution be to eliminate all threats, particularly that of an open relationship, and separate? They might consider forming a business-like partnership to oversee the wellbeing of their child. By putting a different slant on their interaction they might increase their chances of actually falling in love—the kind of love that can tolerate conflict and endure.

One reasonable solution might be for Richard and Nancy to buy a house or rent something for her and the baby nearby, with the stipulation Richard could visit as often as he wanted, and/or establish joint visitation. Nancy could get on with her life, and Richard with his.

"I don't think that would work," he responded. "Nancy wouldn't buy into that."

"Is it Nancy? Or is it your need to control Nancy, and visits with your child, that is important to you?"

He was sincere when he said, "I don't know."

"If you wait five years to see if you can stand Nancy enough to marry her, you might wind up hating each other. Or what if you do marry her then, only to find out it will never work. Your baby will be in school if you divorce. Wouldn't a divorce and all its trappings be far more traumatic then?"

"Lots of people who are miserable with each other stay together."

Yes, but that's not a healthy answer. "Richard, what's best for you? For Nancy and your baby?"

"Right now, I don't know."

"Why do you think I should tell my readers about your story?"

"Because there are a lot of guys out there who think like me. They are trapped in loveless relationships, but they take it."

"And you want the rest of the world to know how miserable you all are?"

"No. I want people to know this is the way it is."

No matter how great his partner is, Richard is the kind of guy who will continually break a woman's heart until he learns an important fact of life: people are not perfect, including him. Once he learns this fact, accepts the realities of marriage and fatherhood, and finds enough fulfillment there, he won't have to play around.

LIVING TOGETHER WHILE MAINTAINING SEXUAL FREEDOM

Because Richard* decided playing around would be his panacea, I need to report that on many occasions—enough to warrant discussion—people I interviewed for this book expressed involvement in or desire to be in an open relationship. The frequency caught my attention, and made me realize love affairs you and I may disapprove of nonetheless exist. Moreover, because I am in contact with a vast number of couples who have been disillusioned by monogamous relationships, these people made me think about aspects of loving in unconventional ways—and also about society's indifference: Once the rules are broken, everybody does it. Does that make it right?

Take a look at one very highly educated, middle-class couple, who decided they couldn't live within the confines of either unofficial or traditional marriage. I wonder what influenced them to redefine the love commitment as we know it. I would expect it in New York, and for sure in Los Angeles. But I would *not* expect that in mainstream America—Portland, Oregon, to be exact—there would be no fewer than four swing clubs. Is this becoming a mainstream phenomenon?

"In lieu of a costly, nasty divorce, and destroying family unity, it's the newest solution," says one of my "cooler" friends who has zillions of cutting-edge acquaintances. "But," said another friend, "what exactly is an open relationship?"

That question is pertinent to this next couple who admit openly to swinging, approve of it, and encourage it. So why bother having a living-together relationship?

Liz* and Ralph* met through a computer bulletin board and courted on-line for many months. She says, "We really started to like each other before we met in person." She is a twenty-three-year-old college student working toward a Ph.D. in anthropology. He is twenty years older and has a Ph.D. in computer science.

Their story fascinated me from the outset. "Ralph and I lived together for over a year, 'non-committally,' when *I* proposed to him to become engaged."

"*Really?*" I responded. "That's unusual. So what does that mean? Did you give *him* a ring?"

"I was only nineteen when we met. Shortly after that we began living together. I decided I wanted to get married to him, but was not ready to get engaged. We agreed that on the one-year anniversary of my proposal, Ralph would then officially propose to me."

"And did you then set a date?"

"Yes, that was part of the plan," she said. "We were to be married eighteen months later."

Did you find much of a difference from living together to becoming engaged and living together?

"Oh yes, we fought a lot for about three weeks," she remembered vividly. "It was really awful. But then things calmed down." Ralph said formalizing their love affair, making it public, having to live up to other people's expectations, made him testy. "It bothered me," he said, "that once we made the transition from being a very private living-together couple to being engaged, everyone was watching me. Before, it didn't matter who *I* was. Afterwards, you become a sitting duck."

Many living-together couples warned me other couples should expect big fights and awkward moodiness once they get engaged. I asked Liz what the reasons for this tension were. Did the ring symbolize that they couldn't look around anymore? Or, that although the test drive was satisfactory, the permanency of monogamy and commitment is threatening?

"Yes and no," Liz said. "We were both really scared of the official side of marriage. Then we went to visit a psychotherapist to talk about that, and the strong differing viewpoints we have on so many topics, and how we could work around that. Therapy gave us a chance for both of us to air old laundry in a neutral setting. Since then, we have been much more able to express ourselves." On the other hand, remaining faithful was not a concern because she said, "We have a different arrangement than most couples."

At this point I had no clue what she was talking about. "What kind of an arrangement?"

"Well...uh," she stalled to size up my anticipated reaction, "Ralph and I have an *open* relationship."

I had heard the term, and had an idea what it meant. But I never talked with anyone who had this arrangement with a

lover before. So rather than pretend, I professed total igno-
rance.

"So tell me, Liz, how does this work?"

She became very serious, and said, "We basically have a set
of rules that goes with our open relationship."

"Like?"

"For example, if I saw a man at school I started to like, and
he asked me on a date, I first have to say, 'Maybe.' I go home
and tell Ralph, 'This guy at school asked me on a date.' I'd tell
him a little bit about the guy, and ask him what he thought
about it. So if we both thought it was a good idea, I'd go on a
date with the guy."

"What if you got serious with him?"

"Then I would introduce him to Ralph," she explained,
"and they would get together, talk, and get to know each
other."

"What if Ralph didn't like him?"

"Then it would be over," she insisted.

Sensing my alarm, she assured me, "It's not something we
do all the time. But to have that freedom is really good for us
and good for our relationship."

Shuddering at the very thought of God blessing this relationship, I was thankful Liz was unable to read my thoughts.
Obviously, she had my attention, and I had no intention of
turning back.

When one of Liz's friends asked her, "Are you concerned
that when Ralph works late at night, he's with another
woman?"

"Not at all," she confidently told the friend. "If he was
with another woman, he would *tell* me."

The advantage is, according to Liz, the arrangement eliminates anyone getting jealous. It doesn't foster competitiveness

because both parties know what's happening. In a monogamous relationship you always have the option of straying, but you do so secretly, while your partner senses that something is wrong. "And if you think something is wrong," she explained, "then maybe you worry that you should think about leaving." In her case, she said, "Ralph can have a regular girlfriend and not worry about losing me."

"Suppose I flirt with somebody," Liz continued. "It's so much more honest than if I did it behind his back."

"And you can deal with that in reverse?"

"Oh, yes," she said.

"Did you discuss this on the computer before you met?"

"No," she said.

Intrigued, I asked, "So how far does it go?"

"We can let it go as far as it can go. That's not our standard practice, though." Liz said it hasn't happened yet. But if it did, that would take a lot of discussion. Ralph has never had an ongoing relationship with another woman. "But if he did, it would certainly fall within our set rules."

"Are these verbal rules you have set?"

"Yes, but we have them written down, too."

Liz admits this kind of relationship is not for everybody, "particularly those who need the security of knowing they are with just one person."

She firmly believes that in the course of a long-term relationship, it is impossible to not be attracted to someone else. "So why hide your feelings," she said, "and not deal with them?

"It also adds variety," she said. "Besides, I enjoy having sex with other people. And it's that someone else who can add a new dimension to your life, which in turn can add a new dimension to your relationship. You both have something else to talk about."

"Did both you and Ralph come to your relationship with this philosophy?"

"Ralph had a relationship like this before," she said. "I hadn't, but I considered it. So basically, he introduced me to it."

You hear that sexual ennui, and ennui in general afflicts, the best marriages and love affairs. But has it come to this? Is fear of boredom so bad that people expect it to happen and initiate damage control measures from the very outset?

"Do you know other couples who operate similarly?"

"Oh yes, quite a few," she said. "We're in a social club where couples who practice open relationships go and socialize. But we also have drifted toward many other open-lifestyle friends who don't belong."

"What happens at the club?"

"It's a nightclub atmosphere," she said, "where we meet other people once a month. And often people use it as a way to meet other people to be open with."

"How many people belong?"

"Oh, at least two hundred couples," she said.

"Are there other clubs in Portland?"

"Yes, they cater to swingers, too, but they're only dance clubs. What those people do is have swing parties at someone's home, afterwards, usually around a hot tub."

"What amenities does your dance club offer that are different?"

"This is an on-premise swinging club," she said, "meaning you can have group sex in front of everyone. Or, they do have private rooms you can use."

"You mean you sit there naked, in front of everyone, watching others get it on and wait for someone to come on to you?"

"Yeah."

"Can anyone join?"

"First you have to attend the orientation. The director gets us all together and asks us if we have any questions, and finds out if there are any areas where we would feel uncomfortable. Then he sets the guidelines." She explained there are two sets of rules: The couples' and the club's. The club rules include: no always means *NO*. On-premise drinking is not allowed. But, she said, "A lot of people drink before they get to the club."

"Can you have dinner?"

"No. Only snacks and soft drinks. It is open from 9 P.M. until 4 A.M."

"It sounds like it might be really expensive."

"Not really," she said. Her club's annual membership fee is only $30. And the cost is $30 per visit.

"I go because I have found it is very easy to meet other couples," Liz said, "that think like we do. I use the club for more than swinging. For instance, if I have a problem with my relationship with Ralph, I'm more likely to go to a friend from the club who understands the open marriage lifestyle." Liz finds she meets a lot of people at the club who have the same set of values.

"You used the word values. On what do you base these values?"

"I base them on the fact we are open and honest and not hypocrites," she said, but realizes "to some people my kind of lifestyle is very offensive—and very threatening. This is not something Ralph and I talk about in general."

"I guess you're not really hurting anyone by it because you only associate with people who also have these same 'values.'"

"True. The values of a monogamous marriage are ingrained in us from birth. So to accept this new arrangement, you are disavowing the values you grew up with."

"There are those of us," Ralph interjected, "who pound away at one marriage after another until we get it right. An open lifestyle might teach them self-acceptance and security to be clear-headed about who they are. I have seen it elevate self-esteem, and elevate a person's level of tolerance, too. The open lifestyle is not perfect either, but at least, through variety, one can appreciate what it means to accept compatibility on different levels. You become more tolerant of your live-in or spouse, with whom you should be in love, and able to cope with his or her imperfections."

"You are a very articulate couple when it comes to defining and reasoning out your own behavior. Do you find other swingers equally as self-aware?"

"Oh yes," Liz said. "I do find, on average, couples practicing an open life-style to be very well-rounded socially and intellectually. I also find they are significantly older than we are."

"Really?"

"Many of them led very monogamous marriages for many, many years," she explained. "But they decided this is what they wanted and needed to spice up their marriages." She informed me she and Ralph are one of the few who have always been this way from the outset of their relationship.

"Are most of these people married?"

"I would say 90 percent are," Liz said. "But for the most part the others live together, or are looking to get into a relationship."

"So what's the point in living together, being able to walk out hassle-free, and being a swinger?"

"I think before you live together," she said, "one person at least thinks it will lead to marriage. It's just cleaner and neater if you both think this is what will happen after marriage. It's best to start it from the very beginning."

"Has there been much written on this?"

"Yes. But most literature only discusses the sexual turn-on, not the emotional or psychological aspects: what bad or good things happen to you as a result of it. If you get on the Internet, you'll find lots of discussions. But it's still very controversial."

"What are the risks?"

It was obvious Liz had given this a great deal of thought. She said, "The risks are that I could fall deeply in love with someone else, and not want to be with Ralph anymore. But I could choose that route if we were a conventional couple and wanted to break up." To prevent that from happening, Liz said her rules include clauses that don't allow them to participate in another relationship when she and Ralph are fighting or having a bad time. "When we're unhappy with each other, we stay monogamous," she said. "I don't want to swing when I am mad at Ralph. I only want to if I'm happy with him."

That didn't make sense to me, but I decided not to pursue it. "What if you decide you don't want to do this anymore?"

"We would discuss it," she said. "And if one of us were really unhappy, we would quit. But right now, it's working for us."

Time out! Have you noticed that throughout the discussions I have had with various LTCs many preface their remarks with "right now?" Why is Liz hedging when she thinks she is in a win/win situation?

Ask yourself this: if marital test drives engender accepting or giving only a feeble amount of security, how is it possible— if the LTC gets married—for them to blot out the living-together mantras: "For now," "Until she pisses me off," "Up to the time that…" and institute living by the marriage vows, 'forever after' and 'for better or worse,' which should engender a great deal of security?

It seems to me that rub plagues a great number of LTCs who get married.

Putting the open relationship aside, I asked Liz, "What advice would you have for living-together couples contemplating marriage?"

Liz said, "If they really love each other, I would tell them to persevere through the worst parts—of which there are plenty after the first year—when you become a lot more committed to each other. But at the same time you have a bigger responsibility toward the other person. Sometimes taking on the other person's problems can be a burden. But I love Ralph so much, and he loves me so much, we weathered each other's misgivings and emotional turmoil over the past four years. And what we have, now, is truly special."

Ralph said, "Before you can make that transition, you have to face what 'I love you' means. Everyone knows what it means when they say, 'I love pizza.' But what does it mean to love another human being? 'I love you' is so badly misused that nobody knows what the *hell* it means."

After working all of that out, this couple says they feel comfortable enough to want to get married and have a family. However, I am still bothered by what happens when the rules change. When one partner doesn't want to participate in an open relationship anymore—say, after the birth of a child—what happens? They could divorce, proving their theory invalid.

Despite that, Liz and Ralph were married a year later. Ironically (to me) Liz went out on several "dates" just before the wedding. But she reasoned, "They were very, very nice people, and reinforced how much I wanted to marry Ralph." She said she can have platonic or sexual relationships with other people, but what she has with Ralph is much deeper. They have a history together.

Two weeks before their wedding, because Liz did not want to go through the fights again that she and Ralph experienced when they lived together and became engaged, she moved out of their house and into her parents' home.

Liz described her wedding as right out of a Norman Rockwell painting, complete with a two-hundred-year-old church and steeple surrounded by a white picket fence. This is not the kind of wedding I thought an open-marriage couple would choose.

Despite this couples' confidence, I doubt this kind of marriage has a future because it isn't marriage anymore than living together is unofficial marriage. My concerns are that one partner might be taken advantage of by the other and manipulated into entering into it. Maybe for this couple, this arrangement will work. It surely wouldn't for me.

LIVING TOGETHER
VERSUS FEAR
OF REMARRIAGE

In his book, *The Pursuit of Happiness*, Dr. David Myers points out: "Although married people are still considerably more likely to feel happy than unmarried people, in recent years the gap has lessened because married women aren't as happy as they once were, while unmarried men and women are happier. In today's world, people are [increasingly] more comfortable staying single. Thus the apparent contribution of marriage to happiness has weakened."

A 1993 survey in *The American Woman* shows, "Of the formerly married, more than one-fifth of women overall were either widowed or currently divorced, compared with 10 percent of men." While writing this book, I talked with over-fifty female subscribers to the W.O.O.M. network about remarriage. Those who were financially secure decided, "I would never get married again." They have been there, done that, put their time in and *appear* satisfied remaining single.[1] Once they get used to being on their own—over the shock of divorce or their spouse's death—thoughts of remarriage are reminders of never-ending responsibility, accountability, and jockeying for free time. Some said that although marriage and raising their children were exciting and fulfilling at the time, putting their goals on the back burner and living life around their family's schedule, opinions, and needs, had a lingering, frustrating effect. One over-fifty said, "Before it was *we*; now it is *me*. Once I got over being scared to be alone, I enjoy doing things important to me I never had the time to do before." Women who want to climb the corporate ladder say they are better off remaining single after fifty.

"On the other hand, these women insist they don't want to be alone. It is then that living together becomes appropriate and has its advantages. Partners are able to hang onto the *illusion* they can come and go as they wish. Interestingly, if men have grown, independent children, they are more eager to remarry. They said they wanted a regular companion, someone to take care of them. However, I have found over-fifty men still involved in the mayhem of parenthood were less inclined to want to remarry. A new wife interfered with their relationships with their children. The catch is, more and more over-fifty men date younger women. But younger women are not satisfied with the living-together set up. They want to get married, and in most cases, start a family.

Informal W.O.O.M. studies suggest the deciding factors for and against middle-age remarriage seem to be the levels of independence and autonomy in a previous relationship, and the level of family responsibility after divorce or widowhood.

In the chapter *Negotiating Your CCA*, the section, "It Isn't Always About Money," discusses how you can contractually declare and defend your independence while living with an unofficial or official spouse.

THE REWARDING JOY
OF DISCOVERING HERSELF
ON MANY LEVELS

"When I decided to divorce my husband in 1972, after twenty-eight years of marriage, I moved to Honolulu to begin a new life as a single. I was forty-eight, ready to put the past—the good and the bad—behind me," said family and marriage counselor Elizabeth Bailey. However, that was a short-lived aspiration when six months later, during a hiking vacation, Liz met 60-year-old, German-born Guy Mussen. "He was the biggest surprise of my life," she exclaimed. "The last thing I was thinking about was getting involved with another man!" Despite misgivings, she did. "It happened very fast. We lived together from that first week for eighteen years, and eventually married in 1990." Liz was then sixty-six years old; Guy, seventy-eight.

Most of us would wonder, *why bother*. Particularly when more and more senior couples are choosing to live together rather than to marry in order to protect assets. "Our wedding came about rather spontaneously," Liz remembers. "Each year, Guy and I would celebrate the anniversary of the day we first met on October 18. Either we would plan a special dinner or take a trip to an outer island." When Liz looked at her calendar in the fall of 1990, she realized they would be celebrating their eighteenth living-together anniversary on October 18. She turned to Guy and said, "Wouldn't this be a fun time to get married? *Well*," Liz chuckled, "Guy's face lit up with a magnificent smile, as if he were a little kid. He looked happier than happy and said, 'Nobody ever asked me that before!'"

Although Liz was perfectly content living with Guy and had no desire to ever get married again, pleasing him was important to her. They put their legal affairs in order, so that Guy's will named Liz as the beneficiary and wouldn't be contested.

"Having achieved what he so desperately wanted," Liz assumes "marriage gave Guy another layer of contentment." The couple, surrounded by twenty-one of their closest friends, were married in a beautiful park in Honolulu. Afterward, they walked across the street to the Academy of Arts for a sit-down dinner. "It was the best party in the world," Liz reminisced.

Unfortunately, their love story has a bittersweet twist. Liz has been fighting the overwhelming isolation, and deep loss of her best friend for the past three years since Guy was diagnosed with Alzheimer's disease. It was such a shock to both of them considering Guy, a computer engineer, had only retired in 1987 at age seventy-five. "After living a wonderful life together including international travel, adventure, and loving intimacy, everything changed," sighs Liz. "I have been given the role of caregiver," a role she identified with as a therapist, but could not identify with personally. "I thought these things happened to other people. Guy was so healthy and remarkably youthful, the switch from his extreme independence to dependence came as a true shock—unimaginable, at first.

"It is shattering to know that we just passed our sixth anniversary and Guy has no recollection of that day, nor any day."

Liz, a University of Hawaii instructor in human development, went into a personal tailspin. "Intellectually and professionally I should have been able to cope," she admits, "but I wasn't prepared for the devastating, profound sadness. The loss of my lover and friend—my companion. I had this big, black space inside me." With all of her professional experience, and yet because it was happening to her, she was unable to connect with the anger she also felt. "I became frightened and knew I needed help." A year and a half after working with a therapist, Liz's recovery began. She has made steady progress to where she is a healthy woman again.

Liz has studied everything about Alzheimer's disease she can get her hands on. Ever optimistic, she has enrolled Guy in a national trial for a new drug. Although Guy is in the early stages, he sleeps 18 hours a day and is almost entirely non-verbal. He reads the same book over and over, but can still take care of himself. "Hopefully, he may not get any worse," she sighed. "But I miss him so much."

At this point, it's an awful question to have asked Liz, but I was thinking about a man I had previously interviewed who did not want to deal with his live-in's chronic illness. While she was in the beginning stages of MS, he eased her out of his home and his life. I asked her, "Would you have reacted differently to Guy's illness if you had remained an LTC? Would the responsibility have been easier to bear?"

"This relationship was so strong before we were married, I know that it would have been just the same. I don't know how much sense this makes, but I don't see any difference between the way I felt before we were married and the way I feel now. Married or not," Liz says, "we have always been married in our hearts, since the day we met. That's the magic. I will always treasure the twenty-five years we spent together."

Staying around when times are difficult is more than love. You have to know yourself—what you can deal with. It's self-awareness and self-evaluation.

"In my case," the counselor said, "Once I rationalized that I had lost my husband to a disease I couldn't do anything about, and that I'm on my own, but also that, I am still here, I made progress and a healthy transition." This attitude can be applied to any relationship crisis.

Because living together is often considered by the partners to be an unofficial relationship, free of responsibility, few consider how they would respond should a crisis occur, Liz says, "When you can say, 'I know this is where I want to be, and even though I have been handed an unlucky break, I feel very good dealing with it,' that's when a person's real character unfolds."

I CAME TOO FAR...

Saddeled with an alcoholic husband whom she left and came back to several times, Denise couldn't take it anymore. She gave up hope of ever salvaging her marriage and moved on with their young child. Several months later, she met an unhappily married, older man twenty-two years her senior.

After three years of dating, Denise felt they should have lived together, or gotten married, but he refused to get a divorce. She stayed for eight years, but eventually broke up with him. "I wasn't happy with him for a long time," she says. "He was a job without benefits." But no matter how mean she was to him, she says, "he just wouldn't get out of my life. He wouldn't accept it was over for me. And because I hadn't met anyone else, he became a habit." Burned by two significant bitter relationships, she lost confidence in men.

Denise had gone out with her present live-in years ago, but she was dating the married, older man at the time, and let Joe know she wasn't available. Occasionally he would run into her and ask her out, but each time she brushed him off. One day, Joe ran into Denise's sister. He asked her, "Please tell Denise to give me just one more chance."

Two and a half years ago, Denise gave him that chance, and she went out with him. "He was my age," she said, "which was a big plus, and had never been married." Just weeks before, Joe was living at home with his mother and sister, who decided to sell that house, and told him they wouldn't have room for him in their new one. "He needed a place to stay for a few weeks until he got an apartment," Denise remembered, "and I let him move in with me."

"Somehow, he got his way," she explained, ignoring the alarm and disapproval of her family, "but at the same time, I was willingly manipulated into it. It happened so fast."

Denise admits on the surface it looked bad. Aside from setting a bad example for her fifteen-year-old daughter, this guy was far less well-off than she. For years, Denise struggled by working day jobs and cleaning houses at night to be able to buy a beautiful home for her and her daughter.

"But what I didn't know was that the debilitating headaches and the awful pain I was suffering from was really a malignant brain tumor," Denise explained. She described how she began doing things she never would have imagined doing before. "I would wake up with those headaches, and I didn't have the strength to resist him."

A few weeks after Joe moved in, a CAT scan revealed Denise's brain tumor. She was rushed to the hospital for emergency surgery and at age forty-one, was not expected to live. Miraculously Denise survived the surgery, and when she finally got home found she was incredibly vulnerable. "But Joe was there for me when I was at my worst," she fondly remembers. "I lost all my hair from the radiation; I had to take steroids. I gained weight." And here was this new relationship. The pretty girl that Joe met was a very different person. "I felt ugly," she says. And perhaps not worthy of his attention.

Denise told Joe she wouldn't be upset if he left. But Joe stayed and helped nurse Denise back to health. A regular churchgoer, Joe encouraged Denise to practice her faith. "You know," Denise said, "on our first date, Joe said, 'You're my destiny. We'll be together forever.' I had no clue what that meant at the time, but I do believe God sent him to me to care for me."

By the time I had spoken to Denise, she had just passed the two-year anniversary of her brain surgery. Now almost fully recovered and cancer-free, she has begun to rethink, or perhaps rework, the live-in situation. Much stronger, she can assess what she and Joe have together, and what needs work. But she always keeps in mind he was there for her when she didn't have a spouse to support her through the most dreadful thing that had ever happened to her. Indebted and also in love, she would like to see it work, but on her terms.

The first issue Joe has to get over is that Denise will never marry him. He's proposed to her repeatedly. "But I have such a negative attitude toward marriage," Denise insists. "I think it just ruins things. I really want no part of it. I own my own home, my own car. I don't need anything." Joe has never had children, and Denise knows she's not going to have any more. "But I'm sure if he wanted children," she rationalized, "he would have been married and had them already."

Joe contributes to the household expenses and pays rent. But Denise is concerned because his job is seasonal, and since it relies on the weather, he doesn't have a steady income. "He'll never have what I have," she boasted, with good reason. "I have a stable job, medical benefits, and someday I'll have a pension. My home is a two-family house, so I have income from that, also."

Joe does talk about opening his own business. But Denise insists she will not front him. And if the business fails, she will not support him. "He's got more to lose here," Denise says. As much as she truly believes in her heart she and Joe will be together forever, her attitude toward him, or any man for that matter, is influenced by her strong feelings of independence. "I did what I had to do to support myself and my daughter, and I will never take a chance on a man again."

Many forty-something women who have been through traumatic divorces and relationships have been so hurt by men that they lose their ability to trust. It may take the next guy who comes along a great deal of compassion, understanding, and patience to break through that barrier.

Put to the test, Joe has taken his marital test drive seriously. Having faced one of the worst crises that can occur in a relationship, he proved he is worthy of more respect than Denise is willing to give him. Denise has put a dollar sign on the relationship, but has failed to see you can't put a price tag on honesty and decency, trustworthiness, and unconditional love. Is it such an affront when we find a woman supporting a man that his good qualities go by the wayside? Reverse the situation. We don't think twice about a woman who is supported by a man.

Is financial independence for women a turn-off that precludes marriage but makes living together palatable? Denise and many other women have to come to terms with the fact that they cannot have independence and be supported, too. When Denise was sick, Joe was her knight in shining armor, but overall, she has to cope with reality. Having it all is a fairytale.

FOR MANY SENIORS,
REMARRIAGE IS NOT AN OPTION

It's simple. When seniors marry the marriage tax penalties are too much for the average older couple. Roberta Kirwan, a writer for *Money* magazine, says, "An estimated 370,000 men and women over age 65 live together." Conservatively, that's over 10 percent of the cohabiting population. According to Ms. Kirwan, "One reason so many stay single is that marriage can erode financial security seniors depend on in retirement." Social Security reductions and taxes deter over-sixty couples from wanting to get married and combining incomes. By filing separate returns, you get to keep more after-tax dollars. Take a look at what this financial writer has to say about it:

➤ SOCIAL SECURITY
"Two singles living together can each have an income of $25,000 before their benefits are subject to tax. A married couple filing jointly is limited to $32,000."

➤ PENSIONS
"Remarriage can mean you forfeit your deceased spouse's benefits. Unmarried partners receive no survivor benefits, but the retiree can take a lump-sum distribution, and buy an annuity with a survivor benefit for the [domestic partner]."

➤ MEDICAID
"Though eligibility rules vary by state, a married couple may have to deplete a significant portion of their jointly-owned assets before Medicaid will pay for long-term nursing-home care for the sick spouse. The assets of the healthy partner of an unmarried couple are not counted in the eligibility criteria. The only exception is property you transfer to your partner in

the three-year period prior to applying for Medicaid, and after entering a nursing home."[2]

"But surely," I asked New Jersey attorney George S. Cowen, specializing in estate planning, "mustn't there be some advantage to over-sixties' couples getting married?"

"Wedded bliss?" he jested.

He did, however, come up with one good reason. "Consider this advantage. Two seniors decide to get married. One of them dies. The surviving spouse is entitled to a portion of the deceased spouse's estate even if the deceased spouse died without a will." The security of marriage will also provide protection when a will exists, but fails—in the opinion of the surviving spouse—to adequately provide for the surviving spouse. Laws may provide for the surviving spouse to "elect" to take a share of the deceased spouse's estate larger than designated. Without a will, an unofficial surviving spouse, residing in a state which does not recognize common law marriage, would more than likely not receive anything.

"Under federal estate tax laws, if the value of the deceased spouse's estate exceeds the exemption amount [$625,000 for decedents dying in 1998, gradually increasing to $1,000,000 by 2006], the deceased spouse's estate will have to pay federal estate taxes on the excess," Mr. Cowen said. "Unless the excess passes to or for the benefit of the surviving spouse."

When the surviving spouse dies, his or her estate will have to pay federal estate taxes to the extent that its value exceeds the exemption amount. "Therefore, if so inclined," the lawyer said, "the surviving spouse could eliminate federal estate taxes being payable by his or her estate by spending or gifting the assets during the remainder of his or her lifetime. So that, upon death, the then value of the estate will be less than the amount then allowed to pass federal estate tax-free." A much younger surviving spouse (let's say she's sixty and he is seventy-five) might need to "spend down" the value of her estate (including inheritances which the surviving spouse received from the other spouse).

Although only a small segment of the senior citizen population is well-heeled enough to worry about federal estate taxation, a person can leave up to $625,000 to $1,000,000 worth of assets (depending upon the year of death) to a non-spouse, without incurring a federal estate tax. However, Mr. Cowen suggests wealthier marital hold-outs weigh the following facts.

➤ If you remain unmarried, then, upon the death of your unofficial spouse, his or her estate will incur a federal estate tax on that portion of his or her estate that exceeds the exemption amount. Suppose the value of your unofficial spouse's estate is $1,000,000 and he or she signs a will leaving you his or her entire estate; then he or she dies in 1998. Upon your unofficial spouse's death, the first $625,000 of assets will pass federal estate tax-free to you but the remaining $375,000 will incur death taxes of $143,750.00! These death taxes will have to be paid by the surviving unofficial spouse's estate within nine months of his or her death.

➤ If you marry, and your spouse wants you to inherit his or her entire estate, then no federal estate taxes will be payable upon your spouse's death. However, upon your subsequent death, federal estate taxes will be payable by your estate if its value exceeds the then exemption amount.

➤ If you marry and your spouse wants you to benefit from his or her entire estate, but your spouse also wants his children to eventually receive his entire estate upon your subsequent death, then your spouse could execute a will that provides for the creation of one or more trusts. This trust(s) would be held and managed for your benefit for the remainder of your lifetime with the remaining balance in the trust(s) being payable upon your subsequent death to your spouse's children. No federal estate taxes would be incurred upon the death of your spouse and the federal estate taxes, payable upon your subsequent death, would be either eliminated or substantially minimized.

"In other words," Mr. Cowen continued, "there are estate planning advantages to being married:

➤ Federal estate taxes could be eliminated in their entirety upon the death of the first spouse to die.

➤ The surviving spouse can enjoy the full benefits of the deceased spouse's estate during the remainder of the surviving spouse's lifetime.

➤ The deceased spouse's children (presumably born of a prior marriage) could receive the balance of their deceased parent's estate, which was held in trust for the benefit of the surviving spouse upon the death of the surviving spouse.

➤ And, depending upon the year of death, between $625,000 and $1,000,000 of assets held in trust for the benefit of the surviving spouse (and which assets were not taxed upon the death of the first spouse to die) will again pass tax-free upon the death of the surviving spouse to the children of the first spouse to die." [3]

Now an unofficial spouse might say, "Leave me the full million! I'll gladly pay the $143,750 of federal estate taxes, and run with the remaining $856,250!" If your unofficial spouse is childless—or if he or she has had a falling out with his or her child(ren)—that strategy might work. However, by not being married, federal estate taxes may be payable upon the death of the first unofficial spouse to die and, possibly, upon the death of the surviving unofficial spouse. In effect, the same assets could be taxed twice if the parties were not married, whereas federal estate taxes could be avoided in their entirety if they were married.

Mull over what the financial advisors have to say about over-sixties getting married, or remarrying. Unless you want to go through the process of suggesting and enacting a prenuptial agreement or in the event that deep love, ego, living in sin, and/or personal convictions are compelling factors, staying single looks like your best bet when your income and assets do not justify sophisticated estate planning. On the other hand, the very rich have a lot more to think about.

Whatever you decide, consult with an expert.

COHABITING WHEN THERE IS A LARGE AGE GAP

ONE WOMAN'S ADVENTURE
LOVING A HOT, YOUNG STUD

It was a potentially boring evening. Sam had a cold; I cooked, or rather I ordered in. Pork fried rice and an egg roll grumbled through my intestines, making me uncomfortable at every turn. While contemplating my fortune cookie message —*The philosophy of one century is the common sense of the next*— the phone rang on my business line.

"Good evening," I answered formally. "May I help you?"

"Beliza! Hi! I'm in the bathtub!" purred an androgynous voice. "Guess what!"

"What! You're about to electrocute yourself?"

"No way!" *it* laughed. "I'm reading about you in *Psychology Today*."

"Oh great! *Pu-leeze* cut me a break."

"No! Wait. Please—I need your help," *it* gurgled and splashed around. " My boyfriend's nineteen. I'm twenty-nine. I'm feeling so-o-o old. Can you help me?"

"Oh lovely!" I chided. "Please tell me how you could possibly feel over-the-hill at twenty-nine!"

"You know how these guys are," *it* moaned, while protesting, "they see one crow's foot, and take a piss on you. It's just so *f——g* hard to keep up!"

"Who the hell is this!"

"Dot!"

"Dot who?"

"Dot Leckner Stein."

"Do you have a gender, Dot?"

"Oh yeah female...every inch of the way! I look like Madonna. Oh, by the way," *she* let me know, "I'm calling you from Germany—Berlin—on my cell phone. How did I ever live without these things? Can you believe this magazine costs eight bucks over here! Actually, I didn't buy it. We Americans sort of pass stuff around."

By now, I was amused. My inner senses tingled—while my itching writer's fingers typed the air.

"I do Mick," she bragged.

At my age, there's only one Mick. Treading carefully, I said, "Mick? You mean Mick—like in the Stones?"

"Yeah," she boasted. "Like is there any other Mick? Isn't he gorgeous!"

Thinking about his big, ugly lips and skinny little ass, I thought, *No, not really*, but didn't answer. First rule of interviewing: The subject talks. You listen—if you want a story. This was promising.

"I do The Grateful Dead, too," she said with bravado. "And Oasis, the famous British group you probably never heard of.

Famous people over here aren't always famous over there."

"*Do?*" I dared to ask. "What do you mean *do*?"

"I'm a masseuse," she replied. "The best and most famous in Germany! Because I'm one of the few massage therapists who speaks English, I've got the whole market tied up. It's incredible! All the rock stars love me.

"Boy could I tell you stories! You wouldn't believe what goes on backstage."

"I want to write a book, too. But it would be just to-o-o scandalous." She belly-laughed. "I've got over three hundred pictures. Good stuff!"

"Where does boy-toy fit into all this?" I asked.

"Oh, Lars is my boyfriend."

"Does he live with you?"

"You mean does he sleep here?" she asked. "Yeah! We're lovers. He sleeps here every night. What a body! He only goes home so his mom can do his laundry.

"I don't *do* laundry," she informed me.

"Oh."

"My grandmother tells me I should get an older man to take care of me instead," she babbled on. "But that's disgusting. You know these young women. They latch onto these old guys, and bleed them dry."

"Well, that's one way of looking at it," I conceded. "So what does Lars do while you're *doing* rock stars?"

"He's a student," she said, "in the American equivalent of freshman year of college. Boy! Do I spoil him," she bragged. "I like to, though. I do very well, so why not? The sex is fantastic! And my seven-year-old is crazy about him. But what if he dumps me, Beliza? What's it going to be like when I'm fifty and he's thirty-nine? Will he be able to stand looking at me?"

Reeling from her inability to cope with their age difference, and aging in general, I said, "You're not really serious about marrying him—are you? Liz Taylor tried that, and it bombed."

"Oh God no! I did that once. I'll never get married again! Fastest way to destroy any romance. Got to have options... Marriage ruins everything."

"You know," I commented, "since you haven't any intention of getting married, why not just enjoy what you've got today? That includes your firm body and wrinkle-free eyes. Worry about tomorrow—tomorrow."

"Yeah, but I love him! Do you think, when he gets older, he'll want to have a baby with me?"

"Ask him," I suggested. "But appreciate the fact that a kid who's got you to pay for his playthings, a mother to do his laundry, and daddy to pay for anything else, may not be so quick to know what he wants—or grow up."

"You've got a point," she concluded.

She then asked me to send her information about W.O.O.M. and my articles on what it's like to be in love with an older man. "Even though I'm the older woman, I'm sure I could relate to a lot of stuff older guys feel—like really insecure."

Thinking this was one confused woman, I softened and said, "Sure...of course."

"Could you send me a postcard sometime, too?" she urged.

"I promise to keep in touch. *Guten Nacht.*"

"Good night and thanks," she whispered appreciatively.

We had talked for over an hour. But when I hung up, I thought, *Just who the hell, and what was that!* I don't know what came over me, but somehow, I believed her *unbelievable* story and sent Dot the information she requested. Three weeks later, a hot-pink and orange tie-dyed envelope embellished with a huge, hand-drawn smiley face arrived. And that's the day I began a long epistolary friendship with Dot.

"Right now, my hands are dying [her way of saying sore]! Because for the last two days, they've been all over Sting's body. Yes, Sting! Mr. Gorgeous Pop Star from Newcastle, England—happily married with six kids.

"Lars is currently sulking because I've been hanging out with Sting and his manager, eating in Berlin's best Italian restaurants. He does yoga two hours every day and looks 20 years old." There was a lot more to the story.

"Ben [her estranged husband] and I are still officially married. Frankly, I am afraid of getting a divorce. It's very cozy the way it is." She's pleased Ben, twenty-eight, has met Lars, and they get along just fine. "No static." On the other hand, Lars's mother would rather her son date a younger, single German woman. They tolerate each other in a catty way only a woman would understand. She wrote, "German women spoil the hell out of their sons, and that makes more work for the girlfriend. Hard shoes to fill."

Dot indulges Lars with a daily massage and daily presents—"I treat him like a king!" Dot boastfully complains that she has spoiled all her past boyfriends, "and I've never, *never* had a man/boy older than me."

So how did she meet Lars?

"Well, I was in a taxi with a girlfriend, raising hell on the main street of Berlin. We spotted Lars and five friends. So, we opened the windows and yelled, "Hey little boy, you want some candy?" Lars looked around, then said, 'Who me?' in English. Our taxi sped off to the bus stop, where we got onto a double-decker bus. We sat up front. And when I took a look back, I saw Lars, and I never turned toward the front again."

Dot and her friend, Pamela, got off at their stop and went into a 24-hour convenience store. When they left the store, Dot said Lars was there and started to talk to her in German. She lied, and said, "I don't talk German, man!" Lars was shy in his approach to Dot *(who wouldn't be?)*, and his fumbling with English made the whole situation comical. They both lied about their ages. She instantly became younger; Lars, older. The two went their separate ways, but Lars got Dot's phone number.

He called a few times, but Dot, on purpose, refused to take his calls. She finally gave in and took his call one evening and invited him over. "We watched *Forrest Gump*," she said. "I gave him a back massage, which ended up in a make-out session, and we have been together ever since."

Dot says, contrary to what we might think, Lars is extremely mature. He and her daughter, Jasmine, have a fabulous relationship, and Lars plays games with her and pays a lot of attention to her. He is a very concerned surrogate parent.

"But I also know Lars needs to be with his younger friends," Dot confides. "So I give him lots of freedom to go out to discos. But mostly he likes to be with me and Jasmine at home."

In one letter I asked her, "What's the status? Do you see this lasting?"

She wrote back, "Do any of us know what the future holds?" Sometimes, she writes, "I cry thinking Lars is just going to use up my good prime years, and dump me for a young girl someday. But any man can do that." Even this die-hard feminist has bought into the notion her looks are the only attraction.

"I'm living for today and enjoying him as much as I can," Dot philosophized. "My grandmom warned me, 'Dot, you can either be an older man's princess or a younger man's slave.' Well, this is my life as a slave, I guess. But because I have good luck and good karma, and because I pay all the bills, I am too stubborn to be taken care of."

When Lars tells Dot how much he wants to marry her someday, she tells him, "I think marriage is an old-fashioned concept that destroys any lust for each other, because married couples suffocate each other."

She says her friends warn her it will never last. "But maybe they're jealous I have a hot young lover," she jokes.

Like Dot, more and more women living with younger men are calling me for reassurance. Although the self-help network I operate is called Wives of Older Men, they hope that I can help them understand inherent problems facing "husbands" of older women. They say that men their age are in search of younger models. Older men don't appeal to them. However, the age issue for women living with younger guys is often a surmised, looming threat. "How long will he hang around with an old bag?" one forty-year-old fretted. She and her younger boyfriend have an eleven-year age difference.

Unlike older men in love with younger women, many older women say even a minimal age difference suppresses thinking about anything permanent—even when every other aspect of their relationship is satisfying. "I'll enjoy it while it lasts" is their mantra. Living together is their salvation, marriage out of the question. So wrapped up with the preconceived notion that it won't be long before she is dumped, the women I spoke with regarded their relationships as short-term flings. "I knew this affair was doomed from the first day we went out."

Society thinks that way, too, and that won't change any time soon. However, since some older women put such emphasis on the negative aspect of the age difference—more so than their younger partners—they have difficulty trusting their men's motives, and eventually shun them. These women run from one relationship to the next, as in the case of one woman I have worked with who has had four live-in younger boyfriends in five years. "They make me feel good," she says, "But I know it's not real."

But what if he thinks it's real? Then generally, there is little doubt about who actually instigates the break-up.

The bottom line is that older women infatuated with younger men have to face the fact that if they base their worthiness on their looks and seek out younger men to affirm that they are still desirable, then don't give these guys a chance to prove their love, they'll constantly be changing their locks and, with few exceptions, coping with a lonely, empty life ahead.

WHEN AN EXCEPTION EVOLVES INTO A MEANINGFUL RELATIONSHIP

My friend had just announced to me she was excited and nervous about having a first date with a much younger man. Knowing she's fifty-plus, I was dying to ask her, "Just how *much* younger?" But I held off. After a couple of glasses of wine at my yacht club on St. Thomas, she mustered up the courage to tell me he was a *lot* younger. Then she giggled like a little girl, and asked me, "So what do you think?"

"I think it's great! If he's fun, and you're having a good time, what's there to think?"

Just then, Kenny, the club's assistant manager, who overheard the last part of our conversation strolled by and said, "I think it's a damn good idea."

I glared at him and thought, *How would he know?*

A little while later, he took me aside. His eyes sparkled as he bragged, "I'm living with a woman 13 years older than me."

"You're kidding!"

"Now, would I kid you about a thing like that?"

A few months later, I called him. Because men are always a little nervous to be interviewed, I warmed him up with, "So tell me how you and this extraordinary older woman met."

"I was the first mate on a tour boat, and she took a job as manager."

"What was the initial attraction?" I pried, catching him off guard.

"Um...I don't know! That's so hard to pinpoint." A second later, he said, "I think it was her attitude. She just seemed like a real good friend. That's all."

"So had you dated a lot of women before?"

"Not really," he said. "I was married once before when I was nineteen, for about six years."

Ken looks twenty-five, so I was surprised when he said he was thirty-two. "I guess, by now you know what's happening in life...where it's at."

He laughed, and said, "Of course *not*."

"What do you find appealing about living with a woman who is older?"

"Definitely, she is more mature. Instead of running around acting like maniacs, we've got some kind of focus going on, which I didn't have when I moved here for no good reason."

"You did?"

"Yeah, I just got tired of the rat race in Texas. And actually, it was the same with Jean. She moved here from California."

"What did you do in Texas?"

"I was the site manager of a construction company." he said. "And even though the money was good, I hated it."

"Was your first wife older than you?"

"No, she was a couple of years younger." Apparently, Ken's dating older women wasn't a pattern.

"You married so young because you thought it was a good idea?"

"Yeah." He laughed. "*Thought* is the key word there."

"How long did it take you to figure out your marriage wasn't working?"

"After about four years, I didn't see any progress. There wasn't a purpose for the relationship. And after awhile, I realized it wasn't going anywhere."

"How long have you lived with Jean?"

"Seven years now," he said. "It's taken me this long to get her to say 'yes,' but we're going to get married next year."

"She gave you a hard time?"

"Well, I had to ask her a few times." He laughed. "She's never been married before, and this will be quite an experience."

Ken said he and Jean get along really well. They worked side by side and lived together twenty-four hours a day for five years while they were in the boat business. "After Hurricane Marilyn, when we switched jobs, it was really empty not having her there with me all the time. And vice versa."

Some younger guys are attracted to older women because they feel taken care of on the domestic front. So I asked Ken, "What's the deal at home chore-wise?"

"I cook. She cleans," he said quashing all my other stereotypical prejudices.

A lot of older women worry, 'Just what would I do with a younger guy while he's playing Super Mario Brothers?' So I asked Ken, "And what are some of your hobbies?"

"We're really into scuba diving and all sorts of water sports."

"So you really stick to non age-related activities."

"Yeah. I'm beyond goofing off."

"Tell me about the age difference. Do you feel Jean tries to mother you?"

"Not at all. I can only *wish* she would!"

"Do you plan on having a family?"

"No, I don't think so. We both feel the same way about that. I've got my two miniature Yorkies, and they're a handful enough. Besides, my parents were divorced when I was eleven. When my dad went on the road, I had the responsibility of raising and keeping an eye out for my little sisters." That was enough child-rearing for Ken.

"What has this relationship taught you?"

"Listen to each other always," he said. "That always works. Even if you aren't listening—pretend!" He laughed. "And argue a little bit."

"Oh?"

"Yeah, a good healthy debate gets everyone's attention. Usually one of us is wrong, which forces us to think about what the other person is saying."

"So is marriage the best answer? Or could you live together forever?"

"Yeah, we could live together forever, but we're a team, now. And all the family's nagging us. So we decided—not just because of that, because we're not going to be separated by anything, except death—'Let's just go ahead and take that last step, and get married.' But she'll keep her last name."

Thinking about it, he said, "It's hard to explain why we decided to do it, but it will help the relationship out a little."

Figuring what they had was darn good already, I asked, "How?"

Ken said, "Instead of saying this is my girlfriend all the time, I can say this is my *wife*. It will mean more. I think it's the ceremonial part of it I want, making it official."

"Will it make your love affair more special?"

"No," he said. "I can't imagine how it could get any more special."

"Do friends ever make fun of your older girlfriend?"

"No, but I do feel a little tension once in awhile. It's hard to explain. But I sense they just don't think it's right. I'll introduce Jean. And they'll say, 'Hi!,' take a second look that says, 'Oh! Oh my gosh, who's this?' They don't say it out loud, but they're reactions speak volumes. Then again, maybe it's just me creating that discomfort for myself ."

"Aren't you afraid marriage will change what you have?"

"Everyone tells you that," Ken replied. "But I have a theory about that. If marriage changes your love for each other, then there was something else wrong with the relationship before that. Other couples might think marriage could fix what was wrong or missing from the relationship. But right now, Jean and I have no ties. We could just bolt, and say, 'see ya.' Therefore, I think some couples go into marriage feeling trapped before they even get married. That's what I think destroys marriage for couples who have lived together."

Ken said a lot of couples don't realize life changes everyday. And when the change isn't for the better, "then they start blaming it on the marriage itself," he said, "when, in fact, the change was going to take place anyhow. And they can't deal with that." Ken feels a lot of LTCs he knows go into marriage assuming that the commitment is going to ruin everything. But if they are that scared already, they shouldn't even be living together. "They should date each other a while longer," he suggested. Or, maybe break up, and try again.

"So what do your friends think about your getting married?"

"Well, considering no one thought it would last anyway," he said, "they are really happy for us."

"Tell me, on what emotional level do you gauge your relationship?"

"It's simple. After Hurricane Marilyn, I felt so betrayed. The island was a mess and nothing was getting better. And although it brought Jean and me much closer together, living every day with such devastation was awful. My personality changed, and I got really irritable. It upset me that this tragedy brought the worst out in people, and I felt helpless. I decided one day, 'I've got to talk to somebody about this.'"

Ken says he called a therapist and went every day for two weeks. "Boy, did that help! I thought therapy would really strain our relationship." He thought maybe Jean would think he was weak. Instead, she was a hundred percent behind Ken. She attended sessions with him a couple of times. "But she was really committed to my getting better," he said appreciatively. That's when Ken knew he never wanted to lose what he had with Jean.

Ken told me, "It's a real shame more men don't get into therapy at certain times in their life, when they see signs of problems they can't control." Even his therapist expressed surprise that Ken, not Jean, initiated the call. But he insists, "No matter how big and tough you are, men have to recognize they can't always work things out on their own. You've got to know where it's at before you can fix it."

Emotionally and philosophically, Ken is way beyond his years, which undoubtedly allows him to sustain a relationship with a woman thirteen years his senior.

Dot's story describes an older woman who has little confidence in her relationship and little confidence in herself. Therefore, she has little chance of taking her love affair to a higher level. Ken's story is reassuring and confirms that when a relationship is based on similar values, the joy of pleasing one another long-term goes far beyond looks, age, and lust. Ken knew he was ready to take the next step. Dot says she'll never be ready. And judging by the basis on which *she* judges her relationship, she's probably right.

If you happen to be living with a person younger or older than you, and you haven't established the confidence it takes to sustain marriage, you might want to think about what it will take to close up those gaps of insecurity. Those gaps may have nothing to do with age. If you are looking to your partner to make marriage happen for you, chances are that expectation will put so much pressure on your partner that he or she will feel blamed for your deficiencies. That pressure can get old really fast. The relationship seldom gets to the higher level of love required to make a successful marriage.

In these cases, living together is a transient phase, a failed test drive, and always a disappointing waste of time.

GLOBAL
LOVE NESTS

This is a global society. If you're available and interested, it's possible you're going to fall in love with someone who doesn't live nearby. However, complications arise when couples have to travel great distances to see each other. Some of the confusion surrounding this relationship comes from the constant disappointment of having to say good-bye and the continual pondering of whether to pack up and move closer to be with the other. Juggling schedules, going to events dateless, trying to work out a domestic partnership make long distance test drives very difficult.

If marriage is on your mind, give this type of love affair a second thought. Some of the best global relationships fall apart when couples are together on a daily basis. On the other hand, some of the stronger relationships I have seen are when couples live together part-time either at his place, her place, or their place. It works best for those who have raised their families and those who want someone in their life, but want to remain unmarried.

Maintaining a measured distance and calculated remoteness can be emotionally draining, especially when you're two thousand miles away wondering just where your love-mate is when you call and get the answering machine.

Will you fuss? Be consumed by clashing emotions? Fret about with whom and where your lover is? And why? Will you wonder, "What's happening behind my back?" It's only natural some people will. But they are not candidates for this type of relationship.

When couples embark on a relationship of such complexity, sticking to boundaries may be daunting. There's a fine line between owning and leasing. If you're insecure in any way, or monogamous and require regular sex, never consider this type of relationship. Lack of control and contradictory feelings of jealousy and a strong desire to maintain your independence will eat you alive.

The upside is, for the footloose and fancy-free, it can work splendidly.

A POSITIVE EXAMPLE

"At this time in my life, I'm not so sure I want to get married again," says Ginny*, a girlishly pretty sixty year old. "I mean, I see Sam* exclusively, and he sees only me, and we do have a committed relationship; but I have lived alone now for seven years. Sam has lived alone for twelve. It would be hard to go back to being tethered to someone or to think of myself as part of a couple. We each have our own space—emotionally and physically."

After her divorce Ginny presumed the road to survival was to meet a man to replace what she lost. "I thought I would be a whole person again by having someone around to share my life. But after awhile, I wasn't finding anyone who lived up to what I had before.

Something else was happening to Ginny. She was developing as an individual, learning to cope with being alone, and she liked who she was becoming. It was with this new-found confidence that she packed up her home and belongings in New York City and moved to Albuquerque.

Shortly after arriving, Ginny got a job in a jewelry store, through which she developed friendships and a social life as a single. "I got my personal act together," she says, "and little by little the devastation of my divorce dissipated. I could almost see how it had happened."

When she realized she could make it on her own, Ginny began to enjoy herself apart from any relationship and decided unless the quality of her life wasn't going to be greatly enhanced, she didn't see any reason to get married again. "I stopped running scared," Ginny revealed.

"So when I met Sam, I saw I was able to love a man from that point of view," says Ginny. "And what I love about us is when we're apart, we talk on the phone every day, share the excitement of our separate lives. When Sam comes home, for three, maybe four nights we are so close, we sleep with our toes practically interlocked, then gradually we simmer down, and resume more independent roles."

Ginny will go off and have dinner with her friends, attend the Philharmonic—which Sam hates. He does his own thing and there's no guilt, no trying to appease or compromise.

"We're both pretty selfish, and it's okay. It can be boring being married. God, if I had cut off my head," Ginny says laughing, "it would have taken my ex-husband three weeks to notice! When you are apart some of the time, you become aware of the little things that make being in love fun."

Several months a year, Sam, a land developer, lives and works in Palm Beach, but during the winter months, he flies west to his home in Albuquerque where he met Ginny six months ago. Even though she maintains a separate home, Ginny and Sam spend every night together either at his house or hers. On holidays, Ginny's three children and grandchildren join their mother and Sam.

"My kids add another dimension," brags Ginny. "I am so totally devoted to them—buy them anything I want—I don't want someone interfering with that. In second marriages, her money and his money—how you separate who pays for what— plays a big role. I don't want to be admonished for spoiling my grandkids. If I want to order rack of lamb, I do it—and pay for it myself if necessary. If I were married, that would be a whole different story."

On the other hand, Ginny feels that very shortly she and Sam will be forced to come to a decision. She says, "We miss each other terribly when we're apart. And yes, there is that wondering just what he's up to. However, right now I'm very happy—definitely not ready to make a decision. Down the road, though, there will come a day when I will want more than a friendship. I'll want a meaningful commitment. Today, the choices are mine."

During our conversation, I tried to get Ginny to tell me what would change this romance into a more committed relationship. I wanted her to define the missing component. Ginny hedged, and came up with lots of excuses, but nothing really concrete until she said, "There are certain things about Sam that bother me. I'm not sure I love him enough to want to put up with them." I got the feeling Ginny was wiped out from giving thirty unconditional years of her life to her ex-husband.

Perhaps, during those worst years, Ginny may have formulated her idea of the perfect spouse and may be expecting that in her next man. I also think she's afraid of getting hurt.

"When my ex-husband and I were first married, he patented a small computer component. We started his business in our garage. I used to spend half my days invoicing and packing the shipments. The kids toddled at my feet while I worked. I was willing then to give my husband everything I had. When the business became a world-wide conglomerate, we were worth millions—all we had left of our marriage in the end. I won't compromise myself ever again."

Taking it slowly, Ginny is considering going to Palm Beach for a few months to see if she and Sam could live together on a more permanent basis—and if she can put up with traveling back and forth. "Practically speaking," says Ginny, "it really is dumb to have four houses."

On the other hand, it may be the four houses and everything else—staying up all night reading a great book when she wants to, the intermittent separations, the lack of money, prenuptial agreement, and inheritance hassles—that make this love affair so wonderful.

A NEGATIVE EXAMPLE

"I met Trevor* four years ago," says the British model, Michelle. "He is a world champion athlete, and I attended one of his races. Afterward, friends of mine introduced us and I invited him to a party I was giving that night. By the time he arrived, I had run out of food, but I fed him party cake and we laughed a lot about that. The next day he asked me out."

Michelle says Trevor fell in love with her because "I am this crazy, fun person who everybody loves. He's sort of a mad scientist—and very introverted," says Michelle, who explained Trevor has his doctorate in chemistry and has worked on some high-powered, national projects. "You know these scientific guys," Michelle laughed. "The difference between Trevor and me is he calculates how to open the bag to get the apples out. I rip open the bag and don't give a damn *how* I get the apples out." The other difference was Trevor was born independently wealthy. She says, "We are complete opposites."

Michelle's carefree lifestyle appealed to Trevor, who retired at the age of 33 to focus solely on his sports career. Michelle says she taught him how to open up and make friends. "This guy lived in a cave the whole time he was in the science program. Through me, he met a lot of different and interesting people. He learned how to dress nicely, what all the hot music was, how to be cool. He's a hundred percent different now."

Michelle lives in Manhattan, but because she was often on location in Los Angeles, she got to see Trevor—who lived there year round—every other week. "After each of my shoots," Michelle said, "we'd meet up, always in these fabulous, posh places. And either he would stay in my hotel, or I would stay in his house in LA. It was always exciting." So exciting the couple lost track of reality.

Michelle juggled schedules and jobs, over the years, so she could visit Trevor. "I always had my bag packed—it was grueling. The bad part of our whirlwind relationship was when I would get back to New York, I found my clients and friends counted me out of doing things because I was never there. I was so lonely. The social life I established in New York was slipping away." Michelle expected Trevor to fill that void.

One day Michelle decided to stop out-of-state location modeling and concentrate on her real estate business. "I wasn't getting any younger. My parents are in England and, with no one to fall back on financially, I had to think about my future and supporting myself."

Nevertheless, she was in love with Trevor, and their unmarried commitment prevailed. Michelle had flown back and forth to Los Angeles for almost three and a half years when she and Trevor started making plans for her to leave New York and move there permanently. "Trevor was so excited about my moving in with him," Michelle remembers. "He had completely redecorated his bedroom for us. That would give us time to find a new place of our own when we figured out where we wanted to live. Together, we made all the wonderful plans young lovers make." Michelle said, "Everything that last week we were together was 'we...we...we.' Trevor never said *we* in all the years we had been together!" Michelle exclaimed. "It was brilliant!"

The following Monday, Michelle left Los Angeles to return to New York to start packing. "I was on top of the world," she said. By the time her plane had landed, Trevor's father had died. And that was the turning point of their relationship.

When Trevor got back to LA after his father's funeral, he called Michelle and got her answering machine message that abruptly informed him, "I had a really bad day. I need a root canal that will cost me a couple of grand, and I just learned my house needs repairs to the roof. I'm in a really bad mood. Don't call me today, I'll talk to you tomorrow."

Trevor, who needed Michelle most at that time, hung up after hearing her message and realized just how different their lives were. Michelle's life revolved around Trevor, but she still had friends and business obligations in New York. He was on the West Coast with his own life and friends. Upset by what appeared to be Michelle's total lack of concern for his grief, Trevor believed that their joining forces would ultimately not work out. Meanwhile, Trevor called Michelle and told her so.

"I do agree I should have put my own shit aside when Trevor was at his lowest point," Michelle regrets. " I should have been there for him."

Although one cannot excuse her thoughtlessness, couples who are not regularly together cannot possibly be attuned to each other's day-to-day emotions. The distance creates discontinuity. Emotions experienced miles away lose their depth.

Michelle says Trevor came to the conclusion their life together was a fantasy. He told her it wasn't fair for her to expect him to be everything to her, nor her to be everything to him. He realized that although they were together most weekends, they each had established separate lives on opposite coasts. The reality of their making a success of marriage was slim. "I don't hate Trevor for that," Michelle decided. "I only hate how it came about out of the blue. He really broke my heart."

But did this end result really come out of the blue? Chances are his father's death magnified whatever misgivings Trevor may have had from the outset and brought them to the surface. Often he had told Michelle, "I can't give you what you want."

"Since then we've been talking," says Michelle. "But I no longer want to see him long distance." But because they're involved in the same sport, she knows they're eventually going to run into each other. They're going to try to stay friends. But Michelle says she begged him, "Tell me when you start to see someone else because it will kill me."

Three months after their split, Michelle knew Trevor hurt her terribly, but maybe he did her a favor. "I was so dependent on this one person for my own happiness. I was willing to walk away from my career, which pays me a lot of money every year. I was willing to walk away from the two duplexes I bought eleven years ago, from which I get rental income. I was living my life for Trevor. I was so blinded by my love for him, I didn't think about what I had here that I had built for myself."

Admitting she can be a bit of a baby, Michelle said, "I wanted him to be my knight in shining armor because I never had that in my whole life, and because he is older than I am—he's thirty-eight and I'm thirty-one." Michelle thinks the pressure of her moving in with Trevor meant he had to live up to everything he promised. "He promised me a baby. He promised me a life together. I thought I'd never have to worry about anything again because he's wealthy, and I'll be wealthy, too, with my career."

Looking back at it now, Michelle knows Trevor didn't want to settle down. Which is why, initially, the global love affair appealed to him. "I really believe now, if I had moved there," Michelle considered, "we would have broken up, and I would have lost a lot.

"It wasn't real. Every time we were together it was a honeymoon, ordering room service or ordering in all the time, making love because we knew I was going to be leaving soon—but we never did the dishes together."

Michelle says she can't imagine being with anyone else right now. "I don't want to touch anyone else. I have to heal." But she knows in the long run she will find someone.

"I was in love with being Trevor's girlfriend," Michelle realizes now. "A woman's got to keep her life. I gave up too much."

The dangerous side of a global love affair is that you can get strung along far longer than if you were living nearby. In Michelle's case, she subjected herself to three and a half years of continual uprooting, exorbitant travel expenses, and turmoil. It is essential to put a time limit on these relationships because when you're apart, you fantasize only the good about the relationship. On the rare times you're together, you choose to ignore problems. In the back of your mind you think, "It's not a big deal because I'm leaving soon." Global love affairs are unnatural and oftentimes staged.

Procrastination and being in limbo cause a relationship's slow death. Without a definitive time frame, global couples can go on for years and often do. If you want to get married and your partner hedges, not knowing where you stand will turn your insides out. Give yourself one year. If you're no closer to marriage, get out.

If a marital test drive serves any purpose at all, it should be tested in a situation as close to marriage as possible. Think about what you would expect from your global partner if he or she lived nearby.

If you're the one doing all the traveling, try this: "I can't afford to come out this weekend. Will you help pay?" Or, "I can't miss work, can you come out here?" If your significant other agrees to visit you, the marital test drive might turn into marriage. On the other hand, if he or she says, "Get here when you can," you know the love affair is doomed.

Only when both partners are willing to put up with the same amount of inconvenience and equally give up and give in should one partner sacrifice his or her lifestyle and make the move. The global relationship offers all the excuses one needs never to marry. "We'll talk about it when you get here." Or, "I'll think about it after you leave," could go on forever unless someone makes a decision.

NONCOMMITTAL;
BUT COMMITTED

I can't help but wonder, "Does everyone over forty have to be married?" Just asking the question is a huge step for me, who started off thinking my eternal happiness—and everyone else's—rested on a marriage certificate. And even if I keep in mind that most of the women I come into contact with would rather be dead than not married, I still wonder if marriage is always the best choice in every situation.

Now that I just turned fifty—and have been happily married twenty-seven years—would I ever want to marry again if something happened to Sam, who's fifteen years my senior? I'm not sure. But I am certain I would not want to be alone. Still, would I want to be a wife again? And what kind of guy would want me if I didn't?

I cannot discount the many conversations I have had with women of all ages who call me year after year for support, whose sole identity rests upon being Mrs. Somebody. And there are those singles "of a certain-age"—never-marrieds, divorcees, and widows—who tell me expectations of getting married is their oxygen.

Not counting the ones pinning their hopes on jerks, other women tell me they aren't satisfied just having a respectable man around. Rather than sit back and enjoy the relationship they grumble because, "He won't commit.... He's avoiding marriage.... I can't get him to sit down and talk about it." These are just a few of the complaints I hear from women.

When I ask them, "Is he good to you? Is he responsible? Does he respect you?" Many say, "Yes...but I want more."

More what? An engagement ring? A marriage commitment—the bills paid? Will that be a positive change? I agree, it's hell to remain single when everyone's wondering, "What's wrong? Why won't he marry her?" But ask yourself, is he capable of delivering? For whatever the reasons, some men aren't, though they are in the minority.

Fewer men than you think have an aversion to marriage. One Harris poll showed over 90 percent of men marry at some point in their lives. Nevertheless, if you're living with one of the few holdouts, and you want marriage, it could mean he'll walk if you dig in your heels.

A lot of women get wrapped up in the chase. First, they think "I need a decent guy in my life." But once they get one, and then focus on convincing him to marry, some men, for various reasons resist. If you're young, want to settle down, have kids, or need the security of a wedding band, a house and white picket fence, then time is of essence. You'd better move on to someone else. In most cases, living with someone won't fulfill those goals.

On the other hand, if you are older, have had a couple of kids, are independent, have a career that leaves little time for wifely duties, don't need a meal ticket, and want a hassle-free companion, living with and loving a guy who's not into marriage might turn out better than you think.

Recently, I had a discussion with Tom. He opened my eyes to what a woman can expect in a man who's not keen on marriage. I knew right off the bat he is a good, decent, honest person. He showed me that a long-term, living-together relationship is doable for some women. I gathered from what he had to say, at this point in his life, he's not out for a marital test drive.

In contrast to the emotional interviews of women who complained about their men's lack of interest in discussing marriage, Tom's dispassionate discourse was refreshing, if a bit chilly. Although he emphasized the financial concerns many live-in men and second husbands have, he convinced me that just because a guy doesn't want to get married doesn't mean he doesn't love you. Many live-ins told me "Marriage is just a piece of paper." They may have a point.

Unlike a lot of the people I talked to, Tom appeared uncertain about revealing too much. He talked fast and covered a lot of ground, but avoided discussing intimate details. I sensed he was not used to talking about loving—and his reluctance could drive a significant other right up the wall! I also sensed he was doing me a huge favor. Getting personal wasn't easy for him.

"If I wanted to have children I would have gotten married," explained Tom, a fifty-four-year-old airline pilot. "I think kids need that stability. For seventeen years, I lived with the same woman, a very successful physician whose career was established. She had two kids and didn't want any more. Still, in my mind, we had a commitment. A lot of guys get married over and over only to divorce. That's not a commitment."

"For fifteen years," he went on, "I had a good relationship that coincided with both our careers and lifestyles. Over the last two years, we grew apart, but it didn't happen overnight. She said over and over again she wanted to talk about it, but we never got around to it." With the exception of the last two years, Tom said their years together were very fulfilling. I have a feeling he was devoted to her, but never told her so. The unofficial marriage may have lasted longer than it should have because Tom was away a lot of the time. "The relationship thrived on our individual autonomy." Tom said. "When we got together, we looked forward to seeing each other. We had something to talk about, and didn't have time to get into hassles about who squeezed the toothpaste the wrong way."

I thought it unusual that Tom felt no need to talk about this woman's physical appearance. He did mention, though, he and his ex liked to scuba dive and ski. He liked to work out, but to her, a walk was a heavy workout. She was into computers; he had no interest. Little by little their lives went in different directions. "She's been living with someone else for the past four years, so I guess she's not into marriage, either," he decided. To him, that was the extent of it.

After their split, Tom was surprised to learn it took her a couple of years to get over it. He was surprised by how much she had really loved him. I am inclined to think it is possible she had second thoughts about bypassing marriage. *One partner almost always wants to get married. One partner almost always gets hurt.*

Still, according to Tom, the break-up was as clean and as neat as the relationship itself. You'd think after seventeen years, some animosity would exist, or perhaps a hint of regret. But he expressed none of that. Throughout my discussion with Tom, I felt no passion. I sensed restraint typical of certain cultures that discouraged members from showing emotion. Yet, I sensed he'd give any woman in need the shirt off his back.

"From the very beginning," Tom said, "I wanted to keep our money separate. She wanted a joint checking account, but I didn't think that was a good idea." The couple bought a house together, and discussed and shared the expenses of major home improvements. When it came to the everyday stuff, Tom told me, "I paid for certain items; she paid for certain items. It came out pretty even." If she wanted to redecorate, his live-in took her own money and just did it. "She didn't ask me." Tom laughed for the first time. "I'd come home and there was a new couch, and say to myself, *'Okay.'* Fortunately, our tastes were similar." If Tom and his live-in went on vacation they split the bill right down the middle. "I think it is unusual that we both were financially independent, and equally capable of living quite comfortably on our own."

For Tom and his unofficial wife, keeping their money separate seems to have been a positive aspect for both of them. He said, "When I talk to people living with partners who don't contribute equally, especially if there is a great disparity in the amounts being contributed, that seems to be a source of considerable tension in the relationship for the one who is putting in the greater amount."

"When we broke up," Tom explained, never going into the details of how and when, "the real estate market was soft. We had a really beautiful home, and neither of us wanted to give it away. I had no problem hanging onto it with her, but she insisted upon buying me out." Within the span of a 30-second phone call, a figure was agreed upon. No quibbling. It was over and done with. Because everything was kept so separate, it was just as easy to *separate*.

Tom passionlessly proved this relationship never got to the level of love needed to sustain a marriage. However, if you are sure you could end a live-in relationship feeling, 'It was good while it lasted,' then you're a candidate for a nonchalant, business-like partnership that throws in regular sex and an escort as perquisites. But it's a long shot that—when put to the test—you'll really be able to handle that.

Curious about Tom's need to be in another relationship right away, I asked him, "Are you living with someone now?"

"No. But I have been dating the same woman—who's ten years younger—since I moved here almost four years ago." Can't knock this guy's loyalty.

I asked him, "Since you're only home four or five days per month, why don't you live with her?"

"I'm there a lot, but I won't stay over if her two kids are there. She doesn't want her eighteen-year-old throwing it back into her face. I do a lot of work on her house. And since she has a nicer home, I really enjoy it." A few years ago when Tom's job relocated, he bought a duplex as a crash pad to rent to other pilots. "It's a real cash cow," he said, "but not a home."

"Is your new girlfriend as financially well-off as your former live-in?"

"Not really. What makes her so attractive to me is that she is extremely wary of ever becoming financially dependent upon me. In a very subtle way that won't embarrass her, I'll write a check, and say this is for the groceries. Or, here's a check, I want this done to the house. Since I'm here so much, this is for me, too." Tom says it makes him feel good to give her these little gifts, but to also know it isn't expected. "That's comforting," he stressed.

Considering Tom is a traditionalist, I wondered what would have happened if his former live-in had needed him just a little bit more and wasn't so independent. Would that have made a difference in the outcome of their relationship? We'll never know. However, women might want to bear in mind that part of a man's innate nature is to provide, safeguard, and watch out for loved ones. If you take away that need to provide, you just may take away some of his need to be with you.

Making no mention of what would happen to his present relationship, Tom said, "When I retire in six years, I'll move back to Florida. I've got a lovely home there. I've got a lot of plans—maybe they're fantasies—about what I want to do then, including traveling."

Compartmentalizing his desire for a regular companion and his need to remain independent, I decided no woman should hold her breath to become Tom's wife. Because he has avoided marriage, I concluded Tom didn't need a wife for the usual reasons—to cook, to clean, to make a nice home, and to provide a family—like so many other men. But I got the feeling he will always have a long-term woman in his life, and look upon her as a trusted friend.

New York City psychotherapist and coauthor of *Cold Feet: Why Men Don't Commit*, Dr. Marlin Potash summed it up: "If you're living together, and you both know that's all it is, that's okay." You can have a lovely time together and have a committed, unmarried partnership as long as you both know the rules.

Curious how he would respond, I asked Tom, "What advice would you offer a guy, who's not into marriage, about living with someone long term?"

"A great deal of honesty is required in a relationship," he said. "And men who aren't honest in their relationships don't usually practice it in their business dealings, or anywhere else in their lives."

Tom answered my earlier question. If I, or any over-forty self-sufficient, career- or goal-oriented mother and wife was in the market for an unofficial spouse, would there be a suitable candidate? If he treated me like Tom treats his significant others—and we both understood that's all it was—I have to say, "yes."

But I have the feeling if you ask Tom's new girlfriend what she would truly like to see happen, she would confide "to be married to Tom."

EXCEPTIONS
TO THE RULE

Throughout this book, I have referred to statistics that prove trial marriage is a short-lived proposition for LTCs. However, there are exceptions. Some LTCs can live together forever and never feel the need to marry. Although they may be an enigma to their families and friends, these are happy, stable couples content with and committed to their relationship. Their experiences prove that in sickness and in health, one can be perfectly satisfied remaining an unofficial spouse.

Forty-six and never been married would be the kiss of death to some women, but not Sarah*. "My sister is getting married for the sixth time," she informed me. "I've lived with the same man for twenty-three years! Now tell me who's more stable? Who's got real security?"

Sarah was twelve when her sixteen-year-old sister got pregnant and had to get married. The revolving-door of brother-in-laws may have made a difference in her attitude toward marriage. "They certainly influenced my attitude about marital soundness—there isn't any. A spouse can walk out at any time. Furthermore, up until two years ago, child support was bullshit." Actually, it still is.

"I never expected marriage laws to protect me," she said. "I should be smart enough to deal with whatever is handed to me. Nobody's going to look after you, but yourself." Sarah, whose father is an attorney, said that she learned from him at a young age that state laws and legal remedies give false security.

During her freshman year of high school, Sarah met Fred*, and they became casual friends. They never dated, but by the end of high school, they were in business together with four other friends. "We ran rock concerts and booked local bands," she said.

By the time the two business associates entered the same university at eighteen, they became best friends and remained so all through college. "But we dated other people," she said. "The romantic part was always there, and I think we knew it for a long time, but we had such a good friendship we didn't want to spoil it."

They felt it was inevitable that something would happen, just *when* was the question. "One Halloween, Fred and I decided we would get dressed up and go out. We had a couple of drinks too many for people who hardly drink." One thing led to another and they never left the house. The duo passed out, and when they woke up the next morning, Sarah looked sheepishly at Fred, "and he looked at me," she fondly reminisced, "and we both said, 'Nah. Couldn't be.'" Relieved they'd finally gotten past their inhibitions, they simultaneously burst out, 'Oh, what the hell!'"

Less than two weeks later, Fred moved in with Sarah. Because the couple felt it would be better to get a new place together—"It wouldn't be either his nor mine"—they spent New Year's Eve, 1975, moving into their new apartment and have been together ever since.

Like married couples who want to get ahead, Sarah took additional jobs like babysitting for her musicians' children and accounting work so she and Fred could save up enough money to buy a house. By then they were managing more famous groups like the Commodores and the original Jackson Five. They bought a recording studio and then sold it a few years later.

More than any other job, Sarah found she loved caring for children. She went back to school to get the proper credentials to open a day care center. In 1980, she opened her own center. She sold the business, but not the property, in 1989.

Fred went on to graduate school and received his Masters of Music. He also took a course in musical editing and started making radio commercials. He is now working on his doctorate in music. In 1990, Sarah took a job with the federal government working for the Head Start Program. She is responsible for policy-making and regulations.

This couple's accomplishments are quite a remarkable tribute to their support for one another and they are totally dedicated to each other and to each other's endeavors. Yet, Fred and Sarah have chosen not to marry.

What irks Sarah is the needling they've received over the years, about when they're finally going to "settle down." How much more settled could they be? Or, how much more married? Remembering in several states they would be common-law partners by now—protected by those state's marriage laws—Sarah and Fred made me aware of the advantages of the laws which allow a common-law couple to remain somewhat anonymous. These couples take the position that provisional, matrimonial happiness is nobody's business.

As parents, many of us might think Sarah and Fred's unofficial marriage sidesteps the total package, which is why I noted that their record of lifetime achievements, thus far, made no mention of having children.

"We thought about having a family, and because I absolutely adore children we actively talked about it quite a bit," Sarah said. "But I don't feel they have to be my children to enjoy them and to have fun with them."

The glitch was that Fred experimented with drugs from 1970 to 1972. Although he has not used drugs nor taken a drink since then, he and Sarah, who never used drugs, worried about birth defects. "So we decided if we were ever going to have children, we would adopt because there were enough children in the world already that need loving parents," she said.

"So basically," I pried, "you never felt the need to get married?"

"That's really it," said Sarah. "I don't need to pay the state five dollars to give me permission to cohabit," she laughed. "I know how devoted Fred and I are to each other—how committed. And even if we had children, we probably would not have gotten married. Fred is a very private person...a very quiet person. For him to get wrapped up in the marriage scene would undoubtedly be more upsetting than it's worth. And I respect that."

From a practical standpoint, however, Sarah said the only way she and Fred would consider marriage is if Fred was offered a full professorship at some university, where she could go to law school for free.

Curious about how the outside world has reacted to them as a long-term LTC, I asked Sarah, "Do you feel you have ever been discriminated against because of your unofficial marriage?"

"Oh yes, when our real estate agent was showing us houses in 1978, she couldn't bring herself to say we were an unmarried couple. She would tell the seller we were engaged. Fred told her, 'Don't say that.'"

"Basically, that was unimportant," she said. "But when we decided upon a house, and the owner found out we had no intention of getting married, he was adamant about canceling the contract." When Sarah and Fred made a huge stink and threatened to sue the deal went through. "But it was really unpleasant."

"What's the quickest and best way to get back at somebody who confronts you with disparaging remarks?"

"Basically," Sarah said, "if they push me about marriage, I stare them right in the face, put them on the defensive, and say nothing more than, 'Why?' Should I have to get married to placate the rest of the world? Or change my status to make it more socially acceptable so *other* people can feel more comfortable? In the long run that could affect my relationship."

"Have either you or Fred ever really tested your level of commitment?"

Without hesitation, Sarah said, "When I was very, very sick about seventeen years ago and went through a major depression, Fred could have walked out in a heartbeat. He didn't."

Wondering if her live-in situation might have caused the depression, I asked, "What brought that on?"

"Major diet pills and a quick loss of seventy-five pounds. In those days diet pills were very common and weren't considered dangerous." Sarah said, even though she was on a prescription drug and being monitored by a physician, "All of a sudden they just made me nuts." She says she was suicidal for a couple of weeks, and went through holy hell for six weeks until her body chemistry straightened itself out. "When it happened, Fred was supportive—with me all the way. And with me afterwards."

"If there is one," I asked, "what's the most aggravating thing that has happened to you as a result of living together?"

"The only aggravating thing about living together and not being legally married is that I can't call a credit card company and straighten out a bill. We have joint ownership of all our real estate and businesses, and we have had a joint checking account since we began living together, but we have maintained separate credit cards. Because I pay the bills, I have to explain it all to Fred so he can get on the phone and call." Sarah said Fred is so disinterested in money matters that even when he calls the credit card company, "it's still all screwed up. Eventually, I have to get back on the phone, and by then straighten *everybody* out!"

"A lot of live-in couples slam the door and never look back when trouble begins in the relationship. How have you and Fred survived that?" I asked.

"First and foremost, Fred and I have a rock-solid friendship. If he came to me and said he wasn't happy, and wanted out, I would let him go. And he would let me go. And I am certain we would still be best friends. But don't think every day is wonderful." Sarah explained that after a certain number of years together, her relationship went, and still goes through cycles. "You'll have your madly romantic stages," she said. "And then you'll have those times when you think, 'Oh my God, I'm still living with *who*!'"

Sarah says, "We all have months where we want to just close the door and say, 'leave me alone.' It doesn't mean you don't love your partner, but that you just don't want to deal with him or her or anybody right now. When you have a spouse or partner who is willing to give you that room, you know the relationship is solid."

Sarah knows her relationship's success comes from being able to tell Fred anything. *Lack of communication* is such an overused term for every relationship malady that it seems trite. It's also one big fat excuse for not wanting to make the effort. How many times have you heard, "We split up because we couldn't communicate." That's malarkey. Get help for yourself and learn how. There are enough books and magazines that suggest such techniques from weekend encounter groups to full-blown therapy. Take advantage of learning to say what's on your mind while test-driving marriage. If you decide to marry that person, you stand a greater chance of having a successful marriage.

MARRIAGE IS A RESPONSIBILITY
I'M TOO YOUNG TO KNOW

Michelle and Ryan, both twenty-four years old, are the only LTC among their circle of friends in Toronto. "All my other friends are married," she says. But her circumstances are considerably different. Michelle is living with Ryan because her strong-willed mother threw her out of the house, not once, but twice. Michelle says it was the best thing her mother could have done because what she has with Ryan is developing into an incredible relationship of love and respect. Michelle has always been loved dearly by her mother and father, but expressing her opinions was not something they wanted her to do.

The fights that resulted in Michelle's evictions were always petty. "The first time I was thrown out, I had told my mother

I couldn't clean my room because I had a university test the next day. I felt doing well on that was more important than making my bed," Michelle explained. The fight—blown completely out of proportion—got physical and Michelle was ordered to leave. She stayed at a friend's house for eight months and says, "You don't know what it's like not to be able to go home when you're young and need your parents."

Even though her mom and dad promised it would never happen again, it did several months later. Michelle vowed she would never go back. She stayed a couple of months with friends, but by then she was twenty-two and had dated Ryan for four years. Michelle needed a place to live, and she says Ryan felt it was time for him to move out of his parents' home and live on his own. They decided to pool resources and get a place together. "At first we moved in for convenience, but having dated so long, we were ready for the next step." Michelle and Ryan haven't opted out of marriage; they're in a holding pattern until they feel they can both handle that responsibility and their careers. Their partnership has lasted fifteen months, and each day it gets better.

"We have these rules," she explained. "The most important one is we are not allowed to swear at each other, or call each other names. Once I got really mad at Ryan. As usual, it was over something really stupid. He put salt in my drink when we went out one night. I was really mad, and I called him an f—ing asshole. I had no idea he would be so upset over something like that, but he said, 'Don't *ever* call me a name again!'" She said Ryan's parents called each other names, and he felt awful when they would degrade each other. Michelle and Ryan's rules require the couple talk to each other, and explain, "I feel really bad because..." and not evade their problems with name-calling.

Unlike other couples who move in together, theirs was an equal partnership from the very beginning. They didn't go through the hassles other couples do when they can't agree on what colors to paint the bathroom or which pots and pans to buy. "We have joint bank-and credit card accounts," Michelle said, "but that got us into a bit of trouble. We had never had a credit card before, and Ryan got carried away with his spending on CDs and gadgets." Because Michelle paid the bills, she says Ryan had no idea where the money was going. "One day I wrote down all the expenses for him, and handed the bill-paying job over to him. I bought a big ledger book, and we both entered everything we bought. Even a pack of gum." Within a few months, Ryan was chastising Michelle for spending two dollars a day on coffee, complaining that that was sixty dollars per month. Michelle now makes her coffee at home and takes it with her. "I could buy a new pair of shoes with that money."

Michelle is waiting for Ryan to propose to her. She knows they will get married one day. But Ryan wasn't ready when she began to talk about marriage a couple of years ago. She told Ryan she would stop bringing it up if he promised one day he would propose. They cut the deal. She knows it will happen, but realizes they are both too young and have too much to do right now. The only thing she insisted he agree upon at the outset was having children. Because Ryan's parents are divorced, Michelle said he doesn't feel good about having kids. But she wants a family, and told him if that wasn't going to happen, she would move on to another relationship. He's agreed to have children.

Their plans to move to Australia in the year 2000 have Michelle and Ryan saving as much money as possible. They both work very long hours. But Michelle is used to that. Since she was fourteen, she's worked. All through high school she held two part-time jobs. Ryan is a recording engineer, which Michelle explains is a tough area to break into and do well in. "Australia does not have a big recording industry, and Ryan thinks he has a great opportunity there." She also is looking forward to the challenge of emigrating to a new country, which will accept them more quickly if they apply as individuals, not as a married couple.

Michelle works at a bank, and her company pays for the graduate courses she is taking. Her undergraduate degree is in political science and law and society. Right now, she is working toward getting her securities and mutual funds license. When she gets to Australia, she would like to teach twelfth grade political science.

Another reason they don't want to marry right now is that Michelle feels she should be well established before she has a family. "I see my friends who didn't go to college, and they are really struggling. I want to be as successful, or more successful than Ryan, before I start a family. Anything can happen, and I want to be prepared for the worst. Besides, the challenge of making more money than Ryan is good for him—good for our relationship."

When Michelle and Ryan first moved in together, he did not know anything about housework and laundry, and Michelle did everything. Because Michelle was going to school and held a full-time and a part-time job, his lazy boy days were numbered. Michelle taught Ryan how to cook and clean, and how to do the laundry. "Now," Michelle brags, "he is a gourmet cook." He's even gotten into baking. "The only thing he refuses to do," she said, laughing, "is the bathroom. He hates that."

When Michelle has a paper due and it's getting late, Ryan will stay up all night with her to type it as she writes. "We're constantly motivating each other to push forward so we can buy a house and a car, and get those things out of the way. I don't want to be struggling financially when we get married." Michelle used to be a homebody, but since they have lived together, Ryan takes her to small clubs to hear the latest groups. Formerly always working and studying, she is now developing balance in her life.

This couple will probably beat the odds against trial marriage because it appears when the time comes for Michelle and Ryan to get married, their test drive will have given them the stability they need to enjoy the rest of their lives together. Neither partner is waiting for the other to make life happen. Individually stable, they have both feet firmly planted. Each could get along just fine without the other. Together they are an extraordinary team and make a good example of what a trial marriage represents. Many LTCs never fully understand why they chose to live together in the first place, and eventually break up. Michelle and Ryan's test drive goes beyond "let's see if we can get along enough to get married." They have learned responsibility, accountability, and that there is a lot more to marriage than making babies—a lesson that will successfully carry them through the duration of this relationship, and, if they do break up, any relationship.

HOW LIVING TOGETHER
CAN BACKFIRE ON YOU

California therapist Dr. Peter Pearson, cofounder of the Menlo Park Couples Institute, recently told a writer from Knight-Ridder, "the presence of underlying love is the key to solving relationship problems. It's not so much the magnitude of the problem, but what lies underneath the problem.

"If people are saying, 'He or she is driving me nuts; I can't stand when he does A, B, or C, but I still love him,' right from there I know [things] can be worked out. People who say, 'She drives me crazy, I don't know why we are together, and I think she's disgusting' are another story," Dr. Pearson says. "When you have that kind of contempt for your partner, that relationship is on life-support. At some point, the best thing is to pull the plug."[1]

As I discussed earlier, many living-together relationships never make it to the altar. Unfortunately, LTCs lose sight that living together is a test drive—a no-guarantees experiment.

Under those circumstances, your extraction in the relationship becomes a fight against the inevitable.

Once the inevitable happens, it's only natural to try to change that part of you that you think caused the break-up. Over time, your self-esteem takes a nose dive.

A stylist for a New York photographer, who has been through several live-in relationships, recently told me, "The more you strike out, the more you feel your approval rating plummeting making you feel less and less desirable to anyone." How you react and feel about yourself after the break-up is often more destructive than the break-up itself.

When a never-married couple dissolves, there's no record of that relationship unless the parties involved have a nasty, public court battle. When Farrah Fawcett and Ryan O'Neal broke off their seventeen-year relationship, they made front-page news. But the rest of the unofficially married population who call it quits have no tabloid clippings, a divorce certificate, or a discarded wedding band to signify their former alliance.

It wasn't until I spoke with many live-in couples who went through splits that I realized they seldom have closure. Many divorced couples have closure because their marriage has been formally terminated by the state in a court of law.

On the following pages, you will discover how former live-ins coped with the mistakes they made while in their unmarried relationships and ultimately, the unhappy endings. I was impressed with how they emerged from the experience wiser than before, ready to enter into a positive, more optimistic relationship—their reward for the years served.

If you think these nasty abuses could never happen to you, think again. The goal of this book is to spare you the heartache that these women endured, and encourage you to apply the lessons they learned the hard way to your relationship.

I JUST COULDN'T GIVE HER
ENOUGH LOVE

You will find many of the people I talk about are from the Virgin Islands. I do the bulk of my writing on Saint Thomas, where I find a cross section of people with a broad range of cultural and societal attitudes.

Two people who have become very special to me are Paul* and Suzie*. Paul owns a water-sports company, and until eighteen months ago, when they took a breather from each other, Suzie and Paul were an item. Separately, they are the two most charming, lovable people you want to know. Together they're catalysts for each other's destruction.

Four years ago, Suzie broke off a marvelous three-year test drive that fell apart when she couldn't deal any longer with her fiancé's meddling ex-wife. For the sake of his kids, she walked away from marrying him.

"I was sick of men, sick of relationships," Suzie emphasized, "and I decided to go to the Caribbean for a long weekend to sail with old friends." She had been on-island for only two hours when Paul walked into a bar and they were introduced. She whispered to her friend, "*That* is my man. This is the guy for me." She couldn't believe it—she had never felt that electric feeling before.

"I can flirt pretty hard," Suzie said, "and so can Paul." The drinks were flowing and within an hour the pair really hit it off. It was a wild night, according to Suzie: "We made fierce, passionate love over and over." By the next day she moved in with him.

Positive this was "it," Suzie flew back to California three weeks later to pack up her old life. She quit her public relations job, and because she honestly didn't think she would need them anymore, gave away bags full of Charles Jourdan pumps and expensive suits and saved the shorts and tee shirts she needed for the island.

It took three years for her to learn "If you don't give yourself six months to a year of relationship fasting, you'll flip-flop from one to the next, and lose who you are."

Paul says, "I'm not sure it was love at first sight, since it was more sexual in the beginning. I'm inclined to think it was lust and then love on both of our parts." Everything the couple did together was great fun, "until after about six months we had our first big fight," Paul said, "and Suzie was on the verge of walking out. And really, that was normal—almost easy for us to accept because we had both dated a lot. We had been through so many relationships—seen them come and go—it would have been easy for us to let it go."

Paul, a handsome thirty-five year old and Suzie, who was once featured in *Playboy* in a college campus pictorial, are well-matched both physically and emotionally. It is easy to see why neither would have to put up with any crap a relationship might dish out.

After their first blowup, Paul said his relationship with Suzie became like a roller coaster. Later fights turned into drunken brawls. "I was never *ever* physical with anyone before, or had someone I love try to hurt me," Paul insists. "But as we became fonder of each other, it became increasingly more difficult for us to walk away from each other." Nevertheless, Suzie packed up and left the island on three different occasions.

Over time, Suzie developed a grave, stress-related disease and had to be hospitalized in California. "I was so filled with rage over never getting my love returned I couldn't stand to look at him, and he couldn't stand to look at me."

Suzie was very much a giver and thought of their relationship as a partnership. "I gave up three years of income so we could put everything back into his business," Suzie says. "I incurred a lot of debt because I never took a paycheck from Paul." It got to the point where she would have to ask him for a dollar to buy a coke. "That was a huge mistake, because I was deluding myself thinking the business was ours. I was wrong."

Paul admitted he was every bit the taker. "And as I kept taking she'd give more." Occasionally, he'd give back, and she would keep hanging on.

I said to Paul, "When Suzie took whatever crumbs you were willing to give her, how did that make you feel?"

Oblivious to my meaning, he said, "I felt secure the whole time. I never worried about Suzie cheating on me. I never had to be jealous about anything. I put my business in her hands and depended on her so much." Now that she's gone, he admits, she spoiled him. He's desperate for someone to help him clean his house, make a decent meal for him; and organize his life as Suzie had. "I didn't have to buy toilet paper for years."

Paul said he thinks Suzie didn't feel secure at all. "I just didn't give her that same security back that made me feel so good," he admits. "And that's what she wanted to get me to understand—that you can stay in a relationship and work things out. Suzie made every effort to get all my love and attention. But in return she wanted to be pampered for doing everything for me."

"And you're not capable of that?"

"Well," Paul thought, "that's what she felt. I think I'm capable of it, but I was concentrating so much on business—putting my business first, her second, I couldn't at the time."

Suzie agreed with that view. "I was the wife," she said, "and his business was the mistress who gets all the goodies."

Paul thinks if he can just get to the point where his business is solidly on its feet, he might be able to achieve more balance in his life. "I always dangled that carrot in front of her. That was ninety percent of the dilemma," he said. " Suzie always told me, 'You make love to your boats.'"

It's important to note that it may not always be an appropriate time to enter a live-in relationship. In Paul's case, he was streched to the limit by extremely stressful situations occuring back-to-back. This may have aggravated his temperment, leading him to act out of character, and reducing his ability to cope with Suzie's demands. Paul has been through four hurricanes since 1989, which would have taken a ravaging toll on anyone, particularly those involved in the watersports industry. Each time the island is hit, you have an ominous uphill climb. On one hand, the challenge of surviving and picking up the pieces can be exciting. On the other, the post-traumatic stress manifests itself in many different ways for years after.

Paul has had other stresses as well. Three years ago, a boat engine blew up and burned all the skin off his legs. He was in intensive care for fifty days. His younger brother died suddenly, and his mother died at any early age. It's easy to see why Paul might need a relationship where he gets more than he gives. That's okay, as long he finds someone willing to play that role.

Suzie says, "I have nothing but good things to say about Paul. If I had to say anything negative, I would say he has limitations like everyone else." She believes his selfishness and need to control his partner are a huge part of his personality and will be hard for any woman to cope with.

Lately, Paul has seen a change in himself. After his brother's death, he says, "I've gotten a lot more spiritual. And I've learned that life really is short and you need to enjoy every day." He and Suzie talk every three or four days. When his brother died, six months after they split up the last time, Suzie didn't hesitate to fly to West Virginia to be with him for five days. "I wanted to take away his hurt and pain—hug him and hold him," she says.

When things were the worst they could get, Paul says, "Suzie was the angel sent to me from heaven. What she did for me was very special."

The former partners are trying desperately to remain friends "and I think we both have this glimmer of hope that one day we might be able to get back together again," Paul said. "Time will tell. If not, Suzie taught me many lessons that I will use the rest of my life about what it takes to make a relationship work."

Suzie says, "I need a man who truly feels he can't live without me," which makes her less optimistic her relationship with Paul can ever resume. "I walked out of there a year and a half ago. If we were going to get back together again, it would have happened already."

Overall, the break-up has been hard for both of them to accept. "I've gone out on a couple of dates. Nothing sexual has happened," Paul says. "But that is going to be the hard part—if Suzie finds someone else, or I do. I'm guilt-ridden, thinking if I just got her back here and loved her…[and gave] her everything she needs, that would be the answer to all the bad things I've done to her, we've done to each other, and to ourselves."

"I was and still am in love with Paul and Paul's potential," says Suzie, who is trying to make a life for herself in California. "I want so much for him to become a success, then apply those same principles to a relationship. But right now, he's not ready to do both. He needs to balance his time both at the job and away from the job because when he's fifty years old, he's going to end up hugging his accounting books. And nothing else."

I asked Suzie, "What would you tell a couple who are going through what you and Paul have put yourselves through?"

She answered as if she'd given this a great deal of thought. "Would you allow somebody you love to be treated this way? Put someone you love in the situation Paul and I put ourselves in and ask yourself, 'Would you allow them to go through that?' Then ask yourself, 'Why am I doing it?'"

When a relationship breaks up, healthy people look back upon the experience as a positive stepping stone to another love affair. If one partner's character flaws caused the break up and he or she was told to change, in the next relationship the "offending" partner should note how those flaws affect his or her new significant other (a control freak to one partner could be positive assertiveness to a different partner). If he or she sees the flaws are producing negative results in the next relationship and it matters, he or she will change.

There is a considerable difference between discovering you need to change character flaws to make your life more fulfilling for *yourself* and having someone ask you to do it for *them*. Mental health therapy plays a major role in achieving self-awareness and how flaws impact someone you love, when you want that love returned.

COPING BY BLOCKING IT OUT

It's amazing who will let go emotionally when you're having a martini at Fifty-Seven Fifty-Seven. Last spring, while I was waiting for Sam at the Four Seasons, I was cleaning up one of the chapters of this book. It was about 4:30 in the afternoon, and the bar was not crowded. A woman sitting at the table next to me asked if I was a writer. I responded, "Yes," and we became involved in the kind of intimate conversation you have when you know you'll never see a person again.

We started chatting about the subject matter of this book, when Suzanne* hesitated, then haltingly said, "I lived with a guy for twenty-four years."

As an American living in Paris, she began, "I don't think Jean-Claude* and I ever chose *not* to get married." "But because most of the women in my family, including my own mother and her sisters have been divorced, I learned early on that there were no guarantees with marriage. Given my emotional state and that I am financially independent, and all the women in my family worked and had many boyfriends, I never gave marriage much thought."

Suzanne said she and Jean-Claude, a well-known French chef, bought a house together and split expenses, as well as closet space. She looked upon their relationship as a marriage. "Except that when we broke up, it was enormously easier because we did not have the hassle of the paperwork of divorce," she said. However, they did have possessions they purchased together, which meant they had to maintain a level of civility while dividing up the household. In the end, Suzanne was able to write a check and buy Jean-Claude out.

"Yet, I never considered a break-up," she said. "There was never any feeling that we would not be together. I know *I* never thought of that."

After two and a half years, Suzanne suspects Jean-Claude was not the right man for her, for all of those years, and that maybe she didn't marry him because somehow she knew that. As if to justify her staying in such a relationship for so long, she asked, "Don't a lot of married people stay together even when they know they're not right for each other?"

"Yes," I agreed. "But when you are married that long, I think people take a longer look at getting out of it."

She remembers they were codependent. Jean-Claude was very insecure. Suzanne provided the confidence, and supported his ego. "He was fun—very good-looking and because he was famous, he opened up all kinds of doors for me. We were comfortable together."

I asked her, "How do you think you have grown from this relationship?"

"In the past, I didn't know how to ask for things. I would much prefer to do for others. Trouble is I get dumped on. After Jean-Claude and I broke up, I learned that those same characteristics were spilling out into my business life. Now, I'm much more demanding in asking coworkers to do things for me. I can say no to people; I don't always have to people-please. I have realized I can't do twelve things at once. I don't have to be perfect—no one's expecting it."

Coping without Jean-Claude, Suzanne says she has now found a place for herself in her own life. "I'm getting to see how much of my independence is real and how much is on automatic pilot." Without Jean-Claude around, she has the time and the inclination to find out if "maybe there's something else going on here," she said. "To get to know myself better." She no longer dates men just to date. "I'd rather go to a party alone than get stuck with someone I don't like, or worry whether he's having a good time."

I sensed her pulling back when I asked, "Did you have a tough time getting over the loneliness?"

"Not really. But I felt blue. It's that child part of me that felt abandoned—or not cared about enough. There's a natural inclination to want to be with someone. Yes, we all like to have someone to come home to, but when you start to need someone for primal reasons, I have trouble accepting that.

"I'll tell you what I really miss," she said. "I miss the day-to-day stuff. Even when we didn't get along, I had someone to share my life with—to understand its everyday, mundane ups and downs. I miss having someone around to let the plumber in, feed the cat, be there when I come home."

Contemplating what she had said, I thought, isn't it at the stage when the fireworks of any love affair begin to die down—yet there's a level of dependency, comfort, forgiveness, and decency left—that the partnership of marriage continues to burn with a steady flame, creating a new level of love? And is it that level most couples who live together without the promise of marriage can't accept or deal with—or don't ever reach? Do they find the less passionate times not good enough, and seek out a new relationship?

While I was still on that thought, Suzanne whispered out of the blue, "We had discussed children, but he didn't want any. And I accepted that. I think people have an evolutionary, almost organic reason why they put off having children. In my case, I was a child myself. I couldn't see Jean-Claude and myself as parents." Just recently, though, she has begun to question her feelings about never having children. She asked herself aloud: "Am I curious? Perhaps. Am I missing something? I'll never know. And do I have regrets? Probably. But life goes on."

I sensed Suzanne constantly fights her need to be independant and seldom allows herself a sentimental moment. I saw how she compartmentalizes her love and protects herself from getting too emotional, when almost as an afterthought, she confided Jean-Claude had an extra- "cohabital" affair with a woman in Nice, with whom he admitted he had two children. When Suzanne found out, they broke up.

I was flabbergasted! It would have been one of the first details *I* would have revealed. But it's almost as if Suzanne was so hurt by the betrayal, she tucked the bad memory into the inner recesses of her mind. The afterthought may have been the only way she could remember it. I wondered if she had ever, *ever* told that part of her story to anyone else.

Her story proves my point: When lovers move in together *one partner almost always wants to get married, and one partner almost always gets hurt.* Suzanne never admitted to herself or to Jean-Claude she might like to get married, never told him she might want to have kids. Did she, by skirting those two major issues, lead him to believe she didn't want either? It's evident she never came to terms with those decisions herself until after the break up.

In many vignettes in this book, you have read these statements, "We didn't touch on that." Or, "Marriage wasn't something we talked about." *Why not?* When people date, then fall in love, they talk about getting engaged, then they talk about when they will get married.

When you talk about the future of a relationship and make plans to be together forever after, you know where you stand and where your partner stands. You know each other's dreams and goals. Maybe what Jean-Claude wanted most was to get married and have children. *But he didn't say it.* Instead, he went behind Suzanne's back and started a family with someone else. Obviously throughout the years he wanted more. If he had said that when he decided it was important to him, maybe years earlier, they would have taken action. They would either have broken up or married. They would not have wasted twenty-four years of their lives and ended up with nothing but bittersweet memories.

You could argue that a couple could be married for the same amount of time and break up. But they don't end up totally empty-handed. They end up with an alliance that went sour, but it was a *sanctioned* alliance, supported by a house of worship and/or the state, and generally the family. When someone reveals that their first marriage ended in divorce, many people react a lot more sympathetically than when they hear that a live-in couple split up. "They'll get over it" meaning "it wasn't real anyway" is the sentiment a forsaken live-in partner usually conjures up.

It is the perception of the seriousness of marriage versus the ephemera of a trial relationship that is the difference, not just to outsiders, but to the parties involved.

I'LL NEVER MAKE THAT MISTAKE AGAIN!

It's hard to believe Brooke*, an all-American beauty and a successful charter boat captain who can also bench-press 110 pounds, would ever have felt insecure about herself. But she did. Two emotionally destructive live-in relationships over several years left her feeling like a failure.

Brooke was eighteen when she moved in with her first significant other. Three years later, she came home one evening with a temperature of 102 degrees. After struggling to get through a 12-hour workday and just wanting to fall into bed, she found her lover in bed with another woman.

Not having a clue as to what I would do, I asked, "What did you *do*?"

"At first, it threw me totally into shock," Brooke remembers. "I didn't yell; but I got really cold towards him. Then I became so angry, I wanted to shoot him!"

"Literally?"

"Yeah, we always had guns in the house for sport. I really thought about killing him."

Fortunately, Brooke called her father first. Knowing she wasn't kidding about shooting him, her dad rushed to her house and managed to calm her down enough to ditch the gun idea. Her boyfriend was pleading, "it will never happen again." But Brooke knew if he did it once, it was only a matter of time before he'd do it again. "And how did I know it hadn't happened in the past?"

"What happened next?" I pried. "Where did his playmate go?"

As Brooke remembers it, she told her to get dressed and leave. "I couldn't really blame her," Brooke said.

After he left, Brooke threw all his belongings out of a second-story window. Unfortunately, this tale doesn't get any better. Brooke and her live-in had a joint checking account. The bulk of the money in the account was Brooke's. After he left the house, his feelings of remorse were obviously short-lived. He took their ATM card and withdrew as much cash as he could after banking hours. The next morning he returned to the bank and cleaned out the checking account to the tune of $8,000. "I was so upset about his screwing around with someone else," Brooke said, "I never thought about the checking account."

After that, Brooke developed ulcers and health problems. She took some time off and visited her brother who lived in Fort Lauderdale. She liked it there. Because she and her ex-partner had so many friends in common, it was difficult to stay in Nantucket, so Fort Lauderdale became her permanent home.

She spent the next year taking it easy, just watching. "I had a lot of 'me' time coming to me," she said. She also changed careers. Before she left Nantucket, she had a high-stress sales job. When she got to Fort Lauderdale, she began studying for her captain's license. "I wore bummy boat clothes, never wore make-up, and just sort of hung out and healed. I had to figure out where I was going with myself."

Two years after Brooke moved to Fort Lauderdale, she met an extremely successful harbor pilot who lived a very glamorous lifestyle. "He was really good for me at the time," Brooke admits, "because I had become really scruffy." To please him, Brooke began to pay attention to her looks again. She and her pilot fell in love and moved in together. However, this time there was no joint anything. In order to make a fast get-away, she initialed all her belongings and kept her personal finances and affairs in order.

Brooke was extremely nervous meeting her lover's tony friends and living up to his expectations. She overreacted to his posh surroundings and began developing feelings of inadequacy. To compensate for what she thought were her shortcomings that led to the failure of her last live-in relationship, and wanting desperately to make this one work, Brooke went overboard thinking she had to be perfect. "I would work all day, which in the boating business means you have to start at 8:00 in the morning and don't often get home until 7:00 at night." Then she'd run home and cook a gourmet dinner, clean up, redo her make-up, and dress up to please her very social boyfriend. "It wasn't long," Brooke said, "before I burned out trying to be something I wasn't." And then decided, "For what?"

Brooke took a hard look at who was putting in the most effort in these relationships. She began to think about a relationship's inequities. "If he insisted we split all the expenses right down the middle, and if he's making a hundred thousand a year, and I'm making less than half of that, he works a three-hour day versus my twelve, why am I allowing him to watch me scrub the floor? Why am I killing myself trying to please him?"

She didn't have to wait to come up with an answer. While she was knee-deep in Mr. Clean, her live-in was having an affair with another woman. "It wasn't all his fault," Brooke said. "Busy being Ms. Perfect, and not letting him know how exhausted I was, I didn't have enough time for him."

Disillusioned by now, turned off by all relationships, Brooke shut down. She needed time to heal. She decided it was time to work on herself. "I was twenty-eight years old, had been through two major, traumatic relationships over a period of ten years. I had nothing but insecurity to show for it. It was time I ditched all the bad feelings to work on myself." The lesson Brooke learned was "You have to be comfortable with yourself before you can be comfortable with someone else. And before you can forgive someone else, you have to be able to forgive yourself."

A year later, Brooke was ready to try again. One afternoon, her brother introduced her to his friend Charlie*. A couple of dates later, they fell in love. Brooke was about to suggest they move in together, when Charlie said, "No way! You've got six months to plan a wedding. Until then, you keep your place, I'll keep mine." They were married last June.

"I'm glad I didn't make the mistake of living with someone again," Brooke said. "This time, I can't walk out the door so easily. Which means each day Charlie and I have to learn a little bit more about each other and develop trust."

SIX AND A HALF YEARS AND POOF! IT'S OVER

Emma* has spent the last year of her life sorting out what went wrong with her six-and-a-half-year live-in love affair. "It upsets me most not knowing what I did wrong," she said. "One day, it was over, but Raymond* never told me why."

Emma was a 28-year-old freelance cinematographer in Los Angeles when she met her boyfriend, Raymond, 29, a fledgling actor, who worked as a mâitre d' at night. Because they both had been married before, they decided to live together and test drive marriage this time around. They split all household costs down the middle, but that's where the equality in the relationship ended. Raymond had a three-year-old son, and an ex-wife who was a drug addict, who had custody of the boy. Emma describes her addiction to cocaine as so bad that "one Christmas morning we went over to Raymond's ex-wife's house to share Billy's* excitement when he opened his Christmas gifts. His mother was so drugged out, the gifts were piled under the tree, but none of them were wrapped!"

After that Emma felt she wanted to get close to Raymond's son and give him some stability. The trouble was, once she showed the boy a little attention, Raymond dumped Billy on Emma during his weekend visitations. The sad twist is that when she first met Raymond, Emma was attracted to his sensitivity and responsibility as a parent. A couple of years after she moved in, they seldom did anything together as a "family." "Soon, I was disciplining the boy," remembers Emma. "That's not what I wanted, but I felt badly that Billy was emotionally abandoned by both his mother and father. I thought I should fix this."

Eventually, Emma, who was a rising star in films, started to turn down jobs to care for the boy. Her career stood still. "That was my fault," she said, "because I was using childcare responsibilities as an excuse not to pursue my career. And I thought Raymond would love me more if I stuck around." Over time—just a few months actually—she found that not only was she assuming the role of the boy's mother and father, she was also expected to do the housework and assume all the household responsibilities. "My mistake was that I allowed that to happen. Because the more I did, the less Raymond wanted to be with me. I used to beg him, 'Can't we have just a night out by ourselves?'" After awhile, she stopped asking.

Over their years together, they never brought up marriage, but other people would. "Raymond always told them, 'We've both been married before; we're not going to do that again.'" To protect herself from Raymond's rebuff, Emma says she went along with him, even though in her heart she was devastated.

I asked her, "You never discussed marriage when you were alone?"

Emma said, "It was really stupid, but we seldom talked about what was good or bad about our relationship." Now she realizes that she was afraid to let Raymond know how much she loved him and wanted to get married. She bent over backwards to send the message that she didn't care. "Maybe he believed it and wanted to protect himself from my turning him down. It was a big mistake not to tell him how much I loved him, and to assume that he knew."

Years went by and Emma began to resent Raymond. "There was never any 'thanks a lot for all you are doing,'" she said. But she was very attached to his son, and didn't want to face the fact that the relationship was crumbling.

Three-and-a-half years into the relationship, Raymond's ex-wife went into a rehab clinic, dried out, and didn't need Emma to care for Billy. "That was the turning point," Emma remembers. "With Billy not coming over as much, I went back to my career, but I felt an emptiness without him—as if I had also lost a part of Raymond." Emma moved out of Raymond's Palm Springs condo and went back to Los Angeles. Raymond hated Los Angeles and refused to visit Emma. She commuted on weekends to be with him, but he was angry she had moved out and showed it by ignoring her. She was angry, too, but held it in. "He just didn't appreciate me, and I was stupid for not telling him how badly that felt." She thinks they held back because they were afraid of getting hurt. "It was a pride thing," she says. "I think we did love each other, but by then it was difficult to turn around and say it or talk about it." Emma says she was emotionally wiped out, too drained to pick up the pieces, to try again—perhaps only to get hurt again.

During the last six months of their living together, Emma sensed Raymond was playing around, but it wasn't until she moved out that friends told her it had been going on for years. "I was crushed," she admits. "I felt betrayed because these weren't girls Raymond would take home to his mother." And because they were one night stands, Emma says, "I don't think he was looking to replace me. But because he was mad at me for not being more demanding, and I was mad at him for not being supportive of me, he dumped on me." By then they were entangled in an unhealthy web.

One of Emma's friends saw Raymond soon after they broke up. He told her, 'I really, really am still attracted to Emma. I thought she was the girl I was going to marry. I don't know what went wrong."

Emma's friend responded, "Well, if you wanted to marry her, why didn't you tell her?" He shrugged his shoulders and stammered, "I don't know."

Emma thinks she made things too easy for Raymond and says she learned a lot that she can use to make a new relationship better and more fulfilling. "First of all," she says, "I am never going to hold back and cover up how I really feel. I realize now I should have taken my chances. Also, I'm never going to live with someone unless we're engaged and planning to get married." Emma says she cheated herself and compromised her career and her self-esteem. She's dating someone new—a friend of hers and Raymond's from before. "I always knew he was a solid, decent guy, with a good head on his shoulders. Isn't it a shame? When I was with Raymond, I didn't recognize that I needed a man who had those characteristics, someone who respects me and my feelings. But I do now!"

Six months after they broke up, Raymond got engaged to a divorcée, who had a house and two kids. When Emma ran into him, recently, she asked, "Are you happy?" he defensively burst out, "Yeah! Why wouldn't I be?" She senses he got used to being with a woman who took over domestic responsibilities, but that he rebounded too quickly and settled. Emma says Raymond's fiancée is very demanding, like his first wife. He likes that. "I was too nice," she admits, "too gullible."

A MISSION STATEMENT FOR LTCS

Drawing from the study *The Division of Labor Among Cohabiting and Married Couples* that I discussed earlier, Dr. Rebecca Stafford and her coauthors made this conclusion:

> "Most members of cohabiting dyads claim to love their partner and to have a warm, supportive, personally and sexually intimate relationship which provides them with emotional security without destroying their individual freedom to grow and mature as persons. *Many claim to be sexually faithful without requiring the same sexual fidelity from their partners* and to be personally loyal without being committed legally to the relationship."

It seems that philosophy could become a component of an LTC mission statement, which in turn spells out the difference between living together and marriage. However, when one partner deviates from the purpose of the relationship, the other partner cannot imagine that person in a more permanent role. He or she has to seek out someone else and establish those parameters from the very beginning. The difficulty of dealing with a role change is sure to result in trouble.

Apply these concepts to the stories you have just read, and you can see why an unmarried live-in can almost expect levels of infidelity to infiltrate even a loyal bond.

The study continues, "The future of these relationships is unclear as some couples anticipate marriage, some recognize the temporary nature of the relationship, and others have no perception of their future together." This finding confirms the "We don't touch on that!" sentiments we've read in these pages.

Imagine working for a firm and not having a clue about whether you will be promoted or fired or whether the company will survive. Wouldn't your job performance reflect these uncertainties? Compare going to work day after day wondering, "Will I be here next week? Next year?" "Am I doing a good job?" After a while, would you give it your all? Probably not.

Many marital test drives resemble this scenario.

When I analyze marital test-drives that backfire, I find several common denominators:

➤ Moving in together is spontaneous. The couple barely knows each other.

➤ Seldom is there a 3-, 6-, 12-, or 24-month game plan established before couples move in together. Few couples know where their relationship is headed.

➤ 90 percent of the time the man is allowed to decide the destiny of the relationship.

➤ In an effort to be in a relationship, the women studied are willing to compromise their careers, personal happiness, and individual security.

➤ Women studied assume living together leads to marriage.

➤ Women studied feel responsible for the failure of the relationship.

➤ To save the relationship, the women studied are willing to lower their original expectations of what they thought an ideal partner should represent.

➤ Once a woman realized her partner was not her ideal choice, she stayed in the relationship anyway and settled.

➤ Long term living together erodes the women studied's self-esteem.

That is not a pretty list in favor of living together. Hopefully, it will provoke you into giving marital test drives a second thought. If you are an LTC and find that this list reminds you of what is happening in your relationship, you might want to pack your bags and move out because when men are ready to get married, they get married. Living together is not an alternative. Only half of all LTCs marry. [2]

DOES BEING ENGAGED CHANGE ONE'S ODDS?

Recently, I was told the following stories about engaged couples living together. I was impressed that even after someone is given the ultimate token of love—an engagement ring—living together before the wedding can still hurt your chances of getting married.

My housekeeper, Nida, was excited about attending her best friend's wedding last June when all of a sudden, two weeks before, it was called off. I heard Nida talking on the phone with her friend, consoling her. One afternoon, she asked me what I thought. Her girlfriend dated her fiancé for about two years before they moved in together. Six months after that, she got pregnant. By the time she walked down the aisle, she would be five months pregnant. I told Nida I thought the guy was having an anxiety attack. Having a baby and a wife on almost the same day might be too much for him.

"What should she do?" Nida asked.

"I would lay low. Not call him. And if he called me and I still wanted him, I would not mention the wedding or the pregnancy. I would give him a chance to grasp what he was about to get into. If he really loves her, he'll come around. It could take a few weeks, maybe even a few months."

Her girlfriend tried my approach, and within two weeks, the guy was back. "There is not going to be any wedding right now," Nida said. "But at least they are together."

In cases like this, women are sometimes so excited about getting married they shove too much down a guy's throat at one time. Men need time to absorb what's happening to them. Thinking about the responsibilities that lay ahead of them can be overwhelming.

At about the same time Nida's friend was going through her troubles, I remembered an engagement announcement I received well over a year ago. I wondered if the couple had eloped or had a small family wedding, because we never received an invitation. One afternoon Sam said he ran into the girl's father. He told Sam, "I've got a thousand dollars worth of engraved wedding invitations sitting in my house, but it looks like we don't have a bride and groom. I don't think there's going to be a wedding."

When Sam asked him what happened, he said his daughter and her fiancé were having trouble working out their differences. Once they started living together, the relationship got worse, not better. "My daughter wasn't used to compromising, not getting her way." She was too immature to accept the give and take that marriage requires, and didn't want to.

A couple of months later, another friend told me her daughter's wedding was off after Mom made non-refundable deposits all over New York City amounting to fifteen thousand dollars, plus a Vera Wang wedding gown. However, my friend's attitude surprised me. She said, "I went through an awful divorce. I'm happy to lose fifteen thousand if it helped my daughter find out that she couldn't stand her fiancé's overbearing need for control."

She didn't know that before? Did she think living together would change him?

These stories tell me a lot of couples don't really know each other well enough before they become engaged and expect a premarital living-together arrangement to fill in the blanks. Often it doesn't. Sometimes it's an expensive lesson.

Other couples who test drive marriage get engaged beforehand only to save face with their families. When everyone gets wrapped up in wedding plans, the pressure on the couple is so intense they bow out never knowing whether they were right for each other or not.

Don't underestimate your family's coolness to your marital test drive. One committee member I serve with who is in her mid-thirties said she won't let her younger sister visit her with a live-in. "She's had four different ones over the years and I think that is a bad influence on my five year old son," she insisted.

If your relatives are opposed to your living together and they are important to you, keep separate places.

MY FIANCÉ'S MISTRESS

Phaedra was vacationing with friends on St. Martin when she met a West Indian man she fell for. "We really hit it off during that week," she said, "and I went back a month later to see him. I returned the month after that, and when I came back the following month, I decided to quit my job in New York City and move in with him." Phaedra's fiancé supported her, and she didn't work for the next three years. "He was a bit of a control- and neat freak," Phaedra described. "If there was a dog hair on the floor, he'd go ballistic. But, all in all, he treated me very well," she said.

"The week after we filed for wedding papers, I found out he had an affair with one of my best friends who *he* introduced me to. I felt so betrayed he would do that to me." As she began explaining to people why she wasn't getting married, Phaedra learned her lover was a womanizer. "People began to spill the beans that he had many affairs on me," she sighed. She felt so stupid that she was the last to know.

"My fiancé used to say that I didn't understand West Indian men," Phaedra remembers. "He meant West Indian men are allowed to have more than one woman." But Phaedra says she knows plenty of West Indian husbands and boyfriends who don't fool around.

"It was beyond belief. My fiancé was actually *surprised* I didn't understand that his love for me was separate from whatever else he did. That these other women had nothing to do with me."

"So did you work it out?" I asked.

"No. Are you kidding! I didn't trust him enough to even try. I left St. Martin the next week."

"Did you go back to New York?"

"No. That would have been too easy. I went to St. Thomas by myself, and opened a skin care salon."

"So tell me," I asked Phaedra, "if you can't cope with your significant others' infidelity, do you keep throwing them out one after the other?"

"Well, that's a big problem. Then we women would *really* be by ourselves," implying men's unfaithfulness is a given. "In my opinion, a lot of guys you're going to live with or marry are going to present you with problems, so it boils down to just what kind of problems you want to deal with."

"So what should we do about it?"

"Well, a woman has to decide," she thinks. "Does she want to be with a guy she's not so passionate about, but who is going to be faithful and treat her well? Or, does she want to be with the one with whom she has a lot of passion, but might not be able to trust?"

"What's the likelihood of finding both?"

"That's highly unlikely."

Burned pretty badly before she had one foot down the aisle, Phaedra still thinks there is someone for everyone. But after four years, she still doesn't think too highly of men. Despite that, she says she's not going to stop dating to avoid getting hurt again.

"How would you go into another relationship differently?"

"Well, this is terrible," she said, "But after it happens a few times, you go into other relationships so guardedly." Phaedra says she feels very protective of her feelings. "On the other hand, women should take control over what they are doing for themselves, make themselves happy apart from their relationship. Regardless of whether you are very successful or not, develop independence and fulfillment so that no matter what happens you can still hold your own."

"Do you think an affair is a wake-up call that other things in the relationship aren't so wonderful?"

"I know one thing, if I think I might have to put up with that much aggravation and hurt again, the next guy's going to have to marry me. I'll never, *never* live with a guy again before we get married."

"And if he was your husband and played around, would it be different?"

"Look, my parents separated when I was eleven years old. They never discussed it with us kids. My dad moved to a loft, but I was told he just needed bigger space for his work. They had problems, but never involved us. We still had family dinners together, and my parents still talked. It wasn't until I was about fifteen, when I put two and two together, that I realized they were separated. So I had a really positive male role-model there; not like the men I've dated."

"Are they divorced now?"

"I don't really know."

What she does know and sees is that her parents still go out together. Her father's an artist; her mom an illustrator. They have a relationship that works for them, their kids, and a sense of keeping the family together. After so many years of marriage, they're friends. "These days that's not bad," Phaedra said.

Six months after I interviewed Phaedra, her ex-fiancé called her after four years of silence. She said to me, "I know what you are going to say, but guess who's coming to dinner?" I guess Phaedra, worn down by not having a steady boyfriend, subscribes to the axiom: *The devil you know is better than the devil you don't know.*

There is no end to the war stories people have been willing to share with me. During a recent haircut, my hair stylist asked me about the subject of the book I was writing. Her next client, Randy, overheard the conversation and said, "I've lived with a few different men. But after I lived with them, knew what I had, saw their spots, I knew I would never want to marry any of them. When I met my husband, I refused to live with him because I knew, if I did, we would never have gotten married."

Randy's parents were divorced; her mother remarried but she didn't get along with her stepfather. When she began dating, she feared commitment. To her it represented hurt and betrayal. The moment a guy fell for her and they moved in together, she'd take a walk. When she met her husband, she says he had all of the qualifications she was looking for. "He was Jewish, smart, caring, and attractive—he would listen to my fears," she says. "I didn't want to lose him, so I went to a therapist to get over my commitment anxieties.

"There are a lot of people flitting from relationship to relationship, sometimes losing the right person because they can't get a handle on what is wrong with themselves," Randy continued. "People should know that once you recognize what the problem is, you will able to cope with problems to which you thought there were no solutions." Randy and her husband have been married eight years.

When a man proposes to a woman and she accepts, they are saying to each other, "I trust you." "I trust myself and this decision." "I trust our love and I trust our future together." When a couple chooses to live together instead of getting married, they are potentially admitting, "I *do not* trust you, myself, this decision, our love, or our future together." Think about it.

THOSE WHO TOOK
THE PLUNGE

"**A**ctually, what is the difference between living together and marriage?" That was the question most pondered by the more than 200 unofficial spouses I spoke with while writing this book. Many defensively answered with a glib "nothing except a piece of paper." Those who weren't as defensive feel, at some time, they might want to get married, but are scared that they might ruin a good thing. On the other hand, I found die-hard opponents of marriage insist, "We're so happy, we don't want to rock the boat."

Meanwhile, a handful of couples, where *both* parties knew the benefits, have opted for marriage in the near future. Nevertheless, for them, test-driving marriage is a convenient holding pattern. In certain cases, that makes sense.

Some good reasons to live together, and put off getting married right away might include:

➤ Saving for an engagement ring and the cost of an expensive wedding

➤ Concentrating on finishing college—without the adjustment of becoming a spouse as well

➤ Waiting to obtain a divorce or annulment from a previous marriage

➤ Being engaged—with a wedding date planned—and the parties have chosen to live together in the interim (But keep in mind the risks.)

In most cases, these couples assume they *will* get married and know exactly when. Unless living together changes their impressions about each other, once they've lived together, they often do marry. Nonetheless, ever present is the statistic that they are more likely to divorce than couples who chose not to, even though few people I spoke to blamed their divorces on living together first.

There is a certain segment of the population whose choice of living together over marrying makes sense. A few examples include:

➤ Older folks who decide not to marry to protect assets, maintain their independence, please their children, or because poor health deems it impractical

➤ Couples who choose not to divorce an existing spouse because of health, religious, or other reasons

➤ Common-law married couples who are protected by common-law state statutes

➤ Those who select to cohabit because of privacy issues ("it's no one's business—including the IRS")

➤ Couples who hold incompatible religious beliefs

If you choose living together to see if you can be compatible, or change offending habits, etc. you fall right into the trial marriage trap.

It's true, you might not have known he snored *that* irritatingly or that she voraciously reads well into the middle of the night. And yes, these are the types of annoying idiosyncrasies you may have preferred to know about before marrying your mate. But would it have altered your decision to get married? I doubt it, because most quirks are tolerable, and married or living together, you get used to it.

The difference between living together and marriage is the difference between the maiden aunt baby-sitting for the day and having children of her own. You can't know what to expect until you've been up all night with your child, who has a high fever and is inconsolable. Likewise a LTC cannot measure the ups and downs of cohabitation versus marriage until they try it both ways, because living together is not marriage's counterpart.

Proponents of living together are often married people who did not live with their spouse first. A gentleman I know has two daughters who have earned professional degrees. His worry is that marriage will cause them to lose their identity and alter their ability to perform optimally their careers. He has concluded, "If it weren't for the stigma attached to children born out of wedlock, I would encourage them not to marry—*ever*."

Another couple I know isn't thrilled with their daughter's controlling boyfriend, but their philosophies surrounding what they would like to see their daughter decide are divided. The mother wants her daughter to live with her boyfriend first. "Maybe she'll get him out of her system." Her father is adamantly opposed to premarital cohabitation and says, "She can always divorce him." There are statistics that prove each of these solutions could prove correct.

Karen S. Peterson, a writer for Gannett News Services, published an article, "Marriage Makes Men Happier and Women More Vulnerable," in which she discusses the happiness/unhappiness ratio of marriage by comparing several formal studies and professional opinions. Included was University of Washington psychologist, Neil Jacobson who said, "'Marriage is an institution that primarily benefits men.'"

Ms. Peterson also points to Dalma Heyn, author of *The Erotic Silence of the American Wife*, who describes wives as "'Women who give up much of what they enjoyed about themselves as well as what their husbands enjoyed about them [before marriage], in order to aspire to a more conventional, more conforming, more proper, and modest and toned-down version of themselves.'" Bowling Green University sociologist Gary Lee punctuated popular trepidation with his statement, "Younger married women may be unhappy [wives] because today couples go into marriage firmly committed to equality, but then the woman usually gets the short end of the stick."[1]

These professionals confirm what some single women told me. They are certain the independence lost when becoming someone's wife compared to remaining someone's live-in lover is enough to dampen their enthusiasm for marriage.

Research studies and professionals I consulted suggest the majority of couples today expect some anniversaries will be more enthusiastically celebrated than others, however, overall, they are happiest being married.

To learn more about the differences between marriage and living-together, I talked to people who got married after various stints of cohabitation. Living through their happy and sad times, I found their stories tell us to take a second look at marital test drives. Knowing the factors that led them to decide to get married offers invaluable insight.

The most important, however, was my discovery that cohabiting couples seem desperate for a lifetime guarantee.

IT NEVER WOULD HAVE HAPPENED IF...

Tonie, an independent businesswoman, and Joe, a novelist, lived together for four years when Joe's oldest friend and his psychologist wife asked them if they would appear on another friend's radio show to talk about living together. Oddly, the station was located in an upstate New York chicken coop. "We were cornered in a room smaller than my linen closet," Virginia joked. "Our host asked the traditional questions: 'Why aren't you two married?' And, 'Why do you live a monogamous relationship, but seem not to be able to commit, totally.'"

Joe and Tonie both responded with conventional answers. She said, "Why marry now? Joe has two grown sons, and I have two sons in their early teens." She explained neither she nor Joe had any desire to have more children, and besides, "I am terrified of the institution of marriage. After one bad one, I do not want a second." The talk-jock continued to badger them, and then concluded his program with his opinion: "Obviously you two cannot commit."

The couple said their good-byes to the show's host and their trouble-making friends, and drove the three-hour ride home. They did not speak the entire way. Another three days passed where they said little more than, "Pass the salt."

A few days after that, Joe caught up with Tonie and barked, "So you don't want to commit!" She didn't reply.

Another couple of days passed when Tonie ran into Joe and confronted him, "So you don't want to commit!" The gibes went on and on for a couple of weeks. Then one evening the couple was having cocktails and decided to talk about it. They agreed they didn't need a marriage license to be committed to each other. After all, isn't a four-year monogamous relationship quite a commitment? However, Tonie said, "We began to notice changes in our relationship which, when I look back on it today, depicted a *lack* of total commitment."

During that discussion, Joe and Tonie quietly resolved to get married at City Hall by a friend who is a judge. She was thirty-seven. He, fifty-three, and has heart disease. She said one deciding factor was one of Joe's frequent visits to the hospital, where Tonie walked into his hospital room and found his ex-wife giving him a back massage. Never mind that his ex *was* a massage therapist, and still friendly with Joe. Tonie was jealous. Enraged, she thought, 'Get your Goddamn hands off my...my...what?' At that moment, it became vividly apparent to her Joe wasn't her husband. And no amount of living together would give her that security. At that moment, her independent attitude gave way to the safety net of marriage.

Their wedding day arrived, and as usual, Joe drove Tonie's sons to school. On the way home, he began to think, "Well, now I must act responsibly. I will have two teenage sons. They'll need guidance from me." On the other hand, conflicting emotions conjured up uneasiness. "I don't want this shit!" he thought. "I want to be a writer...not a husband. What the hell am I doing!"

While Joe was out, Tonie had a panic attack. Her anxious thoughts included, "When this was Joe's house, if I didn't vacuum, dust, and clean, I didn't feel responsible. Now, I'll be the lady of the house and when those things aren't done, it will be all my fault."

On their way to City Hall, Tonie and Joe didn't speak to each other. But then, just before they entered the judge's chambers, he spun around, turned to her, and snarled his last words as a single. "If they make us say love, honor, and *obey*, please don't say that bullshit! We know what our relationship is all about." Tonie complied. Minutes later, the judge's assistant informed them the ceremonially words had been changed to love, honor, and *cherish*. And so they were married. Meanwhile, Tonie got the last chuckle.

On a subsequent visit to the same friends who linked them up with the radio show, the newlyweds went back on the air to inform the listening audience that indirectly they were responsible for their marriage. Joe and Tonie have recently celebrated their fourteenth wedding anniversary.

How have they fared? "Some of it has been boring, like any married couple," Tonie said. Their marriage has had its ups and downs, as well as bouts of elation and disappointment. Joe's heart disease has been with them all twenty-one years they've known each other. He also contracted prostate cancer the first year they were married. "So his penis glows in the dark," she joshed, maintaining the sense of humor that has gotten them over rough times.

Accepting her assignment as permanent caregiver has, at times, been daunting. Over the years, Tonie rewarded herself with eating binges, until one day she burgeoned into a 250-pound blimp. "Eating rage put me in a size twenty-two!"

Four years ago, the couple relocated to Florida. "Joe's ambition was to write one more great novel before his 'near-death time of life,'" Tonie recounted. "Ironically, this was the best time of my life, most ambitious, most successful, most recognition." However, she acquiesced to Joe's needs. "We sold our beautiful home in Connecticut, and my business," she said.

Arriving in Florida was at first, for Tonie, a death sentence. "Joe waiting to die—although he'd been 'dying' since he was fifty," she chuckled. "All the stories that people talk about when they move to Florida to retire are true. Florida is God's waiting room."

Uprooted, Tonie started up her fourth, and hopefully last, staffing business. At first, she called Joe every hour on the hour from her office to make sure he was all right. Then she stopped feeling guilty about leaving Joe. She worked before they were married, and she will continue to work. "Although it scares me when I wake up in the middle of the night, and I don't see him moving. I want to hold a mirror up to his nose to make sure he's still alive. But life has to go on for me, too."

Today, Tonie is svelte. A couple of years ago when she turned fifty she looked in the mirror and had a real heart to heart chat with herself. She went on a "healthy me, for a change, campaign," and lost one hundred pounds. Her business is doing well. Joe is feeling the best he has felt for a long time. Tonie bought him a computer complete with Internet and e-mail capabilities. She says, "It's funny teaching a man who has written a dozen novels on a manual typewriter to use the computer." But more importantly, they reached a stage when they both knew it was time they had to get on with the business of living.

Tonie recognizes, "I bought into this." In spite of themselves, Joe and Tonie's love gets stronger. That's what a good marriage is all about. They stuck it out, and worked at it when, at times, walking out would have been much easier. And now, the rewards are theirs. "We watch sunsets," says Tonie. "They haven't changed. We talk in bed about all the wonderful years we have spent together. We pray for more nights and days together." You see, there are no guarantees.

BEST BEHAVIOR

Being a part of the Elysian Hotel operation on St. Thomas, my family and I routinely watch brides and grooms get married on the hotel's terrace. Some of the brides are lovelier than others, but at first glance *this* one was ravishing, which made me grab for my binoculars and watch her exchange vows from my fourth-story condo. However, it seemed peculiar that my daughter, Ashley, and I were their only guests and only because we snooped!

A few days later, I met Debi Larrison and her new husband, Dennis, at the pool bar, and told her how much fun we had eavesdropping on her wedding. She explained they would have a reception in a couple of months, but wanted their wedding ceremony to be a totally private matter. The ironic coincidence is that she and Dennis live in New Jersey, just minutes from our house. Over the past five years, that chance meeting developed into a very special friendship for all of us.

The Larrisons lived together when they spontaneously decided to get married eight months later. "Shacking up just wasn't for me," Dennis said. "My first marriage lasted twenty years, the second was shorter, but I still believed in marriage, and felt the strong foundation marriage provides would allow me to trust and give more openly to Debi's and my relationship." He says he feels more secure being married.

"Everything happened fast with us," Debi exclaimed. "Dennis moved in with me only three weeks after we met, in April. We got engaged for my birthday in December and by the end of January, we were on a plane to St. Thomas getting married." Debi, whose first marriage ended after eight years, says she probably could have lived with Dennis indefinitely. "It really didn't matter to me." But because marriage meant so much to Dennis, she went ahead with it.

Considering both had been burned by previous marriages, they showed great confidence by being willing to try again. Dennis' confidence is even more impressive because the bad taste of his first divorce was exacerbated by his not seeing his two children and grandchildren. He says, "It's their choice that they rarely visit." But you sense he is terribly hurt. This time around, Debi, a CFO of a large firm—who didn't have children with her first husband—and Dennis, a builder, have decided to skip having children together.

Add it all up, and you could see Debi's side—living together indefinitely.

Dennis, however, took the marital test-drive seriously, "If I didn't have the total commitment, I would have felt as if I was hanging. I wouldn't be able to build a life with Debi. I would hold back. And even if it means making sacrifices," he said, "you can't just live for yourself. How can you expect to get something back if you're not willing to give 100 percent?"

Debi says one negative aspect of getting married after living together may have more to do with the novelty of the relationship wearing off. Before they were married, Dennis would bring home flowers in the middle of the week, and they would have candlelight dinners. "It's a shame," she knows, "but that romantic phase seems to go away after a period of time. If we had lived together, maybe it would have lasted longer."

"The one thing we had going for us was that I was thirty-five when I met Dennis, and he was forty-two," she said. "We both knew where we were going in life." Debi thinks because they were well grounded individually, it was easier for them to risk getting married. She has friends who have lived together for over a decade. Now that she and Dennis are married, she realizes, "Neither one of us would have wanted that," and has determined, "there's enough turmoil in life. Add to that the turmoil of a living-together relationship—and it's not healthy." She feels certain she could have committed to Dennis even if they had chosen to live together, but the commitment meant more when they got married.

Another aspect of the issue Debi discussed is, "When a couple lives together, they're both on their best behavior, afraid to make the wrong move. When you get married, you let down your guard. I've seen this with many of my friends who are in the same situation. Marriage allows you to really see who that person is. The ups and downs may become more apparent, but because you are married, you'll spend more time working them out. Dennis says, "You also learn to keep your mouth shut in certain situations because the awful things you say in the heat of an argument come back to haunt you for years." On the other hand, Debi feels, "Because the edge is off, you gain a lot, too, because you can, in a sense, express your-self more confidently."

Debi told me about a relative whom she feels will probably live with his unofficial spouse indefinitely. "I look at them, and laugh to myself, 'ten years down the road, and they're still split-ting the electric bill!'" Because most living together couples do not combine their money, Debi, a financial officer, brought up a good point. "Suppose one party has a bad year financially. Does that mean the partner who has had a good year can't go on vacation, or go out to dinner because the other one can't afford to? And even if the richer one loans the poorer one the money, what could be more ridiculous and foolish! Living together presents an accounting problem that never lets you get together on solid ground. When it comes down to, 'This is yours,' and 'That's mine,' there's a block on the commitment. You can never have a carefree, true, open, honest, going-forward relationship." She wonders "Could that couple have achieved more together if that obstacle wasn't a factor?"

THE RULES CHANGE

Toni Chambers-Jackson was born an unwavering free spirit. When she moved in with her boyfriend, Frank, he knew that side of her personality wasn't going to change, but Toni thinks he wasn't prepared for just *how* unconventional she was.

When I asked Toni if she and Frank had decided to get married before they moved in together, she hesitated and said, "I think *he* had. Yeah...maybe I had, also."

The couple lived together for one year when they gave in to pressure from Toni's mother and Frank's family to get married. She regarded Frank's integrity and values as something she needed to have in a husband. And because she wasn't a kid—she was twenty-eight and able to support herself—she knew her love for Frank wasn't infatuation. "I was as ready as I was ever going to be to get married," Toni remembers. And for all concerned she thought, 'Wouldn't it be better to just go ahead and do it!'

"The scary part about living together is it was easy for both partners to change the rules on a whim," she reflects. "When you live together the door is always open. You don't have that concrete commitment. Living together made it easy to excuse anything with, 'After all, I'm *not* married.'" Living together is a wishy-washy relationship. If you want marriage to work, you have to accept responsibility and commit.

That was seventeen years ago, and Toni thinks times were different. She recollects living together was considered *de rigueur* among her college friends in the late seventies; and recalls when she was in her last year of college, she and her friends thought, "I'm not just going to get married. I'm going to live with the guy first." However, when Toni told her mother how she felt, "My mother couldn't *believe* that's what I got out of four years of college!" Much to her family's disappointment, eight years later, she moved in with Frank anyway.

Toni, now 45, was the epitome of today's independent-minded woman. She says, "I didn't feel I needed to rush to the altar, nor to get married, nor was I looking for anyone to take care of me." After careful consideration that her mate selection—*Frank*—understood how rigorously she would guard her independence, Toni, who owns Silk Greenery, a retail operation, was sure she wasn't marrying a traditional man—only to find out, "Boy, was that *not* true!" Needless to say, it took her awhile to adjust to being married. "It was a lot more than I expected."

Toni says Frank, a prominent attorney on the island of St. Thomas, was and is an easy-going husband. However, the bulk of their early marriage battles were about her need to remind him who she was and is. She says, "I don't know when the fighting over it ended, but after awhile one or both of us came to grips with my need to be my own person."

Defending that position, she said, "A lot of women just don't want to live like that anymore—they want to keep their careers. Everything isn't by the time clock, and there's a lot more negotiation." As well as eating out, and ordering in!

If a husband can cope with his wife's independence, equal power and control, and equal distribution of responsibilities, then marriage becomes an advantage over living together.

I WANTED A WIFE...NOT A CHILD

Gerard and Marianne had everything going against marriage when they met eleven years ago. Yet, on the eve of their first wedding anniversary, Gerard says he feels good about the frustrating events that blocked their union.

Marianne was twenty-two years old when she met Gerard. Her father had just passed away and Gerard says she had a really hard time with it. She looked to Gerard, nine years her senior, to fill that void and counted on him to handle certain responsibilities. "I knew she was a good person," Gerard says, "but I didn't want to marry a child. I wanted a lover and an equal. I told her I would be there for her, but I wasn't going to be the person she could rely on." He wanted her to learn to depend on herself.

The next nine years were volatile. When they weren't battling, they made annual culinary visits to Europe, "except, our battles left their mark in every city we visited," he said laughing.

Early on, Gerard gave Marianne the nudging, but also the space she needed to learn how to accept more responsibility. For a couple of years, they were miserable because Gerard refused to take a controlling role. "I didn't want to shape, develop, or watch over Marianne because that's what you're supposed to do with children, not a mate." He may not have known it then, but he was right. Throughout the history of W.O.O.M., where I have seen the older man take over, his lover or wife winds up resenting him for doing so later on (I want you to take care of me, but I don't like your being in control). More than half of these fatherlike/daughterlike relationships and marriages break-up because of the control issue.

Over the next few years, Gerard and Marianne drove each other crazy. When Gerard felt Marianne was slipping back to childlike ways, he would break up with her and move. Over time, Marianne would come and stay with him, then stay a little longer. It was a pattern until the time he refused to tell her where he had moved. "We were going through one of those stages where we weren't getting along, and I wanted my freedom," Gerard said. He told all his friends if Marianne called them not to give out any information about where he lived, or his phone number.

One evening, Marianne went to the restaurant where Gerard served as maître d' and sommelier. She was very upset that he hadn't called and she didn't know where he lived. He told her not to make a scene and he would meet her at a local bar after work. One thing led to another and they decided to go to his house. "It was really comical," Gerard laughed. "I drove all these back roads so she wouldn't be able to figure out where I lived." When they got to his place they had talked for a couple of hours when Marianne asked Gerard for his phone number. He told her he didn't own a phone. Shortly after, he ordered a pizza. Marianne wound up spending the night, but left the next morning. That evening, the phone rang. When Gerard answered, he cringed when he heard Marianne say, "Hello, big daddy!"

He shot up out of his chair and screeched, "How'd you get this phone number!" Marianne said, "From the pizza box!" Soon after, Gerard learned Marianne had moved down the street. "Four months would go by, then one month she couldn't pay the rent." He paid it. "But I couldn't handle the two rents, so I would have her move in again with me."

"She certainly was persistent!" I commented.

"Unbelievable," Gerard said. "But that's when I knew if anyone loved me so much, that they'd switch jobs so our hours would mesh and we could be together, and had painstakingly pursued me, then that person was the one for me.

"The biggest difference between living together and marriage is commitment," Gerard says. Years ago, he dillydallied under the guise of testing the waters, and procrastinated a lot, because he basically wasn't ready to commit. "I just wanted to make sure I was doing the right thing," he said. And aside from making sure that Marianne was the right person, he also wanted to make sure that he could cope with the responsibility of having a wife. "I knew that I wanted to get married one time, and one time only," Gerard confided. "It was worth the wait for Marianne to grow up, and for me to sow my wild oats and become balanced, because until I knew who I was myself, how could I give myself to someone else?" So it took a little longer than anyone expected! So what?

I wonder if he served pizza at his wedding?

AFTER AWHILE, LIVING TOGETHER
DIDN'T FEEL GOOD ANYMORE

Anne's second marriage was on the rocks when she met recently divorced Vince twelve years ago at work. She had earned a master's degree in nutrition, but became bored with that field years later and went back to school to get a beautician's license. Two months later, while Anne, then thirty-six, was giving Vince a haircut, she mentioned that she had left her husband. They discussed how each was coping with the dating scene. Complaining that it had been so difficult to find intelligent and decent men to go out with, Anne confessed she was thinking about placing an ad in a personal's column. "What do you mean?" Vince said, jumping at the chance. "You don't need a dating service; I'm right here!"

It was Christmastime, and Anne had moved in with her brother. Taking Vince's offer seriously, she invited him for dinner. "I could not believe how beautifully she had decorated the house," he bragged. "It was very countrylike and warm." Over a bottle of wine, they talked most of the night. "I was so up," Vince says. After feeling lousy about his divorce and losing confidence, he chuckles, "I was flying." The couple has been together ever since.

Anne, already burned twice, wanted nothing to do with marriage. She loved Vince and knew how good they were for each other, but she turned down his offers over the years to get married. "I was scared and wanted to make sure." Over the eleven years they lived together, they sporadically talked about marriage, but nothing came of it even though Vince's daughters, with whom Anne has a very special relationship, would have liked it very much. "We found we were more committed than most of our married friends, many of whom were getting divorced," Anne said. "Their splitting up made me think maybe we should stick to status quo." Eventually, after the death of Vince's father, which brought them much closer, and family pressure to get married, Vince, by now fifty-five, decided on Super Bowl Sunday 1997, that they should get married three weeks later on Valentine's Day. "I felt Vince wanted to end the uncertainty of that part of our lives," Anne said. "As we watched our parents age and pass away, it became apparent our getting married would be more meaningful to everyone—including Vince and me."

After eleven years of living together, I didn't expect Anne to know so soon after they married, but I asked anyway, "Have you noticed any significant change since you married Vince?" Her answer surprised me.

"At first it didn't seem different because we were on our honeymoon," she said. "But later on Vince seemed to be more committed to me as far as helping around the house. After we got married, he became a lot more helpful all around." Anne insists she has always felt secure with Vince. "But now, the relationship feels more stable and definitely more settled." After the couple married, they bought a house at the very same time many of their friends were selling their homes and moving into condos. Anne realizes, "We have always been close friends, then we became business partners, but the house made us feel very married."

During the mid-1980s Vince started a company that manufactures arts and crafts novelties and decorative rubber stamps. "A few years later, I was going through a rough time financially," he says, "but Anne came in and was right there to help me through it." He says Anne is very creative and has come up with stamp-art ideas and business plans that really catapulted the company.

The couple has worked together for the past seven years. "But now that we are married everything has fallen into place," Anne says with conviction.

Without hesitation, Vince responded, "I don't see any difference between how I feel about Anne now and when we lived together. Except, I guess in the back of my mind I may have thought, 'If things don't work out, I'm out of this.' I don't think living together is bad—you learn a lot from that—but I feel that after awhile you need to make a decision. Now, we are whole. We have decided, 'I love this person, I don't want to be with anyone else, so why not take it to the highest level of commitment?'"

Anne says, "If a couple has been happy for a very long peri-od of time, why not get married? It's not going to get any worse, it can only get better."

"It's important to laugh together," Vince interjected. "If you can't maintain a sense of humor, everything gets too intense while you're looking for things to be perfect. Annie and I have learned that lesson well."

Notice how often LTCs say, "At first, we talked about marriage, then after a few years, we dropped the subject." Whether it is complacency or fear of yet another rejection for the partner who wants to get married, or a little of both, it's important to discuss the question from time to time, as Anne and Vince did. If not, how could you possibly know where you stand? Assuming you know how your partner feels isn't good enough. Ask him or her every few months, "Does living together still feel good to you?" Be prepared for the answer. It might take you by surprise. *One partner almost always wants to get married. One partner almost always gets hurt.* But at least you'll know.

THEY BEAT THE ODDS

Meandering through Jack's* glorious gardens and the vistas he has created on his riverfront property, one would find it unfathomable that Jack was once a walking corpse, beaten down by cocaine and booze, while his live-in lover, Laurie*, not only endured his insidious habits, but coaxed him out of the addictions. Today Jack is clean, sober, alive, and happily married to Laurie. However, their story serves as a reminder of the difference between living together and marriage. Their horrific ordeal shows how easy it is to get wrapped up with a charmer who could turn out to be a loser.

Fifteen years ago, Laurie, then 27, was offered a high-powered position in the fashion industry, and moved from Rochester to Manhattan. Shortly before her move, she met a vice president for Goldman-Sachs on a Rochester-bound airplane. "I guess I fell in love," she said, "and when I started my job in New York, I moved in with him, which was to be a temporary arrangement of convenience. But I never moved out."

Toward the end of that three-year relationship, which Laurie describes as perfect in the sense that, "Neither of us had been married before, he was four years older, successful and stable, we were both Catholic, came from good families, and my mother was thrilled. But he definitely was *not* my type," Laurie met Jack, a gregarious rascal who was separated from his wife, had two kids, and chased and bedded glamorous women all over New York City. Any similarities between the two men ended after the good job part. Yet, there was no doubt Jack *was* Laurie's type. And there was no doubt Jack was impressed with Laurie, who, nevertheless, felt she had to have her own place and break up with the broker before she took up with a new partner.

Although Laurie was reluctant to break it off completely, she did begin to build a townhouse in Norwalk, Connecticut, while lunching regularly with Jack. Six months later, she decided she would like to have a relationship with him— although Jack had decided he'd like to have a relationship with her the first time he met Laurie.

The beginning of a more serious relationship stalled when Jack thought Laurie stood him up on their first official date. "I wanted her to meet all my friends," Jack said. "And here I thought I was such a cocksman—bragging about this outrageous, knockout blond—and she doesn't show up! God! Did those guys bust my balls!"

Laurie tried to explain she never promised she would meet him, but Jack did not want to hear her excuse. When finally, he asked her out again, this time to a company party, he added, "You probably won't show, but..."

"Now remember, we were six months into doing lunch, and hadn't even kissed," Laurie emphasized. "We were very, very attracted to each other, but there was nothing sexual going on. To prove to Jack I would show up, I promised him, 'If I'm not there by nine o'clock—I mean it—I'll give you a blow job.' *That* got his attention!"

On her way to keep her promise, Laurie couldn't find a cab. Feeling doomed, she ran down into the subway. Having never taken one before, she had no clue which train to take. "Knowing this would be it for Jack and me if I was late, I was frantically running around the subway, can you believe in my mink coat!" The clock was ticking, and Laurie was completely lost. She hopped onto what she prayed was an uptown train and managed to race into the party at what she thinks was 9:01. Naturally, Jack said it was 9:03.

All was forgiven, she thought. They had a great time at the party, left there, and went to a nightclub. Before long it hit Laurie that Jack was with another date! "I was furious," she vividly remembers. "I couldn't believe he needed a back-up in case I didn't show!" Laurie stomped out of the club and went home to her still-live-in (by now roommate) broker's apartment. She decided she never wanted to see Jack again, and had second thoughts about breaking up with the broker.

"I was *bad*! A really, really bad womanizer," Jack said. "It was nothing for me to have affairs with two or three women—from models to corporate types—at the same time. I liked them all equally. So sometimes I would take them all out at once."

Surprised these women would put up with that, I said, "You mean you'd line them up like trophies?"

"Yeah, sort of. And even when we broke up, we always remained friends."

A couple of weeks later, Jack called Laurie. She caved in. And the couple started dating more seriously. It wasn't long before the trysts heated up and turned sexual, even though she was still living with the broker. "I don't know if he ever caught on," Laurie said. "However, I couldn't live with myself knowing I was playing around behind his back, so I rented a fully furnished apartment in Stamford until my condo was completed." That's when the dumped broker started sending her roses, and making every effort to try to get her back, but to no avail.

After Jack's separation, he wanted his kids to stay in their house, but he couldn't afford to do that and rent an apartment. As soon as Laurie got her own place, he started to spend more and more time at her apartment and later at her newly built condo.

"So he moved in for economic reasons," I interrupted.

"Oh *absolutely*," Susie burst out. "And to be honest with you, he did not contribute at all." He didn't clean or cook either.

"Yeah, but I did wind down all my other affairs one by one," Jack assured me.

"At this point, Jack was an alcoholic," Laurie said. "I didn't know it because most of our dates were at restaurants, or parties, or we met at local bars after work." Then Jack got involved with cocaine. "I also knew the combination of coke and booze was going to kill him. But what happens when you live with someone who drinks all the time is you start to drink more and more yourself. I also began to do cocaine once in a while on weekends."

However, Laurie came to grips with her life in the fast lane when her career catapulted. She said to herself, "Hey! Wait a minute, we have a problem here." And when Jack's drug and alcohol abuse began wrecking their relationship, she stopped dabbling in drugs as fast as she started. But because the first year was so wonderful, and Jack hid his addictions so well, Laurie didn't really get how bad it was until "Jack started to not come home."

"You are a beautiful woman," I interrupted. "You had everything going for you personally. What possessed you to stick with this nightmare of a marital test drive?"

"When Jack was sober, we were very compatible. I wanted this relationship to work so badly. I was in such denial, I bawled myself out for making more of it than it was." She replayed the good parts over and over again to erase all the bad. "But worse, Jack kept promising 'it will never happen again.'" And Laurie believed him.

The first two and a half years were hell, but the last year was torture. Because Laurie was already head over heels in love, she put up with it and excused his behavior. "But what a lot of people don't understand is, even though you're in love with someone you never really know how bad addiction is, although, I knew it was putting a lot of strain on our relationship."

That notwithstanding, Laurie felt she could fix it. "But eventually, I couldn't look the other way. The drugs conquered me." Laurie became the enabler, making excuses for Jack, not just to the outside world, but worse—to herself.

At the height of Jack's coke addiction, he was always sexually aroused, she says, but he could not perform. "Our sex life was very unsatisfying," Laurie complained. And after Jack came down from a binge, he was so moody, nothing she did—

including cleaning her own house—was ever good enough for him. Yet she stayed with him. "The denial was so bad," Laurie explained, "I couldn't tell right from wrong." Laurie says she knows she needed help for herself, but everyone thought she was so perfect, she was afraid to let on how bamboozled she was by Jack's charm and false promises. She couldn't let go.

"It got so bad," Jack said, "I dropped into a bar I hadn't been to in a couple of years. When the bartender turned around and saw me, her eyes popped open. She struck at my heart when she said, 'You're still *alive*!'" At that point Jack went off the deep end.

Eventually, his kids came to hate him. They were very disrespectful, and Jack was on the verge of losing his job. Instead of spending time with Laurie, who no longer participated in his habits, he ignored her, went out with his drinking cronies, and found other playmates to cheat with. Jack makes it very clear, "Druggies have no scruples. Once you get in over your head, whatever morals and spiritual values you had go out the window." Nevertheless, Laurie was crazy about him. She put up with all types of abuse and supported him, too!

"One day, I came to the realization, 'Wait a minute, I'm really the asshole here! I'm living with a guy who's got a drug problem, who's got a drinking problem, who cheats on me, has an ex-wife, two kids, alimony payments, and a W2 form that reads $9,000.'" To top that, Laurie had also agreed to rent an apartment on New York's West Side in both of their names.

Three-and-a-half years into their relationship, Laurie woke up one morning and said to Jack, who was moments away from getting fired, "That's it! I don't know why I am here. You have to get help. You've hit bottom, and you're not taking me down with you." She took everything she owned out of the New York apartment and walked out on him. "I finally realized I've got my own house, my own car, a great job. I don't need this."

She didn't hear from Jack for two weeks. She went back one evening to see him and to see if her leaving him had made a difference. When Laurie saw he was in the same state, she told Jack she would never be back. The next morning Jack called her.

"I knew I had hit rock bottom," he said. "I would wake up in the morning and beg God not to let me drink. Then I'd have that first drink, and any desire to quit vanished." This time though, he called a friend, a recovering alcoholic, who said, "I've been waiting too long for this call." When Jack told Laurie he was going to a rehab clinic, that he needed help, Laurie said, "Yeah, sure."

Jack enrolled in a thirty-five day program in Pennsylvania. When Laurie saw he meant it, she stood by him, and drove two-and-a-half hours each weekend to see him. When Jack got out, he and Laurie went back to their apartment and her Connecticut townhouse, which she had scoured to remove any trace of booze and drugs. Jack embraced the entire Alcoholics Anonymous program where he went through the ninety meetings in ninety days. However, during one of the counseling sessions, the therapist told Laurie, " If you're going to stick by Jack, you're going to have to hang around for at least a year. Don't make any changes."

She agreed to follow through. "And that's when our relationship moved to a whole, new level," she said. "I was really committed to Jack, and to his getting better."

"Laurie made me realize I had something to live for, to stay sober for," Jack said. He spent the better part of a year making amends with his children and co-workers, and getting his life back on track. He also began contributing to household expenses and purchases. Already a success when he was drunk, when Jack was sober, his commissions soared!

However, Laurie was questioning her devotion. Could she cope if Jack went back on booze and drugs? Could she go through the humiliation of his drunken womanizing and another rehabilitation period? At the same time, she wondered if Jack would turn out to be an AA holy-roller who couldn't be around anybody who drinks. Would she have to alter her lifestyle also? Laurie was used to being in control of Jack's life. After he got back on his feet, she realized that her control wasn't working. Intense therapy helped her relinquish some of that control. "But to this day," Laurie says, "my assertiveness gets in the way."

Jack stopped drinking, forever, on September 17, 1986. A year-and-a-half later he proposed to Laurie. "By then, he wanted to get married the next day," she laughed. "But we waited until August." In the interim while they were looking for a house in the country, Laurie discovered all sorts of wonderful hobbies Jack used to love to do that he gave up when he was always drinking—especially boating and gardening.

"Now, Jack needs to go to Gardener's Anonymous," Laurie joked. "What a hoot! I can hear him now. 'Hi! I'm Jack. I haven't planted a bulb in three days!' He traded one addiction for another," she said, giggling.

"Yeah," Jack said. "I've lived two lives in one life."

The couple just celebrated their ninth wedding anniversary. And because of Laurie's commitment to Jack and Jack's commitment to sobriety and Laurie, they have a great chance of spending the rest of their lives together. The success of their marriage hinges on the trust Laurie developed when Jack went into rehab before they were married.

When pinned down, Laurie admits her marital test drive wasn't rational. To anyone else she looked like a successful woman in control, when in fact, she went through sheer hell. And Jack doesn't know whether she'll stick around if he falls off the wagon again. But what he does know is, if he falls off the wagon, he'll die.

The burden of their marital test drive was on Laurie. The success of their marriage is up to him.

Alcoholics and drug addicts can recover. However, proceed with utmost caution. This type of relationship could be hazardous to *your* health. If you feel you are in an abusive live-in relationship, get help for yourself. Laurie and Jack are the exception.

A COLLEGE ROMANCE
TURNS INTO A SEVEN-YEAR
LIVE-IN RELATIONSHIP

"The advantage of living together first, especially for women who want to finish their formal schooling and find careers that make them happy, is that you have time to become a more well-rounded person, and thus a more well-rounded component in the relationship," Rose began.

She met her husband, Michael, when she was nineteen years old. "That had a lot to do with why we didn't get married early on," she says. "I was too young. Later on, I wanted to get established as an art dealer and appraiser before becoming a spouse, where I would have yet another identity. Marriage is a huge commitment, and you have to be prepared for it." If not, she says, you'll resent the relationship, hate your spouse, and get lost in how you perceive you should conduct yourself to please others.

"Most marriages I know that are very problematic have partners who went into it not knowing what their goals in life and expectations are," she continued. "Some women may think they want to have decisions made for them, but they'll never know what options are available to them." In the long run, will they stand up to the stresses of modern marriage?

From Rose's point of view, individuals change, and should. "But I think when you are young and impressionable, change occurs very frequently. It is an added burden if those people have to worry about conforming too strictly in their personal lives." Living together gives you freedom and the leeway to develop autonomy. "Michael and I grew a lot when we lived together, which was very interesting. And in many ways we grew apart. It was terribly important to find who we were as individuals before we got married."

"And you could do that while living together?"

"We did," she said. "I think because we maintained some-what separate lives in terms of friends and our very diverse careers. That was healthy for both our living together rela-tionship and marriage. We came together on a lot of things, but maintained a healthy separateness we have carried into marriage."

"Tell me what immediate advantages you enjoyed when you married."

"I thought it was sort of a giggle to introduce ourselves as Mr. and Mrs.," Rose confessed. "And there was an easiness about making hotel reservations. From a financial aspect, it was easier conducting business as a married couple. And of course, we definitely had a nod of approval from our families who weren't that big on our living together."

"That seems to be a big issue among unofficially marrieds," I commented.

"In our case, that was true," Rose agreed. "Michael and I did not tell our parents we were living together until three years later, after I graduated from college."

"So you didn't go through any big adjustments when you got married?"

"No. Not really. We bought a home while we were living together, which might have been easier if we had been married. But that's all."

"A lot of people I have talked with say they go to great lengths to make the wedding special. In your case, you bought a home. To go from the church back to the same house you lived in together doesn't suggest change. In a sense, the blush was off the rose. Or, am I wrong?"

"There were a variety of things we did to make it a special step in a different direction," Rose explained. "Before we married, Michael and I felt we really needed to talk things out when we discussed the commitment we were making to one another. After we were married, there was a more comfortable silence between us. It was assumed things would be a certain way. Because we lived together, the parameters of the relationship had been established. Before, we spent excruciating moments establishing the rules. Living together eliminated that stress after we married."

"What was one of the biggest benefits of getting married?"

"In the past, if Michael was invited to a relative's wedding, I might wonder if I was going to be invited. How would I be introduced? Would I be invited to the rehearsal dinner? That sort of social ambiguity is gone. It was easier for everyone else when we married. You immediately feel like you aren't just a girlfriend. You feel as if you are a specially chosen person rather than 'and guest.'"

"What worried you most when you decided to get married?"

"Initially, I was hesitant because I was afraid to rock the boat. Everything was working so well."

"What convinced you to get married?"

"My dad had recently passed away. I felt I took away a dream he always had to walk me down the aisle. I got married for him."

Originally, when Rose and Michael planned to get married, she especially wanted a very small wedding at which the two of them would confess their love to one another in an extremely private ceremony. "It sounds very flower-child-like…New Age," she giggled, "but I wanted the exchange to be ours alone. Then one day, a friend explained her own philosophy. She thought making this profession of love in front of her family and friends would give her marriage much more of a bond; give her marriage strength and would make it a more serious and significant commitment. That's when I realized I wanted to go in a different direction than we initially planned, and had a big wedding. My friend made me see how important it should be to me, also, to share my happiness with the people I love."

There is something to be said for the community coming forth to rejoice in the new couple's happiness. Which is why, after conducting a variety of interviews, I have concluded that living together, to some people in our society, is offensive. Because the relationship isn't officially sanctioned, some people view it as tantamount to thumbing your nose at something they believe in. In these circles, couples lack status, and friends and family not only shun the relationship they shut the couple out, isolating them from their community.

Rose and Michael have been married for nine years and been together for seventeen years in all. I asked her, "What do you think are the differences between being married and living together?"

"There were many rewards in taking the next step. I didn't know what they were because many of them were very subtle. Until I took that step, there was a little bit of blind faith involved. I almost felt a sigh of relief. I had the feeling I was now part of a unit," Rose said.

"How do you view living together today?"

"I still can't help but think the trial run for Michael and me was positive. We were better prepared for the nuances of daily life that emerge from being official partners. Living together prepared us to know that we can live together in a designed space that we both agree upon and want to be in. I can't think of anyone who shouldn't test drive marriage first."

"So, you truly are an advocate of premarital cohabitation?"

"Oh, absolutely. It went against the religion I was brought up in. And it went against the mores of my family. And I am sure a lot of people regarded it as being radical. But I was often surprised they couldn't see the logic to it. It makes such sense, and offers people more flexibility. Living together teaches couples so much about themselves as individuals, and also how they will react as partners."

UNNERVING PROCRASTINATION

If you are not careful, the living-together relationship can turn out to be a nightmare of indecision and procrastination.

Living with someone who cannot decide whether he or she wants to marry you destroys you. The antidote is: Don't allow it. However, when both parties suffer from indecision, the immobility is frustrating. If allowed to continue over a period of time, it can destroy a relationship.

In Kay's* and George's* relationship, indecision was their way of life. George, well into his forties, had never been married. Living with Kay perpetuated his innate procrastination. George could not decide whether he wanted to be a husband or not. He could not decide whether he wanted to be a father or not. At the same time, Kay desperately wanted to be George's wife, but waited for George to call the shots. "I promised myself I would never go through another long-term dating period," she says, "only to fall into the same trap again." At seventeen, she met her first husband. They dated for seven years, got married, and two years later, divorced. Then Kay met George, and although she chastised herself for doing it, she put herself through another seven-year ordeal.

After four years of dating the couple decided they would like to get married. But neither party pushed it, George because he had been a bachelor for so long, Kay because she was too weak and embarrassed to assert herself and pin him down.

"We weren't brave enough to just go ahead and get married," she regrets. The interim comfort zone they chose was for Kay to move out of her apartment into George's condo. "That answered the 'What do we do next?' quandary," she said. However, Kay emphasized *she* assumed that marriage was only a step away.

Six months later, he finally gave her an engagement ring, but balked at setting a wedding date. One year agonizingly turned into two, which soon added up to six. And still, the couple hadn't discussed *when* they were going to get married. By now, Kay was frantic. At the same time, it shamed her to admit that their two-year marital test drive had veered off course.

Anxious about her future, Kay worried, "Maybe he doesn't love me anymore. Should I start looking for an apartment?" Afraid to bring up the subject of marriage again, she quietly steamed. "At first you talk about it, then you kid about it," she remembers. "But after so many years of not getting a response to any mention of getting married, you drop it, and assume it isn't going to happen."

The couple lived together in limbo. "No one said anything," Kay sighed. "I was walking on eggshells all the time—deflated by false hopes. It was shaky ground for me." She says it became evident she had lost control, and she felt paralyzed to do anything about it.

Kay's mother had started making wedding plans, but then was at a loss as time dragged on. "George is a very private person," Kay said. He didn't really want a big wedding. "But I kind of did." So once again, even though George says he always knew they would get married someday, Kay had to endure the insecurity of not knowing where she was headed. So she just waited.

I asked Kay, "Would you have ever had the guts to say, 'George, just when are we going to get married?' Or, 'George, I've set the date. Will you show?' Or, 'George, do you still want to marry me?'"

"I wish I had," she said. "But I wasn't the person then I am today." She admitted she is very passive and needs to work on that.

Soon after, Kay's mother died. "I was at my lowest ebb," she remembers. "I was very depressed and not communicating. And nothing George did could snap me out of it." George told a friend about Kay, and he recommended she visit a psychologist. When George called and made the appointment for Kay, the therapist suggested he come in with her, also. However, Kay revealed, "George resisted that notion, and said, 'it was her mother who died and it's her problem.'"

She says the counselor countered with, "'But I treat couples. And this is your problem, too.'"

Reluctantly, George went. And after they talked about Kay's mother's death, and dealing with the natural grief surrounding it, the counselor zeroed in on an underlying problem: the indecision to get married. Kay says the counselor pried open a can of worms when he asked Kay, "What's that on your finger?"

"It's my engagement ring!"

"How nice. When did you get engaged?"

Kay told him, "Two and a half years ago."

"What are your wedding plans?"

"We don't have any," she sighed.

"Why not?" The therapist went on, "Do you want to be engaged? Or do you want to be married?"

"That's true!" Kay said. "I was so excited to get the ring. Our family and friends were so happy we were engaged, I dropped the ball and didn't push about getting married."

Kay says George hedged, "Well, we're like waiting. Kay's mother died…We don't know what kind of wedding to have…I'm not sure I want a baby…" and made one excuse after the other.

After a few sessions full of excuses, the counselor cut to the chase. "Is there anything you don't know about each other you need to know after all these years?"

"No, not really," Kay and George responded simultaneously.

"Then, since you have all the data on each other," the therapist reminded them, "and since nothing awful is going to pop up that will drastically alter your feelings about each other—and since George has agreed that if you want to have a baby he won't stop you—what you need to decide is either to get married, or to break up." It's as simple as that. "Living this way is not healthy for either one of you," he said. "Your relationship can only go up from here."

When the couple left the psychologist's office, they were dazed. "Someone had challenged us to do something," Kay said. "It gave us such energy." The change in their relationship was significant. "We both felt more secure. Our love affair was finally going somewhere." On that high note, the couple ran to Borough Hall and got a marriage license. Next, they found somebody to marry them. A week and a half later, they were pronounced man and wife without fanfare.

"A lot of people think it's only the woman who feels insecure when she lives with a man," Kay related. But she learned after they were married that George had often worried, "Would she pack up and leave?" The trouble is neither Kay nor George shared these feelings with each other.

Looking back, Kay says, "When we decided to move in together, we both thought we felt committed. It felt warm to close down my apartment, move in together, and become a family. Although it was nice, we never felt like we established a solid foundation." Kay says she can describe that difference only now that she is married but she often wondered when she was living with George if marriage would change the good feelings they had.

"I don't really know whether living together helped our cause, but, for us, it all worked out." When she learns a couple has chosen to live together, she says, "I'm not all that keen on it. There was nothing I learned about George after living together I didn't already know through dating." However, she said, laughing, "If I had lived with my first husband, I never would have married him." But then again, the odds were against her. She was only seventeen years old when she met him.

"Now that George and I have been married for three years—have been together for ten, I'm going to muster up the courage and finally hang some pictures on the walls and make this place mine, too." Since then, Kay and George have become parents.

It's too bad it took so long for them to get to this point. But at least they made it. A lesson here is that it's always worth asserting yourself, especially when your demands are reasonable. Had Kay pushed for marriage sooner, they would have had more happy years. And maybe even another baby!

SO WHAT DO
YOU THINK?

When I had completed the first draft of *Test-Driving Marriage*, my husband, Sam took me to André and Rita Jammet's La Caravelle in New York City to celebrate. It's a glorious restaurant, especially for festive occasions. With champagne glasses raised, we toasted each other, then he said, "So, what do you think?"

I said, "I think there is never any perfect answer when it comes to love, loving, and being in love. We cannot rely on levels of love to be constant. It's not always a reliable emotion. What worked yesterday doesn't work today. And some days are wonderful; others defy us."

Because most living-together couples worry about getting everything perfect before they marry, they can't cope when something goes wrong after they tie the knot. They have left no margin for error. And you know what invariably happens when the pressure is on to perform perfectly—we blow even the simplest thing. Therefore, chances are when an unattainable level of perfection is expected in a relationship, it usually becomes *imperfect*. Sadder still, maintaining perfection is a distressing, insurmountable, ulcer-producing burden.

When a couple marries *before* having lived together, most of them don't expect to know all the answers. And because they don't, they fumble around as they work at making things better. LTCs *think* they have it all figured out. Therefore, things can only get worse if they marry. By operating under this assumption, individuals distrust love and distrust falling in love ever again.

Cohabitation is marriage's parody, which is why, in my opinion, living together makes one or both partners feel especially vulnerable. The insecurity attached to not being legally attached creates self-doubt, which spills over to every area of a living-together couple's lives.

After conducting the many interviews I needed to write a balanced book, I still believe living together is iffy at best. Before I began, this opinion was an intuition. No longer conjecture, my opinion is now substantiated by my research and people's firsthand experiences, and I understand the reasons why I came to my initial conclusion. It is my hope that, as a result of my efforts, you are beginning to understand trial marriage better, too.

While writing these first two sections, I realized another reason why couples are impatient when coping with relationship problems. As we zoom through the electronic age toward the next millennium, there is little we do that takes more than a few minutes. We can e-mail a brother across the country, fax a girlfriend living in Paris, order a pizza from our car. Computer-driven results to anything we want to know are at our fingertips. The Internet puts us instantly in touch with anything we want to know. Yet ironically, there is no zippy software that fixes relationship problems.

Spoiled by speed, we haven't developed the patience it takes to work out problems in a relationship. Learning how to communicate with a loved one takes time. Results are slow. Used to built-in obsolescence and speedy technology, we may find it simpler and faster to get rid of "that one" and start afresh. We mistakenly think it's easier to sweep relationship idiosyncrasies under the rug, rather than face them head on. But if we don't get the bugs out, they'll only return to zap us the next time around.

I've pointed out before most living-together relationships don't make it down the aisle. Remember the first couple we met? Joseph and Serena broke up last February, bearing out the statistics that unmarried couples usually break up. Taking a hiatus from getting seriously involved with a woman, Joseph has embarked upon a worldwide sales pitch for his art (an idea stemming from Serena's marketing expertise).

Serena is back in Miami, where she has taken a job with a newly formed advertising agency and is working on her abandoned graphics art hobby. You remember that their relationship was all about perfection: If you were just a little more this. A little less that. If you saw things my way. If only you were more perfect. Unfortunately, they burned out.

Yet, oddly enough, their break-up was perfect. They've remained friends. And probably always will be. "I'll always love Joey," Serena said with a great big smile.

Working at any relationship is a formidable task. Staying together is a challenge. However, when we care enough to take the risk, we end up with a lifetime love affair, a companionship that is far greater than the sum of its parts.

When people call and seek my opinion, and after I give it, I find it more revealing to probe, "So, what do *you* think?" I hope I have provoked you sufficiently so that you can answer that one for yourself.

STILL NOT CONVINCED?

If you are dead set against marriage or insist upon living with your significant other before marrying, the next two sections of this book deal with intricate unofficial marriage snags, financial, legal, and cultural matters you should be aware of *before* you actually move in together. You'll give your marital test drive its best shot by accepting that it might not work. Be prepared. Learn how to protect your possessions, your reputation, and yourself from an ugly court battle.

The invaluable advice offered next by those couples who made it, those who broke up, and the experts who helped them with the paperwork required to successfully opt out of marriage, could, in your case, make the difference between a simple, amicable transition and one headed for doom.

THE CULTURAL
ASPECTS OF
LIVING TOGETHER

MOM, THIS IS MY...
WHATCHAMACALLIT!

G oing out with someone new? You've got a date with a *date*. Get a bit more serious and your date evolves into a girl- or boyfriend, a steady, beau, sweetheart, significant other, or even a honey. Fall deeply in love and get engaged, you'll be promoted to fiancé(e), bride-to-be, or an intended. Collectively: lovebirds. Marry, and everyone's calling you new-lyweds or honeymooners. Individually—husband or wife, although it's becoming more popular and politically correct to use the generic: spouse. Romantic men refer to their wives of many years as "my bride." Less used is "my old lady." Nevertheless, these common names work. Everyone knows who you're talking about, and what the relationship is.

When couples live together, tongue-tied partners often fumble when reaching for an apt label. Somehow, "Oh hi, this is my spousal equivalent, Mary Jane," doesn't cut it. Using just his or her name may lend an air of suspense, but it leaves people cold—especially when those close to the LTC are dying to know where this relationship is going, but don't want to ask.

Thinking over titles couples could use, I considered roommate—but that's not terribly romantic. Friend? Not even close! Few jump into bed with just friends. In this book's introduction, I discuss Judge Ben Lindsay's 1920 proposal of the "companionate marriage." Although the motion was rejected by the courts, companionate has a mystical air. Chamberpal has a new-age twist. The truth is there isn't a term in the English language for unofficial marrieds.

In 1990, when the United States Bureau of the Census first documented the number of live-in-lover households or heterosexual, cohabiting couples, the acronym POSSLQ, pronounced poss-l-q's, (Persons of the Opposite Sex Sharing Living Quarters) came into use. Yet, day to day, it's impossibly cumbersome.

At a Christmas tea I gave last year, my interior designer Mary Fran Brassard told me a bittersweet story about a business associate. When this fellow's mother called her son's house, she would rudely ignore his live-in; even refused to speak to her if she answered the phone. When the couple became engaged, she acknowledged and spoke endearingly to her future daughter-in-law—her son's *fiancée*. Same live-in scenario, even though a wedding date had not been set. However, the young woman had gained significance in her mother-in-law's eye.

"Cohabitation has so recently become established as a lifestyle that societal norms have not yet had time to develop," writes family and marriage researcher Lloyd Saxton.[1] "The absence of a commonly accepted term for a cohabitor underlines the ambiguous nature of cohabitation in our society."

Partners may not realize how the lack of an appropriate term affects them, but not having a descriptive niche may eventually compromise the relationship, other friendships, and family acceptance.

SOCIAL AND
BUSINESS PROTOCOL
FOR THE LTC

When we plan to get married, there are loads of etiquette books and experts offering advice on how to
plan for "the big day" and life together. Most also discuss
proper social protocol when one is involved with a divorce.
However, advice on what is politically correct when a couple
moves in together is still evolving. Most etiquette experts
agree that how an unmarried couple should and should not
act—both privately, publicly, and at work—boils down to
using good taste and consideration.

Deciding how to proceed can be a problem for the couple,
their families and friends, coworkers, and bosses. Out of igno-
rance, critical mistakes can be made by all parties, such as: you
may be elated your boyfriend has asked you to move in with

him, but should you run around the office screeching the good news? Some coworkers will disapprove, and even though it may not seem fair, a prudish boss could use it against you.

BUSINESS ETIQUETTE

Good Housekeeping magazine etiquette columnist and author Peggy Post, great granddaughter-in-law of etiquette authority Emily Post, has recently issued the sixteenth edition of Emily's first book. She says, "As far as telling everybody you work with you are living with someone, you may casually want to mention your relationship to coworkers, but weigh each situation individually." She advises that you really don't need to announce your relationship to your business associates. "However, if it should come up in conversation, do not lie nor hide. Living together has not replaced marriage, but it certainly has found a place in our society." In that respect, Mrs. Post told me, "The key thing for the couple to consider is what all of this means to them personally. Though you do want to think about other people, as well."[1]

As for couples moving in together who work at the same firm, Columbia, South Carolina business etiquette consultant, Ann Humphries, president of Eticon, Inc., (Etiquette Consultants for Business) and writer of the business etiquette newspaper column, "The Right Moves," said, "If this couple conducts their relationship with dignity, everyone will be happy for them." However, she warned, "they must pay close attention to not show extreme, open displays of affection. A peck on the cheek is acceptable, an exaggerated back rub is not."

The same discretion applies to the ups and downs of your personal life. "There is an element of excitement at the office when someone has a new boyfriend," Ann said. "And it is okay to reveal that, but if you talk about it too much, then it becomes burdensome." The same rule applies if a coworker has problems at home, or his or her relationship breaks up. It is appropriate to mention you may not be yourself because your live-in walked out, but anything beyond that is not professional during work hours.

On another front, Ms. Humphries and I talked about the fine line between unofficially married couples and married couples when it comes to a firm's nepotism policy. She said, "Bearing in mind the ethical component, unrelated, domestic partners who work together are operating within a gray area." If a couple knows their company has this rule then, Ann warned, "they are going to have to be extremely discreet." In her view, this duo should not be perceived as a couple. "They're going to have to make a choice. Do they want to be a couple, or do they want to be employed at the same company?"

In response, I said, "I can see some precedent-setting lawsuits here."

"Yes," Ms. Humphries said, "you may be right. An attorney would probably know the answer to that." On the other hand she said, "There are times when you need somebody to push the envelope…we all need people to break down barriers. Despite that, it can be really awkward."[2] When people are breaking the rules—creating a conflict of interest—an element of trustworthiness diminishes.

ETIQUETTE AT HOME:
RESPECTING FRIENDS AND FAMILY

Speaking practically, Peggy Post suggested the first person you need to contact is your letter carrier and advise him or her of the additional party residing at your address. "After that, or concurrently," she said, "you should tell your family—whether or not you think they will approve."

I wondered, "To help friends who may telephone the residence feel comfortable when they call and get a strange voice—and a quick way for them to get to know his or her name—would it be appropriate to send announcements saying something cute like: 'Mr. John Doe and Ms. Mary Smith are now romantically linked and live together at…'?"

Peggy laughed and said, "You can, but certainly do not send out anything engraved. You will want to keep it simple. A change of address card or simple note card is appropriate."

We have learned live-in lovers don't have a proprietary position such as wife, husband, spouse, fiancé(e)…even mistress. So how do you address your unmarried couple status? Mrs. Post said, "Fifteen years ago, etiquette books referred to these couples as POSSLQ's but that term bombed out." Today, when you are introducing your live-in to a new or casual acquaintance, she said do not feel obligated to identify him or her by anything other than his or her name. On the other hand, if you are with company you know well, it is perfectly appropriate to say: "This is the person I live with."

In order for everyone to feel comfortable, and your significant other to feel welcome, don't assume people know that you are living with someone. If you know you and your live-in companion are going to be invited to a function of a friend of yours, you may want to mention you will be attending with your live-in and give his or her name, and follow up with a note.

And what about invitations? Should two separate ones be sent to the same household? Is it polite to place both names on the outer envelope? Or, should one of you be referred to as the "guest" "Once a couple is living together," Mrs. Post informed me, "invitations are generally handled the same way as a married couple." In this case, you address the envelope by putting one person's name on one line and the other person's name on the next line, except you drop the *and*. I thought it was interesting the woman doesn't necessarily go first. Mrs. Post said, "Either way is correct, but it's nice to write the name of the person you know best on the first line."

Gracious behavior will go a long way to make your living arrangements comfortable for all concerned. If grandma does not approve of your marital test drive, make every effort to let her get to know your partner. Invite her for dinner or visit her together, often. However, don't flaunt the sexual aspect of your relationship by hanging all over each other. Once she gets to know what a princely guy or gal you've chosen to shack up with, she may not approve, but she'll probably adjust to it.

INFRINGEMENTS UPON SPACE, BOUNDARIES, AND PRIVACY

After the novelty has worn off, a couple often finds getting down to the nitty-gritty of living together a nerve-racking experience. Century City, CA psychologist, Dr. Hollie B. Rice, also an assistant clinical professor in the Department of Psychiatry and Behavioral Sciences at UCLA, feels couples live together to hold on to a certain level of independence. She says, "More so than marriage, maintaining a separateness by respecting space, autonomy, and independence are important factors if couples want to develop a healthy, fulfilling living-together relationship.

"When one partner crosses over the boundaries of living-together and assumes a more possessive marital-type role," says Dr. Rice, "the reasons couples chose to live together over marriage are challenged." Consider typical behavioral mistakes new LTCs make that can be real relationship wreckers:

1. INSISTING YOU HAVE TO BE TOGETHER
AROUND THE CLOCK

Too much togetherness can suddenly be yuck! Couples can O.D. from each other, too. A bit of distance is an essential elixir.

There may be friends you want to see on your own, after-work job responsibilities, or networking events you may have to attend—and he/she hasn't been invited. A jealous partner forces you—unfairly—to make a beeline to the exit door.

2. NOT LETTING YOUR PARTNER
GO IT ALONE ONCE IN AWHILE

You may love to go to the ballet, but he hates it. It is perfectly normal and appropriate to want to continue doing the things you like to do. Go alone or with a friend who shares those interests.

3. NOT RESPECTING YOUR LOVER'S PRIVACY

Some people simply want to be alone; they enjoy their own company. Be mature enough to know that doesn't mean he/she doesn't love you. I spend a lot of time at the library doing research. On many occasions I run into a friend of mine who lives with someone. One day, I said, "Gee. I see you in here all the time. You must love to read."

I never thought he would respond, "Not as much as I need my space."

People do need their space. When the partner they live with does not respect their lover's autonomy—their individuality—that's violating boundaries.

4. VIOLATING BOUNDARIES

Walking in on someone without knocking is an obvious way of violating boundaries. But so is not letting your lover say what he/she thinks. Or insisting someone agree with everything you say. Or knocking him for not liking the same colors you do, or the same restaurants, or your friends. Being overbearing violates boundaries, and after a while causes damage to any relationship.

Meddling with someone's identity or career advancement and potential is another cause for the break up of a marital test drive. Pay attention to your lover's moods. Could it be you're not showing him any respect? Or perhaps you are dumping your dishes in the sink, expecting her to clean up, taking her for granted, or dumping on her. Walking all over someone violates boundaries, as does telling your partner how to spend or not spend his or her money. Disrupting or disrespecting your partner's individuality by insisting things should be done your way should be avoided, too.

5. HOGGING THE BATHROOM

There are no official statistics to prove it, and don't laugh, but I'll bet LTCs split up more quickly when they have only one bathroom. Bonnie Segall, my publicist at Barricade Books, says she and her twenty-something friends are certain a LTC's love affair might survive having one checkbook, but two bathrooms are essential to keeping a relationship going.

It makes perfect sense. Think about all the reasons we use the bathroom. I use it for solace. When I'm really peeved, or need to get away from my husband and kids, I can sit in there for hours. And where do you go, and feel confident enough to lock the door when you want to sob, check out your figure, or try on a new dress for the first time? Where else can you hide out to pull your cheeks back and dream about how fantastic you could look with plastic surgery or a new hair style? To many of us, the potty is a sanctuary.

6. MOVING IN BEFORE TESTING THE WATER

Recently, Sam and I took a trip to Paris. When we got to our hotel room, because I was writing this book, I paid particular attention to how we settled into our new digs. The first question Sam asked was: "Which side of the bed do you want?" My next thought was if we both need to get up and out at the same time and he's in the bathroom, where will I put on my make-up? The full length floor mirror and the floor became my vanity. There was one tiny desk that Sam decided right off the bat would be his catch-all. Which left me the top of the TV. When I was freezing, he was hot, so we took off the down comforter, raised the air, and I put on a sweatshirt. The fact that there were two night stands, with separate reading lights—so I could read and he could sleep—balanced the drawbacks. We coped by asking each other, "What do you prefer?" And compromised.

I wondered how different the circumstances would have been if Sam had arrived at the hotel a day earlier, and I got whatever drawers and closet space he left me, and became *his* guest.

Because I equated that experience with living together, I realized a good test for any couple contemplating moving in together would be to try a hotel room first. It doesn't have to be The Plaza or a fancy resort. Try a Days Inn. See how you adjust on a couple of different occasions. Stay about four days, since anyone can cope with a weekend. Watch who hogs all of the closet space; who is inconsiderate when using the bathroom. Who leaves dirty socks by the side of the bed? If you survive the long weekend, you'll have a good indication of what's to come when you move in together permanently, or as permanently as this type of relationship allows.

7. NOT GETTING A BRAND NEW PLACE

If the partners live at home, have recently separated from a spouse, or have just graduated from college, it makes sense to get a new place together. And when you do, input from each party makes it easier to compromise on decisions like decor, which side of the bed he'll sleep on, household chores, maintenance problems, and who will use the shower or the phone first.

Because you established your household together, territorial problems are usually reduced. "When one partner moves into the other's Love Shack," wrote Kenneth Blanchard for *Mademoiselle* magazine, "it sets up an unequal power axis, and the situation gets sticky if the homeowner gets territorial."

IT'S MY HOUSE!

Katie and Glenn have lived together since July 1993. She says, "In the beginning, it was a difficult adjustment, especially for him. He has five grown children; mine are ages fifteen, thirteen, and eight." Since that time, her two older boys went back to live with their dad. What irks Katie is Glenn is not willing to help raise her young daughter. She says, "I suppose I agree with him when he says he feels it is not his place to discipline her." Yet, she vacillates and says, "Except he's living in my house, and when I run into difficulty, he could at least step in and help out, rather than criticize from the sidelines. Under those circumstances," Katie says, "I don't want your opinion."

Although Katie is the first to admit her relationship on the whole is a good one, she realizes, "After three years of living together a certain comfort level sets in, which can be an advantage, or a disadvantage because couples can so easily take each other for granted." She would rather be married to Glenn, but because he had a thirty-six year bad marriage, she understands why he's not eager to marry again. "I used to be insecure about not being married, but Glenn and I share expenses and household responsibilities, and respect and love each other almost as if we were married. However, the exception is he is living in *my* house."

Katie says she bristles when Glenn criticizes how she keeps house, or says, "Boy, how can you stand driving around in that messy car?" Or when he doesn't understand how hard it is to work full time and singlehandedly raise a young daughter and participate in her school and after-school activities. Considering there are only twenty-four hours in a day, any woman in that position could easily understand why making the beds and vacuuming the car are not high priorities.

"This *really* irritates me," she pointed out. "It's *my* house and *my* car!" And even if she chose never to clean it up again, she repeated to me, "It's *my* house!"

If you move into your boy- or girlfriend's house, it will take a very long time for you to settle in. He or she has had a routine way of doing things, and it's going to be tough to share closet space, adjust to your taste in music, let you move in furnishings from your old place, cope with your sloppiness, or adjust to your work schedule.

Since you're the newcomer, you may feel you have to give in. And if you do without discussing your rights beforehand, you're probably headed for splitsville. As inconvenient or expensive as it may be, avoid, at all costs, moving into someone else's place.

Learning to compromise—being flexible, and establishing rules and considerations of all sorts from the outset—makes the adjustment to moving in together a lot easier. And if you do make it down the aisle, that's one less newlywed hassle you'll have to deal with.

NONNUPTIAL CONTRACTS MAKE STRANGE BEDFELLOWS

IGNORANCE
IS NOT BLISS

Here is a real-life situation that illustrates why you need
to pay attention to all the legal nuances and ramifications surrounding unofficial marriage discussed in this section.
Francine's* naiveté shows how you can unwittingly get caught
in a dangerous financial and legal situation if you have no clue
about what you're getting into when you invite someone to
live with you.

A few months ago, Francine, a psychologist from Cincinnati,
was relieved to learn about my support group from an article in
Mademoiselle. She called my office. Not expecting to find me at
the other end of the telephone—and sure I would brush her
off—she exploded with, "Beliza, I have to have your advice!
Please just give me a minute."

Used to dealing with desperate people, I said, "If you calm down—take a deep breath—we'll get to the bottom of this a lot faster."

"I've been seeing this guy who's sixty for the past year and a half; I'm forty. He wants to move in. But I'm not sure."

"Well, do you love him?"

"Oh yeah! After my divorce, he took real good care of me. You know. He helped me move. And I have some pretty heavy furniture to lift for a sixty-year-old guy. After that, he kind of hung around to make sure I was all right. Pretty soon, we fell in love. And now he wants to move in with me. My mom is having a fit!"

"Why?" I asked, but thought I knew the answer.

"Well, he's a bartender," she said, "and broke! You know that's kind of a cash-type business. And now, he doesn't have a pension or much to fall back on. He's fallen on hard times and can't afford to pay the rent on his apartment. I'm trying to help him by taking a loan out for him to start his own business. But should I have him move in with me?"

Without hearing further details, I was shaking my head thinking, "Brother, this lady may have a psychotherapy degree, but certainly not one in common sense." The daytime tabloid shows on television would die to air this story: "Female Suckers!" Cosigning a loan, no less!

"Are you that comfortable financially?" I pried.

"Oh yes. I have a beautiful two-bedroom apartment. I also receive child support; but not alimony 'cause I made more money than my ex."

"Well then, have you thought about a relationship agreement?"

"What's that?"

"It's a legal contract that might protect your assets if this guy is after your money. And if he's not, it will validate his love for you. If he signs it, you'll know his heart's where it belongs. If he refuses, I would dump him."

"How do I get one?" she asked.

"Ask your divorce attorney to write it, or ask for a recommendation of someone experienced at drafting these documents. But make sure to find out if she's ever litigated one first."

"Wouldn't that be expensive?"

"Not as expensive as possibly losing your shirt!"

"True, but how much would it cost?"

"Well, you get what you pay for in this business," I warned. "The key is, time costs money. If you go to someone who's done enough of these, he can write it in fifteen minutes. You'll save a bundle, both now and later—if you have to go to court—versus using an attorney who hasn't got a clue, goes to school on you, takes weeks to bumble through it, and charges you for the privilege."

"Oh," Francine muttered, taking a few seconds to absorb the brief course on protecting her assets (Why is it so many women still can't grasp they have a net worth?) But apparently, that went right by her. Still not convinced, she whined, "Do you *really* think I need to do that?"

"Why do you think I have spent the last twenty minutes giving a perfect stranger free advice a lawyer would financially clobber her with? Of course, I think you *need* to do that. Have you talked to your mother about the loan, and his moving in?"

"Oh yes! She's really upset. She can't believe someone so smart, so beautiful, gets caught up with all these losers."

"Maybe she has a point. Shouldn't one divorce be enough?"

"Well, I'm not really divorced," she said.

"Oh my God! What do you mean? You said you were divorced!"

Come on! How did she think she could get a cohab agreement without a divorce certificate?

"I'm divorced under Jewish Law—I got a Get."

"That doesn't cut it in civil court, Francine."

"No, I guess not. He's not divorced either."

"You've *got* to be kidding!"

"It's not as it appears. He's been separated for ten years, but he hasn't gotten divorced because his wife has great insurance, and she keeps him on her policy."

"Isn't that sweet." *Talk about a freeloader of the worst order!* "What makes you think he's not involved with *you* for the money?"

"Oh, that would never happen," Francine assured me. "He's so nice. Tells me I'm gorgeous. Picks up my kids at school. Even if he's tired, he takes me out whenever I want to go and loves a good time."

"Who pays?"

"Well, um, I do. But he contributes when he can."

"Oh *really*. Wonder how long that's going to last?"

Francine still wasn't seeing the big picture when she said, "He really can't afford to live alone. Do you think it's a good idea for him to move in with me?" *And she counsels people!*

Common sense told me to hang up. My conscience screamed to give it another shot. Worn out, I hissed, "Not at this point. Let him get on his feet first, Francine. Besides, play the field for a while. Are you so desperate for a man you'll compromise everything you own? Next you'll open up a joint checking account and add his name as an authorized user of your credit card. You're responsible, Francine, for overdrafts."

I must have hit a raw nerve when she moaned, "Maybe my mother's right."

"She wasn't born yesterday, you know."

Lordie! If I didn't hear it with my own ears! What would you do? Let him move in and play it by ear? Or date indefinitely? If your answer is let him move in, I don't want to know about it.

POSTSCRIPT:

During a meeting with my publisher, Carole Stuart, she asked me, "How many people really have non-nuptial agreements?"

"It's hard to say," I replied. "But with the advent of computer programs that make it really easy and cheap to crank one out, and because the prenuptial agreement has become almost commonplace, more people than you think have living-together agreements, but less than I wish."

FINANCIAL TRAPS SURROUNDING COMMON-LAW MARRIAGE LAWS

Another trap LTCs fall into is common-law marriage. A popular belief is if a couple lives together for seven or more years, they are considered common law marriage partners. Not necessarily. In states where this archaic practice exists, two people could pen love notes declaring their marriage, and, in most situations that simply written vow would be enough to establish legal wedlock.

However, actions that would qualify a couple for common-law marriage status—in states that allow it—would be a woman adopting her lover's name; the parties signing the hotel register as Mr. and Mrs.; the couple filing joint tax returns; and generally conducting themselves openly as a married couple.

Unless contested, certain states protect common-law "spouses." Their children are automatically entitled to an inheritance, and the surviving spouse can collect life insurance.

With the exception of omitting the ceremony, common-law marriage sounds like the real thing to me. However, Indiana University historian Michael Grossberg, author of *Governing the Hearth: Law and the Family in 19th Century America* contends, "Common-law marriage provides a level of individualism and privacy recorded marriage cannot."[1]

The fundamental difference between common-law marriage and living together involves legal structure decided by each jurisdiction. If a couple cohabiting as man and wife terminate their relationship in a state that recognizes common-law marriage, the case will be heard in family, not civil, court. And even though the parties did not marry, a "divorce" certificate must be obtained in order for one party to sue the other, or remarry. Caught unaware of those states' matrimonial laws, you could unwittingly find yourself liable to pay alimony. In other states where cohabitation is legal and common-law marriage unrecognized, living-together disputes fall under contract law. If not settled out of court, a jury could decide the suit.

THE PITFALLS OF COMMON-LAW MARRIAGE

Ever hear of Shannon and Spinozi? They are the Howard Stern wannabes at *KRXO* radio in Oklahoma City. A few months ago, the caustic duo invited me to appear on their talk show. Aside from a few really distasteful, below-the-belt gibes directed at my husband, Sam's and my *naughty* fifteen year age difference, I thought their ribbing was fun.

If you can take the abuse, early morning radio interviews spice up an author's otherwise isolated life. Still in my pajamas, sipping vanilla-laced coffee, I can travel the airwaves hawking my books from LA to London. I also get to meet a variety of new friends, who call in live with comments that may find space in my next book. Shy listeners call me directly afterward. That is how I met Susan, an avid *Shannon and Spinozi* fan.

"Can it be possible, Beliza? I never heard of such a thing!"

"Let me in on your little secret, Susan, and I'll tell you what I think."

"My friend's boyfriend threw her out of the house. Can you believe it!"

"Happens all the time," I reminded her.

"Yeah but you don't understand!" she screeched, "He won't give her her stuff back."

Thinking she meant a few bras and panties, various sundries, and his and her vibrators, I asked, "Did she have anything of value?"

"To her it is," she snapped at me. "I'd say a dining room set she paid for herself, some appliances, and pictures are pretty important. They lived together for a couple of years. All that little stuff adds up."

Concerned, I queried, "Did she go to the police?"

"No, but she went to her lawyer," Susan spilled. "You know what he told her, Beliza? She'll have to get a *divorce* in order to sue this guy. They weren't even married! Did you ever hear of such a thing?"

"Yup!" I chuckled at the predicament's irony. "You guys live in Oklahoma which recognizes common-law marriage. Just ask baseball player, Dave Winfield, how he got stuck paying $210,000 in legal fees and $10,000 a month in alimony to former flight attendant, Sandra Renfro, with whom he has a child. Few could believe the outcome of his Houston trial. His lawyer,

Tom Alexander was enraged. 'It was legal blackmail!' he told *Newsweek*. '[Winfield] was never married to that woman.'"[2]

"*Nevertheless*," I was very specific to Susan, "if you live together in Oklahoma, fornicate, play house like husband and wife, and fight like husbands and wives do, Oklahoma, like any other common-law state, litigates your domestic spats as if you are a ceremonially married couple."

"That's preposterous!" Susan protested.

"Maybe so. But in order to change the law, you'll have to talk to your local congressperson."

Common-law marriage, a holdover from pioneer America, still endures in fourteen states and the District of Columbia: Alabama, Colorado, Georgia, Idaho, Iowa, Kansas, Montana, Ohio, Oklahoma, Pennsylvania, Rhode Island, South Carolina, Texas, and Utah.

HOW YOU CAN GET ENSNARED
BY COMMON-LAW MARRIAGE QUIRKS

One might wonder how a bright guy like actor William Hurt, who has access to good legal advice, got trapped into an expensive, noxious common-law marriage battle. It's easy when you are involved with a former girlfriend who feels she's entitled to compensation for time served, emotional abuse, and suffering. Ballerina Sandra Jennings found an unofficial marriage legal loophole which allowed her to claim a portion of Hurt's $10,000,000 earnings, as well as give him a serious case of aggravated heartburn. It could happen to you, too.

Ms. Jennings, who lived with previously divorced Mr. Hurt in New York, joined him in South Carolina while he was filming *The Big Chill*. She lived with him in South Carolina for *only* five weeks of their three-year, live-in relationship from late 1982 to early 1983, yet she claimed they established a common-law marriage. Mr. Hurt denied participating in any ritual that gave Ms. Jennings the notion they were "married." He took this position even though their relationship produced a son, Alex, now age fourteen, followed by annual child support payments of $65,000.[3]

The couple's relationship ended in defeat for Jennings in a Manhattan courtroom in 1989. "Sandra wound up with nothing," New York attorney, Raoul Felder, told me, but she managed to bad-mouth Hurt in the press and on nationwide talk shows. Meanwhile, the just or unjust common-law aspect turned the squabble into a national, circus-like debate. "After one of these television shows," Mr. Felder blurted out, "Ms. Jenning's attorney started cursing me for not taking the case. She didn't have a case! It was a public thing."[4] In turn, Mr. Hurt accrued huge legal fees over a six-year period for the privilege of defending his position. Here's how Ms. Jennings' suit got as far as it did.

New York—where William and Sandra resided—acknowledges legitimate, out-of-state common-law unions, even though it does not recognize common-law marriage itself. When Ms. Jennings claimed she and Mr. Hurt entered into a common-law marriage while visiting South Carolina, New York was forced to examine the validity of her allegation, but ultimately denied it.[5]

If you are dead-set against marrying your significant other, it would be wise—before you arrive in a state which validates common-law marriage—to contractually confirm you are:

➤ Not married
➤ Have no intention of getting married
➤ And have offered no promise of marriage

Safer yet, maintain separate homes. Or, fly home to visit on weekends. People in the military, out-of-state college students, and those who accept temporary out-of-state job offers should be particularly wary.

COMMON-LAW AND ACCOUNTABILITY

The flip side of the Hurt/Jennings outcome protects men and women who have entered into legitimate, long-term, common-law marriages. If they split up, the parties are held legally culpable for their actions. Common-law states and juries may view shirking obligations as inhumane, particularly when the abandoned spouse is left to assume the responsibility for raising the couple's child(ren) and maintaining the home. People involved with support networks like myself, mental health therapists, family members, the clergy, and welfare agencies are left to clean up another person's dirty work.

BUT IT DOESN'T END THERE...

There are not two, but *three* sides to every story. His, hers, and the truth. I have learned the lesson so well that even while listening to the most vacuous news report, I drive everyone crazy with my personal sense of justice. That's why I gave Mr. Hurt the benefit of the doubt until all the chips were in.

On the whole, women—myself included—are slow learners when it comes to recognizing some philanderers are incapable of changing. Nevertheless, while not being directly responsible, these men or women can temporarily flatter and influence an insecure woman or man to make some unwise choices.

In piecing together my research on Mr. Hurt, I took a long look at his behavior toward women, as well as his behavior in general. I concluded I'd be a lousy character witness on his behalf. I also concluded that Sandra Jennings should have won her common-law battle from a moral standpoint, even though it could be argued that Mr. Hurt fulfilled his financial obligation to her by supporting their child. On the other hand, Sandra (and all women who are willing to compromise their chances of getting married by living together first) should have known she was playing with fire.

Beyond the common-law marriage dispute, Mr. Hurt's love 'em and leave 'em sagas go on and on. In 1975 he divorced actress Mary Beth Hurt, whom he married in 1972. While his case with Ms. Jennings was still pending, he was drying out at Minnesota's Hazelden treatment center, where he fell in love with Heidi Henderson, bandleader Skitch Henderson's daughter. They married in 1989, had two children, and four years later, Mr. Hurt was back at Manhattan family court seeking a divorce from Heidi. An unusual prenuptial agreement, which tied alimony payments with both parties' ability to stay clean and sober, complicated matters; and Heidi challenged the contract's validity. [6]

The contract was riddled with promises of intent. And anyone preparing, or considering signing any type of prenup/nonnup agreement, should be aware that promises of intent to lose weight, keep off the computer, stay sober, etc. are inappropriate. But against her lawyer's wishes, Heidi signed. And before her divorce was final, William was living in the guesthouse of their Sneden's Landing, NY estate with actress Sandra Bonnaire, who had recently given birth to his fourth child.[7]

Curious, I wondered how many star-struck ladies can't say 'No!' to men who have a reputation of casting off one woman after the other, and believe that *with her* it will be different?

"Too many!" says Allegra, my single friend from Los Angeles. "I've never lived with a man. Never been married. Maybe that's *my* fear of commitment. I figure if I'm going to live with a man, I want to know he's going to be there—forever.

"What I'm hearing from the men I date," she emphasized, "is that if I am not willing to drop everything for them, I don't love them that much." Yet, if you do drop everything, people believe you are an easy catch, and also easy to dump. "Women should be more aware of what some men can do to them emotionally in the long run," Allegra insisted.

Oprah Winfrey once asked me on her show, "Wouldn't it be a good idea if we got the low-down on our lover from their ex-whatevers before we committed to them?" If people would be willing to heed the advice given, Oprah makes a good point—worthy of *serious* consideration.

STAKING
YOUR CLAIM

Some of you may think that because you are not as financially comfortable as Francine in chapter 21 or William
Hurt, a living together break-up won't cost you. Not so. It
always does.

Ronald Rindfuss, professor of sociology at the University
of North Carolina's Carolina Population Center in Chapel
Hill, says the average cohabitation lasts about twelve months.[1]
Knowing this, and how much accumulated junk a couple could
collect in the course of a year, live-in lovers may want to mark
his and her CDs, computer programs, appliances, electronic
gear, household items, and so on with different colored stick-
ers. Get a laundry marker, and initial his and her sheets and
towels. However, if your grandma gave you her silver flatware

when you got married the first time, think about putting it in your safe deposit box.

It's amazing how everyday, ordinary possessions become precious commodities when a couple splits. Put an X on your Victoria's Secret silk boxer shorts (circa Christmas 95 from your former live-in) and other clothing she loves to borrow, including your Giants' football jersey, an O on her Clinique pimple cream and conditioner you use more often than she. (Get it? *XO*.) Sounds silly, but the effort will facilitate a quick and relatively hassle-free departure.

Try to avoid going halfsies. How would you split a fax machine? Keep a running tally, an actual ledger book, and alternate who pays for expensive household purchases (he the washer, you the dryer). Set a figure: He'll buy groceries one week, you the next. If you buy a condo or home together, the departing partner often has to wait for the sale to get his or her money back. Rent is easy, you just split it (two checks, please, so you can establish credit if you need to get your own place). If you've moved into his/her home, you could pay the taxes, split the phone and utility bills. Don't buy a vehicle together.

Custody of the dog and visitation rights could get hairy. It's better to decide those arrangements in a computerized, notarized agreement (which is often good enough for a couple without a great deal of money). I'm aware that sorting it all out can be petty. But add up how much it would cost you to replace the squabbled-over items and it makes sense.

Another thing! Lots of women living with men more well-off than they are get trapped by this one. Find out if expensive gifts are yours for the duration, or yours to keep. For instance, the Honda he leased for your birthday: Is your gift the *lease*, or the "option to buy" payment when the lease is up? And for goodness sake, since you really don't know this person, do *not* open joint checking accounts or change the beneficiary on your insurance policy. I could go on and on, but I think you get the point.

In other words, be the author of, and remain in control of, *your own* contingency plan. You'll be less likely to make a wrong decision or stay in a compromising relationship.

By the way, if you do not have enough money to contribute to all of the above consider yourself a kept person with no rights (Yuk! I'd rather live with my parents) unless you have a palimony agreement that reimburses you for services rendered. But be careful! You could be considered a gigolo or meretricious spouse (one who gets paid for sexual services), and the agreement may not hold up. Believe me, though, if you're looking for free room and board, you'll probably do a lot better working for an escort service, and the hotel's housekeeping department will iron his Calvins.

On the other hand, if you are a twenty-five year-old with a million-dollar trust fund, a rich divorcee, a well-provided-for widow or land baron or baroness, own your own home, or lost a bundle on your last live-in experience, you've got a lot more to lose. Hire a lawyer today, and pay close attention to the advice offered in the following chapters. Living together can be a scary experience. But you'll only know that the day you break up!

BROACHING
THE FINANCIAL
AGREEMENT

THE CONTRACTUAL COHABITATION
AGREEMENT (CCA)

It may appear cold-hearted to discuss break-up settlements
and equitable payoffs just when you've decided to test drive
marriage. But since the biggest problems start not when you
move in together, but when the relationship sours, such discussions are definitely a good idea. Note that state laws that
provide alimony, separate maintenance, and equitable property division statutes for married couples don't do so for unofficial marriage. Legal and financial experts emphasize putting
monetary affairs at the top of your list of relationship booby-
traps to resolve—before you move in together!

DIFFERENT AGREEMENTS FOR DIFFERENT FOLKS

There are a variety of agreements, and it is important to learn the vocabulary that surrounds trial marriage. A *nonnuptial contract* was thought up by Los Angeles attorney Marvin Mitchelson as a transaction between two parties who live together without the benefit of marriage. However, during his 1976 *Marvin v. Marvin* case discussed earlier in this book, the media referred to the document as a *palimony agreement*, and coined a new word. "If a couple was engaged to be married," Mr. Mitchelson explained, "I intended their document to be referred to as a *prenuptial contract*." [1]

Other lawyers describe living-together contracts as *relationship agreements*. However, isn't that rather vague? After all, married or otherwise, two people living together form a relationship, even if they are platonic roommates. Mistresses could have a relationship agreement with live-in or live-out married lovers. *Premarital Agreement* is equally nebulous. What if the couple never wants to marry? LTAs—*Living Together Agreements*—don't explicitly define present and future intentions and purposes of the relationship. One could live with a parent, sister, or friend and sign documents that protect each other's property.

I have discovered that lawyers and judges alike, as well as common folks, remain confused when assigning the proper name to the appropriate document for individuals living together. Laws lag behind the constantly changing times and the jargon of clever, high-powered attorneys. Contractual living-together agreements and their pursuant arguments, even twenty years after their inception, are still too new.

When discussing agreements between any unmarried couple cohabiting under the same roof, regardless of future wedding plans—heterosexual or same-sex—there was no question what information I wanted to obtain from experts, attorneys, and judges. But it was a bulky explanation requiring a great deal of clarification. I was looking for a clear-cut label that would include the verb *cohabit*.

Here, I will call a spade a spade: *Contractual Cohabitation Agreement* or *CCA*. I think that term gets the message across clearly. It refers to non-affianced couples living under the same roof who are involved in an unlicensed, marriage-like, sexually-uniting love affair.

Taking into consideration each state's individual laws, you will always get the best advice when you know exactly what type of agreement and specific content is best suited for your situation. But remember Ivana Trump? All relationship agreements can be contested. However, win or lose, the legal fees that skyrocket when you make your case could clobber you!

"IT'S A TERRIBLE IDEA!"

Illinois courts consider any deviation from marriage a transgression against the sanctity of that union. That state does not recognize any relationship agreement. And although she personally doesn't view living together as immoral, Marta Coblitz, chair of the Chicago Bar Association's Matrimonial Committee who has been married for twenty years, "thinks it's a terrible idea."

Ms. Coblitz described how couples, in an effort to assume responsibility for the other person, paper over ceremonial commitment by getting powers of attorney to make health care decisions for the other partner. She has seen twenty-year-olds signing wills to make sure their significant other inherits something, and non-committing sweethearts concoct and sign business-type arrangements to jointly share property. "When in fact, if they *honestly* cherish their affinity for one another to that extent," she concludes, "the easiest way to contract a relationship is to get married."

Ms. Coblitz explained that she has represented spouses who lived together for a decade or more. They decide to marry. Then, suddenly, a year later they are getting divorced and are seeking ten-years' worth of benefits. "But you've only been married a year," the attorney points out to the couple. "Still the disgruntled spouse finds it inconceivable that she is not entitled to anything for the ten years she put in beforehand. I tell them, it *doesn't* matter."

"The party line may be, 'we both like it this way,'" Ms. Coblitz said. "But when you penetrate the façade, one of them isn't letting on how truly unhappy, even *insulted*, he/she is that the partner refuses to make that trip down the aisle." *One partner almost always wants to get married. One partner almost always gets hurt.*

"On the whole," Ms. Coblitz has decided, "I'm not able to view living together as a really positive relationship."

PUTTING THE MORAL ISSUE ASIDE, WHY YOU SHOULD CONSIDER DRAWING UP A CCA

I've seen grown men cry and women turn into retaliating bitches because they put off establishing financial parameters and contractually stipulating the status of their live-in relationships. I'd hate to see any of you compromised by procrastination, or because you felt too awkward to approach the subject.

If a couple has few cash assets, preparing a financial agreement is quite simple. As we discussed earlier, a notarized, signed letter of agreement might do it. Unless a child is born to the couple, or one member of the team won the lottery, ex-lovers can part company relatively unscathed.

The same goes for those who began the relationship well-off enough to survive on their own. In many cases, unless the couple has made joint investments, financially independent live-ins tend to brush off petty quibbling over who owns the blender. They often take back from the toppled relationship only what they personally put in. A practical business-type agreement that addresses breaking up, division of individual and mutually acquired assets, and reimbursement clears the way for couples to concentrate on staying in love.

On the other hand, when one party has considerably more money than the other, the situation is more difficult. We've all read about celebrity court battles when a wealthy movie star's hairdresser moves in for a year and a half. The relationship falls apart and all hell breaks loose when the scorned party ("Generally," according to Mr. Mitchelson, "it's a woman"[1]) thinks she's entitled to a larger portion of his assets than he's willing to give.

Without a financial agreement, don't ever bother going into court. Lawyers get rich on cases bickering over what he said or she said which also wastes court time. If the defendant is lucky, she walks away with a humiliating good-will pittance minus gigantic legal fees. Although jury decisions vary, particularly in states that do not recognize common-law marriage, a written, well-prepared contract is the best insurance policy a person can have in an unofficially married relationship.

A lot of couples wait to see if their live-in love affair works first, or reaches a more serious plateau, before they talk about financial agreements. Don't fall into that trap. The longer a couple lives together, the more complicated a breakup can become. The simplest agreements can be amended regularly, as the relationship progresses, with codicils or newly created documents. But be aware, if they change their minds and choose to marry, that could negate any unmarried couple contract in some jurisdictions, particularly community property states. The drafting of a marriage agreement, which must correspond with state disclosure laws but can most likely contradict marriage laws, is almost always required. And since only a handful of lawyers have actually drawn up cohabitation agreements, keep a careful eye on what the contract implies. At best you and your attorney have entered into a complex, still-gray area of law.

Because this section speaks in generalities, it is not intended to be a state-by-state unofficial-marriage legal handbook. All states where cohabitation is legal use former cases to set precedent and develop judicial continuity. Since the law is developing around former decisions that do not necessarily account for all types of living-together situations, I cannot stress enough how important it is to learn your state's predisposition pertaining to non-nuptial cohabitation agreements. Each case is litigated almost as if it were a first.

TWO FORMERLY COHABITING ATTORNEYS
SHOW YOU THE WAY

Anthropologist, and self-help law attorney-turned-publishing graphics artist, Toni Ihara speaks a mile a minute. You're still absorbing her last sentence while she's halfway into the next. She co-wrote and published *The Living Together Kit* (Nolo Press) with her husband, attorney, Ralph "Jake" Warner. This is a nuts and bolts guide to designing your own living-together agreement. From soup to nuts, it's very well done.

The *"Kit"* was written from personal experience when the Berkeley, California couple examined the practical and legal aspects of their own nineteen-year live-in situation, adding firsthand credibility to what they have to say.

"Actually, it's even crazier," remembers Toni. "Jake and I lived together *and* separately for the first twelve years. I've always thought any relationship works better if the other guy has a place to go."

However, as practical as it sounds, that's a luxury few can afford for very long. So Jake and Toni moved into one place together before they married six years ago. Because many married couples split or wish circumstances would allow them to call it quits after twenty-five years, I queried, "Why did you *ever* bother to get married?"

"That's a really funny story." Toni laughed. "Our daughter, Miya came home from school one day, saying one of her schoolmates insisted she couldn't be six years old if her parents weren't married. Like parents have to be married to have babies—how could you be here?" It didn't take long for their little one to start pressuring them to take the plunge.

In her sweet way, Miya needled and nagged. One weekend, soon after the school-yard incident, her parents sneaked away to South Lake Tahoe. With their cowboy preacher from Tahoe's Little Wedding Chapel in tow—backpacks, jeans, boots, and all—Toni and Jake exchanged civil vows intertwined with religious country poetry on a Native American ritual beach. Afterward, a celebration breakfast at Dunkin Donuts, followed by a vigorous hike, captured the essence of the quixotic milestone. The newlyweds set the record straight without fanfare. "Without Miya, too," says Toni, "who hasn't forgiven us for not inviting her to the wedding."

Giving their friends (and themselves) time to absorb the complete surprise that two proponents of living together finally broke down and tied the knot, Toni and Jake wound up making a lavish wedding celebration for a few *hundred* friends two months later. Bowing to tradition, they left immediately after for a two-week post-nuptial honeymoon in Paris. "In the meantime, our slightly confused—but apparently much relieved—daughter enjoyed visiting with her grandparents," chuckled Toni.

Below, I have listed issues Toni and Jake elaborate upon which LTCs who are thinking about having children out of wedlock should settle right from the get-go.

➤ Having children
➤ Paternity and parenting agreements
➤ Sharing/keeping separate property
➤ Wills and existing families

In its eigth edition, the Ihara/Warner collaboration covers contracts from struggling artists to those for people in school, and many other idiosyncratic living arrangements.

"When you think about it, the worst problems with domestic relationships happen when nothing's been said," cautioned Toni. "One partner may just assume the other person's thinking along the same lines, when in fact, they're on completely different frequencies."

Ms. Ihara says, "Horrible fights end up in court when one party assumes: This is how *I* thought we were going to handle property distribution, incoming assets, etc. And when you're mad at each other, it can turn really nasty." A cohabitation agreement is a safety net that can be referred to when a spat winds up being an antagonistic break-up.

Furthermore, I said, "Without one, you're always going to be up against the biases of a judge or the courts."

"And because of these biases and certain societal antipathy toward cohabitation," Toni agreed, "you never want to get there—it's always an unhappy ending." So do everything in your power to avoid this situation. "The courts are such a horrible system to decide these cases," she warned. And when you come out of it, all the assets you fought over are often spent litigating a battle you could have prevented.

"So whether you go to a lawyer or develop your own agreement," advises Ms. Ihara, "couples have to come to a basic understanding. Meanwhile, when people take certain precautions, they end up in court less frequently." The mere presence of an agreement, which reflects a mutual understanding, usually avoids embittered confrontation.

WATCH OUT WHEN PREPARING
YOUR OWN CCA

Unlicensed relationships are governed by contract law, and disputes may be decided by a jury in civil court. Therefore, "Preparing your own document," says Manhattan attorney Raoul Felder, "is like doing your own appendectomy." *Ouch!*

With the expert advice of an attorney, mediator and/or financial planner and accountant well-versed in your state's laws and cohabitation pitfalls, unmarried partners can feel confident that specific clauses that pertain to their particular situation and estate will be included.

Since unofficial marriage contests baffle even the most skilled attorneys I spoke with, I asked Mr. Felder, "How is a cohabitation agreement different from a prenuptial contract?"

"Because it involves a state of grace that is not recognized by the law," he said. "In other words, you can get a marriage license or a divorce certificate. However, there is no such thing as getting a certificate that says you can live together."

"If you're married," he continued, "there is a whole body of law that says what your rights are." When you live together without any promise of marriage, the security of those laws is not there. A lawyer may refer to general contract law, perhaps, "but it's very difficult," Mr. Felder forewarned. It can keep you on legal pins and needles. "So what you try to do is opt out of present law, and instead maneuver around it with a law that doesn't exist. These are very tough cases. Not that many of them have been litigated."

Knowing the answer, I asked anyway, "Do you do a lot of these agreements?"

"Oh yes," he boasted, with reason. "I think we have the largest practice in the country. As a result we handle a lot of these cases."

He added, "If you don't attempt to do too much with the agreement, it'll probably hold up. You start putting in who's going to take out the garbage…walk the dog, how many times a week you'll make love—that sort of silly stuff [indicating intent]—you're inviting trouble."

If you have absolutely no intention of getting married, "keep it simple," advised Mr. Felder. He described a bottom-line, no-strings-attached agreement that might be something like, "We are now jointly signing a lease, and at the break up of the lease, I will have three months to vacate the apartment. Or, we have a joint bank account to be shared in the following manner.…And computation will be made as per each person's respective income and will be divided up as per that.

Unmistakable contract-like partnership statements, which cannot be misinterpreted, probably won't be any problem."

Depending upon the judge, you might get away with other items your lawyer might include such as:

➤ No claims can be made on property in my name.
➤ _____has no rights to my assets or income.
➤ All earnings and appreciation on assets belong to the owner.
➤ _____and I are not married.
➤ We will use our own names.
➤ If we split, no claims can be made upon the physical or monetary assets of the other.

Obviously, the greater your holdings, the more sophisticated and complicated the agreement becomes, as well as the size of the fee for preparing it. Nevertheless, notice the negative connotation of words like *may* or *may not, probably, won't, might, shouldn't be* sprinkled throughout various sentences of the advisors I've contacted. Any contract can be contested. There are no guarantees.

"Yet, as ugly as it is to work one of these deals out, it's only prudent to have one," Mr. Felder concluded.

NEGOTIATING YOUR CCA

You are thinking about moving in with your steady, but recognize you need to have a CCA before you do. Some people are so uncomfortable discussing the subject, they have their lawyer bring it up, or hide behind the excuse that a parent or business partner insists upon it. Assuming *you're* not that spineless creature, how do you approach this delicate subject?

Experts advise that you remain calm, open, and honest from the very outset. "I love you and can't think of anyone else I'd rather be with, but the reason we're living together, rather than getting married is because: I'm/we're not sure it will last; we can't agree on certain conditions; we can't agree to have children or not; I can't get along with your kids; I want a long-term commitment; your mother will *never* approve of me; etc.

"Under such circumstances, it is quite reasonable to suggest it would be in both our best interests to establish the rules of our unmarried relationship." It's a short step from here to signing a CCA.

Be prepared for all sorts of reactions. *Relief*: "I'm glad you brought it up, I didn't know how to." *Practical*: "Probably not, but if I leave my job to go fishing with you, I'll need some type of financial compensation." *Guilt-provoking*: "What do you mean? I'll take care of you!" *Evasive*: "Oh yeah, we'll get to that." *Jealous*: "You must love your kids a lot more than me." *Denial*: "What are you worried about? We'll be together forever!" And so on.

If you know your partner well enough to move in together, you should be the best judge of how to handle his/her response. Be careful. It's natural that your request will generate some hurt feelings.

Dr. Lori Gordon, acclaimed author of several self-help books including *If You Really Loved Me...* and creator of the internationally respected program Practical Application of Intimate Relationship Skills (PAIRS), comments about the contradictory message a cohabitation agreement sends. "This is an utter paradox: The romantic desire to be together combined with the legalities of a break-up." Illustrating that relationship contracts are usually the opposite of love, Dr. Gordon said the message being sent can be disturbingly confusing: *If you really loved me you wouldn't need to discuss our love affair with an attorney.* "[This is] What I refer to in my books and conferences as a 'love knot,'" says Dr. Gordon.

"For instance," she described, "a love knot is caused by subconscious assumptions; about love, about families, about what we can and cannot talk about, that we bring to our intimate relationships. It tends to act like a land mine: if touched, it explodes. It erodes relationships."

Significantly different than ceremonial marriage, which focuses on hope and optimism and developing trust, the cohabitation agreement—or worse, a premarital contract—centers around despair and pessimism, betrayal and lack of trust. "Just when you are thinking about life, you are really going into this type of relationship thinking about its death," emphasized Dr. Gordon, who describes the end of a love affair or divorce as synonymous with demise and loss. "It's about trauma and heartache," she described, "and so at the very time you are feeling the most positive, you are being asked to think about the most negative possibilities."

I asked Dr. Gordon, "Can a person physically and emotionally handle that?"

"Well," she said, "it is difficult," because the emotional part of the brain is focusing on love, pain, excitement, pleasure and joy, sex and sensuality. If you suddenly ask the coldly logical thinking brain to focus on the relationship, conflicting emotions are often bewildering. "The consequences of having to sign such a thing may put you in such a state of pain and fear, you may decide you do not want to go forward," cautioned Dr. Gordon.

WHAT IF HE/SHE SAYS "NO!"

Judging by the reactions of both men and women I talked with, if a man is determined to have his lover sign an agreement and she refuses, his retort leaves little doubt he is going to get his way, or *else*: "Then I won't be able to do any more favors for you." Or, "This is the only way I'll have it."

Whether seeking to have an agreement signed, or being asked to sign one herself, the women I spoke with were less succinct. Generally speaking, many agreed sticking with a non-verbal reply, processed through body language, might get them an affirmative response. *I'll hang in there until I can cajole him to change his mind. Or, I lose mine!*

"The guy usually feels a little guilty insisting the woman sign," says Los Angeles attorney, Robert Nachshin, revered for drafting bullet-proof cohabitation agreements. "And the woman. . ." he paused, contemplating his response, "acts like she can't *believe* he is making her do this."

There is little room for compromise unless one party can be swayed to give up his/her demand for an agreement altogether. However, before admitting defeat, review the reasons why the concept was proposed. As Dr. Gordon says, "Try to untangle the love knot by talking things out in such a way that does not obscure the issue with assumptions about each other, concerns about power and who wins an argument, or apprehensions about how the other will respond."

The need for an agreement may initially pose a threat. However, when a couple openly discusses misgivings, each may recognize the value in putting things on paper.

Contrary to the ugliness of a prenuptial agreement, where an often demeaning and devious, final-hour price tag is put on a bride or groom's head, contradicting marriage laws and state-protected entitlements, a CCA can be a positive experience.

"The interesting thing is," insists Mr. Nachshin, "in a cohabitation agreement you can do something for somebody. Without a cohabitation agreement, that person would get nothing." Legacies—confirmed and secured by trusts, wills, and insurance policies—land in the hands of the person(s) designated.

Mr. Nachshin illustrated, "Let's assume I'm living with this woman, and let's assume through my employment I have a million dollars worth of life insurance. I could state in this living-together agreement that, should I die, she is the irrevocable beneficiary of the policy. Meaning I can't change it. I can promise her the same thing without an agreement, but my promise is meaningless because I can change the beneficiary tomorrow."

GOOD FAITH STIPENDS

One partner could give an annual stipend to his live-in for his/her contribution to the relationship. If all or part of the stipend comes in the form of transferred stocks, pensions, or insurance, an irrevocable trust could be set up to show good faith. The funds could be invested, and interest accrued. She (the principal) could either name the donor as the agent, or another person, then subsequently leave the assets of her trust to either the donor or someone else, for example, her children from a previous marriage.

Thirteen years ago, then-Playboy chairman Hugh Hefner had a stroke. His live-in lover, ex-Bunny and cover-girl Carrie Leigh, nursed him back to health before he dumped her. Hefner offered Carrie a settlement of $10-50,000. Returning the insult, Carrie and her lawyer, Marvin Mitchelson, sued Hef for $35,000,000. The suit was eventually dropped.

Perhaps, while Hef was sick and relied upon her care, Ms. Leigh might have been able to encourage him to set up an irrevocable trust—giving her a more reasonable amount of money—to compensate her for the five-year relationship and seeing him through his illness. But she loved him, and trusted him and after the fact, those years of devotion turned into an unappreciated gift.

Unless what is being proposed is a chattel-doc (an agreement that stipulates no provision for the abandoned partner) I strongly suggest anyone embarking upon an unlicensed love affair to jump at the chance to initiate the dialogue. Talk about being in charge of your own destiny! To everyone's benefit, the CCA could serve as a financially-enhancing, protective mechanism, a contracted declaration of love, and in its own way— commitment.

If your partner is adamantly against it, that might be a red flag alert. And just possibly you should be on your way out the door.

IT ISN'T ALWAYS ABOUT MONEY

"As a divorcee, I spent a lot of time developing my individuality and strength. Yet, I was scared to commit to any man." says Jacqueline Rickard, author of *Complete Premarital Contracting: Loving Communication for Today's Couples.* "I was afraid if I got married again, I would either give up on who I had become, or concede this newly-found autonomy to the traditional cultural expectations surrounding marriage. Yet, when I met Bob, he was totally different from my first husband and the men to whom I had been exposed throughout my life." Still skeptical, Jacqueline insisted upon an instrument that would help them develop trust in each other.

"When I brought up a premarital agreement initially, Bob was surprised I needed this assurance. However, when I explained my reasons, he understood my request. So we talked about the fears we bring to our relationships and acknowledged that they really had little to do with one another. New partners have to deal with the repercussions of past history and old baggage," confided the former legal assistant and technical writer. "I harbored a lot of deep anxieties which, until we did our contracting, held me back from marrying Bob."

Jacqueline insisted upon guarantees on two levels. "Yes, I wanted to protect my assets, and also ensure, when I die, that my children will receive the bulk of my estate. But more importantly, I needed to have in writing how I wanted to establish the character of our marriage—including our mutual pledge to respect our individuality and to commit to our partnership. We did not want to be trapped by outdated role-model expectations."

However, after a bit of investigative work, Jacqueline and Bob quickly realized that conventional nuptial agreements, simply outlining financial restrictions, were not what they really wanted. "Those agreements seemed to be divorce decrees in advance," she says. Wanting something more user-friendly, "it soon became evident we would have to create our own." Ironically, crafting the process is what motivated the author to write about relationship contracting.

Emphasizing the importance of developing private contracts as well as legal contracts, Ms. Rickard suggests you take advantage of the acute romantic phase of your relationship, "when it is a very flowing, loving time—to talk about issues that are important to you." Frequently, when you pledge commitment to one another, partners may still have doubts. This feeling of vulnerability may have nothing to do with anything your lover has conveyed, but more often than not, encompasses past grievances and experiences. "Premarital contracting can build joint trust based on realistic solutions to your concerns."

In Ms. Rickard's case, she did not want marriage to turn her back into the person she left behind. Thus her private contract served as a constant reminder not to slip back into the role of subservient wife. "I wanted to be a true partner, not just a support system," she acknowledged. "And I wanted Bob to declare some responsibility for his goals, too."

"Whether we are talking about living-together or married couples, same sex couples, or older couples who have fallen in love, but don't want to lose their financial security and benefits by marrying, it is important to get to know each other better," insists Ms. Rickard, who discussed the two-level process of developing a relationship, supported by a contract. One phase is the legal document in which you include clauses that can be upheld.

The other phase—which you enter into without the need for legal counsel—operates on a more intimate level. Expanding on the notion of what a relationship agreement represents, couples shape how they want their marriage or live-in relationship to evolve. "This is your relationship," explains Ms. Rickard. "You may as well be the authors of your future happiness."

Written as a love letter in your own handwriting, taped, or videotaped, Ms. Rickard encourages couples to record loving declarations demonstrating how much they care for each other. "There will be many emotional subjects to discuss," she says, "and for each partner they can be different, yet like the legal document, this contract should not cause fear or exude control." Periodically, Ms. Rickard encourages partners to schedule a commitment ceremony. Set a romantic, loving, caring tone—a candlelit dinner, picnic in the park, or weekend away—where emotional and legally bound promises are reviewed, and vows and pledges remembered.

Thought of as hokey by skeptics, this kind of communication is really the heart and soul of the relationship. To belittle or mock the significance of instituting a process that rekindles the fire, recognizes each individual, and establishes routine dialogue shortchanges any love affair.

"If couples reach obstacles in their discussions, working through these roadblocks with a mentor—a psychotherapist, an accountant, family planner, or clergyperson—who can help them sort out what it is they are trying to resolve, [it] eases them through the process," advises Ms. Rickard, who is also a trained mediator. For example, falling under the guise of a money dispute, an emotional issue may be misinterpreted or become entangled with financial aspects. "When in fact an objective third party may discover the real problem has nothing to do with money, but instead the stalemate may be a resurfacing security or control issue."

It does take some effort to decide what you want to write in your personal and legal contracts. "However, don't get discouraged," Jacqueline encourages couples. "Stick with it until your contracts say what you mean them to say."

QUESTIONS
A LAWYER ASKS
WHEN DRAWING
UP A CCA

According to matrimonial attorney Brenda Winters of Bradley Beach, New Jersey, "It's absolutely critical each party understands what their intentions are. What do they want to accomplish?" Ms. Winters advises couples to be prepared to answer the following questions when they visit *their* attorneys separately. Avoid—at all costs—joint meetings, which confuse issues and exaggerate demands:

➤ Do you intend to share a bank account and pay joint expenses together?
➤ Is your intention to preserve what you owned prior to coming into the relationship?

➤ How do you want to treat the property you already own?

➤ How do you want to treat the property you acquire together?

➤ Once you move in together, how do you want to handle the increase or decrease in the value of the property you own separately?

➤ How do you want to conduct your life as a couple?

"These are some of the basic guidelines," says Ms. Winters, "and your lawyer will help you organize the contract, but you and your partner have to work out the answers."

Retired New Jersey Superior Court Judge, Burton L. Fundler concurs, and added to Ms. Winters' list:

➤ A CCA should include terms relating to issues that might arise in the event the couple has a child—even if the woman promises not to. The father (once it's proven to him he is the biological father) is bound by paternity law. By the same token, the mother can't say, "I'll have the baby, pay all the expenses...you don't have to support it. And by the way, I don't *ever* want to see you again."

"She cannot waive receipt of child support, nor bar visitation in New Jersey or other states whose laws concur," added Ms. Winters.

➤ The CCA should cover property which is separate and apart beforehand, "But even if they mix it up," Judge Fundler said, "it's still separate and apart unless your agreement stipulates otherwise."

The term *property* doesn't have to be a fancy condo on Fifth Avenue. It could be something as simple as your car or your grandfather's pocket watch.

UNEXPECTED MARRIAGE

Suppose a couple has absolutely no intention of getting married. They're off skiing in Tahoe, and in a weak moment of dizzying passion, elope. "Provision should be made for unexpected marriage by way of a nuptial clause," suggested the Judge.

"However, be careful," Ms. Winters warned. "Full disclosure may be required in some states when drafting a nuptial agreement." And this could pertain to a nuptial clause. Yet, full disclosure is not required when a couple is preparing a CCA because an unlicensed relationship, without promise of marriage, makes its own rules. If you are married (and in some states that could include common law marriage), and do not have a nuptial agreement that contradicts the law, the state looks after your best interests.

"YOU WANT THE ROLEX BACK!"

Regarding gifts, most states with equitable distribution laws divide equally those treasures that married partners who divorce have acquired. Because a CCA does not have to follow state-by-state marriage laws, the distribution of financial reimbursement of such gifts should be spelled out.

Ms. Winters illustrated: "If your live-in gave you a gold Rolex, is he going to want it back if you break up?" Better find out in writing if the gift *is* a gift. Or is the gift for your use while you're together?

Couples often don't comprehend the vast consequences of getting involved in an unofficial marriage. Once you move in together, every item you buy together or separately—even if you have an agreement—is subject to a fight unless you have a personal canceled check to prove you bought it with your own money. This is the time for scrupulous record keeping.

YOUR COHABITATION'S EFFECT ON A FORMER SPOUSE

Unmarried living-together and corresponding arrangements can get complicated when there is an existing family and an ex-spouse. "Couples should take a hard look at legal particulars," said Judge Fundler, "if either party was previously married." Will the cohabitation arrangement trigger any event for their former spouse that concerns their children or finances? How free are you to develop a new relationship when a former spouse or the courts are looking over your shoulder?

A former spouse may feel her ex-husband's living-together arrangement with a young bimbo or another man is not in the best interest of their children. Or, an ex-husband may find it inequitable his ex is living with a *Fortune 500* CEO while he's still struggling to make alimony payments. "The law is evolving in that area," says Ms. Winters, who has litigated these types of cases.

"The court will take a look at that situation by way of a modification," comments Judge Fundler, "to determine whether the new arrangement has reduced the financial needs of the dependent former spouse. Depending upon the facts, the court could modify the alimony, or eliminate it altogether."

"In simple terms," said Ms. Winters, "if someone else is helping an ex-wife financially, then she might not be entitled to the same or any financial help from the former husband." It's a highly litigious area, though.

Brenda explained, "Today in a property settlement agreement in a divorce, when we speak about terms of ending alimony, there is often—if not almost always—a clause that states alimony will be terminated if there is cohabitation in avoidance of marriage."

However, "Proving that frequently requires a costly and lengthy post-divorce visit to court: a full hearing to decide if the live-in is there all the time, not just Thursday to Sunday, July to September," says Ms. Winters, who referred to two significant New Jersey cases dealing with this issue: *Garlinger v. Garlinger* [1] and *Gayet v. Gayet.* [2]

In both of these cases, the divorced husband sought to eliminate or reduce alimony awarded to his ex-wife by suggesting her habitual, post-divorce cohabitation with another individual may have alleviated her need for spousal support. Interestingly, the principles of the earlier Garlinger case have been referred to, over the years, by other courts in determining termination of alimony.

During their trial, it was proven Joyce Garlinger's boyfriend lived in her home from early November 1973 until March 2, 1974. Because it appeared to the court "the paramour did not contribute anything toward the cost of food or such household expenses as utilities, and that part of Mrs. Garlinger's alimony support benefited her friend—" her alimony payments were suspended for the two-month cohabitation period stipulated by counsel. The opinion suggested, "It might be unconscionable to compel the husband by his daily labor to support the divorced wife in idleness and adultery." Despite this small finding in his favor, Bernard Garlinger was ordered by the Appellate Division to clear up all other back alimony payments.

"Several jurisdictions cut off alimony upon post-divorce cohabitation. Since 1934, New York law has authorized termination of alimony if the dependent spouse is habitually living with another man, and holding herself out as his wife, although not married to such a man. In 1974, California enacted a law terminating alimony upon proof that the dependent spouse was living with another person of the opposite sex and holding herself out as the spouse of the person for a total of thirty days or more. And Illinois terminates alimony, 'if the party receiving maintenance cohabits with another person on a resident, continuing conjugal basis.'" [3]

On the other hand, existing laws and court trials prevent the providing ex-spouse from getting off the hook that easily. In *Gayet v. Gayet*, George Gayet's trial case against his ex-wife's on and off cohabitation with another man was decided in his favor; yet the modification was reversed by the Superior Court. Taken a step further, "the Supreme Court affirmed the reversal of that court's decision and the case was sent back for a hearing and factual determination of the extent of his ex-wife's actual economic dependency on alimony from her former spouse," explained Judge Fundler.

In the opinion of the Court, delivered by Judge Daniel O'Hern, he cited, "The majority of jurisdictions have adopted an economic needs test to determine whether cohabitation requires modification of an alimony award."

These types of cases are tough on the dependent spouse. *You're damned if you do*: If the receiver of the alimony invites another party to live with him/her, and that person doesn't put his hand in his pocket, that gives reason to take a look at having alimony reduced because you've used your ex-spouse's hard-earned money to support this new love affair. *And damned if you don't*: If the dependent spouse is being supported by a third party, and his/her life has been financially enhanced during cohabitation, there may be justification for a reduction of alimony because you don't need the money anymore (alimony is based upon maintaining the dependent spouse's standard of living before a divorce).

But what if the dependent spouse gets dumped again, or terminates the cohabiting love affair? That person has to go back to court to get the alimony reinstated.

Ex-wives who want to have his money and *his* money, too, beware! Little by little, the courts' empathy toward double-dipping, dependent ex-spouses may be eroding in favor of reducing or suspending alimony allowances.

I'LL SCRUB THE FLOOR.
YOU PAY THE BILLS

The financial support of a richer significant other may feel secure at the outset, yet that feeling of security is often short-lived. In the long run, the partner being supported develops a subservient demeanor. After a while, being a kept man or woman is psychologically devastating and eventually plays havoc with your self-esteem. Not being able to hold your own financially interferes with how you act and react within the relationship, and begins to control the love affair. But there's a way out of this position, which can be uplifting for both parties. This is an agreement based on documented reimbursement.

"Like any contract," wrote Ronaleen Roha for *Changing Times*, "there has to be something of value on both sides. M. Dee Samuels, a San Francisco family lawyer, says that can be the sharing of any responsibilities. 'They don't have to be equal either,' she points out. 'If you provide homemaker's services and your partner provides the money, that's okay.'"[1]

Ms. Roha suggested chores such as entertaining, cleaning the pool, manicuring the dog's toenails, gardening, painting a room, cleaning, and washing and ironing are services that can be calibrated contributions. You should document days, hours spent, and what it would cost to hire someone to provide those and other household duties you perform. In addition, stipulate which household bill you want to equate the value of those services: i.e. the mortgage, utilities, taxes, etc. It won't take long until, when both on paper and emotionally, you'll accumulate a great deal of face value while retaining your self-worth. Because it's tough to suddenly change old habits—and that includes taking someone for granted—it's best to establish this contractual understanding from the outset. However, if you haven't, it's not impossible to ease into it after you've moved in together.

Case in point: Over the years, I have created computer-generated documents and brochures for my husband's dental office. If I did not have the ability to create these services for Sam, he would have to hire and *pay* someone to format them. Early on, I would not have dreamt of charging him, although these favors were beyond the call of wifely duty. Nevertheless, that got old real fast when I was taking time away from my writing career to help him. At first, Sam was a bit put off when I suggested some type of financial compensation—renegotiating our deal. But when I insisted we barter my costly printing bills in exchange, we both got the best of the new bargain. It's hard to place a value on something you get for free. Those who bow down to an individual for the sake of a love affair inevitably develop doormat syndrome and eventually feel used. Meanwhile, this syndrome can ruin a potentially good relationship.

Being a live-in, without security and the benefits of marriage, demands that you pay attention to out-of-the-ordinary—other than sexual—favors you provide (remember you are *not* married). The value of these favors must be controlled by the person who grants them. At some point, you might want to ask yourself, "Why am I doing this?"

I see a lot of this soul searching in my W.O.O.M. subscribers, particularly when they move in with older men who want them at their beck and call. The younger woman can't hold a significant job because that would interfere with the dynamics her lover set for their relationship. Before long these women find they are not employable. Resentment sets in, and soon the love affair is on the rocks.

"In a lot of these cases, having false security just isn't worth risking your livelihood," cautioned Ms. Samuels during our recent interview. "When you think about it, this is a very dangerous situation for a woman. To jeopardize pension rights, health insurance, and work related benefits," Ms. Samuels explained, "is shortsighted and unfortunate." Yet, she knows of two female clients, who had been very successful in their professional careers, and did exactly that. "So now all I can do is urge them to get themselves named as beneficiary of an insurance policy and insist upon annual monetary gifts." Furthermore, she advised, "As mercenary as it sounds, tell these women not to get swept away. Be tough, and save every dollar she can get her hands on."

Questioning Ms. Samuels about her comments in the 1990 *Changing Times* feature compared to how she now feels in 1998, she told me the services-rendered contract has been found tough to prove, even though they are still being written.

"But women are not the best bookkeepers," insisted the Bay-area attorney.

Here's how you might approach the development of a services-rendered document:

"I'm flattered you want me to move in with you. However, I would feel like a parasite unless we establish a contractual understanding of my contribution to your well being and the household. For that (depending upon the economic level of the parties), I will need $500-$2,000 put in my bank account each week. Additionally, since I gave up my career and advancement possibilities, I will need $25,000-$100,000 in cash at the outset, and a similar annual gift."

The stakes should get higher as you rack up years of unmarried domestic bliss. If your live-in cannot financially handle this arrangement, you won't be able to quit your job anyway. In that case, you need an agreement dividing up who does what household jobs (which are no longer *just* woman's work), who pays for which expenses, and a break-up clause.

The majority of cohabitation agreements Ms. Samuels drafts center around the house issue. Somebody either has a house, or they want to buy a house, "and that is dealt with up front," she says, "by deciding what the contributions are going to be." If you give your partner ten thousand dollars toward the down payment, make certain to document that contribution. "Or else," Ms. Samuels warned, "if you part company, you have no proof and will probably never get it back." A contract will decide—if the couple separates—who is going to move out, who is going to have the right of first refusal, and the parameters of dividing accrued equity.

In Ms. Samuels' experience, clients seem reluctant to discuss anything beyond that specific issue, perhaps because the house is something concrete. Couples harboring different agendas, the attorney confided, often choose not to talk about spousal compensation, or any other estate planning. "Philosophically, if you look at this from the big picture, the laws that we have, although they may not be perfect, do serve a purpose."

The shortcoming of this type of relationship agreement is that it is hard to assess responsibility for emotional damage control. How do you mend a broken heart? Partners should safeguard their loved ones from contracts that unjustly deny one partner any monetary benefits for staying in the relationship, or they will instigate its slow death.

"If someone were to design an ideal world," Ms. Samuels concluded, "we would have the two attorneys, a financial planner, and a psychologist all meeting with the couple together, bringing everything out in the open." Not such a bad idea, is it?

OTHER CONSIDERATIONS
WORTH MENTIONING

I consult with women from Great Britain, Australia, Canada, New York to Los Angeles who leave home, quit their job, and uproot their lives to move in with lovers. A reimbursement agreement for them might include compensation for moving costs to the new locale. Depending on their lover's level of affluence, women can ask for return visits to see family and friends, their former weekly salary times a few months to find a new job, and compensation for missed raises, bonuses, and promotions. In case the relationship doesn't make it, insert claims to include:

➤ Expenses to cover the cost of moving back
➤ Enough money to live on while you find another new job
➤ Deposits for a new apartment
➤ Pocket money

➤ Perhaps a psychologist (which many of us need when a love-affair goes awry)

➤ Doctor visits.

Seasoned in defending these documents, the Wilshire Blvd. attorney Robert Nachshin says in his experience, "Service-rendered based contracts are 99.9 percent enforceable." But if they are poorly prepared it could be a long day in court. A few years ago, Mr. Nachshin represented one of baseball's highest-paid players, San Francisco Giants' Barry Bonds, during his domestic-relations trial. Unfortunately, the center fielder's prenuptial agreement—which was entered into the day before his wedding—was drafted by lawyers who had never prepared one before. "We ended up in a fifteen day trial just to prove the validity of the prenuptial contract. We prevailed in spite of it," the lawyer explained. "However, I think the reason we won was because courts like to uphold contracts."

Concluding our conversation, I asked, "If there is no promise of marriage, why do people stay in a relationship that so strictly revolves around self-imposed restrictions?"

Implying prenuptial agreements may only be slightly less self-governing than cohabitation contracts, Mr. Nachshin responded, "In my mind there isn't much difference between marriage and living together anyway—other than the ceremony." Pope John Paul II may beg to differ.

FEELING PRESSURED TO SIGN
AN INEQUITABLE AGREEMENT

Of course, there are many loving and balanced live-in relationships. There are also plenty that aren't. Nonetheless, *long term* (two years or more) living together without a firm commitment often preys on the weaker partner who lives in a constant state of uncertainty. Compound that with the stronger partner suggesting an inequitable, one-sided relationship agreement and that spells t-r-o-u-b-l-e.

A great number of phone calls I receive are from live-ins who have signed one-sided CCAs. They really wanted to marry the man with whom they are living, but accept whatever kind of relationship he is willing to give, hoping he will change his mind. I can offer them only two options: Stay and insist upon a firm a commitment within a specified period of time. Or, if that isn't resolved, move out in a specified period of time. In my opinion, two weeks after two years or more cohabitation is ample time to make that decision. Few listen because to move out takes guts.

Before you sign any relationship contract, weigh who is getting the most out of this love affair for the least amount of effort. (That includes those who lunch with friends all week, shop with their lover's credit card, get oodles of spending money, drive around in a provided luxury vehicle, and don't do much else.) A person should feel totally comfortable with what the agreement says. If you feel intimidated by the contract, hold off. Walk away and think about whether having this relationship is an equitable trade-off for signing away your self-esteem.

"Women are unbelievably willing to compromise themselves just to have a man," says Dianne E. Brinker, professor of psychology at the University of the Virgin Islands and private, U.S.V.I. therapist. "Especially if she moves in with him—and that's generally the case. Female clients I see in my private practice feel as if they have to toe the line." Fearful they'll get thrown out, Dr. Brinker explained these women feel pressured to be on their best behavior.

"So why do they put up with this abuse?" I asked "What separates these women from those who won't?"

"I think it's cultural conditioning," responded Dr. Brinker, who agreed women of the 1990s are Freudian misfits. "Some women have it in their heads they're not worth anything unless they're in a relationship, whereas most men have more important things like their careers." Even some women who are more successful than their male mates are taken in by the glamour of a love affair.

"We buy into the stereotype," confirmed Dr. Brinker, "falling in love with Mr. Right." Meanwhile, the movies and the media reinforce this fairy tale to the point that some women compromise their futures, potential personal success, and even their lives! "Statistics show men commit suicide over loss of a job or money. Women commit suicide over losing a man. I think that says it all," Dr. Brinker said. "And until women can develop self-respect derived from their own accomplishments, not from anyone else, it's not going to change."

To go forth into uncharted territory, only to find out you are unhappy with the conditions, doesn't make sense. Before you sign a CCA, or even a prenuptial agreement ask yourself:

➤ Is this agreement favorable to me?
➤ What am I expecting the future of this relationship to be?
➤ Have I compromised myself?
➤ What do I end up with if I sign it?
➤ Can I buy myself a one-way ticket out of here if it doesn't work out?
➤ If it doesn't work out, is there some compensation for my trouble?
➤ Have I given up more than I will ever recoup?
➤ Am I doing this to get out of supporting myself?
➤ Do I have a contingency plan if living together doesn't work out?

If you write down your responses and take yourself seriously, the answers to whether this relationship is worth it or not will be right there on the paper in front of you.

"HE PROMISED TO TAKE CARE OF ME
FOR THE REST OF MY LIFE!"

Seeking revenge after the fact sucks! Lawsuits based on a love affair gone sour drag on and on and are ugly and demeaning. Furthermore, by getting involved in a palimony trial, you may develop a reputation that will hurt your chances of settling down with a nice guy who might even marry you. My advice is to forget the litigation, even if you have to wait tables to make a fresh start and get on with your life.

Next time—and there will be a next time—learn to manipulate and control when the heat burns in his loins. Hit him between the eyes with your demands in the beginning when he thinks he can't live without you.

Nonetheless, if you feel your love relationship is winding down and want to get even, you may want to reexamine dragging your man or woman into court. Winning on an oral promise is a tedious process. Your suit will take years to come to trial. To make any case, you will be forced to traipse former housekeepers, friends and relatives through the courts to testify on your behalf. This type of trial is pure smut! Few credible attorneys look forward to getting wrapped up in these cases. Win or lose, you will spend tons of money that you probably don't have initiating and carrying out the suit. Whatever the outcome, expect appeals.

If you don't believe me, look at Barbara Neugass' case against Hollywood actor, Jack Klugman. Can you imagine how degrading it would be to read about *your* sagging boobs and post-menopausal problems at the local greengrocer's? That's what these cases are all about.

"I had served Klugman well for many years," the *Globe* reports his fifty-four-year-old ex-pal said in court papers. "I developed infirmities of age. And like any racehorse with bad knees who was no longer of any use, Klugman, seventy-four, chose to turn me out to pasture."

Barbara says she and the former *Quincy* star lived together from 1974 to 1992. For that she wants, "$1,000,000 for physical and emotional damages," over and above the monthly checks he did send her for years. Insisting she and Jack agreed they would share everything including his pension plan, and that he'd name her in his will, court papers also contend the couple agreed that "she would help raise his kids, and serve as a companion, homemaker, housekeeper, cook, hostess, consultant, and confidante."

So be it. She wasn't his wife. What did she expect? Living in Los Angeles, the Mecca of palimony arrangements and love battles, and since Mr. Klugman obviously wasn't planning to marry her, shouldn't Barbara have been a little nervous about "what ifs" long ago? Few live-in relationships get better with age. Often, without a wedding date, they sour bitterly.

In Mr. Klugman's financial bracket, the $1,000,000 demand is a pittance. Break it down. That's $55,000 for each year she lived with Jack. To hire someone to perform all the duties Barbara claims she performed would have cost far more. Despite the equitable amount, and as unjust as it may appear, I don't think she's going to get it. We'll see.

The irony is, contractual palimony agreements can be a bargain in the long run compared with a court battle. Mr. Klugman could have agreed early on to something like a $30,000 per year annual stipend; a quarter- to a half-million dollar irrevocable insurance policy, a half to one percent of all television and movie royalties while living together. Tag on a small percentage of his racehorse or other winnings, personal upkeep expenses, a comparable vehicle, and annual clothing allowance, and for someone in Mr. Klugman's bracket, that would undoubtedly save future heartache and aggravation for both parties. Think about it, guys.

On the other hand, there are those of us who think if a woman plays by the rules set by her lover, he hasn't made her a victim, she's done it to herself. Unlike some marriages, there wasn't a ball and chain around this woman's foot. So be it.

WHERE THERE'S
A WILL
THERE'S A WAY

A s she lay close to death, thirty-six-year-old Roberta Cone thought about the will she and her live-in lover, Larry Dabolt, drafted a short time before their auto accident. Larry's will includes provisions for his children and grandchildren, and especially Roberta. Likewise, Larry is to receive the bulk of Roberta's estate for lifetime use. In case the couple should perish together, living arrangements for their dog, Barney have been stipulated. "He has an inheritance, also," Roberta commented.

"It seems ironic. We both thought Larry, who is thirty-one years older than I am, would naturally die first." Yet, when that van barreled through the crosswalk in Laguna Beach and hit the walking couple head-on, the reality of the fragility of life, at any age, loomed loud and clear.

Roberta spent six weeks in the hospital, Larry nine days. During her arduous period of rehabilitation, they both realized that not being married could have been a big problem. "We had a notarized durable power of attorney for health care concerns," says Roberta. "Live-ins have to have one in case one party is incapable of making a life decision," especially if they want that decision made by the person with whom they are cohabiting. More and more, among domestic partnerships —same-sex and heterosexual—the durable power of attorney has protected unmarried couples from the unsolicited advice of family members and business associates who could meddle with the outcome of a person's personal affairs if such an agreement doesn't exist.

"This is especially important in Larry's situation," Roberta explained in an early discussion, "His children didn't always have his best interests in mind, and they considered me a gold digger." During a subsequent discussion several months after their accident, Roberta confided that near-death tragedy had an unforeseen benefit—a renewal of family ties. "As awful as the accident was, we've received a lot of gifts from it," Roberta said. "Larry and I value each other even more." Meanwhile, he and his children are developing a closer and better understanding of one another. Roberta has sensed an inkling of acknowledgment that their dad's live-in lover—younger than both of his kids—exists. "Once my lover's daughter got a chance to meet me, and get to know me, I felt her disapproval soften. She and her father worked a lot of things out after the accident. I think she sees the good in me, now."

Roberta and Larry met while attending meetings of ACOA, Adult Children of Alcoholics, and soon developed a fond friendship. "We were buddies for about three years before we became lovers," remembers Roberta, who admits sex easily could have come much sooner if she had not decided otherwise. She and Larry spent a great deal of time together going to self-help functions, antique shopping, and bicycling. "We signed up for any type of seminar dealing with growth and development."

When it became evident the couple had fallen deeply in love, the foundation of their love affair was the strong friendship they had cultivated. "I'm so glad I held off," says Roberta, who explained the depth of their relationship has been based upon considerable understanding of each other's respective attitudes about life, morality, values, and political and ethical inclinations. "An early-on love affair may have confused those values.".

Roberta is self-sufficient and astutely persuasive. She needed to know that Larry accepted her on her terms, including her desire to attend graduate school for clinical psychology. She made it very clear from the outset she couldn't live with the conditions evolving from typical marital shifts, the traditional spousal role, and the hidden agendas marriage sometimes breeds.

"When our friendship evolved into a romance three years later," Roberta confided, "Larry and I visited one of the clinics of the late pop-psychologist David Viscott." After only one session the couple left with their psychotherapist's blessing. All concerned recognized their love affair was founded upon mutual respect and love. "After a great deal of interpersonal searching, we both felt well-grounded in who we were. Moving in together felt right," Roberta said.

Yet, before they made the decision to rent a house, Roberta and Larry, a successful inventor and designer of medical equipment, discussed plans about how they wanted to handle their personal assets. Clarifying her staunch independence,

Roberta planned to purchase their rental herself. "We went into our relationship with open eyes," she said. "Knowing this was a very serious commitment, we were clear about the sacrifices we were making in choosing to live together." Striving to be the very best they could be both individually and as a couple re-enforced the bond. As she promised, after moving in, Roberta entered graduate school to study clinical psychology.

Curious, I asked, "Roberta, you are not getting any younger; what about children? Have you thought about having a family?"

"Oh, yes. At first, I thought Larry and I would marry when we have a child. We've since changed our minds about getting married, but I definitely plan to have a child after I graduate. I want to be financially secure enough to hire the right people to help me care for a baby."

"Are you concerned your child might be stigmatized by having parents who are not married?"

"We have worked that all out. Larry and I will *both* change our names to Cone-Dabolt to match the baby's."

"Oh, really," I responded with a raised brow. "How unusual."

"Isn't it? I said to Larry, 'You had the honor of having a woman take your name for thirty years. Now, hand over some of the control here.'" And he did! Roberta's surname will be listed first.

"I think marriage is beautiful—a lovely tradition for someone else," Roberta confided. Yet, she can't fathom a possible loss of autonomy—a loss of personal identity that marriage may induce. "Friends tell me I may get desperate when I turn forty, and will want to marry," Roberta said. "But I don't think so."

Leery about Roberta and Larry's will, I asked Roberta if she feels secure about it. Does she think a will is enough? Families can pull some ugly pranks after a relative passes on. I saw a potential problem where a sixty-seven-year-old father of a child born out of wedlock ignored his original family and provided for his thirty-six-year-old live-in paramour. Some could argue Larry was coerced into signing such a will. "Yes, you have made a good argument for sealing our partnership with something more than a will," Roberta decided. "But, everyone's been provided for fairly. That should be enough."

I hope so.

PLANNING THE COHABITING COUPLE'S WILLS

First and foremost, don't delay—do it today—make a will! Losing a loved one is awful enough without compounding the surviving partner's grief when no will exists, or, worse yet, is so outdated it defeats its purpose.

The repercussion of abandoning someone you love dearly with perhaps no home, no money, no vehicle, nor the loving possessions and mementos collected throughout a relationship, borders on abusive. In essence, if your significant other dies and doesn't have a will or other appropriate planning, the surviving live-in partner often can't collect a penny.

When New Jersey resident Edilberto Vega was struck down and killed in a violent automobile accident, he left behind his live-in companion, Ana Felipe, and their five year-old daughter, Sueheidi Alexis Vega. Because he died *intestate* (not having a valid will), his father, Lino, was appointed as administrator of Vega's estate. Ana had no right to claim her lover's body because she is not a spouse, and New Jersey does not recognize common-law marriage.

Edilberto's father arranged for him to be buried close to his home. Grief-stricken, disoriented, and unsure of her right to object and take a more aggressive position, Ana went along with the funeral arrangements. She visited Edilberto's grave regularly—placing small religious articles upon her improvised shrine. Lino, somewhat distanced from his son while he was alive, seldom, if ever, visited.

Aside from her continuing affection for Edilberto, and her desire to keep the memory of her surrogate husband alive, Ana believed visits to the grave reinforced Sueheidi's memory of her father and her identity with him. These visits, though, became an ordeal. Ana's fear of driving meant she had to impose upon family and friends to take her to the cemetery.

Two years later, assuming the court permitted the move, Ana made arrangements with a Roman Catholic priest to perform the appropriate religious rites. Bearing all costs of the removal of Edilberto's remains and reburial, Ana hired an attorney and petitioned the court to disinter and move the body to a cemetery within walking distance of her home. Despite the fact Ana did not have legal status as a spouse, permission was granted. The court was persuaded that Ana's continued love and devotion to Edilberto is a substantial force in her and Sueheidi's life, and bore no significant impact on the father's emotional needs or his ability to visit the new grave site.

Exhuming a body is always a sensitive issue, more spiritual than legal.[1] A simple will would have saved Ana from all of this heartache.

Whether a will exists or not, laws favor married couples. State and federal tax structures favor married couples. Cohabiting couples don't count. So far, laws ignore this type of union even though, as in the case of Ana and Edilberto, gradual changes are taking place. Living together means you will have to create the measures that will protect your estate and significant other. This process is far more complex than if you were a married couple protected by state laws. Spouses can contest even a valid will; children and relatives, or anyone else cannot.

Wills are not just for old people or rich people. Everyone should have one, or some equivalent protection, even if it only says where you want to be buried, and next to whom.

SIMPLIFYING THE PROCESS

How can a cohabiting couple best address the drafting of wills and make sure their plans are enforceable? New Jersey attorney John L. Pritchard, who specializes in estate planning, says he would prefer to see unmarried partners draw separate, specific documents. As awful as it is to think about death, we all need to plan ahead if we want to have any control over the disposition of all we amassed in this life.

The first question I had for Mr. Pritchard was the most basic. "Is a will the best document for cohabiting couples?"

Hedging for a moment, he replied, "It can be, depending upon the circumstances. More reliable yet, unmarried couples could go ahead and do something which is *irrevocable* where they give assets to each other while they are both alive." But that's permanent and firm. If you change your mind, or the status of the partnership changes, there is nothing anyone can do to reverse that decision when you die. Alive or dead, you can't get your gift back. "There is more leeway and flexibility when you assign your estate, [or portions of it], to someone in a will when you pass away," the lawyer pointed out. However, under those circumstances, the beneficiary could wonder, "If I'm not a good girl, is he going to change it?"

A spouse cannot be disinherited. In New Jersey and many jurisdictions, spouses—even if they have been cut out of the will—have a right of election to take up to one-third of their husband or wife's estate, unless a signed agreement between them stipulates otherwise. Live-ins can easily be excluded and forgotten. Without some proof (a promissory letter or, at the very least, an oral promise), a live-in has little chance of making a case.

An alternative to a will might be to set up a **revocable trust**, which can be canceled or annulled. The party can even name him- or herself as trustee. Mr. Pritchard explained, "You can have a trust agreement which says, 'I am holding these assets in trust for myself and my friend.'" Wealthier unmarrieds may consider titling the assets like a **brokerage account** (which is handled by a firm like Merrill Lynch or Charles Schwab, or the trust department of a bank) in the name of a trust such as, *The Bill and Laurie Trust*. "Very definitely you can include stocks and bonds," Mr. Pritchard emphasized. "A house can also be deeded to a trust."

In a live-in situation where the future of the relationship isn't secure, you would probably consider the revocable trust agreement, which commonly stipulates the original owner can take property or assets back at any time he or she wants while alive. But your lover may not have faith in this decision, and insist you develop an irrevocable trust to permanently allot at least some assets.

"Sometimes, trusts can serve as a will substitute," Mr. Pritchard said. "But only if you take *all* of your important assets and put them into the trust. However, you should still have a simple will, or **clean up will**, to pour-over other assets not yet entered into the trust, at the time of the principal's death."

Bear in mind, though, if a wealthy spouse passes away, he can leave unlimited assets to his spouse, and no estate tax has to be paid. "However, if he leaves those same assets to a live-in, after the first $625,000 (higher thereafter), the balance is subject to a federal estate tax which starts at thirty-seven percent," said Mr. Pritchard. Similarly, in most jurisdictions that collect inheritance tax, spouses are exempt. However, if an inheritance is left to an unrelated person (a live-in), the tax has to be paid. Marriage is looking more and more attractive!

To further protect a party's wishes, a separate document, which Roberta Cone mentioned, is the **durable power of attorney**. Not a part of anyone's will, the durable power of attorney is enforceable while a person is still alive and often takes effect the moment it is signed. Mr. Pritchard explained, "This is the type of document the agent (the live-in, if so desired) would take to a bank in order to cash checks, and pay salaries and bills such as the mortgage and the telephone company when the **principal** (the person who gives power of attorney to someone else) is unavailable to do so." The agent can step in and make professional and personal decisions on the principal's behalf, until the principal gets back on his or her feet.

Even if the principal is sound and healthy, the agent's responsibility takes effect the moment this document is signed, and, if specified, the durable power of attorney can remain in effect in the event of the principal's complete disability and even disappearance.

A flashback illustrated his point. My friend, Joseph Cicippio, was captured and held hostage by the Lebanese for five years. An extreme example, perhaps, but it illustrated how at any time we all need to have such a document at hand.

"Essentially, a **springing power of attorney** is the same thing, except the agent's responsibility kicks in *only* when it is determined the principal is incapable of making decisions.

The agent only gets the power to act when his/her physician says, 'The principal is not able to manage his own affairs effectively,'" Mr. Pritchard clarified.

WHAT ABOUT MEDICAL WISHES AND DECISIONS?

An advance medical directive, sometimes called a medical power of attorney or **living will**, is another type of document cohabiting couples should consider drafting. This document is particularly pertinent because it assigns an agent (your lover or someone else) to the medical decision-making process. "This document would be put in the patient's chart at the hospital," Mr. Pritchard suggested. Here is what this document covers and should include:

A. Confirm in writing that you do not want medical treatment to continue if you go into a coma, or will never lead a meaningful life again. In other words, "I want the machinery turned off." Or, on the other hand, "I want the maximum treatment to keep me alive."

B. Appoint another individual (an agent or your live-in friend) to make the decision to cancel life-support and make all other medical decisions if, "I am no longer able to lead a meaningful life."

By being appointed this agent, a live-in cannot be frozen out by family members who, like warhorses, may charge right into the middle of the seriously ill patient's care. They could move the relative to another hospital, fire his/her doctor, and alter treatment plans and medical decisions. They could also kick their relative's spousal equivalent out of the hospital room.

When the principal dies, the agent's responsibility ends. An **executor** (also appointed by the principal) wraps up the estate.

WHAT ABOUT THE HOUSE?

As we have discussed, there are many ways to handle the right of ownership of a house if one live-in partner dies. Right off the bat, though, consider two basic options: joint tenancy and tenancy in common. After that, you and your attorney will sort out what is best for you.

If an unmarried couple purchases a house together, they could select to share **tenancy in common**. Each of them owns fifty percent of the property. Should one party die, the deceased's one-half portion of the property will pass either according to his will, or, if there is no will, by the intestacy statute to his closest relatives. On the surface, this might appear to be the best route to go for an older LTC who chooses to leave their 50 percent equity in the house to children from a previous marriage. But consider the drawbacks. In order to stay in the house, the surviving partner will have to buy out the inheriting party. Hopefully, he/she can afford to do that. If not, assuming the inheritor wants his money now, the surviving partner will be forced to sell the house and split the proceeds.

"If you want your partner to be able to stay in the house," Mr. Pritchard warned, "then you'd better take title as **joint tenants**." In this case, the house becomes the property of the survivor.

Suppose, a man is wealthier than his live-in lover. He wants to buy a house for her, but chooses to bequeath the house to his children, or another party upon his death. Rather than leave it to his live-in to ultimately leave to her children, or perhaps her next live-in or new spouse, he can set up a **life estate**. Under those terms, his live-in may stay in the house for lifetime enjoyment. However, upon her death, the house reverts to the inheriting party of choice since that party holds

the remainder (the inherited property, its income, or remnants thereof).

Certain tensions are created by developing a life estate. Remember, the intended beneficiary(ies) will not receive their inheritance until their father or mother's (or their guardian angel's) lover passes away. That could make life quite ugly for the surviving party.

Furthermore, read the small print! A zinger can be written into the life estate that specifies the former live-in lover cannot remain in the house if involved in another love affair, or marries.

In deciding what would be the best scenario, the living-together couple has to confront the issue and decide *up front*, in the case of the death of one party, who they want to get their share of the property.

A NOTE ABOUT INSURANCE

"The first chore is finding insurance companies amenable to insuring cohabiting couples. Here, the rules seem to vary with the type of insurance," advises my insurance agent and advisor, Murray Guth of Fair Haven, New Jersey. Until societal attitudes toward cohabiting same-sex and heterosexual couples change, here are a few insurance pointers, of which, Mr. Guth forewarns, you should be aware:

LIFE INSURANCE:

"The initial application will require that the beneficiary have an **insurable interest** (generally, a spouse or relative). Naming the beneficiary as fiancé(e) will usually pass the underwriter's scrutiny, whereas, 'friend' may not. It is ironic that this scrutiny applies only to the initial application. Once a life insurance policy is issued, the policy owner may change the beneficiary at his/her whim to his estate, his friend—his cat."

AUTO INSURANCE:

"The trick is to insure more than one car on a single policy, thereby enjoying a multi-car discount. That will usually reduce the premium on each car by about twelve percent. Insurers will always permit the cars to be owned (registered) by either spouse, as long as they reside in the same household. However, the downside is insurers will usually not allow this two-car policy when the cars are owned by household members not married to each other. In almost every case, cohabiting couples who each own a car will not be acceptable under a multi-car policy, unless married to each other and residing in the same household. Significant others who choose to live together must, generally, forfeit the discount and carry two separate policies. Or, they may re-register the cars to either cohabiting party. Or, rarely done, register all cars in both names."

PROPERTY COVERAGE:

"Most insurers accept cohabiting couples as coinsureds when both are named on the deed as co-owners of the property. It is common for business properties to be owned by unrelated co-owners, partnerships, etc.; and recently, for unmarried, domestic partners to purchase a home jointly. Most insurance companies will eagerly issue a homeowner policy naming both cohabiting parties as the insured."

"Renters, however, may encounter a problem when not related to each other. Many insurance companies will decline to issue a homeowner-tenant policy to those who want to be coinsured, but are not related. However, these couples should not submit to purchasing two separate tenant policies right off the bat. With a bit of persistence and searching, there are insurers who will accommodate them."

However, living-together couples may have to pay a higher premium than a married couple.

COMPANY OFFERED INSURANCE BENEFITS

Although societal pressures are gradually forcing change, to date, few employers extend health insurance benefits to unmarried partners.

We have already discussed contracts and documents that prevent your lover from getting his/her hands on your assets, while *curbing* any power that individual may feel he/she has over your estate. This chapter has covered documents that *assign* power, and, oftentimes, money to your live-in. It also deals with death, disappearance, and infirmity. I have only scratched the surface of unlimited possibilities and document combinations. With the help of your attorney, financial planner, accountant, and insurance agent, effective after-death and disability priorities—designed especially with the cohabiting couple in mind—can be implemented.

Each of these professionals has his/her own style. For the most part, the job will be well done if you stay on top of the situation. Self-governing an unofficially married relationship means you can feel covered and secure if you know your stuff. Don't be intimidated. Ask a lot of questions. I did. Even if you know the answers, ask anyway to test the extent of your expert's knowledge. Be aware, laws and policies regarding unmarried, domestic partners are changing as demands override the objections.

Once you have established that your live-in union is here to stay, and taking into consideration your state's laws, don't delay creating, at the very least, the following shopping list of documents:

A. Wills

B. Powers of Attorney

C. Medical Covenants

D. Tenancy Agreements

E. Insurance policies

WHEN ALL IS SAID
AND DONE…

I t's pretty hard to remain biased one way or the other about living together when half of the people you talk to think it is a great idea, while the other half thinks it's awful. I hope I have been open-minded and fair when weighing and reporting my findings. Trial marriage stories quickly become redundant. My point was to cover a variety of scenarios and opinions. The amount of experts, ex-lovers, and married and unmarried couples who gave us the obvious and arguable pros and cons surrounding living together is impressive.

Still, I haven't changed my original position: If two people love each other, shouldn't the appropriate next step for them be to confirm their love and get married?

A black cloud hangs over couples when one partner is pushing to test drive marriage and the other doesn't want any part of it, or only reluctantly gives in. I stand by the message

I've sent throughout this book: *One partner almost always wants to get married. One partner almost always gets hurt.* Measure *how badly* and that becomes the most practical consideration when judging whether you are for or against living together before marriage or indefinite living together.

The thirty-year-old daughter of one of my friends recently said to me, "Personally, I want to move in with my boyfriend. But he's adamantly against it; he doesn't think it's right. We can't afford to get married right now so that means if I live with my parents I can save money for our wedding. But in all reality, I'm too old to be living with my parents."

"Another thing," she said, "I'm not sure I want kids, which means I don't really have to get married." But her boyfriend wants to have kids. If he gives in and the couple lives together, it could easily look as if he is backing down from his desire to have children. If he doesn't stick to his guns, living together will prolong the pain of not knowing: does she love him enough to give him the children he so desperately wants?

Marital test-drives habitually send the wrong message.

One of the premises of this book was to discuss how one partner is willing to accept whatever crumbs of a relationship the other partner is willing to give, in order to be in a relationship. Our nineteen year-old son, Sean, has been seeing a woman, slightly older than he is. An old boyfriend who treats her badly resurfaces every once in awhile and disrupts whatever relationship Sean thinks he has with this woman. Sean asked me, "Why do some women put abusive losers at the top of their short-list of men they want to love them—and keep going back for more?"

There are myriad reasons why. Wouldn't we all be healthier if we knew all the answers! At the same time, I asked him,

"Why do *you* keep going back for more?" He said, "Well, I have learned a lot about women from hanging around."

"R-e-a-l-l-y?" I groaned. "In other words, you want to see how much you can take before you go insane and I go crazy hearing you complain?" That exchange sums up why over five thousand people have called me over the past ten years seeking my opinion and solace.

It worries me that the institution of marriage has become such a debacle. Many people become loose cannons when they decide to make their own rules in search of a cure-all. What is wrong with marriage is that we are expecting it to fulfill every dream and fantasy. It can't. Selfishly, we want it all, even if we have to hurt those who are dearest to us.

Recently, I gave a ride home to a gentleman and his "stepdaughter" who were working on a project with me. He has lived with his girlfriend, the "stepdaughter's" mother, for eleven years. At first, she wanted to get married, but when he balked she accepted the arrangement on his terms. Her daughter is a preteen and attends a Catholic grade school. Catholicism doesn't condone living-together relationships. I asked my passenger, more from a curiosity standpoint than disapproval, "Isn't what you are doing confusing to your girlfriend's daughter? It seems she is embarrassed by your behavior or she wouldn't refer to you as her stepdad." I give the man credit; he really thought about what I had to say.

He agreed it isn't an ideal situation for her to be in a household where her mother isn't married to the man with whom she is making love. He defended the situation by telling me, "I love her mother very much." However, it's obvious he doesn't love her enough to get married. He implied, the daughter should "do as I say, but not as I do."

Think how ashamed his "stepdaughter" must feel when her mother's misleading relationship chips away at the very foundations of her child's religious upbringing. At school, she is taught one set of rules. At home, she sees those rules challenged. In many ways, living together turns people into hypocrites.

What worries me most about this young girl? When she grows up, will she ever be able to trust love? And how far will *she* stretch "Do as I say, not as I do?" When I conveyed that thought to my passenger, there was complete silence. It was as if he had never thought about what he was doing from that point of view.

ACKNOWLEDGEMENTS

Writing a book takes an enormous effort to organize what you have to say, write it, and *finish* it. My friends think I died—I farmed Sean and Ashley out to every last one of them. Meanwhile, Sam has had to wing it on his own in more ways than one. But knowing I did it has given me an incomparable high. As I write these last pages, I'm filled with emotion. It's very difficult to say good-bye. You see, my stories are about real people—with real lives, real feelings, real needs, and they have been a part of my life for the past year and a half. But the day has come to let go. *Test Driving Marriage* has been born.

Most importantly, this has been an incredible journey. From talking with hundreds of people about love-relationships over the past year, we have received a priceless gift of insight. I wrote this book, but I want to thank those who bared their souls to provide the invaluable, true stories. I am deeply grateful to all of you who participated. You are really good sports.

With each book I write—each person who consults with me and each talk show I appear on—I mature and grow and emotionally change what I think about life in general. What I thought were indelible beliefs at the outset, have been tested, and my outlook has changed to a large degree. If I have done my job, I will have provoked and encouraged you to open up the way you think about relationships, too.

I especially want to thank Sam, Sean and Ashley for their never-ending support. I love you.

And there are so many others. Please accept my heartfelt thank you for your contribution to the success of *Test-Driving Marriage:*

The librarians at New Jersey's Monmouth County Library and the New York Public Library, Maria Larsen, librarian at Monmouth University, Carol Blunda, on behalf of the Monmouth University Library Association's speaker's program for her confidence in me as a speaker.

Liz Bailey, instructor in Human Development at the University of Hawaii for her contribution to this book and friendship. My certified public accountant, Nicholas A D'Apolito; author and counselor, Margorie L. Engel; and author Sondra Forsyth, for their encouragement. Beverly Hills/Palm Desert attorney, Dale Gribow; my friends, Diney Goldsmith, Lori Huddy, Rose O'Connor-Gawoski and Debi Larrison, who insisted it was *all* in the name.

Then there are those behind the scenes: Gene Sudziarski, manager of Elysian Hotel's Condo Association who puts up with receiving all of my faxes and hawks my books. Dr. Mark Reuter, who helped round up the experts. Gene Barnes, public relations consultant, who is always there for me. Lisa Beck, my former director of subsidiary rights, and Bonnie Seagall, my publicist at Barricade Books. My hairstylist, William Renner, who keeps me looking my best on the talk shows as well as serving as my after-hours publicist. Sergio Vacca, maitre d'hotel at Harry Cipriani in New York City and Jean-Marie Ancher, maitre d'hotel at Taillevent in Paris who lighten me up, make me laugh, and force me to not take all of this too seriously. And Joe Amiel, owner, The Old Mill Inn for giving me the best stories for my books, and treating me to the most amazing book-signing parties.

I sincerely appreciate the mental-health professionals, authors, sociologists, lawyers, and physicians who have graciously granted interviews for this book.

To my readers, thank you for taking me on my terms.
Good Luck!
Beliza Ann Furman

I welcome your letters:
1029 Sycamore Avenue
Tinton Falls, New Jersey 07724

And faxes
732-389-0304

NOTES

A BRIEFLY CHRONICLED ROLL IN THE HAY

[1]Carroll, Ginny, *Newsweek*, "Marriage by Another Name," July 24, 1989, p. 46.

[2]Odem, Mary E., *Encyclopedia of American Social History* "Sexual Behavior and Morality," p. 1964.

[3]Odem, Mary E., *Encyclopedia of American Social History* "Sexual Behavior and Morality," p. 1969.

[4]Levy, Robert J. "Alimony," Microsoft™ Encarta® 97 Encyclopedia© 1993-1996 Microsoft.

[5]In answer to the high divorce rate, abandoning no-fault divorce is being considered in certain legal circles.

[6]Talbot, Frederic R., M.D.* *Ladies Home Journal*, "Should Doctors Prescribe Contraceptives for Unmarried Girls?" January 1968 p. 37. * fictitious name

[7]Lobbia, J.A., Feb/March 1987, *Mother Jones*, p. 18.

[8]According to the same *Mother Jones* article, in 1983, political consultant Joan Horn and her six-year live-in lover, university dean Terry Jones, were sued by the town of Ladue, MO. Told to marry,

split up, or get out of town, the lower courts upheld Ladue's law. American Civil Liberties Union attorney Leonard Frankel requested the case be sent to Missouri's Supreme Court. Before the case was reviewed, the couple succumbed to pressure and married in 1987.

[9]Smith, Lynn, writer for the Los Angeles Times, "Commit or Split '90s Mantra" as taken from the Asbury Park Press "Essentials Section," February 25, 1996, p. D1.

[10]Chiumento, Joyce, Dr., personal interview with Beliza Ann Furman, February 26, 1997, St Thomas U.S.V.I.

PHYSICAL AND EMOTIONAL IMPLICATIONS
SURROUNDING LIVING TOGETHER TODAY

[1]Kelly, Kitty, *The Royals*, Warner Books, 1997, p. 79.

[2]London, Kathryn A., Cohabitation, from *Vital and Health Statistics of the National Center for Health Statistics*, "Marriage, Marital Dissolution, and Remarriage: United States, 1988," Number 194, January 4, 1991.

[3]Costello, Cynthia and Krimgold, Barbara Kivimae, editors, *The American Woman*, 1996-97, Table 1-4, p. 261.

[4]It is interesting to note the legal and cultural inroads over three and one half million unmarried, living-together heterosexual couples have made over the past thirty years as a result of class-action and grass roots legislation brought about by members of the gay and lesbian population (one-third the size) seeking broader domestic partnership acceptance. For example, a successful lawsuit brought about by a gay couple fighting to adopt their foster child in December 1997, resulted in New Jersey becoming the first state to allow unmarried and gay and lesbian couples to adopt children in state care.

[5]Saxton, Lloyd, *The Individual Marriage and Family*, Wadsworth, 9th edition 1996, p. 216.

[6]Fisher, Helen, Ph.D., *Anatomy of Love*, Fawcett Columbine, New York, 1992, p. 111

[7]Saxton, Lloyd, *The Individual Marriage and Family*, Wadsworth, 9th edition 1996, p. 217.

[8]When I mentioned I was writing this book to friends, professional cohorts, mental health professionals, and acquaintances, they gave me reason to believe *one* in *five* couples are involved in a domestic unmarried partnership—even though formal surveys suggest it is one in seven.

[9]A starter marriage is usually when a couple marries in their late teens to early twenties, and they divorce, or annul that marriage within one to three years.

[10]McGowen, Jo, "There's no such thing as trial marriage." Her article and survey of responses appearing in *U.S. Catholic's* "Sounding Board," December 1992, pp 22-27.

COPING WITH THE NUANCES OF UNOFFICIAL MARRIAGE

[1]In his book, *The Pursuit of Happiness*, award-winning social psychologist, David G. Myers, discusses the results of seven studies of cohabiting couples; three of which were national surveys. In a U.S. survey of 13,000 adults, one-third were likely to separate or divorce within a decade; a Canadian survey of 5,300 women found that 54 percent were likely to divorce within fifteen years; a Swedish study of 4,300 women revealed trial-marriages resulted in a whopping 80 percent greater divorce rate. These numbers belie the popular, but *mistaken* theory that marriage stands a better chance if couples live together first. In 1993, slightly more than half of all cohabiting unions resulted in marriage. Trial partnerships were less likely to lead to marriage among black than among white women: 54.4 percent versus 42.1 percent respectively.

[2]Levitt, Shelly, *Reader's Digest* pp 57-64, October 1995, "What Women Don't Know About Today's Men," Condensed from *Cosmopolitan*, April 1992.

WEIGHING THE DECISION TO MOVE IN

[1]Dr. Edward Dengrove, a prominent psychiatrist from West Allenhurst, New Jersey, has been in practice for forty years. A cou-

ple of years ago—because he has seen so many marriages go down the tubes—he placed an ad in the paper offering a free premarital counseling session to couples contemplating marriage or living-together. Much to his surprise, not one couple called. His results demonstrate vividly that lovers are blinded by infatuation, and often throw words of caution to the wind.

MOVING IN WITH SOMEONE ELSE'S KIDS

[1]Franz, Dennis, December 1996, *In Style*, pp 101-102.

LIVING TOGETHER VERSUS FEAR OF REMARRIAGE

[1]I said *appear* because the over-fifty-year-old women who consult with me want to know if they can be happy with a man ten or more years older than they are. My case studies reveal that when these women learn about the problems inherent in these relationships—particularly that an older man's demands and needs can rival those of a young family—the prospect becomes less appealing than remaining single. I talk at great length about middle-age, female relationships with senior-aged men in my book, *Younger Women— Older Men*.

[2]Kirwan, Roberta, July 1995, *Money Magazine*, "Why Seniors Don't Marry," p. 100.

[3]Cowen, George S., Esq., Hackensack, New Jersey. Personal Interview with Beliza Ann Furman conducted August 8, 1997.

HOW LIVING TOGETHER CAN BACKFIRE ON YOU!

[1]Knight-Ridder Newspapers syndicated article, "Unmarrieds Sometimes Need Counseling, Too," reprinted by the *Asbury Park Press*, October 27, 1996.

[2]*Jet* Magazine, "2.6 Million U.S. Couples Living Together: Census," February 4, 1991.

THOSE WHO TOOK THE PLUNGE

[1]Peterson, Karen S., Gannet News Service, "Marriage Makes Men Happier and Women More Vulnerable," Reprinted by *The Virgin Islands Daily News*, April 24, 1997.

MOM, THIS IS MY WHATCHAMACALLIT!

[1]Saxton, Lloyd, *The Individual, Marriage, and Family*, 9th edition, publisher: Wadsworth, 1996, p. 225.

**SOCIAL PROTOCOL FOR THE
UNOFFICIALLY MARRIED COUPLE**

[1]Post, Peggy, Personal Interview with Beliza Ann Furman, conducted June 12, 1997, *Elizabeth Post's Etiquette*, 16th edition, published by Harpers Collins. The Emily Post Institute, Burlington, VT 05401.

[2]Humphries, Ann Chandler, Personal Interview with Beliza Ann Furman conducted on June 13, 1997. Eticon, Inc. http://www.Eticon.com/.

**FINANCIAL TRAPS SURROUNDING
COMMON-LAW MARRIAGE LAWS**

[1]Carroll, Ginny, *Newsweek*, "Marriage by Another Name," July 24, 1989 p. 46.

[2]Carroll, Ginny, *Newsweek*, "Marriage by Another Name," July 24, 1989 p. 46.

[3]*Life* Magazine, "Jennings v. Hurt," January 1990

[4]Felder, Raoul Lionel, personal interview with Beliza Ann Furman, January 9, 1997.

[5]Felder, Raoul Lionel, personal interview with Beliza Ann Furman, January 9, 1997.

[6]Bellafante, Gina, *Time* magazine, "Another Round in Court," November 1, 1993.

[7]*People* magazine, "His Life in Court," November 8, 1993, p. 83.

STAKING YOUR CLAIM

[1]*American Demographics*, "Cohabitation is a Premarital Step," November 1991, p. 20.

BROACHING THE FINANCIAL AGREEMENT

[1]Mitchelson, Marvin, personal interview with Beliza Ann Furman, May 1994, full text appears in *Younger Women/Older Men*, Barricade Books, September 1995.

QUESTIONS A LAWYER ASKS WHEN DRAWING UP A CCA

[1]*Gayet v. Gayet* argued October 25, 1982, Decided February 14, 1983. Cite as, 92 New Jersey 149.

[2]*Garlinger v. Garlinger* argued September 8, 1975, Decided November 3, 1975. Cite as 137 New Jersey Super.

[3]Written into opinion delivered by Superior Court Judge Daniel O'Hern, *Gayet v. Gayet*, argued October 25, 1982, Decided February 14, 1983. Cite as, 92 New Jersey 149.

I'LL SCRUB THE FLOORS; YOU PAY THE BILLS

[1]Roha, Ronaleen R. author, Blum, Adrienne, Research, *Changing Times*, October, 1990 p. 70-76.

WHERE THERE'S A WILL THERE'S A WAY

[1]*Ana Felipe v. Lino Vega*, Decided November 15, 1989. Superior Court of New Jersey, Chancery Division, Atlantic County. Cite as, 570 A.2d 1028 (N/J/ Super. Ch 1989).